Geomedia Studies

The present book offers a substantive introduction to geomedia studies, an expanding interdisciplinary research terrain at the intersections of media studies and geography. The concept of geomedia is used as a lens to theorize spaces and mobilities in mediatized worlds. By addressing imperative questions about the implications of geomedia technologies for organizations, social groups and individuals (e.g. businesses profiting from geo-surveillance, refugees or migrants moving across national borders, or artists claiming their rights to public space), the book contributes to the ongoing academic and societal debates in our increasingly mediatized world.

Karin Fast is Senior Lecturer in Media and Communication Studies and one of the Geomedia Research Group coordinators, at Karlstad University, Sweden. She has published her work in journals such as *Journal of Computer-Mediated Communication, International Journal of Cultural Studies, European Journal of Cultural Studies, and Media Culture and Society, Communication Theory.*

André Jansson is a Professor of Media and Communication Studies and Director of the Geomedia Research Group in the Department of Geography, Media and Communication, Karlstad University, Sweden. His most recent book is Mediatization and Mobile Lives (Routledge, 2018).

Johan Lindell previously postdoctoral researcher at Karlstad University, is Senior Lecturer in Media and Communication Studies at the Department of Geography, Media and Communication, Karlstad University, Sweden. Lindell is a media sociologist seeking to understand class discrepancies related to globalization, mediatization and news media use from a Bourdieusian perspective. Lindell has published his work in, for example, *Distinktion: Journal of Social Theory, Journalism Studies, International Communication Gazette, European Journal of Communication and Communication Theory.*

Linda Ryan Bengtsson is Senior Lecturer in Media and Communication Studies and coordinator of the Geomedia Research Group at Karlstad University, Sweden. An interdisciplinary researcher with a wide and varied background, her work investigates the relations between creative life, interactivity, media, and place. Her PhD thesis, *Re-negotiating Social Space: Public Art Installations and Interactive Experience*, laid the groundwork for her current projects: Music Innovation Network Inner Scandinavia (MINS), which examines the contemporary music environment and its digital echoes in the border region between Sweden and Norway, and Interactive Place-Based Tourism, which investigates enhanced experiences in digital tourism in the province of Värmland.

Mekonnen Tesfahuney is Professor of Human Geography at the Department of Geography Media and Communication Studies, Karlstad University, Sweden. Questions of mobility, power, space and geophilosophy are his research concern. Amongst his latest publications are the anthologies *Privileged Mobilities: Tourism as World Ordering* (Tesfahuney & Schough, 2016) and *The Post-Political City* (Tesfahuney & Ek, 2018).

Routledge Research in Cultural and Media Studies

For a full list of titles in this series, please visit www.routledge.com.

106 **Affective Sexual Pedagogies in Film and Television**
Kyra Clarke

107 **Tracing the Borders of Spanish Horror Cinema and Television**
Edited by Jorge Marí

108 **Screen Comedy and Online Audiences**
Inger-Lise Kalviknes Bore

109 **Media Representations of Anti-Austerity Protests in the EU**
Grievances, Identities and Agency
Edited by Tao Papaioannou and Suman Gupta

110 **Media Practices, Social Movements, and Performativity**
Transdisciplinary Approaches
Edited by Susanne Foellmer, Margreth Lünenborg, and Christoph Raetzsch

111 **The Dark Side of Camp Aesthetics**
Queer Economies of Dirt, Dust and Patina
Edited by Ingrid Hotz-Davies, Georg Vogt, and Franziska Bergmann

112 **The Materiality of Love**
Essays on Affection and Cultural Practice
Edited by Anna Malinowska and Michael Gratzke

113 **Fashion and Masculinities in Popular Culture**
Adam Geczy and Vicki Karaminas

114 **Geomedia Studies**
Spaces and Mobilities in Mediatized Worlds
Edited by Karin Fast, André Jansson, Johan Lindell, Linda Ryan Bengtsson, and Mekonnen Tesfahuney

Geomedia Studies
Spaces and Mobilities
in Mediatized Worlds

Edited by
Karin Fast, André Jansson,
Johan Lindell, Linda Ryan Bengtsson,
and Mekonnen Tesfahuney

LONDON AND NEW YORK

First published 2018
by Routledge

2 Park Square, Milton Park, Abingdon, Oxfordshire OX14 4RN
52 Vanderbilt Avenue, New York, NY 10017

Routledge is an imprint of the Taylor & Francis Group, an informa business

First issued in paperback 2019

Copyright © 2018 Taylor & Francis

The right of the editors to be identified as the authors of the editorial material, and of the authors for their individual chapters, has been asserted in accordance with sections 77 and 78 of the Copyright, Designs and Patents Act 1988.

All rights reserved. No part of this book may be reprinted or reproduced or utilised in any form or by any electronic, mechanical, or other means, now known or hereafter invented, including photocopying and recording, or in any information storage or retrieval system, without permission in writing from the publishers.

Notice:
Product or corporate names may be trademarks or registered trademarks, and are used only for identification and explanation without intent to infringe.

Library of Congress Cataloging-in-Publication Data
CIP data has been applied for.

ISBN: 978-1-138-22152-9 (hbk)
ISBN: 978-0-367-88465-9 (pbk)

Typeset in Sabon
by codeMantra

Contents

Acknowledgement ix

1 Introduction to Geomedia Studies 1
KARIN FAST, ANDRÉ JANSSON, MEKONNEN TESFAHUNEY,
LINDA RYAN BENGTSSON AND JOHAN LINDELL

PART I
Theorizing Geomedia 19

2 The Necessity of Geomedia: Understanding
 the Significance of Location-Based Services and
 Data-Driven Platforms 21
ROWAN WILKEN

3 Mapping Geomedia: Charting the Terrains of Space,
 Place and Media 41
PAUL C. ADAMS

4 Space, Place and Circulation: Three Conceptual Lenses
 into the Spatialities of Media Production Practices 61
HELEN MORGAN PARMETT AND SCOTT RODGERS

5 Media, Materiality, Mobility: Understanding Geomedia
 as Infrastructure Spaces 79
MIMI SHELLER

PART II
Geomedia Spaces 95

6 Look Inside^{TM}: Corporate Visions of the Smart City 97
GILLIAN ROSE

7 'The Sounds of Silence' – Writing Urban Spaces 114
   TINDRA THOR

8 City as Backlot: On Location in San Diego 132
   CHRIS LUKINBEAL AND LAURA SHARP

9 Unimaginable Homes: Negotiating
   Ageism through Media Use 152
   KRISTIAN MØLLER AND MAJA KLAUSEN

PART III
Geomedia Mobilities 171

10 Mobilism in Translation: Putting a New Research
    Paradigm to the Test 173
    MAREN HARTMANN

11 Artists Out of Place: The Invalidation of Network
    Capital in a Small-Town Cultural Community 195
    ANDRÉ JANSSON & LINDA RYAN BENGTSSON

12 Geographical Imaginations, Politics of Hospitality and
    the Media in the European Refugee Crisis 215
    KAARINA NIKUNEN

13 Fast Media 234
    JOHN TOMLINSON

14 Afterword: Geomedia: In Praise of Unruly Conjunctions 249
    SCOTT MCQUIRE

List of Contributors 261
Index 267

Acknowledgement

The idea of this book was born with *Geomedia: Spaces and Mobilities in Mediatized World*, an international research conference that gathered over 100 researchers from 16 countries in Karlstad, Sweden, in May, 2015. The conference received financial support from The Swedish Foundation for Humanities and Social Sciences and was organized by the Geomedia Research Group at the Department of Geography, Media and Communication, at Karlstad University. Providing a genuinely interdisciplinary ground for research at the crossroads of geography and media studies, the conference served as an arena for what we in this book call 'geomedia studies'. It became a space for absorbing conversations on matters of relevance to all of us who try to understand the intricate relationships between media, space, and place, in our increasingly mediatized, connected, and mobile world. We, therefore, take this opportunity to thank all of you fellow 'geomedians' who attended the 2015 *Geomedia* conference as either keynote, panelist, paper presenter, artist, or audience, our invited speakers to the *Geomedia Speakers Series*, and all those who in one way or another contributed to the critical and stimulating research exchanges that inspired this book project. We are also grateful to Karlstad University for all the support we have received.
Thank you all!

The Editors, Karlstad,
May 15, 2017

1 Introduction to Geomedia Studies

Karin Fast, André Jansson, Mekonnen Tesfahuney, Linda Ryan Bengtsson and Johan Lindell

Introduction

If the map was nothing less than a revolution in geomediating and imagining the world in the 'age of discovery', digitalization and the gamut of new media proffer a second revolution in geomediating and imagining the world. In contrast to the mappa mundi of old, the new media engender novel ways of orienting and re-envisioning the self, the world and one's place in it, not only in the intimate and embodied sense of orientation, but also in terms of making and remaking the world and one's place in the scheme of things. *Geomedia studies* tries to capture and make sense of the new cartographies that have emerged in the wake of new media, that recast presence/absence, here/there, subject/object in radical ways and chart and problematize their manifold histories and consequences. How to capture the power-geometries and differential geographies of geomedia? Which constellations of capital in the wake of the revolution in mapping and orientation emerge in the era of widespread digitization? What are the historical roots and trajectories of these developments? As we all know, there is no revolution without motion. As Hardt and Negri (2000: 362) hold, the human community is in itself constituted through circulation. Therefore, this book attends to the manifold mobilities and flows that are necessary to the very constitution of the social.

When the 'World Wide Web' and 'The Information Highway' gained momentum in the 1990s, telecom companies, in unison with many politicians, policy makers and researchers, praised the 'revolutionary' potentials of the Internet (Mosco, 2004). Today, when the Internet has become an integral part of everyday modern life, a new type of revolution has surfaced – one driven by *mobile* and *connected* media. Nowhere is this discourse as prevailing as in statements left by technology inventors. For instance, IBM's visionary report, *The Individual Enterprise: How Mobility Redefines Business* asserts that 'mobile networks – and the devices that exploit them – are radically changing the way we interact with the world' (IBM, 2017: 1). Along the same line, Swedish electronics giant Ericsson's report *Networked Society Essentials* predicts that connected devices leave us 'on the brink of an extraordinary revolution that will change our world forever' (Ericsson, 2017: 2). 'Mobile connectivity', the Ericsson report continues, 'is empowering us as individuals' (2017: 8).

While companies like IBM and Ericsson have an evident self-interest in promoting the 'revolutionary' aspects of the technology they sell, it is arguably hard to deny that contemporary media devices and the networks that connect them have an impact on how we lead and organize our everyday lives. At the very least, it is reasonable to claim that mobile media and their software, under certain circumstances, change how we relate to time, place and other people. The smartphone is perhaps the device that most effectively symbolizes our new, mobile and connected media life, in which temporal and spatial constraints might feel less imposing. However, if we can share with innovators and businesses the notion that media-induced changes *are* currently taking place, and that they *do* have an impact on our lives, as researchers we should endeavour to offer nuanced, critical and potentially contrasting interpretations of, and perspectives on, those changes – as well as of latent continuities. Such questions may pertain to issues of inclusion and exclusion, empowerment and exploitation, justice and injustice, equality and inequality. Indeed, as the contributors of this book make evident, the 'empowering' potentials of mobile connectivity might be hampered by existent power structures that determine what technology is being used, when, where, how and by whom.

This book introduces the research field of geomedia studies, which deals precisely with such critical questions. The intensification of various mobilities (notably tourism and migration) and the huge expansion of digital media systems (notably various forms of geopositioning systems and location-based services) speak to the need for interdisciplinary research at the intersection of media and communication studies and geography. Geomedia studies, as a field, reflects the *communicational turn* in geography (Adams, 2009; Adams and Jansson, 2012) and the *spatial turn* in media and communication studies (Falkheimer and Jansson, 2006) and hence borders on, nurtures from and feeds into related research fields or subject areas, most notably perhaps communication geography (Adams, 2011; Adams and Jansson, 2012). However, whereas the communicational turn is currently taking place *within* geography and the spatial turn emerges *within* media and communication studies, geomedia studies is in essence an interdisciplinary endeavour equally driven by geographers and media and communication scholars (as well as scholars from adjacent disciplines and fields). Thus, the *geomedia* in geomedia studies is first and foremost meant to signal the truly interdisciplinary nature of the research field. Geomedia studies constitutes, as McQuire suggests in his contribution to this volume, a *space of encounter*. Additionally, the term geomedia, as it has come to be used by both businesses and scholars, signals the new technological regime that

IBM, Ericsson and other agents describe with great enthusiasm. Importantly, though, whereas new and old media technologies are accepted as potential drivers of change and gain attention from many geomedia researchers, geomedia studies, as the chapters of this book make evident, engages not so much with the technology per se as with questions about *the role of media in organizing and giving meaning to processes and activities in space*. In what follows, we attempt to bring further clarity into what geomedia studies is – and what it is not.

What is Geomedia Studies?

Geomedia is a relatively new term that has been given only a few definitions so far (see Thielmann, 2007, 2010; Lapenta, 2011, 2012; McQuire, 2011, 2016). What these definitions have in common is that they refer to geomedia as a particular technological condition. This condition, in turn, is associated with the most recent decades of rapid digital development, which has led to the interweaving of 'locative media' and 'mediated localities' (Thielmann, 2010). Thielmann argues that geomedia should be seen as the subject area of media geography, whose relevance is currently revolutionized by the spatialization of media and corresponding digitalization of place. While the former part of this development has been discussed in the rapidly growing literature on 'spatial media', 'geo-tagging' and other articulations of location awareness in media (see, e.g., Elwood and Leszczynski, 2013; Wilken and Goggin, 2015), the latter part has been explored by, for example, Kitchin and Dodge (2011) in their influential book *Code/Space*, where they show how various spaces (also taking into account the built environment) have become dependent on computer infrastructures and software for their functioning. Thielmann's point is that these realms collapse into one another due to technological change.

Lapenta (2011) has suggested an even more technology-centred definition that includes only the first element of Thielmann's argument. Lapenta (2011: 14) defines geomedia as 'platforms that merge existing electronic media + the Internet + location-based technologies (or locative media) + AR (Augmented Reality) technologies in a new mode of digital composite imaging, data association and socially maintained data exchange and communication'. In this definition, geomedia is thus a label of media technology per se. McQuire (2016), in turn, points to much broader technological *and* social transformations and highlights four intersecting features of geomedia: ubiquity (that media are continuously available, even while people are on the move), real-time feedback (that many-to-many flows of information can be circulated immediately among users), location awareness (that media flows and contents are increasingly adapted to the users' locations and movements) and convergence (that different media technologies, genres and institutions are fused together, and traditional distinctions are thus breaking down). In McQuire's understanding, the transformation 'from media to geomedia' signifies the emergence of an entirely new technological regime that has far-ranging consequences for social life in general and urban life (where the density of media is particularly high) in particular.

A simple way of defining geomedia studies would thus be to refer to it as 'studies of geomedia', understood in the abovementioned sense and including the duality that Thielmann (2010) highlights. It is also possible to identify such an area of study, which has expanded rapidly during the last decade, despite that the very term geomedia has rarely been picked up. The intersections of 'locative media' and 'mediated localities' have been analysed perhaps most prominently in relation to urban spaces and the so-called media city (McQuire, 2008). For example, several studies have looked into how location-based and hybrid-reality mobile games amalgamate with the overall social fabric of urban space (e.g., De Souza e Silva and Hjorth, 2009). Licoppe and Inada (2012: 57) speak of urban public places becoming "hybrid ecologies' in which different forms of access to a particular place (e.g., through embodied presence and through various screens and terminals) are somehow articulated'. In another study, Licoppe, Morel and Rivière (2015) explore how urban dating practices are reshaped under the influence of location-based dating services, whereby the boundaries between visibility and invisibility, public and private, are altered. Similarly, Polson (2016) discusses in her analysis of female Western expatriates in Bangalore how new forms of 'geo-social media' contribute to altered perceptions of the city and a sense of security and control when navigating foreign terrains. These and other studies point to the pervasive consequences of geomedia technology in today's society.

In this volume, however, we want to advocate a more inclusive and less technology-centred understanding of geomedia. The notion of geomedia may then refer not just to the epochal shift that we currently witness in the area of spatial (re)mediations and spatialized media, but also to the expanding interdisciplinary research terrain at the intersections of media studies and geography where various ontologies and epistemologies of space/time and mediation/mediatization come together. Our suggestion is that geomedia should be taken as a *relational* concept that captures the *fundamental role of media in organizing and giving meaning to processes and activities in space*. This role has been exercised in various ways in different historical periods, through, for example, maps, compasses and newspapers, and is thus not restricted to recent developments within digital geomedia technologies. Geomedia incorporate both mediated representations of space/place and the 'logistical' properties of media that 'arrange people and property into time and space' (Peters, 2008: 40; see also Rossiter, 2015; Young, 2015). Whereas in the latter case the very notion of 'media' becomes slippery, ultimately pointing to pervasive cultural techniques like clocks and calendars, it is important to keep both aspects within sight in order to understand the historical roots and complex remediations (Bolter and Grusin, 1999) that make up and define contemporary forms of geomedia.

We thus argue that geomedia studies should take into account not just geomedia technologies in the narrow sense, but also the geographical qualities of media at large (texts, technologies and institutions), for example, the flows of digital signals between particular places and the infrastructure carrying those flows and how these both assemble and reconfigure social and material relations (see Wiley, Moreno, and Sutko, 2012). As already mentioned, this is not a new concern, and it takes us far beyond the confines of geomedia as a distinct technological category or regime. Similar questions were famously addressed by Innis (1951) in his study of how the dominant 'biases' of media have shaped entire civilizations in history. They were further developed and given a more phenomenological import by Meyrowitz (1985) in his analyses of how the rise of mediated communication paved the way for negotiated understandings of place, placement and belonging. There are also more recent examples in this tradition, such as Zook's (2008) work on the geographies of the Internet industry and Parks' (2005) work on how the development of satellite infrastructures, as well as discourses surrounding these infrastructures, altered people's perceptions of the world, while at the same time extending the hegemonic power of the West.

A related issue concerns how commercially driven media discourses and technologies take part in the geosocial positioning of people and groups. Thurlow and Jaworski (2010) have shown in their analyses of tourism discourses, found in genres like inflight magazines and television holiday shows, how different types of mobility (and thus different tourists) are socially and ideologically coded. Yet another important area regards the ways in which spatial media representations per se have developed in different eras and sociocultural contexts and how these developments are related to society at large. A key question that has arisen in the wake of 'big data', for example, concerns the usefulness and power of data visualization. While new visualization techniques may help us understand the complex patterns of social relations, practices and experiences, we should also, as Wilken and McCosker (2014: 155) highlight, 'be cautious about fetishising the sublimity of "beautiful data"'. The enticing fantasy of total knowledge is to be countered by critical discourses of symbolic power. This type of work furthers the various tasks and challenges of data collection, evaluation, (geo)visualization and management that geomedia studies should engage critically and put into historical perspective (see also Rose, 2016; Stadler, Mitchel, and Carleton, 2016).

Altogether, geomedia studies should analyse and problematize the relations between any and all communication media and various forms of spatial creativity, performance and production across material, cultural, social and political dimensions. Such analyses are bound to raise important political and ideological questions pertaining to, for example, the development and adoption of communication infrastructure and the spatially uneven patterns of access to such technologies. This unevenness underlies the often-critiqued digital divide or rather a host of different divides that mark access inequities between men and women, rich and poor, white and nonwhite, global north and global south, old and young and so on. It also brings us to the critical question of *mediatization*, which provides the structural context of this book.

Spaces and Mobilities in Mediatized Worlds

The growth in connected and mobile media devices over the last three decades is astounding. According to the World Bank report, *World Development Indicators 2017*, in 2015 there was nearly one mobile cellular subscription for every person on earth, while in 1990 fewer than 2 per 1,000 people had one. The number of Internet users worldwide reached 3.5 billion by the end of 2016 (ITU, 2017). Overall, there is strong statistical support for the notion that we are currently undergoing a shift in terms of personal and professional media use. In this book, we use the notion of *mediatization* – and, by extension, *geomediatization* – to approach this shift. Importantly, though, the notion of mediatization points to processes that cannot be reduced to merely the voluminous increases in media devices or media content. Mediatization, as used in this book, involves new ways of *understanding* and *relating to* media – as content, technologies, institutions and social platforms. In line with previous definitions, we understand mediatization as a meta-process that, in parallel with other meta-processes (such as individualization, globalization and commercialization), reconfigures social life (cf. Krotz, 2007; Couldry and Hepp, 2013; Krotz, 2014; Jansson, 2013, 2018).

Mediatization research, thus, should attempt to capture the complexity of what it means – for citizens, governments, businesses, societies, etc. – to *live* with media. Analyses of the implications of the quantitative increase in new, mobile and connected media for various agents demand great levels of sensitivity to what Jansson (2018) refers to as the *dialectic* of mediatization. On the one hand, the media might come across as potential sources of emancipation, empowerment, autonomy, resistance and, ultimately, social change. Indisputably, the new technological regime liberates us from (certain) spatial restraints by offering the 'magical' possibility of 'being in two places at once' (Scannell, 1996: 91) and affords new forms of mobilities. They provide new public spaces, facilitate community formations and allow us to connect with other people, 'wherever' and 'whenever'. On the other hand, and concurrently, the media might be viewed as agents of estrangement, exploitation, dependency, isolation and, in the end, hegemony and domination. The 'liberating' connectivity and mobility of new media – and inbuilt geo-positioning features especially – also render possible new forms of surveillance, new means of commercial exploitation and new consumer needs, for example. Mediatization, thus, should be understood as a non-normative concept that point to media-induced changes that cannot, in any simple way at least, be evaluated as either inherently positive or negative.

Relatedly, researchers interested in the interplay between media technology and the social should be attentive to *inequalities* of mediatization, or, to frame it differently, to the possibility that mediatization plays out differently in different social contexts (Jansson, 2013). If technology *is* indeed 'empowering us as individuals' (Ericsson, 2017: 8), then questions about access and closure, inclusion and exclusion, possibilities and impossibilities, positions and dispositions, become acute. Marvin's (1988) seminal account of 'old technologies', such as the electric light and the telephone, teaches us that technology is never just for anyone, but always geared towards certain groups while excluding others. On a global level, quantitative data alone reveal that sociotechnological divides (whether digital or analogue) remain to this day, irrespective of the alleged new technological 'revolution'. While mobile devices and Internet connections are on steady increase worldwide, still only half as many have access to the Internet in the developing countries compared to developed countries, with a ratio of 40/80 per hundred inhabitants (ITU, 2017). Consequently, mediatization research should engage with questions about how our use *and* non-use of various media *conditions,* and *is conditioned by,* social life at large, including existent power structures. As the reader will note, the contributions of this book have in common that they bring these questions to the fore.

If people's uses of mobile and connected media spur mediatization processes, meaning that these media become all the more indispensable to individuals, groups and organizations, then certain traits of these media make for what we denote as *geomediatization*. In a narrow, technology-oriented sense, the term speaks to the increased prominence of geopositioning systems and place-based services in today's media landscape and in everyday modern life. Currently, almost all digital mobile and connected media have built-in components that reveal and exploit the user's geographical coordinates. As we use our smartphones' GPS to navigate a new city, 'check-in' at a certain venue on Facebook, hunt for virtual gadgets in a location-based augmented reality game, connect with potential partners on a geotagging dating app or simply buy an electronic bus ticket based on our current location, our device communicates with its surroundings. In a wider sense, which is more in line with our understanding of geomedia per se, geomediatization is not limited to specific media technologies (i.e., digital, mobile and connected) but points to the accentuated and socially pervasive interplay of media users, media technologies and the geosocial surroundings on the whole. Ultimately, geomediatization denotes the coming of a social regime where human subjectivity, media and space/place are co-constitutive of one another. Against this background, this book is an attempt to overview how media – old and new – interplay with (moulding and being moulded by) the social production of *spaces* and *mobilities*.

This brings us to the structure of the book, which in turn is reflected in the outline of this chapter. Our volume is organized around three key parts, namely 'Theorizing Geomedia', 'Geomedia Spaces' and 'Geomedia Mobilities'. The first, theorizing, section brings together perspectives and insights that serve to further contextualize geomedia as a theoretical domain and position geomedia studies in relation to previous research, whereas the second and third parts are thematically organized around 'space' and 'mobility' respectively – two notions that are central to this emergent research field. The book ends with a reflective and forward-looking contribution by Scott McQuire, author of *Geomedia: Networked Cities and the Future of Public Space* (2016) and a key contributor to geomedia studies. In the remainder of this chapter we introduce each of the subsequent parts and the individual contributions that constitute them.

Theorizing Geomedia

Geomedia is an emergent field that studies the complex dialectics of space, mobility and media. Theorizing Geomedia is about making sense of the complex processes and forces of coding, transcoding and decoding that mould societies, territories and bodies. Geomedia examines (new) power geometries of digitization and digital colonization of planetary space. It signals to a concern with material, lived and imagined spaces that are engendered through geomediatization processes. Beyond studying various reconfigurations of territories, societies and bodies, Theorizing Geomedia is also about delineating the terrain of the emergent field of study, attending to the underlying ontologies and epistemologies that delineate the field itself.

The papers that are included in this section muse on these issues from different angles. While invoking the necessity of *geomedia*, Rowan Wilken (Chapter 2) alerts us that geomedia has a long pedigree and ought to be seen as the most recent contribution in a long line of scholarship that seeks to explore the interdisciplinary possibilities that arise from conversations between, and the intersections (if not convergence) of, two key fields of research: geography and media and communication. Wilken stresses the novelty of geomedia – the gamut of 'technological developments that have contributed to a profound reshaping of our everyday engagements with and understandings of space, place, communication and social interaction'. Three such technologies are identified.

The first involves the democratization of mapping technologies, i.e., availability of geolocation services *en masse*, on different devices, which make everyone a geographer of sorts. Second, smart phones, consolidation of the mobile Internet, and the rise of a vibrant app economy – new assemblages, or dynamic spaces and relations, that fuse producers, consumers and developers of new media technologies. Third, following McQuire (2016: 6), Wilken maps out the implications on current research on location-based services.

Using a crowd gathered on a convenience store watching the semifinal football of the UEFA-2015 match in a small town in Iceland as a point of departure, Paul C. Adams (Chapter 3) proffers a synthesis of geomedia – modelled as a quadrant consisting of media *in* spaces, media *in* places, spaces *in* media and places *in* media. We are taken on a tour, which begins with the fundamental observation that communication (pretty much as everything else) '*takes place*', understood somewhere, and the corollary axiom that media create space and place, with the proviso that we should apprehend the quadrants as intertwined and complementary. The coming of the digital era ruffles the quadrant so to speak, and as Adams notes although useful as a taxonomic device, we need to transcend the quadrant by moving perpendicularly (transvessally á la Felix Guattari). Adams identifies new directions: modular identity, *dividuals* and the key role played by codes in defining who gets access to which spaces and power as access to networks, i.e. code/space (Kitchin and Dodge, 2011), the forest of cookies and filter bubbles. What does the notion of publics mean in a digital era? asks Adams. In an era defined by the selfie, where do we locate the (mobile) public? Questions that touch on perennial issues of presence/absence, here/there, subject/object. Perhaps one could claim that Derrida's metaphysics of presence has little bearing on the ontologies and epistemologies that define geomedia.

By asking 'where is the locus of contemporary media production?', Helen Morgan Parmett and Scott Rodgers (Chapter 4) chart the new and changing geographies of the media. Pertinent in an age of fake media, this question examines the ontologies and epistemologies underlying geomedia as well. Wherefrom to theorize geomedia? For those familiar with Heidegger, topos and logos, place and epistemology are intertwined. How to theorize geomedia in a context of multiple, deinstitutionalized and deterritorialized loci of media production? How to theorize geomedia in an era of the mobile and fleeting? The conjunctive notion of geomedia is taken as indicative of the 'arrival of a broadly shared *environmental* view of media'. Space, place and circulation are deployed as conceptual lenses to examine the spatialities of media production. Beyond the fuzzy boundaries of media production and consumption, it has become more difficult to discern what is and what is not a media product. However, 'media environments instead retain marked power asymmetries, not just in terms of content production, but also in design, operation and ownership of new media forms, commodities, devices, data, platforms and infrastructure'. 'We are witnessing a complex reshaping of how media-related professions, organizations and technical platforms attune with, speak to, and act on behalf of others'. Their musings lead them to three postulates regarding media production spatialities, viz., (a) as practices within *circulatory* processes; (b) as a radically contextualized habitus (a relational conception of space such that it is part of what it produces); (c) as practices positioned and oriented towards dispersed field *spaces* of production (technical and social). Inspired by the 'circulatory turn', a relational ontology and epistemology of theorizing geomedia is proposed.

Mimi Sheller (Chapter 5) draws on materialist approaches to media studies, critical logistics studies and critical mobilities theory to offer a novel approach to theorizing geomedia. Sheller's take underscores differential/uneven material geographies of geomedia by foregrounding the politics of uneven topologies, dissonances, speeds and frictions, drawing on theories of 'infrastructuring' as an active practice. The complex processes and forces of coding, transcoding and decoding that reconfigure territories, societies and bodies are not only horizontal, but also vertical. Sheller attends to the 'horizontal and vertical geographies of mediated mobilities that span planetary scales'. In so doing, Sheller provides an account of geomedia that combines the metaphysics of flow and fixity, the grounded/rooted and the fleeting/nomadic to shed light on how horizontally and vertically 'networked infrastructures of mobility and communication are being imagined, extended, contested and appropriated'. Sheller theorizes geomedia studies as an emergent field that weaves geography, geoecology and geopolitics. By drawing attention to the differential, contested and political dimensions of geomedia, Sheller signals to the necessity of critical geomedia studies.

In conclusion, it may be noted that theorizing is an active process. It is averse to closure; this spirit runs through the chapters included in this section.

Geomedia Spaces

The second section of this book engages specifically with how space and place are closely intertwined with media and communication. The authors explore how visual representations, media practices and the media industry *are shaped by space* as well as *shape space* themselves. It is this, the complexity within and interconnection between how *media is shaped by space* and how *media shapes space* that emerges as the core of this section. Each chapter uses different theoretical angles and different empirical material to clarify these ongoing asynchronous processes and how they are entangled with the past, occur in the present and affect the future. However, a close examination of these chapters reveals recurring themes within these processes, where the most prominent is *power relations*. By closely studying a specific situation or setting, the chapters illuminate different aspects and levels of power.

Gillian Rose (Chapter 6) illustrates the ways in which media play a role in shaping the future city. Rose links today's planning of the future urban city to corporate films promoting the 'smart city'. 'Smart city' has become a term to describe the future urban city, where 'smart' refers to the ability to harvest big data and to analyse this data to build cities, adjustable to the needs of growing populations. Rose notes that the notion of the 'smart city' has come to have a great impact on how cities around the world plan for the future, suggesting that these films are representational as well as operative: they portray how the future city looks and functions and define the problems our urban cities will face in the future. However, these corporate media productions also enact smartness, thus defining today what the citizen might need and want in the future. In Rose's text, the power dimensions emerge in the way these promotional films shape our perception of future cities and technology, also on a political level. In her conclusion, Rose discusses how the leaders represented in these films are overwhelmingly male and that citizens portrayed in the animations enact conventional gendered stereotypes. This also brings absence into focus: what is not represented, who is not portrayed, and how are power structures enacted and reacted to in these productions?

The next chapter of this section takes us on a journey through urban space, where we 'tag along' with Tindra Thor (Chapter 7) on her walks and interviews with graffiti artists. Through the concept of in-betweenness she uncovers the dimensions of graffiti, between the hidden and the present, between celebrated art and disgust, between humour and seriousness, as well as how graffiti, while existing in the periphery, are often at the centre of public attention. By elevating these dimensions, Thor demonstrates that an act of communication – a graffiti painting – functions as a disturbance of the hegemonies of the urban. The chapter points out the resistance and empowerment of graffiti artists, but also how politics and institutions push their actions to the periphery, thus illuminating ongoing negotiations of power and power structures. A silent scribble on a concrete wall can make a sound that reverberates throughout the whole city.

Chris Lukinbeal and Laura Sharp (Chapter 8) use San Diego, US, as a case to investigate in which ways a city emerges as a 'Backlot' – a term used for the area behind a movie studio for outdoor scenes – and why certain locations get picked for filming. By following the development of the film industry in San Diego, they identify traits that are of importance: the location's look, political agenda, access to skilled labour and infrastructure. However they also identify implications for the citizen to live in a 'Backlot', where filming on location disturbs the citizens' everyday life. Focusing their study to one specific location over a longer period of time, Lukinbeal and Sharp draw out continuous negotiations between local politics, location and distance and the media industry and show that negotiations between location and the media industry appear at different levels and among different partners.

After visiting the future city, walking through hidden places with graffiti artists and travelling through the San Diego Backlot, we finally end our journey in the home. Kristian Møller Jørgensen and Maja Klausen (Chapter 9) present their study on how elderly peoples' media practices play into shaping their homes. Through the concept of 'flows of bodies' they map how media engender continuous intrusion of strangers into home spaces. The reader gets to follow elderly peoples' experiences of the media as 'The Other', an uninvited nuisance in their home, while at the same time a necessity to their social life and constitutive of their homemaking. By placing the home at the heart of the study, Møller Jørgensen and Klausen are able to capture how hegemonic and counter-hegemonic cultures are at play in elderly peoples' mediatized homemaking.

These chapters, in different ways, describe and disentangle the intricate web of media, communication and space. All in all, they give both methodological and theoretical insights to the field of geomedia studies, pertaining above all to how power permeates the interactions of space/place and media and is constantly negotiated and renegotiated.

Geomedia Mobilities

The third and last section of the book comprises four chapters that in different ways set out to understand the complex relationship of media, space and mobility. While differently attuned both methodologically and theoretically, the chapters of the last section come together in a joint emphasis on the coalescing of media on the one hand and mobility on the other. The section testifies to the fact that it is increasingly difficult to understand one without the other in times of *geomediatization*. By extension, the argument on the necessity of *geomedia studies* (theorized by Wilkens in Section 1) is further illustrated and corroborated by the following chapters. Maren Hartmann (Chapter 10) begins by proposing a new research paradigm for the empirical study of geomedia. The concept of 'mobilism', she argues, combines mobility with momentum and as such has the potential to account for the social inertia and change that are crucial to understanding 'the social'. The chapter takes as its starting point the mobility turn in the social sciences and pursues to explicate the concept of mobilism, which may help to understand contemporary societies 'on the move'. The concept's empirical applicability is explored via the media use of Berlin's homeless – a social segment 'fixed in mobility'. Hartmann demonstrates, thus, the potency of the research paradigm of geomedia. Her chapter provides a concrete platform from which empirical research in this emerging field of inquiry may evolve in ways that not only promote an understanding of outstanding dynamics of our geomediatized worlds but also hold political and societal relevancy.

The mobilities turn has meant that the social sciences are increasingly occupied with movement and with space, and the emerging power dynamics connected to them (Sheller and Urry, 2006). Yet, as André Jansson and Linda Ryan Bengtsson argue (Chapter 11), we still know very little about how these dynamics play out in practice in specific social, geographical and cultural milieus. Jansson and Ryan Bengtsson present an interview-based study that examines how the network capital of artists is renegotiated when relocated to a new social, cultural and geographical milieu – the provincial, small town of Arvika, Sweden. Focus is put on the social costs involved in the attempt to translate one's capital accumulated in one social field (the largely urban-centric artistic field) to another (the local social space that is the sum of the struggles over positions in a small provincial town). As such, the study constitutes an addition to previous research on the (re)negotiations that come with migration and mobility, which Jansson and Ryan Bengtsson argue have tended to focus on movement from the global south to the global north. Via their interviews, Jansson and Ryan Bengtsson proceed to unearth a paradox of contemporary mediatization. The network capital of artists is devaluated when recontextualized, yet the artists become increasingly dependent on various technologies of communication to sustain themselves as artists, precisely because of their relocation to the small town.

Kaarina Nikunen (Chapter 12) tackles one of the outstanding traumas of our increasingly mobile world – the European refugee crisis (which has been referred to as 'the worst refugee crisis since the Second World War') that has resulted in thousands of deaths at the European borders and in the Mediterranean Sea. Nikunen adopts an ethnographic approach stretching over 14 years covering the village of Badolato located on the Italian south coast. The aim is to understand the geographical imaginations – the understanding of place and its connection to social processes and its construction – put in motion in connection to the arrival of refugees at the shores of Europe. During the 2015 refugee crisis, the media and political decision making promoted a particular geographical imagination. By and large, this imagination was one of fear – guided by images of an overwhelming and uncontrollable influx of refugees into Europe. By welcoming the 300 refugees who, almost two decades earlier, were shipwrecked along the Italian coast, the locals of Badolato challenged such an imagination. At least initially, the locals' (an ageing population wherein many were unemployed) reception of those in need was one guided by a cosmopolitan hospitality. Refugees were greeted with cultural meetings and festivals promoting cross-cultural interaction and the rejuvenation of a depopulated small town. These contrasts between the micro (localized practice) and the macro (European politics and media images), lead Nikunen to wind up her chapter with a normative call for media coverage to be attentive to the actual practices that play at the local and place-based level and to give voice and political subjectivity to migrants, particularly in times of uncertainty and increased mobility.

Closing the section, John Tomlinson (Chapter 13) unravels the dynamics of 'fast media'. Since the end of the last century, significant parts of social scientific inquiry have revolved around globalization, not least its cultural significance. Those of us who have been concerned with the role of media in and for globalization may, according to Tomlinson, have been too preoccupied with the notion of *proximity*. Media, approached from this perspective, are understood – broadly speaking – to succeed or fail in creating McLuhan's 'global village'. We have, in other words, put our focus on the media's capacity to create or hinder the formation of belongings and connections across space and time. Tomlinson's contention is that the cultural significance of media throughout modern history is also another one. Throughout modernity media have imparted a shift in tempo by promoting *immediacy* (see also Tomlinson, 2007). This compelling and significant insight – which crucially adds temporality to the study of mobility, space and media – is exemplified by a look at some of the peculiarities of both 'old' and 'new' media. Tomlinson's examples range from the banality of the speeding up of end-credits of television programs and the news ticker, rushing by in the margins of our screens as the anchor presents the news, to the Apple watch and drone-delivered wine to people's homes. In a world where the promise of *immediacy* has been fulfilled the gap between desire and its fulfilment is closed, argues Tomlinson. A key challenge for geomedia research is to further delineate the cultural significance of *immediacy*.

What Is on the Horizon of Geomedia?

While rooted in previous research – most notably communication geography – and informed by more or less classical theory from media, geography and nearby traditions, geomedia studies is a relatively new reseach field, whose future orientation we can only attempt to predict and whose object of study – at least in terms of 'media' – is caught up in a continuous metamorphosis. In the fourth and final part of this book, an Afterword rubricated 'Geomedia: In praise of unruly conjunctions' (Chapter 14), Scott McQuire offers reflections on the present-day media landscape, on the media landscape that we might presage in the horizon and on the potential implications of these developments for research. Greater diversity in situations of production and use; new capacitites for devices and platforms to use location-awareness and changing temporal patterns of communicative exchanges are identified as some of the most important characteristics of contemporary media development.

What this complex media landscape demands, according to McQuire, is 'a new commitment to *unruly* thinking, predicated on systematic and creative engagement between humanities and social science scholars in fields such as media, geography, cultural studies, sociology and journalism with those working in areas such as computer science and geospatial sciences, but also in areas such as law and public policy'. In looking to the future, McQuire ultimately requests a media theory that is not media centric, but grows out of a 'messy' encounter between disciplines. Geomedia studies, he suggests, may provide the space in which such encounters might begin to be elaborated. Such a vision of this emergent research field – as a brave and innovative meeting place between disciplines – is indeed in line with the overall thrust of this book and our underlying imagination of what geomedia studies should be about. This book, we would like to think, is evidence alone of the fecundity that such endeavours might bring about, in terms of multifaceted and rich approaches to media, space/place and mobility.

References

Adams, P.C. (2009). *Geographies of Media and Communication: A Critical Introduction*. London: Wiley-Blackwell.

Adams, P.C. (2011). A taxonomy for communication geography. *Progress in Human Geography*, 35(1), 37–57.

Adams, P.C., & Jansson, A. (2012). Communication geography: A bridge between disciplines. *Communication Theory*, 22, 299–317.

Bolter, J.D., & Grusin, R. (1999). *Remediation: Understanding New Media*. Cambridge, MA: MIT Press.

Couldry, N., & Hepp, A. (2013). Conceptualizing mediatization: Contexts, traditions, arguments, *Communication Theory*, 13(3), 191–202.

De Souza e Silva, A., & Hjorth, L. (2009) Playful urban spaces: A historical approach to mobile games, *Simulation and Gaming*, 40(5), 602–625.

Elwood, S., & Leszczynski, A., (2013). New spatial media, new knowledge politics. *Transactions of the Institute of British Geographers*, 38(4), 544–559.

Ericsson (2017). *Networked Society Essentials*. Retrieved from www.ericsson.com/res/docs/2013/networked-society-essentials-booklet.pdf.

Falkheimer, J., & Jansson, A., eds. (2006). *Geographies of Communication*. Göteborg: Nordicom.

Hardt, M., & Negri, A. (2000). *Empire*. Cambridge, MA.: Harvard University Press.

IBM (2017). *Individual Enterprise: How Mobility Redefines Business*. Retrieved from www.ibm.com/blogs/insights-on-business/oracle-consulting/wp-content/uploads/sites/13/2015/02/The-individual-Enterprise-How-Mobility-Redefines-Business.pdf.

Innis, H.A. (1951). *The Bias of Communication*. Toronto: Toronto University Press.

ITU (2017). *Global and Regional ICT Data: Statistics*. Retrieved from www.itu.int/en/ITU-D/Statistics/Pages/stat/default.aspx.

Jansson, A. (2013). Mediatization and social space: Reconstructing mediatization for the transmedia age. *Communication Theory*, 23(3), 279–296.
Jansson, A. (2018). *Mediatization and Mobile Lives: A Critical Approach.* London: Routledge.
Kitchin, R., & Dodge, M. (2011). *Code/Space: Software and Everyday Life.* Cambridge, MA: MIT Press.
Krotz, F. (2007). The meta-process of 'mediatization' as a conceptual frame. *Global Media and Communication*, 3(3), 256–260.
Krotz, F. (2014) Mediatization as a mover in modernity: Social and cultural change in the context of media change. In K. Lundby (Ed.) *Mediatization of Communication (Handbook of Communication Sciences, Vol 22)*. Berlin: De Gruyter Mouton.
Lapenta, F. (2011). Geomedia: on location-based media, the changing status of collective image production and the emergence of social navigation systems, *Visual Studies*, 26(1), 14–24.
Lapenta, F. (2012). The infosphere, the geosphere, and the mirror: The geomedia-based normative renegotiations of body and place. In R. Wilken, & G. Goggin (Eds.) *Mobile Technology and Place*. London: Routledge.
Licoppe, C., & Inada, Y. (2012). When urban public places become 'hybrid ecologies': Proximity-based game encounters in Dragon Quest 9 in France and Japan. In R. Wilken & G. Goggin (Eds.) *Mobile Technology and Place*. London: Routledge.
Licoppe, C., Morel, J., & Rivière, C.A. (2015). Grindr casual hook-ups as interactional achievements. *Media, Culture, and Society*, Published ahead of print, September 9th 2015.
Marvin, C. (1988). *When Old Technologies were New: Thinking about Electric Communication in the Late Nineteenth Century.* New York: Oxford Univ. Press.
McQuire, S. (2008). *The Media City: Media, Architecture and Urban Space.* London: Sage.
McQuire, S. (2011). Geomedia, networked culture and participatory public space. In R. Hinkel (Ed.) *Urban Interior: Informal Explorations, Interventions and Occupations*. Baunach: Spurbuchverlag.
McQuire, S. (2016). *Geomedia: Networked Cities and the Future of Public Space.* Cambridge: Polity Press.
Meyrowitz, J. (1985). *No Sense of Place: The Impact of Electronic Media on Social Behavior.* Oxford: Oxford University Press.
Mosco, V. (2004). The Digital Sublime: Myth, Power, and Cyberspace. Cambridge, MA: MIT Press.
Parks, L. (2005). *Cultures in Orbit: Satellites and the Televisual.* Durham: Duke University Press.
Peters, J.D. (2008). Strange sympathies: Horizons of German and American media theory, In F. Kelleter & D. Stein (Eds.) *American Studies as Media Studies*. Heidelberg: Universitätsverlag, pp. 3–23.
Polson, E. (2016). *Privileged Mobilities: Professional Migration, Geo-Social Media and a New Global Middle Class.* New York: Peter Lang.
Rose, G. (2016). Rethinking the geographies of 'objects' through digital technologies: Interface, network and friction, *Progress in Human Geography*, 40(3), 334–351.

Rossiter, N. (2015). Coded vanilla: Logistical media and the determination of action. *South Atlantic Quarterly*, 114(1), 135–152.

Scannell, P. (1996): *Radio, Television & Modern Life*. Oxford: Blackwell

Sheller, M., & Urry, J. (2006): The new mobilities paradigm. *Environment and Planning A*, 38(2), 207–226.

Stadler, J., Mitchel, P., & Carleton, S. (2016). *Imagined Landscapes: Geovisualizing Australian Spatial Narratives*. Indianapolis: Indiana University Press.

Thielmann, T. (2007) You have reached your destination!: Position, positioning and superpositioning of space through car navigation systems. *Social Geography*, 2(1), 63–75.

Thielmann, T. (2010). Locative media and mediated localities: An introduction to media geography, *Aether: The Journal of Media Geography*, V.A, 1–17.

Thurlow, C., & Jaworski, A. (2010) *Tourism Discourse: Language and Global Mobility*. Basingstoke: Palgrave.

Tomlinson, J. (2007) *The Culture of Speed: The Coming of Immediacy*. Los Angeles, London, New Delhi, Singapore: Sage.

Wiley, S.B.C., Moreno, T., & Sutko, D. (2012). Assemblages, networks, subjects: a materialist approach to the production of social space. In J. Packer, & S.B.C. Wiley (Eds.) *Communication Matters: Materialist Approaches to Media, Mobility and Networks*. New York: Routledge.

Wilken, R., & Goggin, G. (Eds.) (2015). *Locative Media*. London: Routledge.

Wilken, R., & McCosker, A. (2014). Rethinking 'Big Data' as visual knowledge: the sublime and the diagrammatic in data visualization. *Visual Studies*, 29(2), 155–164.

Young, L.C. (2015). Cultural techniques and logistical media: Tuning German and Anglo-American media studies, *M/C Journal*, 18(2).

Zook, M. (2008). *The Geography of the Internet Industry: Venture Capital, Dot-coms, and Local Knowledge*. Oxford: John Wiley & Sons.

Part I
Theorizing Geomedia

2 The Necessity of Geomedia

Understanding the Significance of Location-Based Services and Data-Driven Platforms

Rowan Wilken

Introduction

In this chapter, I explore how questions of location have become a central part of our experiences of an expanding suite of smartphone applications and services and a necessary part of the technological developments and corporate arrangements that underpin them (the business deals, monetization strategies, platform-specific data extraction methods, algorithmic sorting, etc.). Given the complexity of these developments, I wish to argue that the need for thorough, robust and nuanced accounts of 'geomedia' has become urgent.

In exploring these concerns, I begin by providing a brief account of key scholarship – particularly by Scott McQuire, Jesper Falkheimer and André Jansson, and Paul C. Adams – that seeks to examine the creative coming together of media and communication and geography. A number of these texts appeared at the time of significant technological change that, among other things, fed the rise of location-based services. In the second part of the chapter, I describe three generations of these location-based services, with specific attention given to two of them: Banjo and Foursquare. In the final part of the chapter, I relate these developments back once more to Scott McQuire's (2016) account of the concept of geomedia, which, I argue provides a productive framework for extending and further sharpening present critical engagements with geolocational technologies.

Geomedia, Mobile Media, Locative Media

In his book *Geomedia: Networked Cities and the Future of Public Space*, Scott McQuire (2016) develops the title term as a conceptual means of making critical sense of the complexities of the contemporary urban condition. Geomedia, according to his formulation of the term, is fed from, and should be understood as forming at, the intersection of four different sources:

1 *Ubiquity*: 'mobile and embedded media devices, coupled to extended digital networks, recreate the city as a media in which content and connection are seemingly available "anywhere, anytime"' (2), and where 'the ubiquity of social media is currently transforming the social space of the city in complex ways that extend well beyond the choices to individual users' (3);
2 *Location-awareness*: 'when the everyday movements of millions of individuals through the city can leave discernible traces, location-awareness assumes a new prominence in urban experience' (4);
3 *The 'real-time orientation of contemporary digital networks'*: 'what is different in the present is the way the distributed architecture of digital networks opens the potential for "real-time" feedback from many-to-many, supporting novel experiences of social simultaneity' (4); and,
4 *Convergence*: which, for McQuire, describes not just 'a narrow technical logic', but also 'a broader process of remaking, impacting on business, institutional and regulatory settings as much as social, political and cultural practices' (5).

Geomedia, I would suggest, ought to be seen as the most recent contribution in a long line of scholarship that seeks to explore the interdisciplinary possibilities that arise from conversations between, and the intersections (if not convergence) of, two key fields of research: geography and media and communication. While this particular line of research can be traced back a long way, there has been a noticeable (re)flowering of critical interest in these concerns from the early 2000s onwards, with the publication of a number of key books, including: David Morley's (2000) *Home Territories: Media, Mobility and Identity*; Nick Couldry and Anna McCarthy's (2004) *MediaSpace: Place, Scale and Culture in a Digital Age*; David Morley and Kevin Robins' (2005) *Spaces of Identity: Global Media, Electronic Landscapes, and Cultural Boundaries*; and, even more explicitly, Jesper Falkheimer and André Jansson's (2006) *Geographies of Communication* and Paul C. Adams' (2009) *Geographies of Media and Communication*.

In the context of the present book, the specific contributions of the last two titles in the above list in advancing thinking around the commingling of geography and media and communication require special mention. In their introductory chapter to *Geographies of Communication*, co-editors André Jansson and Jesper Falkheimer (2006), who come at this issue from the direction of media studies, argue that a 'spatial turn' in media studies is not so much required as already underway. Given this, what is needed, they suggest, is a detailed account of 'the full potential of this ["turn"]' (9). In response, the two editors set out to gather contemporary Nordic scholarship spanning media studies and geography and drawn from a range of other specialisms, with each contribution responding to the research question of '*how communication produces space and how space produces communication*' (9 – original emphasis). Jansson and Falkheimer (2006) frame the resultant collection as mapping out 'what might become a new subfield within media and cultural studies: *the geography of communication* (or communication geography)' (9 – original emphasis). The result is an important synchronic account, or snapshot, of the diversity of media and communication research being undertaken within a Nordic context at that time.

Meanwhile, in *Geographies of Media and Communication*, Paul C. Adams, who comes at the same issue from the direction of geography, suggests that a so-called 'cultural turn' that was occurring around that time within 'various geographical specializations' is, in fact, perhaps best understood as a '*sensitization to communication*' (Adams, 2009: 11 – original emphasis), a 'communicational turn' (10). Rather than sketch the contours of what such a subfield might look like, Adams sets himself a more ambitious aim: to provide a survey 'of the major ways in which geographers have dealt with the idea of communication' (3), while also interweaving 'hints [...] of pathways leading from geography to communication and vice versa' (3). The ensuing analysis of geography's engagements with media and communication is framed around Adams' now well-known 'quadrant' schema (comprising media in spaces, space in media, media in places and places in media), which is structured around two intersecting axes: space versus place and geographical representation versus geographical organization (4). The result is an important book that provides a comprehensive, diachronic account of geography's engagement with media and communication. In combination, these two books – along with the other titles mentioned earlier – are significant for the ways they draw out and explore what in this book is referred to as 'geomedia': the various intersections between media and communication and geography, and the ongoing importance of exploring these intersections.

In addition to scholarly interest in geomedia, around the time that Falkheimer and Jansson's and Adams' books were released, at least three major sets of technological developments were underway that have since contributed to a profound reshaping of our everyday engagements with and understandings of space, place, communication and social interaction.

The first of these involves the democratization of digital mapping technologies. As I have noted elsewhere, 'since Google's embrace of geolocation services in 2005 – with the fascination attracted by Google Earth and Google Maps – mainstream interest in and uptake of locative media services flourished', such that 'consumers are now well accustomed to using sat nav devices in their cars or while walking, Google Maps on desktop and laptop computers and mobile devices, and geoweb, geotagging, and other mapping applications' (Wilken and Goggin, 2015: 5).

The second set of developments follow from the launch of the Apple iPhone and Google's Android operating system in 2007–2008, which led to extraordinary growth in smartphone take up and use and the consolidation of the mobile Internet (see Hjorth, Burgess, and Richardson, 2012). The rise of the smartphone – the 'iPhone moment' as Gerard Goggin (2011: 181) refers to it – led to a number of additional and significant developments: an acceleration of 'the trend toward the crossover between Wi-Fi (wireless internet) and cellular mobile networks and devices', such that handsets, applications and users now switch with ease among networks (Wilken and Goggin, 2015: 6); an associated 'evolution of network architectures and infrastructures, as telecommunications and mobile networks – especially next generation networks and 4G and 5G mobile networks – merged with Internet protocol and data networks' (2015: 6) and the rise of a vibrant 'app economy' servicing platform owners, mobile application developers and smartphone end users (Goldsmith, 2014; Wilken, 2017).

The third set of developments concerns the 'enormous growth in personal, private, and machine-based information and processing [that] has been associated with a wide range of consumer and enterprise technologies and networks, which adds significantly to mass personalized user, device, and network data concerning location' (Wilken and Goggin, 2015: 6), among other things. These developments are often associated with RFID technologies (Rosol, 2010; Frith, 2015a), the interconnection, via the internet, of computing devices that are embedded in everyday objects (the 'internet of things') (Greengard, 2015), and with globe-spanning industrial and software-related logistics industries (Rossiter, 2016). These increasingly miniaturized computing chips and sensor technologies, coupled with advances in machine learning capabilities, thus come to play a vital role in *connecting* people, goods and other material things, and in facilitating and tracking the *movement* of people, goods and other material things.

Commensurate with the above developments – particularly that of the advent of the smartphone with incorporated mapping capabilities – was the rise of location-sensitive mobile social networking (LMSN) services. Characteristic of these services was the ability to register one's physical presence at a particular location or venue that was then communicated to one or more people, either those within the individual's social network or fellow users of the same service unknown to that individual. A significant body of scholarly work has emerged in response, which seeks to chart and make critical sense of LMSN and broader locative media services (see, for example, Farman, 2011, 2013; Gordon and de Souza e Silva, 2011; de Souza e Silva and Frith, 2012b; Hjorth and Richardson, 2014; Evans, 2015; Frith, 2015b; Wilken and Goggin, 2015; Evans and Saker, 2017). Little discussed in existing literature is the extent to which, since the advent of the smartphone, the means by which one's physical location at particular venues could be registered within location-enabled social network applications and by end users of these services has shifted subtly yet significantly, passing through a number of iterations, or generations. In the following section, I aim to detail what I see as the three main generations of these services, before returning to McQuire's conception of 'geomedia' and to an exploration of why his formulation of this term is productive for thinking through what is at stake in current forms of location-based applications and associated parent platforms.

The Rise, Evolution and Maturation of Location-Based Services

Contemporary smartphone-enabled location-based services can be described as having passed through at least three iterations or generations. 'First generation' location-based services required the active registering of one's location by end users, often in the form of 'check-ins'. Several of these predate the release of the first iPhone and were thus designed to operate on older mobile handsets and associated infrastructures. A pioneering early example was Dodgeball (co-founded by Dennis Crowley in 2000 and subsequently sold to Google in 2005) (see Humphreys, 2007, 2010). Other, related services followed, such as Loopt (founded in 2005), Whrrl, Brightkite and Gowalla (all founded in 2007), Foursquare (co-founded by Dennis Crowley in 2009, the same year that Google discontinued Dodgeball) and Chinese Foursquare clone, Jiepang (founded in 2010). Of these, only Foursquare continues to survive as an independent operation: Brightkite sold to HDmessaging (formerly Limbo) in 2009, Whrrl to Groupon in 2011; Gowalla to Facebook in the same year and Loopt to Green Dot in early 2012; having undergone a significant redesign in 2013, Jiepang closed in 2016.

'Second generation' LMSNs, also known as 'ambient social location' or 'social search' applications (Lee, 2013: 27–28), involved 'passive' location disclosure, tracking and compatibility pairing of end users. Indicative of these 'second generation' LMSNs were applications such as Glancee and Sonar (both founded in 2010) and Highlight and Banjo (both founded in 2011). The first of these, Glancee, tracked a user's location in the background and linked to the user's Facebook and Twitter accounts to show the user 'people who are using the app [nearby] and their shared social graph interests and Facebook picture' (Burns, 2012); it also included a 'radar' function to reveal their physical proximity (Lee, 2013: 27). As with those of the first generation, very few second-generation applications have survived as ongoing independent operations – not least due to consumer perception that they were inherently 'creepy'. Glancee was purchased by Facebook in 2012 and closed; support for Sonar app was halted in 2013 (Ha, 2013); Highlight ceased operation in 2015 following a 'talent acquistion' by Pinterest (Lynley, 2016). Only Banjo survives in altered form, and I will return to discuss what has become of this service below.

The 'third generation', and arguably the dominant present form at time of writing, are more broadly defined location-based services that involve what I am here referring to as *ubiquitous geodata capture*. For these services, location remains fundamental to their operation but is integrated at both the front end (the interface) and the back end (algorithmic processing, database population, monetization efforts and so on).

Uber is a good example of a 'native' third-generation service in that geolocation and geocoded data are seamlessly integrated into, and vital to, the operation of the service at all levels. For the end user, the ability to book an Uber ride and then track the position of the approaching car on a map is one of the key features of the app interface. For Uber, the app does this and much more: it 'incorporates fleet driver management, social interaction between driver and passenger, taxi hailing and payment' (McGregor, Brown, and Glöss, 2015). The bundling of all these functions and operations into the one app is also what makes Uber disruptive at an industry level: 'The threat posed to the incumbent taxi service providers, regulators and users', as McGregor et al. (2015) write, 'resides in the transfer of control over aspects of an entire industry – such as pricing, discrimination and work allocation – to whoever controls the software'.

In addition to newer entrants like Uber, established search and social media firms, such as Facebook and Google, have effectively become 'third generation' location-based services platforms, insofar as they have both reshaped, to varying degrees, their operations (and, in Facebook's case, those of its subsidiaries) so as to facilitate the integration, at a range of scales, of ubiquitous geodata capture across their operations (see Barreneche, 2012a; Wilken, 2014; Barreneche and Wilken, 2015). Indeed, for Facebook, as I have argued elsewhere, geodata should now be viewed as a 'fourth pillar' that is interconnected with and informs the firm's other three pillars: its newsfeed, timeline and graph search (Wilken, 2014: 1098).

Of the specifically location-focussed applications discussed above, the two that have survived – Banjo and Foursquare – have done so by undergoing significant transformation from first- or second-generation location-sensitive mobile social networking (LMSN) applications to third generation location-based services (LBS) or platforms, where location has become a core component of a wider suite of offerings. What follows is a brief outline of what Banjo's and Foursquare's respective reorientations have involved, before turning to a discussion of the larger implications of third-generation location-based services.

Banjo

Banjo began as an ambient 'social discovery' (Perez, 2011) and 'location-based social media tagging platform' (Keohane, 2015). In its original incarnation, Banjo's ambition was twofold: to integrate social media data into 'one streamlined service, offering a one-stop shop for updates from Facebook, Twitter, and more' and, in so doing, facilitate 'serendipitous moments', and the making of 'nearby social connections in real time' (Carr, 2011). As Austin Carr (2011) explains, first-time users of the Banjo app would receive 'updates from the 16 closest users of any network that Banjo taps into'; however, when synced with a user's social networks, the service would narrow results to 'nearby friends'. If friends were not nearby, the service would yield tips and updates from other users of the app in the immediate vicinity (Carr, 2011).

Since these early days of operation, the Las Vegas-based firm has undertaken a dramatic shift in focus – and a significant injection of funds with a US $100 million private investment in 2015 by Japanese multinational telecommunications and internet company SoftBank (Bradshaw, 2015) – with much of its energy now directed towards a subscription enterprise software service, called Banjo Enterprise, that provides large-scale real-time location-sensitive visual and social media analysis. Where once 'users could see what others were publicly sharing across various social networks in locations around the world', now the Banjo app 'displays results based on location and the event taking place there' (Yeung, 2014).

This change of strategic direction was said to have been prompted by founder and CEO Damien Patton's realization during the aftermath of the Boston Marathon bombings that, by following social media posts accessed through the Banjo app, he and his staff 'were learning about events on the ground faster than reporters were – and faster even than the police' (Bourne, 2015). As Patton put it in 2014, 'We are witnessing a transformation in the way content is created and consumed. This perfect storm is being fed by the convergence of three powerful and distinct forces: Mobile + Social + Cloud = Real Time Web' (quoted in Yeung, 2014).

The Banjo Enterprise system, which is pitched primarily to major news organizations and other large corporations, involves image-driven data mining and predictive analysis of social media posts in high volume. Very little detail on how their data matching system operates is revealed by Banjo – beyond, that is, describing it as the product of its 'secret algorithm' (Yeung, 2014). What is discernible from press reports is that each social media post that the Banjo Enterprise systems accesses and analyses is overlaid onto a world grid comprised of 35 billion squares (Pierson, 2015). When social media posts emerge that 'deviate from the norm' – say, by noting something like a building fire or earthquake – the

Banjo staff is alerted and clients are notified. Banjo claims that, in performing these analyses, its computer systems are making 'a quadrillion computations every 10 seconds' (Pierson, 2015).

While the company has private deals with social networks that facilitate access to social media content, it is still heavily reliant on its own app which explicitly asks users to 'share access to their social media accounts', whether they be Twitter, Instagram, Weibo or Vkontakte (Pierson, 2015). This access to combined social media data provides Banjo with the requisite information richness for its service to work.

Foursquare

In Foursquare's case, the New York-based firm, while still often thought of as a mobile social networking and venue 'check-in' service, has in fact, since 2013, undergone a much-publicized reorientation of its business operations. Among other things, this has involved the splitting of its operations into two apps – Swarm (for check-ins and social networking) and Foursquare (for search and recommendations). Together, these two apps combine mobile, social and place-based interactions with past and present user data to generate real-time and predictive venue recommendations for Foursquare clients and end users.

Foursquare's data scientists are able to achieve this by combining the insights generated by two (interconnected) data sets: social data (Foursquare's 'social graph') and location data (their 'places graph'). Both graphs are composed of 'nodes' (things) and 'edges' (the connections between these things) (Shaw, 2012). With respect to the *social graph*, the nodes are Foursquare's subscribers and the edges are the connections that link these users to each other, which include friendships, follows, 'dones' (tips offered by one user to other users), comments users leave and the 'co-location of people [who are on Foursquare] in the same physical space' (Shaw, 2012). Meanwhile, with respect to Foursquare's *places graph*, the nodes are the places that are registered in its points of interest database, and the edges comprise a variety of different things: flow ('how often people move from one place to another'), co-visitation ('how many people have been to the same place before'), categories (the sorting of venues based on similarities between them), and menus, tips and shouts (described as data that 'connects places because they share the same characteristics') (Shaw, 2012).

Foursquare's aim is to develop from these combined data sets responses to queries generated through the Explore feature of its app in order to produce for users 'realtime recommendations from signals [that combine] location, time of day, check-in history, friends' preferences, and venue similarities' (Shaw, 2012). The larger ambition of Foursquare's engineers is to understand the points of intersection between these two graphs. As Shaw (2012) asks, 'What are the underlying properties and dynamics of these networks? How can we predict new connections? How do we measure influence?'

Thus, by drawing in place-based insights from its own users, and as a result of extensive and crucial cross-platform partnerships involving a range of other services (including Evernote, Flickr, Path, Pinterest, Snapchat and Uber), Foursquare has been able to build a rich places database – all part of its longer-term ambitions to position itself as the 'location layer of the internet' (quoted in Panzarino, 2014).

Further repositioning has followed since, this time towards a 'location marketplace' providing place-related data and analytics services[1] to social media and other businesses and to the advertising industry (Kaplan, 2015). The first service, called the Foursquare Audience Network, involved a partnership in 2013 between Foursquare and ad-targeting firm Turn (McDermott, 2013). Under this partnership, advertisers could target display and video ads to Foursquare's users' desktops and mobile devices (McDermott, 2013). These ads are based on Turn's analysis of 'which shops [Foursquare] users have checked in to and when' (McDermott, 2013) and could be targeted to these users in real-time or ex post facto.

The second service, called Pinpoint, launched in 2015. Where the Foursquare Audience Network allowed marketers to target users of the Foursquare app, Pinpoint allows 'marketers to reach non-Foursquare users, too' (Marshall, 2015). Pinpoint works through Foursquare's partnering with third-party apps and other firms 'to gain access to consumers' GPs locations' (Marshall, 2015). It then compares 'that location information with its own database of places to add context and to build profiles about consumers' real-world behaviors' (Marshall, 2015). For example, it might retrospectively target an ad for a restaurant chain based on a past visit to a similar style of restaurant, or it might track whether a store is visited after a user views an ad for this store.

In a significant further development, in late 2016, Airbnb announced it signed a licensing deal that gives it access to Foursquare's trove of 500 million photographs in order to bring greater 'authenticity' to Airbnb's new local Guidebooks (Yeung, 2016).

The Implications of Ubiquitous Geodata Capture

The key point I wish to draw from sketching the above developments is this: third-generation location-based services, as I am calling them, involve the capture and circulation of geodata at a scale, speed and level of complexity that is markedly different from earlier incarnations of similar services. In this final section of the chapter, I wish to consider the importance of the challenges we face in trying to make critical sense of what is involved – and at stake – in the move towards ubiquitous geodata capture. Just as rich geodata is a necessity for third-generation platforms, so, too, is the formulation of new critical perspectives a necessity if we are to understand the impacts and importance of these platforms.

In developing his conceptualization of geomedia, Scott McQuire seeks to differentiate it from what he sees as the narrower focus on 'specific types of new device' in mobile media studies, as well as from a focus on 'single functions' in, say, locative media research. In contrast, McQuire suggests that geomedia, as he formulates it, aims to conceptualize 'the different *condition* that media enters in the twenty-first century' (6 – emphasis in original), a condition, as set out earlier in this chapter, that is characterized by the confluence, particularly in urban contexts, of four different streams: ubiquity; location awareness; real-time orientation of contemporary digital networks and convergence. My contention is that McQuire's four-part formulation of geomedia has the potential to significantly enrich existing location-based services research for two reasons. First, third-generation services, as I have detailed above, move well beyond a narrow focus on the single function of location/locatability; while the question of geolocation remains important, geodata are integrated in and are now part and parcel of a larger suite of data-driven platform services. Second, the impact and importance of larger data-driven platforms can be better grasped by considering them in light of each of McQuire's four sources and their confluence.

Ubiquity

Ubiquity, as McQuire (2016: 2) conceives of it, involves 'mobile and embedded media devices, coupled to extended digital networks', to 'recreate the city as a media space in which content and connection are seemingly available "anywhere, anytime"'. Or, as Jeremy Packer and Stephen Crofts Wiley (2012: 12) put it, the 'materiality of communication' and how 'communication infrastructure [including cell towers and Wi-Fi networks], transportation and mobility, mobile technologies', work to shape and produce 'urban, regional, and translocal spaces'. This process, of course, is part of a long series of historical developments that, to use McKenzie Wark's (1994) formulation, involved the overlaying of the 'second nature' of the geographies of cities with the 'third nature' of information flows (see Graham and Marvin, 1996; McQuire, 2008).

Also enrolled in these processes have been parallel developments in cell phone technologies. Writing on the cusp of the release of the first iPhone, Gerard Goggin and Larissa Hjorth (2009: 4) remarked on the shift from mobile phones to mobile media, noting that not only have mobile phones been a 'strategically important site of innovation, change, and re-invention of older, existing media', but also, at that time, 'being reimagined as media' through the 'advent of forms such as mobile books, mobile television, mobile Internet, and mobile games'. These developments and subsequent growth in mobile media use has also been dependent, at least in part, on parallel developments in mobile network (3G/4G/5G) standards (see Goggin, 2006, 2011; Frith, 2015b: 27–44).

The recreation of 'the city as a media space' (McQuire, 2016: 2) has been further hastened by the development and take up of location-sensitive mobile applications and practices that work to shape users' experiences of and engagements with urban space and place by allowing them 'to interact with the digital information embedded in that space' and thereby 'control how they manage their interactions with nearby people and information' (de Souza e Silva and Frith, 2012a: 273). This has involved the forms of LMSN applications discussed earlier in this chapter (see Saker and Evans, 2016; Frith, 2014), as well as others, such as augmented reality applications like Layar (see Farman, 2011; Verhoeff, 2012; Liao and Humphreys, 2015). Nevertheless, while such work is important for drawing attention to the manifold ways that mobile-mediated experiences, engagements and interactions with urban spaces are inevitably 'tuned' by pervasive digital media (Coyne, 2010), they are only one small part of an evolving urban condition characterized increasingly by the mutual constitution and co-production of software and spatiality, which Kitchin and Martin Dodge (2011) refer to as 'code/space'.

As McQuire (2016: 3) goes on to note, 'the ubiquity of social media is [also] currently transforming the social space of the city in complex ways that extend well beyond the choices to individual users'. For example, Raz Schwartz and Nadav Hochman (2015) detail how the scraping of social media data, combined from a variety of LMSN services, can provide detailed portraits of what they term 'the social media life of public spaces'. More pointedly, in Carlos Barreneche's critical accounts of how geodata are extracted and commercially exploited by firms like Foursquare and Google, he gives explicit attention to developments around 'geodemographic profiling'. Combining careful reading of patent documents and the technical language and tools of computer science (k-means algorithms, nearest neighbour rules, points-of-interest databases and so on), Barreneche explores how companies like Foursquare and Google employ data mining and aggregation practices that utilize 'records of location trails [and past check-ins] to produce the socio-spatial patterns that make up the segmentations that enable inferences about users' identity and behaviour' (2012a: 339; 2012b). As a result of 'user activity made possible by ubiquitous interactivity', Foursquare and Google are able to construct increasingly detailed and fine-grained accounts of social media users, 'thanks to an unprecedented ability to capture and store patterns of interaction, movement, transaction, and communication' (Andrejevic, 2007: 296).

Location Awareness

In light of the above discussion, any understanding of contemporary mobile device use needs to be situated within an understanding of urban environments as spaces of ubiquitous data capture, especially data concerning one's location. This capture is facilitated by various sensor infrastructures and our interactions with them, including through accessing wireless networks and Wi-Fi hotspots, by registering our indoor position via Wi-Fi and beacons, and from cell tower triangulations and Global Positioning System (GPS) 'trilateration' (Frith, 2015b: 27–44), among other means. The capture of positional data is also enabled by 'distributed mobile sensors' (Andrejevic and Burdon 2015: 22), where 'our cars, phones, laptops, [...] GPS devices, and so on allow for the comprehensive capture of the data trails users leave as they go about the course of their daily lives' (20). Such location awareness, McQuire (2016: 4) argues, 'assumes a new prominence in urban experience' (4), the impacts of which have been configured in a variety of ways.

For Adrian Mackenzie (2010: 5), the 'contemporary proliferation of wireless devices and modes of network connection' are best understood as part-and-parcel of 'wirelessness' – a term he deploys to capture our 'entanglements with things, objects, gadgets, infrastructures and services'. These wireless networks, Mackenzie argues, 'effervesce on the edges of media change, activating and catalyzing experiential change' (3), including to how we interact with and experience urban space and place.

Meanwhile, for Mark Andrejevic and Mark Burdon, location-sensitive wireless networks are enrolled in processes of sensor-derived datafication, whereby mobile devices are working to generate more data *about* those using them than *by*. This, in turn, has given rise to automated processing to keep up with and make sense of the 'large volumes of information captured by a distributed array of sensing devices' (Andrejevic and Burdon, 2015: 27). These automated processing systems, they argue, privilege 'a perspective that focuses on information as a pattern-generating form of behavior and not as ideational content' (28). This is very much the focus of Banjo's large-scale image and social media search analytics efforts and of Foursquare's examination of the intersections of their social and places graphs; both firms are concerned with pattern recognition, with anomalous trends or spikes drawing immediate attention (Sklar, Shaw, and Hogue, 2012).

Real-Time Orientation of Contemporary Digital Networks

The distributed architectures of digital networks detailed above, McQuire (2016: 4) suggests, also 'opens the potential for "real-time" feedback from many-to-many, supporting novel experiences of social simultaneity' – developments that have been well documented in the social media literature (see, for example, Weller, Bruns, Burgess, Mahrt, and Puschmann, 2014, on Twitter, and *New Media and Society* journal volume 16 number 7 (2014) dedicated to '10 years of Facebook'). What is interesting about these desires to facilitate 'novel experiences of social simultaneity' in light of the discussion of this chapter is that these desires formed the specific impetus for second generation LMSNs (like Banjo when launched), and continue to motivate third-generation LBS and social media firms such as Banjo Enterprise and Foursquare Labs Inc (and their desires to draw significance from the signals and cues of mediated social simultaneity), as well, of course, as major players such as Facebook. One key strand of Internet research focuses on algorithmic sorting and seeks to examine the manifold ways that many-to-many feedback is organized by parent platforms and made visible (or not) to end users and third-party clients (see, for example, Bucher, 2012a, 2012b, 2013, 2016; Gerlitz and Helmond, 2013). While some important work of this nature has been undertaken to date specifically on LBS (most noticeably by Barreneche, 2012a, 2012b; Leszczynski, 2015), the wider platform integration of geodata warrants significant further attention and analysis.

Convergence

Finally, to turn to the last of the strands from which McQuire's conception of geomedia is woven: *convergence*. As noted at the outset of this chapter, McQuire's (2016: 5) understanding of convergence extends beyond 'a narrow technical logic' to also refer 'to a broader process of remaking'. This expanded understanding of convergence is useful in directing us towards a key aspect of 'remaking' for the forms of data-driven platform discussed in this paper: interoperability and cross-platform data sharing. The facilitation of interoperability (and, with it, data sharing), I would suggest, is a vital concern for, and a key aspect of the economic ambitions of the firms who control social media applications. This is the case regardless of whether these are large scale 'closed networks' like Facebook (which, at the time of writing, has 1.18 billion daily active users), or – and especially for – smaller scale firms like Foursquare (which, at the time of writing, has 55 million monthly active users) that rely on access to data streams of other platforms in order to survive and thrive. Given the stakes involved in these 'networked media', as José van Dijck (2013) collectively refers to them, it is of little surprise that key players within the social media, search and analytics ecosystem 'have a vested interest in erasing the boundaries [between one service and another] and rendering its operational logic invisible' (van Dijck, 2013: 171). Van Dijck (2013: 163–164) describes these inter- and infra-firm arrangements as 'chains of microsystems', a useful term for framing the various corporate arrangements that shape the flow and monetization of data. What is not included by van Dijck (2013) in her account of 'chains of microsystems', however, but is becoming increasingly important to understanding the internal logics of interoperability and data transfer, is focussed consideration of the (often quite low profile) companies that form the links in these chains, the 'interstices between platforms' (156) – that is, those firms (like Button and IFTTT, as well as Microsoft's Flow service) that provide infrastructural and service support so as to facilitate social media platform interoperability and data flow and form vital nodes in larger networked app ecosystems and economies.

To return to McQuire's (2016: 5) argument, he also makes the point that the developments around convergence he describes impact on 'business, institutional and regulatory settings as much as social, political and cultural practices'. This is particularly true of the kinds of data-sharing and cross-platform partnerships described above and earlier in this chapter. The data that Banjo and Foursquare draw on to populate their respective databases are increasingly 'motile' (Coté, 2014). Generated through an array of location and social-media applications, these data are stored in and shift between multiple proprietary servers and, increasingly, move outside of end-user control (Coté, 2014: 123). Thus, as Jordan Frith (2015: 105) points out, given that Foursquare powers the geolocation features of a range of social media and other applications, those using these other services are likely to be 'interacting with Foursquare data without even knowing it'. As a recent *Wired* magazine article puts it: 'Whenever you tag a tweet with a location, ask Microsoft's digital assistant Cortana about nearby restaurants, or add location to a photo on Pinterest, you're using Foursquare' (Finley, 2016). The data associated with these actions are moving about and are monetized in many different ways.

What is more, the privacy implications of these forms of data motility are significant if not, I would suggest, at all well understood. As *Wired* journalist Klint Finley (2016) puts it,

[While] we're fairly used to the idea of seeing ads in a free app [...] the idea of our location information from one app being used to power ads in another app is less familiar, and less easy to see. [And] Foursquare's use of third party data makes the privacy situation even murkier, since users of the original apps may not understand how their data is being used, either.

Despite the inclusion of third-party sharing clauses in terms of service documents, an iPhone user granting Foursquare access to their photos is not necessarily going to be expecting or even aware that images they have posted to Foursquare might, say, reappear in an AirB&B guidebook.

Even if application end users think they are clear about their own privacy settings, the entangled nature of the app ecosystem and their own (likely partial) knowledge of corporate arrangements and deals, algorithmic processes, terms of service documents, device settings and so on, complicates matters considerably. These are forms of convergent 'remakings', then, that, due to their scale and opacity carry significant privacy and other implications that existing policy and regulatory regimes seem ill-equipped to deal with (Andrejevic and Burdon, 2015: 32).

Conclusion

In this chapter, I have outlined three generations of location-related services (which correlated with a gradual shift from a specific focus on location-sensitive mobile social networking to a broader orientation towards location-based services), sketched the transformations that the surviving two services (Banjo and Foursquare) underwent and then related these back to Scott McQuire's notion of 'geomedia'.

McQuire concludes *Geomedia* (2016) by examining the various potentialities associated with his conception of 'geomedia', including opportunities for fostering 'embodied-connected micro-publics initiated by urban media events' (155), 'public civility' (156) and the recomposition of public space as a 'contact zone … for relating to others' (158). These possibilities are outworkings of what is a key argument of his book: 'that the nexus between geomedia and public space is today a vital arena in which new elaborations of the digital and the technological might be attempted' (167). In articulating these 'new elaborations', there was opportunity for a return to, and more explicit engagement with, the 'four related trajectories' (2) of geomedia that were detailed early in the book. Additionally, there was opportunity for further reflection on their wider applicability, and of their larger policy implications.

In drawing on McQuire's work, the central argument of this chapter is that, just as rich geodata is a necessity for the commercial health and sustainability of third-generation data-driven social, search, and analytics platforms, an equal necessity is the formulation of new critical perspectives if we are to understand the impacts and importance of these platforms. My contention has been that McQuire's four-part conceptualization of geomedia holds wider application and indeed provides a robust and productive framework for extending critical engagement with these contemporary technological developments and their potential larger impacts. It is the task of those who continue to work in this area and who seek to understand these developments to ensure that these conceptual and critical formulations are further tested, refined and extended.

Note

1 For example, as a result of analysis of foot traffic and social media cues, Foursquare was able to predict, with a high degree of accuracy, that, in the US, Apple would sell between 13 and 15 million iPhones the weekend the

iPhone 6S was released (Finley, 2016); they were also able to predict Q1 2016 declines in sales of restaurant chain Chipotle (Glueck, 2016), and a drop-off in stays at Trump hotels in the lead up to the US Presidential election (Foursquare, 2016).

References

Adams, P. C. (2009). *Geographies of Media and Communication*, Chichester, West Sussex: Wiley-Blackwell.

Andrejevic, M. (2007). Surveillance in the digital enclosure, *The Communication Review*, 10: 295–317.

Andrejevic, M., & Burdon, M. (2015). The sensor society, *Television & New Media* 16(1): 19–36.

Barreneche, C. (2012a) Governing the geocoded world: Environmentality and the politics of location platforms, *Convergence: The International Journal of Research into New Media Technologies* 18(3): 331–351.

Barreneche, C. (2012b) The order of places: Code, ontology and visibility in locative media, *Computational Culture* 2, http://computationalculture.net.

Barreneche, C., & Wilken, R. (2015). Platform specificity and the politics of location data extraction, *European Journal of Cultural Studies*, 18(4–5): 497–513.

Bourne, W. (2015). The most important social media company you've never heard of, *Editor-at-large, Inc.*, April, www.inc.com/magazine/201504/will-bourne/banjo-the-gods-eye-view.html.

Bradshaw, T. (2015). Banjo latest California start-up to attract big funding round, *Financial Times*, 7 May, www.ft.com/content/4a98a712-f4a1-11e4-9a58-00144feab7de.

Bucher, T. (2012a) A technicity of attention: How software "Makes Sense", *Culture Machine*, 13, www.culturemachine.net/index.php/cm/issue/view/24.

Bucher, T. (2012b) Want to be on the top? Algorithmic power and the threat of invisibility on Facebook, *New Media & Society* 14(7): 1164–1180.

Bucher, T. (2013). Objects of intense feeling: The case of the Twitter APIs, *Computational Culture*, 3, http://computationalculture.net/article/objects-of-intense-feeling-the-case-of-the-twitter-api.

Bucher, T. (2016). The algorithmic imaginary: Exploring the ordinary affects of Facebook algorithms, *Information, Communication and Society* 20(1): 30–44.

Burns, P. L. (2012). SXSW 2012: The year of the ambient social location app, *arc3|communications*, 27 March, http://arc3communications.com/sxsw-2012-the-year-of-the-ambient-social-location-app/.

Carr, A. (2011). Social media app Banjo aggregates all your Tweets, Facebook posts, Instagram pics', *Fast Company*, 22 June, www.fastcompany.com/1762145/social-media-app-banjo-aggregates-all-your-tweets-facebook-posts-instagram-pics.

Coté, M. (2014). Data motility: The materiality of big social data, *Cultural Studies Review*, 20(1): 121–149.

Couldry, N., & McCarthy, A. (eds) (2004). *MediaSpace: Place, Scale and Culture in a Media Age*, New York: Routledge.

Coyne, R. (2010). *The Tuning of Place: Sociable Spaces and Pervasive Digital Media*, Cambridge, MA: MIT Press.

de Souza e Silva, A., & Frith, J. (2012a). Location-aware technologies: Control and privacy in hybrid space. In J. Packer & S. B. Crofts Wiley (Eds.), *Communication Matters: Materialist Approaches to Media, Mobility and Networks* (pp. 265–275), London: Routledge.

de Souza e Silva, A., & Frith, J. (2012b). *Mobile Interfaces in Public Spaces: Locational Privacy, Control and Urban Sociability*, New York: Routledge.

Evans, L. (2015). *Locative Social Media: Place in the Digital Age*, Houndmills, Basingstoke, Hampshire: Palgrave Macmillan.

Evans, L., & Saker, M. (2017). *Location-Based Social Media: Space, Time and Identity*, Houndmills, Basingstoke, Hampshire: Palgrave Macmillan.

Falkheimer, J., & Jansson, A. (Eds.) (2006). *Geographies of Communication: The Spatial Turn in Media Studies*, Göteborg: Nordicom.

Farman, J. (2011). *Mobile Interface Theory: Embodied Space and Locative Media*, London: Routledge.

Farman, J. (Ed.) (2013). *The Mobile Story: Narrative Practices with Locative Technologies*, New York: Routledge.

Finley, K. (2016). Foursquare's plan to use your data to make money – Even if you aren't a user, *Wired*, 19 January, www.wired.com/2016/01/foursquares-plan-to-use-your-data-to-make-money-even-if-you-arent-a-user/.

Foursquare (2016). How the Trump Presidential campaign is affecting Trump businesses, *Medium*, 4 August, https://medium.com/foursquare-direct/how-the-trump-presidential-campaign-is-affecting-trump-businesses-c343178e3c03#.8ygfztunz.

Frith, J. (2014). Communicating through location: The understood meaning of the Foursquare check-in, *Journal of Computer-mediated Communication*, 19: 890–905.

Frith, J. (2015a). Communicating behind the scenes: A primer on radio frequency identification (RFID), *Mobile Media and Communication*, 3(1): 91–105.

Frith, J. (2015b). *Smartphones as Locative Media*, Cambridge: Polity.

Gerard, G., & Larissa, H. (2009). The question of mobile media. In G. Goggin & L. Hjorth (Eds.), *Mobile Technologies: From Telecommunications to Media* (pp. 3–8), New York: Routledge.

Gerlitz, C., & Helmond, A. (2013). The like economy: Social buttons and the data-intensive web, *New Media & Society* 15(8): 1348–1365.

Glueck, J. (2016). Foursquare predicts Chipotle's Q1 sales down nearly 30%; Foot traffic reveals the start of a mixed recovery, *Medium*, 12 April, https://medium.com/foursquare-direct/foursquare-predicts-chipotle-s-q1-sales-down-nearly-30-foot-traffic-reveals-the-start-of-a-mixed-78515b2389af#.6ar4e8qk5.

Goggin, G. (2011). *Global Mobile Media*, London: Routledge.

Goggin, G. (2006). *Cell Phone Culture: Mobile Technology in Everyday Life*, New York: Routledge.

Goldsmith, B. (2014). The smartphone app economy and app ecosystem. In G. Goggin & L. Hjorth (Eds.), *The Routledge Companion to Mobile Media* (pp. 171–180), New York: Routledge.

Gordon, E., & de Souza e Silva, A. (2011). *Net Locality: Why Location Matters in a Networked World*, Boston: Blackwell-Wiley.

Graham, S., & Marvin, S. (1996). *Telecommunications and the City: Electronic Spaces, Urban Places*, London: Routledge.

Greengard, S. (2015). *The Internet of Things*, Cambridge, MA, MIT Press.
Ha, A. (2013). Yep, social discovery startup sonar is dead (and its CEO explains why), *TechCrunch*, 17 September, https://techcrunch.com/2013/09/17/rip-sonar/.
Hjorth, L., Burgess, J., & Richardson, I. (Eds.) (2012). *Studying Mobile Media: Cultural Technologies, Mobile Communication, and the iPhone*. New York: Routledge.
Hjorth, L., & Richardson, I. (2014). *Gaming in Social, Locative, & Mobile Media*, Houndmills, Basingstoke, Hampshire: Palgrave Macmillan.
Humphreys, L. (2007). Mobile social networks and spatial practice: A case study of dodgeball, *Journal of Computer-Mediated Communication*, 13(1): 341–360.
Humphreys, L. (2010). Mobile social networks and urban public space, *New Media & Society*, 12(5): 763–778.
Jansson, A., & Falkheimer, J. (2006). Towards a geography of communication. In J. Falkheimer & A. Jansson (Eds.), *Geographies of Communication: The Spatial Turn in Media Studies* (pp. 9–25), Göteborg: Nordicom.
Kaplan, D. (2015). With Pinpoint, Foursquare's now a location marketplace, *Geomarketing*, 14 April, http://www.geomarketing.com/with-pinpoint-foursquares-now-a-location-marketplace.
Keohane, D. (2015). With recent $100M funding round, is Banjo tech success Vegas has been waiting for? *Pando*, 7 May, https://pando.com/2015/05/07/with-recent-100m-funding-round-is-banjo-the-tech-success-vegas-has-been-waiting-for/.
Kitchin, R., & Dodge, M. (2011). *Code/Space: Software and Everyday Life*, Cambridge, MA: MIT Press.
Lee, N. (2013). *Facebook Nation: Total Information Awareness*. New York: Springer.
Leszczynski, A. (2015). Spatial big data and anxieties of control, *Environment and Planning D: Society and Space*, 33(6): 965–984.
Liao, T., & Humphreys, L. (2015). Layar-ed places: Using mobile augmented reality to tactically reengage, reproduce, and reappropriate public space, *New Media & Society*, 17(9): 1418–1435.
Lynley, M. (2016). 'Pinterest acquires the team behind highlight and shorts, *TechCrunch*, 14 July, https://techcrunch.com/2016/07/14/pinterest-acquires-the-team-behind-highlight-and-shorts/.
Mackenzie, A. (2010). *Wirelessness: Radical Empiricism in Network Cultures*, Cambridge, MA: MIT Press.
Marshall, J. (2015). Foursquare launches new location-based ad offering, *The Wall Street Journal*, 14 April, www.wsj.com/amp/articles/BL-DGB-41288?responsive=y.
McDermott, J. (2013). Foursquare selling its location data through ad targeting firm turn, *Advertising Age*, 31 July, http://adage.com/article/digital/foursquare-selling-data-ad-targeting-firm-turn/243398/.
McGregor, M., Brown, B., & Glöss, M. (2015). Disrupting the cab: Uber, ridesharing and the taxi industry, *Journal of Peer Production*, 6, http://peerproduction.net/issues/issue-6-disruption-and-the-law/essays/disrupting-the-cab-uber-ridesharing-and-the-taxi-industry/.
McQuire, S. (2008). *The Media City: Media, Architecture and Urban Space*, London: SAGE.

McQuire, S. (2016). *Geomedia: Networked Cities and the Future of Public Space*, Cambridge: Polity.
Morley, D. (2000). *Home Territories: Media, Mobility and Identity*, New York: Routledge.
Morley, D., & Robins, K. (2005). *Spaces of Identity: Global Media, Electronic Landscapes, and Cultural Boundaries*, New York: Routledge.
Packer, J., & Crofts Wiley, S. B. (2012). Introduction: The materiality of communication. In J. Packer & S. B. Crofts Wiley (Eds.), *Communication Matters: Materialist Approaches to Media, Mobility and Networks* (pp. 3–16), London: Routledge.
Panzarino, M. (2014). Foursquare gets $15M and licensing deal from Microsoft to power location context for Windows and mobile, *TechCrunch*, 4 February, https://techcrunch.com/2014/02/04/foursquare-cuts-15m-deal-with-microsoft-to-power-location-and-context-for-windows-and-mobile/
Perez, S. (2011). Creepy/awesome Banjo app now pings you when your friends are nearby, *TechCrunch*, 27 October, https://techcrunch.com/2011/10/27/creepyawesome-banjo-app-now-pings-you-when-your-friends-are-nearby/.
Pierson, D. (2015). Banjo's ability to track events in real time gives clients competitive edge, *Los Angeles Times*, 20 June, www.latimes.com/business/la-fi-0621-cutting-edge-banjo-20150621-story.html.
Rosol, C. (2010). From radar to reader: On the origin of RFID, *Aether: The Journal of Media Geography*, 5A: 37–49, http://geogdata.csun.edu/~aether/pdf/volume_05a/rosol.pdf.
Rossiter, N. (2016). *Software, Infrastructure, Labor: A Media Theory of Logistical Nightmares*. New York: Routledge.
Saker, M., & Evans, L. (2016). Locative mobile media and time: Foursquare and technological memory, *First Monday*, 21(2), http://firstmonday.org/ojs/index.php/fm/article/view/6006.
Schwartz, R., & Hochman, N. (2015). The social media life of public spaces: Reading places through the lens of geotagged data. In R. Wilken & G. Goggin (Eds)., *Locative Media* (pp. 52–65), New York: Routledge.
Shaw, B. (2012). Machine learning with large networks of people and places, *Vimeo*, http://vimeo.com/39088490
Sklar, M., Shaw, B., & Hogue, A. (2012). Recommending interesting events in real-time with Foursquare check-ins, paper presented at the 6th ACM Conference on Recommender Systems, 9–13 September, Dublin, Ireland.
van Dijck, J. (2013). *The Culture of Connectivity: A Critical History of Social Media*, New York: Oxford University Press.
Verhoeff, N. (2012). A logic of layers: Indexicality of iPhone navigation in augmented reality. In L. Hjorth, J. Burgess, & I. Richardson (Eds.), *Studying Mobile Media: Cultural Technologies, Mobile Communication, and the iPhone* (pp. 118–132). New York: Routledge.
Wark, M. (1994). Third nature, *Cultural Studies*, 8(1): 115–132.
Weller, K., Bruns, A., Burgess, J., Mahrt, M., & Puschmann, C. (Eds.) (2014). *Twitter and Society*, New York: Peter Lang.
Wilken, R. (2014). Places nearby: Facebook as a location-based social media platform, *New Media & Society*, 16(7): 1087–1103.
Wilken, R. (2017). Social media app economies. In J. Burgess, T. Poell, & A. Marwick (Eds.), *The SAGE Handbook of Social Media*, London: SAGE.

Wilken, R., & Goggin, G. (2015). Locative media – Definitions, histories, theories. In R. Wilken & G. Goggin (Eds.), *Locative Media* (pp. 1–19), New York: Routledge.

Yeung, K. (2014). Location-based service Banjo overhauls its mobile apps to display social posts sorted by live events, *TNW*, 17 January, https://thenextweb.com/apps/2014/01/16/location-based-service-banjo-overhauls-mobile-apps-display-social-posts-sorted-live-events/.

Yeung, K. (2016). Airbnb's guidebooks now features photos powered by foursquare, *Venture Beat*, 7 December, http://venturebeat.com/2016/12/07/airbnbs-guidebooks-now-features-photos-powered-by-foursquare/.

3 Mapping Geomedia
Charting the Terrains of Space, Place and Media

Paul C. Adams

In my previous research, I have developed a taxonomic system for situating work in the nascent field of geomedia. This taxonomy organizes the field into four quadrants separated by the classic geographical distinction between space and place, and an orthogonal division between media as containers and media as contents. Over the past few years, researchers have explored a pair of related issues that do not fit neatly within this scheme. First, as personal identity emerges from interactions with virtual spaces and places we are pushed to rethink the subtleties of what we mean by 'virtual' as well as identity. There is growing attention to communicational processes that fragment or modularize identity while extending agency in various ways. Second, the formation of social collectivities evolves in response to the new processes forming personal identity. New kinds of publics emerge through digital data flows, and these redefine the nature of mobility. When one moves with a digital device that links to distant locations while constantly updating the location of the user, and the device both shapes and tracks the user's movement, distinctions of space, place, content and context break down. This chapter builds off the quadrant diagram to provide a sense of where we are headed with these developments.

Prologue

My wife and I are on vacation in Iceland and stop for gas at a small town. We join a crowd that has gathered in the gas station convenience store to watch the semi-final match of Euro 2016 (the European football championship) between Germany and France. There are old and young people in the room, speaking Icelandic, French and English. Families, couples and groups of friends cluster together in the narrow space between the lunch counter and a wall-mounted screen – some thirty persons jammed in a place designed for ten or twelve. They are exchanging comments and occasionally shouting about attempted goals. My wife captures a picture of the scene on her cell phone to post on Instagram. I wonder, is the situation as it appears, with many people gathered in a single place, watching the same soccer game? Or are we all encased in experiential bubbles – an Icelandic bubble, a French bubble, an American bubble – multiple senses of place occurring in this one physical place, and different game experiences with only a few similar elements? If so, what is the impact of this particular gas station on the various experiences of the audience? And what brings these moving images across more than 2,000 kilometres? I'm thinking here not just of all the hidden financial and technological arrangements that make viewing the game possible – how this screen in Iceland relates to the flows of money that make the game profitable, and what routes are taken by the digital signals through various spaces and substances between the distant field and the crowded gas station – but also how we can conceive of all of this when it includes so many locations of audience members around the world who are seeing the game and those who forward, comment on or 'like' social-media responses to the event?

To answer such questions I believe it helps to return to place and space, terms that capture key dialectics identified by geographers: stasis and mobility, private and public, small and large, near and far, concrete and abstract. The pull between such opposites is evident in a typical daily routine as one oscillates between home and work, moving through spaces (the road system, sidewalks, public transit) and between particular places (the home with its comfort and domesticity, the workplace with its efficiency and productivity, a restaurant or bar with its conviviality and sensory indulgence). Yi-Fu Tuan offers in-depth treatment of these distinctions in *Space and Place* (1977), in *Cosmos and Hearth* (1996) and elsewhere. Place is a pause in movement that eventually becomes a focus of care and a centre of individual and group meaning, while space is the awareness of potential movement as well as the opportunity for movement or interaction through a structured field of relationships and opportunities (Tuan, 1977; Sack, 1980; Cresswell, 2014).

Going a bit deeper, Agnew and Duncan (1989) argue that place consists of three complementary elements: location, locale and sense of place. These correspond to place phenomena that are geometrical/physical, social/cultural and experiential/emotional, respectively. Location represents a position in space, whereas locale designates the routinized social relations occurring in that location, and sense of place is 'identification with a place engendered by living in it' (Agnew and Duncan, 1989: 2). The elements of the triad are complementary, and the richest discussions of place manage to take all of them into account.

Space is a structural framework or matrix involving the ways in which 'people and things are connected together' (Gould, 1991: 10) but also a matter of enablement: 'that which allows movement' (Tuan, 1977: 6, 52–53). Space forms relationally, which is to say it emerges out of particular relationships between places (Massey, 2004; Jones, 2009). A space can also be seen as a system of systems, where the systems in question include territories, places, scales and networks (Jessop, Brenner, and Jones,

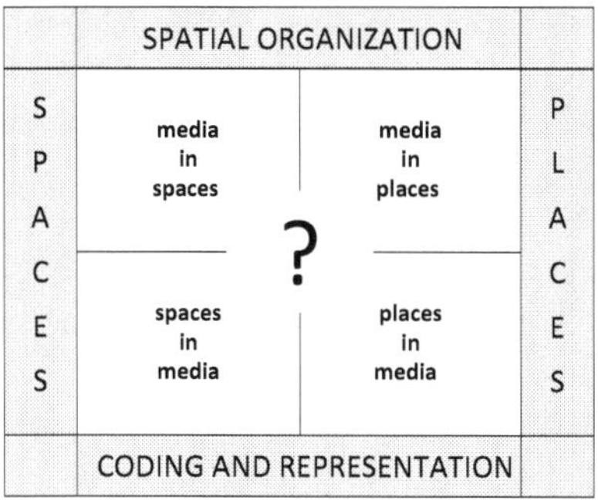

	SPATIAL ORGANIZATION		
S P A C E S	media in spaces	media in places	P L A C E S
	?		
	spaces in media	places in media	
	CODING AND REPRESENTATION		

Figure 3.1 The Quadrant Diagram: a map of the ontological and epistemological terrain of geomedia studies. After Adams (2010: 48). The term 'media', employed in earlier versions of this diagram has been replaced by 'communication' to more explicitly indicate the range of phenomena under consideration.

2008). There are many spaces, including mythical and magical realms, the grids of Euclidean geometry, technical spaces defined by science and engineering, Einsteinian space-time, networks of human mobility, legal jurisdictions and so on (Sack, 1980).

Media appear as distinct phenomena when considered from the vantage point of space versus place, and different understandings of what media are and how they work imply different understandings of space and place. Insofar as careful reflection on the space/place dialectic can enrich the study of geomedia, my 'quadrant diagram' (Figure 3.1) has been offered in previous research as a map of the pertinent ontological terrain (Adams, 2010; Adams and Jansson, 2012). Here we will take a quick look at this map then indicate two related research paths that carry us beyond this terrain.

The Quadrants

Let us start a tour of the heuristic space of geomedia by noting that an act of communication is an event that occurs somewhere – it *takes place*. The place where communication occurs radically impacts what is communicated and what communication does. The soccer example in the prologue suggests this; we can imagine a German couple stepping into the gas station partway through the game and noticing the French fans cheering for their team. The public nature of the place (as opposed to viewing the game at home) will thereafter shape the viewing experience for the German tourists. They might exercise restraint at moments when they would otherwise cheer for the German team, or alternatively, they might exchange looks or words with the French fans. Likewise, the privacy of the place, insofar as a gas station is private property, also affects the viewing experience. The establishment may prohibit drinking or smoking on the premises, so alcohol and tobacco may be subtracted from the experience of anyone who would drink or smoke while watching the game. Thus place shapes communication, not merely with regard to interpretative or 'decoding' activities, but also with regard to embodied engagement and social interactions arising from communication. These observations point to a broad set of concerns I have previously grouped under the heading media-in-place.

From here, we turn to place-in-media by recalling that watching a televised sporting event means encountering a place in video form. Many stadiums have distinct histories and strong local identities, but the stadium circulating as a video has a life of its own, separate from but related to that of the physical stadium (Gaffney, 2010). A video image of a sporting venue could be characterized as a 'virtual place', but we must be very careful about the term virtual. Common interpretations simplistically see virtuality as the opposite of reality, while more complex interpretations acknowledge that virtual is held in tension with various alternative states such as the abstract, the concrete and the probable (Deleuze, 1966). Virtuality therefore represents 'a multiplicity which can be actualized in different ways' (Shields, 2006: 285), so the broadcast version of the game actualizes the same events in many different ways, depending on the place of viewing (as noted above). Thinking more systematically, we could dissect virtuality into particular aspects such as intangible architecture, sensory fragmentation and distanciation (Adams, 1992, 2013). Intangible architecture actualizes including and excluding functions analogous to those of physical barriers such as walls and doors (Mitchell, 1995; Kitchin and Dodge, 2011). People 'enter' via one or two senses (typically vision and hearing) rather than with all of the sensory modes, and their social relations are stretched out through space, disembedded from the local situations in which they previously occurred (Giddens, 1984). As Doreen Massey famously pointed out, a place is not a container 'with boundaries around' but rather 'a particular constellation of social relations, meeting and weaving together at a particular locus' (1991: 28). The place-in-media perspective permits consideration of the constellation of social relations meeting and weaving together in the ephemeral 'container' created by mediated experience.

The phenomena of media-in-place and place-in-media are complementary; each shapes the other, and many studies integrate place-in-media and media-in-place, while emphasizing one or the other. For example, when Cupples and Glynn write of the 'overwhelmingly negative and disempowering iconography of Africa as the chaotic site of famine, disease, war, and political instability' (2013: 1004), they are emphasizing place-in-media. In contrast, when Jones and Merriman (2009) explore road-sign vandalism (or resignification) in Wales, they are emphasizing media-in-place. But what of the observation by Shaw and Warf that,

'Video games are virtual worlds, each with its own, distinctive spatiality' (2009: 1332)? These authors interpret computer games as a kind of space made up of codes, algorithms, computers, players and signals, which people create, access and inhabit by using interactive, digital media. Here we are on new ground that I would describe as space-in-media. A rather different example is an experiment by Defense Advanced Research Projects Agency (DARPA) of the U.S. Department of Defense in which red weather balloons were released at various locations throughout the U.S. as part of 'a nationwide scavenger hunt designed to test how modern methods of social networking might facilitate group contact and information-transfer within the United States' (Pinkerton, Young, and Dodds, 2011: 115). The idea of space-in-media is also evident in Rose's (2016b) observation that: 'in an online archive we scroll, zoom, crop, download, follow links, share. Digital images very often invite not contemplation, but action, navigation into the larger mass of images of which they are a part' (2016b: 340). Returning to the soccer example, the use of Instagram to share a photo indicates a space of connectivity defined by a person's social network, quite often including acquaintances, relatives, work associates and friends. Within these networks of social connection the main structuring force is who 'knows' (or 'follows' or 'likes') whom, rather than who is necessarily physically close to whom. The space-in-media approach draws attention to topologies of interconnection and exchange rather than proximity on the earth's surface.

The final quadrant is media-in-space. Returning to the case of a live soccer telecast, the focus now is on the digital signals (sounds and images) sent from one or more video cameras within the stadium to a nearby truck outfitted as a newsroom/production studio. Multiple audio and video feeds are intercut and text added, then the edited video is transmitted onwards. This may occur via microwaves to an antenna leased by the television station, by special kind of cell phone relay or via a live satellite uplink. In any case, such transmission paths can be mapped relative to the earth's surface and also through vertical space, anywhere from a few metres below the earth's surface (fiber-optic cables) to thousands of kilometres above the earth's surface (communication satellites) (see Chapter 5). Other examples of the media-in-space perspective are Malecki and Wei's (2009) study of the evolving global network of fiber-optic data transmission cables and Sheller and Urry's edited volume (2006) on the 'mobile technologies' that monitor, control, augment and stratify human mobility in urban spaces.

To summarize and illustrate all four perspectives: the image of a soccer field (place-in-media) moves through topological spaces defined by networks of organizational affiliations and personal acquaintances (space-in-media) and, at the same time, through a material space defined by infrastructure and its organization in the mapable space of geographical proximity and distance (media-in-space), to arrive at screens in public and private places where encounters happen in ways that incorporate local place meanings as well as embodied physical relations (media-in-place). The quadrant diagram (Figure 3.1) captures these four aspects of communication. All four quadrants are profoundly interdependent and come together in every communication event, although one aspect or another may be more apparent.

The taxonomy embodied in the diagram provides a rough map of the ontologies and epistemologies employed in geomedia studies. Encapsulating ontologies as the things we know (or think we know) and epistemologies as the ways we go about gaining such knowledge, the quadrant diagram maps geomedia's key ontologies and epistemologies. We can summarize a few of these, starting again with media-in-space. Scholars have explored communication infrastructures most often by employing maps, charts, descriptive statistics and other empirical approaches (Zook, 2008; Christophers, 2009; Lukinbeal, 2012; Warf, 2012; Graham, Hogan, Straumann, and Medhat, 2014). This approach is consonant with the epistemology of empiricism. Moving to place-in-media, discourse analysis and content analysis point to this quadrant, as well as critical historiography, social theory, cultural theory and postcolonial and feminist theory, all of which draw on constructivist epistemologies (Pickles, 1995; Cosgrove, 2001; Gandy, 2003; Cupples and Glynn, 2013; Rose, 2016a). The media-in-place quadrant focusses on transformations occurring in people's sense of place as a result of media use and can be explored with qualitative methods such as ethnographies, interviews, narrative reflections and vignettes, all of which sit most easily within the epistemological framework of constructivism (Morley, 1986; Dodge and Kitchin, 2005; Pratt and Johnston, 2007; Kitchin and Dodge, 2011; Longhurst, 2013). Finally, questions about the social network topologies that enable and channel communication flows (spaces-in-media) often draw on the rationalist epistemologies underlying topological theory, mathematics and algorithmic modelling (Gorman and Kulkarni, 2004; Liben-Nowell, Novak, Kumar, Raghavan, and Tomkins, 2005; Ratti et al., 2010; Warf and Sui, 2010).

Ontologies are more elusive and abstract than epistemologies. Examples include objectivism, relativism, subjectivism and possibly phenomenology.[1] Objectivism is most at home in the media-in-space quadrant where it substantiates the importance of mapping and measuring communication infrastructure (treated as objectively real things). Relativism is suited to the place-in-media quadrant, where it justifies the attempt to interpret how people collectively define the meaning of mediated place-images (as realities that vary as different groups make meaning of them). The assumptions underlying subjectivism illuminate the space-in-media quadrant by lending support to the idea of a virtual rather than a tangible kind of space (something we know through subjective experience). Finally, phenomenology permits crossing between the place-in-media quadrant and the media-in-place quadrant since, for example, the soccer game and the snack food one eats while viewing the game are both, in Heidegger's terminology, ready-to-hand (1962).[2] Strict adherents to one or another ontology will tend to view media from a limited range of quadrants so the diagram as a whole encourages an integrative approach.

This list of examples across various approaches is in no way exhaustive, but it demonstrates that the quadrant diagram is not only an epistemological terrain but also an ontological terrain. The diagram provides a way of recognizing the productivity of contrasting ontologies and epistemologies. It can engender cross-fertilization between various theoretical and philosophical positions.

Beyond the Quadrants

The quadrant diagram (like all maps) is incomplete. Part of what it cannot show is how a particular research project may bring together certain quadrants, how opposite sides or corners of the diagram might fold or blur or weave into each other if we ask certain questions. It also misses what happens when we discard familiar distinctions like here/there, part/whole or near/far and bring less obvious non-dichotomous distinctions into the spotlight. To offer one example, as Rose argues (2016b) not only have images and texts multiplied with the rise of the Internet and other digital technologies, but images have become so mutable and their authorship so distributed that the choice to study any given image becomes increasingly arbitrary. We are better off focussing on a constantly changing flow of imagery and treating this flow as inextricable from the networks carrying the images, the interfaces by which we encounter the images in any of their many different forms and the friction acting on this flow (firewalls, corrupted files, forgotten passwords, unwanted advertising and the like). Such an approach troubles all of the distinctions in the diagram. I increasingly suspect that if the quadrant diagram is to be useful we have to be ready to transcend it and move into new epistemological and ontological terrain. Recent research indicates lines of investigation that do exactly this, moving perpendicular to the diagram's grid or into another dimensionality altogether. Here we will briefly survey a few of these new directions, progressing from ideas of modular identity to publics, surveillant practices and digitally augmented mobility.

Modular Identity

Whereas it was once obvious that a person is the same person whether working, banking, spending time with family, seeking medical care or playing a game, new contexts of interaction and communication permit and in fact encourage the establishment of multiple identities for these various activities and roles. A person moves from one service provider or domain of administrative control to another not simply by changing places and tasks, but by entering a different password or scanning a different card, at which point he or she takes on a new life, activating rows or columns of captured data, or 'capta' in a different database (Kitchin and Dodge, 2011).

Fragmentation of identity has become a practical necessity, at least for the majority of people in developed countries. As early as the mid-1990s, Sherry Turkle observed people's tendency to 'cycle through' various identities while online (Turkle, 1995), but now by some accounts the 'traditional vision of a single and unique identity is obsolete' (Jaquet-Chiffelle, Benoist, Haenni, Wenger, and Zwingelberg, 2009: 76). It increasingly seems that fragmentation is not quite the right theoretical construct to capture this change. Each emerging aspect of self has a certain logic and coherence rather than being a randomly broken shard. Instead of fragmenting, the self is modularizing. The depth and intensity of this modularized identity is indicated by the fact that an identity crisis can occur if divides are breached, for example, between one's gamer identity and one's professional identity or between one's financial identity and one's medical identity (Nissenbaum, 2010). In such situations, when the components of self are brought back together there is a disruption that ranges from mildly annoying to profoundly traumatic.

A related shift is indicated by the rejection of the term individual for the neologism *dividual* (Deleuze, 1992). Dividuals emerge in relation to a wide range of services (health care, education, banking, energy, water, etc.). Not only do people maintain different usernames and passwords in these different contexts, but the consequent multiplication of identity has also come to dominate the more coherent, integrated sense of self. The constitution of subjects as dividuals serves the interests of a complex society in which people are treated in specialized ways out of practical necessity. This is of course a longstanding trend, but an emerging tendency is the avoidance of responsibility to the whole person by constructing the person only through narrowly specialized areas of service provision. In this connection, Deleuze refers to the *'limitless postponements* of the societies of control' (1992: 5) where control is exerted not by containing the body but also by managing when, where and how a dividual can gain access to spaces, resources, services and connections. It is easy to postpone, evade and work around responsibilities to any dividual if it has an element that falls between established categories or fails to meet predetermined criteria – much easier than in a system where there is some formalized responsibility for the welfare of the whole person.

Adding to the challenging nature of this modularization of personal identity is the fact that 'some identities may also be shared by different persons or even by things' (Jaquet-Chiffelle et al., 2009: 76). If one loses a 'coded object' like a cell phone, credit card or computer (Kitchin and Dodge, 2011) it suddenly becomes evident that such things are integral to personal identity. If John's smartphone is stolen, it can continue to relay locational information, make purchases and send correspondence as if it were John, no matter who is using it. Even the loss of a single number can permit a serious breach of one's professional, social or financial identity. It makes sense to think of people as modules of identity acting in conjunction with nonhuman stuff, dividuals created and controlled by spatially distributed assemblages that enrol coded objects, digital records, accounts, activity-logs, online habit profiles and networks of 'friends' and clients (Kitchin and Dodge, 2011).

Hybridity has been of interest for more than two decades, as culturally hybridized identities were linked to political resistance (Bhabha, 1994; García Canclini, 1995; Jackson, 2008) and as human and nonhuman elements were shown to come together in more-than-human assemblages and actor-networks (Haraway, 1985; Latour, 1987, 1993; Lulka, 2009). We are more hybrid than ever, and in ways that radically transform the terrains of domination and resistance. In recent years, we have seen digital media enable progressive, emancipatory movements but also reactionary, nationalistic and politically regressive movements, with the Arab Spring movement and the 2016 U.S. presidential election as two conspicuous examples (Howard and Hussain, 2013; Tufekci, 2013; Albright, 2016; Rutenberg, 2016). At the most general, the key to understanding such changes is to recognize that cultural and political changes occur in tandem with technological changes and that these changes fundamentally arise from and enable new ways of constituting personal identity. Dividuals are not without power, but 'divide and conquer' serves as a reminder of the opening this modular identity formation creates for manipulation and exploitation.

These observations link to issues that André Jansson and others have associated with the term mediatization (Jansson, 2013; Ekström, Fornäs, Jansson, and Jerslev, 2016). The crux of mediatization is the shift from discrete messages and acts of communication towards a meta-process in which 'spatial practices in general and mobility in particular become dependent on and saturated with a broadening range of technologies and institutions for mediation' (Adams and Jansson, 2012: 302). The question of mobility will be treated in greater depth below, but here we can expand a bit more on these observations regarding personal identity by noting that the Internet offers increasingly custom-tailored information environments, ultimately forming what Pariser (2011) calls 'filter bubbles'.

To understand what is meant by this term, we can start by noting that whether one is using a seemingly impersonal search engine like Google, catching up with one's social network on Facebook, shopping online or reading an article from an online news source, one's experience is now almost always personalized through the use of behaviour-tracking 'cookies' installed on one's computer. These bits of code are installed when visiting websites – sometimes with a notification, sometimes without. The code minimally identifies the user's identity but also quite often collects and forwards more-or-less detailed information about the user and his or her online activities. One purpose of such information is to guide algorithms that personalize each user's online experience, reworking 'the web' as a personalized space and effectively hiding large parts of it. In many cases, however, the primary purpose of the cookie goes far beyond this. It works to gather data about the person whose computer it inhabits, as well as social networks, behaviours and attitudes.

Cookies therefore have a rather paradoxical role. On the one hand, they create an evolving boundary around each user, a bubble that keeps out whatever each user is likely to find uninteresting, disagreeable or offensive while letting in whatever most strongly supports the user's preconceptions. Of course, one's online 'friends' serve a similar filtering and directing function, and user-directed search habits compound the tendency towards isolation. Thus, people end up living in what others have called 'echo chambers' (Sunstein, 2007; Bessi, 2016; del Vicario, Zollo, Caldarelli, Scala, and Quattrociocchi, 2016; Quattrociocchi, Scala, and Sunstein, 2016). On the other hand, cookies assist in exposing multiple aspects of identity to the world, potentially undermining efforts to maintain control over one's self-disclosure. This occurs in ways that are not immediately apparent to the computer user, even if the user at one time ostensibly read and signed user agreements allowing the use of his/her personal data. People forget that their online activities are being recorded, catalogued, anonymized, profiled, sold and resold. Cookies undermine the modularized ways in which people want to present themselves, surreptitiously reintegrating them, as dividuals, into opaque technological assemblages.

Together these elements produce fragmentation of experience and ultimately radical divergence in what various groups of people see as real and true. A study of online habits confirmed that 'partisan groups tend to reference nonoverlapping information resources in online discussions' (Jacobson, Myung, and Johnson 2016: 887) while a study of 50,000 U.S. web users showed 'an increase in the mean ideological distance between individuals' as measured by their web browsing histories (Flaxman, Goel, and Rao, 2016). Such studies indicate that information-seeking behaviour in the current digital information environment is less likely to promote shared understandings of the world than to foster filter bubbles or echo chambers. The image of an informationally isolated citizen trapped in his or her bubble or chamber suggests a one-dimensional person – something *too* coherent. However, a paradox we must come to grips with is that even as people's worlds are encapsulated, the individuals within the capsules are becoming less coherent and self-contained as their experiences are subtly shaped by special interests, a kind of fragmentary partisanship manifested opaquely in algorithms employed for a dizzying array of commercial, political and social purposes. So, identity is both encapsulated and subdivided at the same time.

These transformations of identity do not fit easily within the logic of the quadrant diagram, though we could say that filter bubbles are a bit like places. But they are alternatively seen as peculiar, custom-tailored spaces such that what a person encounters as 'the world' (for example, the headlines one finds first when browsing news online) becomes a highly filtered context in which personal identity develops. Yet these experiences may enter the bubble from quite remote locations, even from countries one will never visit and cannot find on a map (Silverman and Alexander, 2016). People have been boundless in some sense for thousands of years (Adams, 2005), but digital communications have enabled a development of self-identity that is much more scattered and disintegrated than before. Such a subject is both here and there, yet neither here nor there in the way it once was.

Publics

To build on such notions regarding the evolution of identity, we must revisit the perennial question of how people come together to form collectivities. Michael Warner helpfully uses the term 'public' to indicate a group or collective that shares a certain mediated experience. What makes a public different from a mere collection of people is that although they may be separated in space, the participants inflect their experience with the awareness that unseen others are sharing the same communication. Such publics are analogous to the small groups that formed for shared experience in premodern times (and to a degree today as well) through congregation in particular places such as churches, theatres and sports arenas. The publics of Warner's model still exist within a larger sphere we could designate as 'The Public' even if its centre no longer holds. To follow Warner in thinking through a public as 'a space of discourse organized by nothing other than discourse itself' (2002: 67) points us in the direction of space-in-media. However, the implications of Warner's argument point no less strongly to media-in-place, as a 'text' is broadly defined in his argument to include 'visual advertising or the chattering of a DJ' (2002: 68) either of which tends to be encountered in and inflected by particular urban places. An additional, crucial, piece of his argument is the notion that society includes counter-publics, which is to say publics marked by subordinate status, marginalized and in some kind of tension relative to the larger public. This brings us back to space through such notions as marginality and centrality, creating an interesting parallel: just as material, tangible places are situated around the margins of geographical spaces, Warnerian publics are situated at the margins of the spaces of mediated communication. Spatial thinking is helpful as we attempt to understand how dividuals change and evolve and how political processes work in a world where people are semi-sequestered in bubbles while contributing to social processes through international networks – in short, how people are linked more than ever to the world while being cut off as agents and modularized internally.

Important questions to be addressed include what happens when we intersect this concept of the self and the public with the digitalization of media and the prevalence of mobility. Mimi Sheller provides the beginning of an answer in her concept of 'mobile publics'. The use of GPS is only a small part of what Sheller means by the 'embedding of mobile information and communication technologies into architectures of mobility' (2004: 39). This embedding also includes new concepts in public transit and new ways of merging private with public transit. It includes 'the convergence and blurring of spaces and times of business, leisure, travel, and inhabitance for certain groups' (Sheller, 2004: 43) as technologies untether communications from fixed locations and permit the breakdown of predictable associations between activities and locations.

Stepping back for a moment in order to contextualize her argument, let us think of the road map as a medium. Since it represents a particular area, it is a kind of place image, a place-in-media. However, if one carries a street map of a city while walking or driving through that city, the map becomes a medium-in-place. The two functions were traditionally connected, albeit with frequent glitches, through human effort and the application of learned wayfinding skills. But what about a device with a built-in map that tells the driver where to go, responding in real time to his/her movements through space and rolling out new maps wherever one goes? Indeed, if we think about using a GPS device and the related 'convergence of moving vehicles and moving screens' (Sheller, 2004: 40) then all distinctions between place-in-medium, medium-in-place and medium-in-space become untenable. GPS devices in effect talk us through the landscape, meaning that one's spatial representation actually performs as part of the space one inhabits, unfolding into new configurations depending on where one moves, just like space and place. Mediated-mobility therefore bridges between corners of the quadrant diagram, embedding each within the other. Add to this the insight that the GPS-with-car-and-driver is an assemblage, and its actions are hybrid spatial performances (Shaw, 2014), then GPS-augmented mobility is predicated on a paradoxical relationship in which the navigated landscape is constantly transformed from communication content to context and back again by a hybrid actor that is both human and nonhuman, a nonhuman communicator embedded within a kind of hybrid performance. In short, digitally guided mobility involves forms of communication that seriously complicate the orthogonal divisions of the quadrant diagram.

At this point, we can return to the discussion of publics by asserting that the dividual is part of something more general: a *mobile public* (Sheller, 2004). Here again we see the undermining of personal control and autonomy. We tend to think of a person's movement through the landscape as an expression of personal volition that is neither immune to systems of social and spatial organization nor entirely determined by them (Certeau, 1988). Traditionally as one moved through urban space one benefitted from anonymity, moving through what Lyn H. Lofland called a 'world of strangers' (1973). Part of what made space public *was* this quality of anonymity, although it was punctuated by chance encounters with acquaintances, friends and sometimes enemies. Now, however, by carrying locationally aware devices such as smartphones, that voluntarily or involuntarily upload one's locational data, the city dweller becomes part of a shifting constellation of knowable persons sharing real-time locational data. The mobile body is no longer off the map, no longer anonymous, as its mobility is shared and reshared, traced and recorded, analysed, sold and resold (Andrejevic, 2014; Humphreys, 2014). This situation arises because the apps people load on smartphones increasingly include locational data as an input, and this in turn involves assenting to share one's location with software and databases housed on a remote server. This data is 'anonymized' and sold to third parties, but there is a substantial risk of one's data being deanonymized because this can be done using a few known locations, and one's location can be deduced by third parties who simply use the app's functionality to extract personal data (Montjoye, Hidalgo, Verleysen, and Blondel, 2013; Summers, 2014). To be part of a mobile public is therefore to be trackable and traceable, both voluntarily and involuntarily. So, in a world where place-in-media and media-in-place are blending together, the flows of locational data automatically constitute mobile publics marked above all by the unreflective and/or involuntary sharing of more than just locational data.

Digitally augmented mobility also mixes up what we think of as private and public. Part of the longstanding appeal of public urban space was the anonymity it afforded. Being away from home in the public space of a large city afforded privacy from friends, acquaintances and family members. It may be a bit of an exaggeration to claim that 'great expanses of public anonymity stretched unbroken for miles, like a pre-twentieth century Amazonia' (Doyle and Veranas, 2014: 207), but the increasingly pervasive capture of digital traces via portable communication devices like cell phones, 'smart' cards (RFID tags), credit cards and video cameras has made public space much less anonymous than it once was. Likewise, the home ceases to be wholly private because much that occurs in the home also leaves digital traces. Viewed optimistically we become part of a 'network of human sensors [with] over 6 billion components' (Goodchild, 2007: 218), but in joining this actor-network we have lost fundamental elements of privacy that were long associated with both public and private space.

This transformation has potential benefits including increased security, but it also suggests 'exposure to the unblinking (if not always all-seeing) eye of the surveillance camera [which] may either provide a sense of security or a sense that certain civil liberties, liberties closely tied to the ability to remain anonymous in public or to engage in activities not directly regulated and approved a priori by the state, are being undermined' (Mitchell and Heynen, 2009). In a convergent trend, people engage in 'social surveillance' (Marwick, 2012) by allowing others to spy on their daily activities while reciprocally spying on the activities of others. In this odd evolution of friendship, human relationships are established and maintained through the nexus of locationally aware technologies, new modes of social networking and mobile lifestyles. Posting from an interesting or out-of-the-way place takes on value as a kind of social capital while, more insidiously, human locational data also becomes a valuable commodity in the 'big data' economy, embedded in all kinds of new calculative spaces (Graham, 2005). Everything one does, in developed economies and increasingly in developing economies, creates a data shadow (Zook, Dodge, Aoyama, and Townsend, 2004). Adaptations people make to such surveillant practices are perfect examples of mediatization, because rather than particular instances of mediation, they involve broad across-the-board transformations of routines, expectations, attitudes and even sense of self.

Historically, privacy was not a function only of the private realm but rather arose from a particular relationship between public and private places. This relationship has now largely been replaced because of interlinking developments in communication technologies, practices, norms and opportunities. These observations pertain most fully to developed countries in the Global North, but similar processes are underway in most places with the rapid diffusion of the cell phone and social media into developing countries and the Global South. All of these changes rework the meanings of public and private, space and place, here and there, self and other, bringing elements of each into the other and prompting radically new ways of maintaining these distinctions. What emerges is not an undifferentiated world, but a set of somewhat different distinctions revolving around 'new modes of public-in-private and private-in-public that disrupt commonly held spatial models of these as two separate "spheres"' (Sheller, 2004: 39). This shift ultimately unsettles how human identity itself is constituted. The concept of a commodified 'mobile public' made up of surveilled dividuals living in filter bubbles therefore troubles all of the distinctions embedded in the quadrant diagram, pointing to a new sort of geographical order with contours we are still struggling to understand.

Conclusion

As a tourist who combined travel abroad with GPS-guided mobility, with the consumption of broadcast media, with social media use, with encounters of others, with the accumulation of digital photos for teaching, with the use of a credit card, ATM card and passport, I thoroughly took part in this new geographical order. It was far easier to do so than to gain an understanding of its contours. I remain uncertain about how to apply concepts of space and place, communication content and context to much of this excursion. One thing that is clear is that the experience in its entirety, tangible and virtual, contributed to the substrate of my evolving sense of self.

Segmented worlds arose with modernity, offering a continuum of places and spaces ranging from the very public to the very private (Tuan, 1982). As Tuan argues, this evolution in space and place supported a deepening of subjectivity, stretching the continuum of self from the polished, opaque and thoroughly public self to the mysterious and untamed recesses of the private self. In short, the evolution of spaces and places enabled a complementary and deeply interlocking evolution of the self, including all aspects of subjectivity and identity. Now, in response to the emerging phenomena of dividuals, hybrid and distributed selves, digital surveillance, filter bubbles, mobile publics and other related transformations, the self will be enabled to evolve in new ways. Or rather it will be compelled to evolve because, as much as one may want to stay the same, one interacts with others whose understandings of space, place, public and private, mobility and stasis are all evolving in response to new and emerging conditions. One cannot opt out of these changes. One can at best choose between welcoming or enduring them.

The arguments laid out here also suggest that identity has come unstuck from place in a new way even as the self has come unstuck from the body's location in a new way. Assumptions about the anchoring of identity in the body and the anchoring of the body in space have often gone hand in hand (Adams, 2005). Indeed these relationships are worked out in detail by the ontological and epistemological traditions mentioned above, as they have addressed questions of media, communication and geography. Likewise, the processes of detachment, modularization, mobilization and digitalization affect selves and publics; they strain against the ontological and epistemological distinctions I have given some organization with the quadrant diagram.

I have sketched the applicability of the quadrant diagram to the task of understanding a rather ordinary situation – the viewing of a soccer game – but have also suggested that in various ways new geomedia research points to a new theoretical terrain that cannot be situated within the heuristic space of the quadrant diagram. We confront the conundrum of growing experiential isolation combined with increasing mobility and exposure of one's data shadow, bringing together dividuals, algorithmic surveillance, mobile publics, hybrid performances, segregated digital worlds, locationally aware technologies and encoded spatial logics. In the process, established distinctions between space and place, communication content and communication context dissolve. While these concepts remain useful, the attempt to understand self and subjectivity must recognize the emergence of new trajectories off the grid, because these will tell us where people are going, in a literal and a figurative sense.

Notes

1 Phenomenology is understood as either ontology or epistemology depending on whether one builds on the works of Husserl or Heidegger (Cohen and Omery, 1994).
2 A phenomenon that is ready-to-hand is understood in terms of its potential uses, in this case as a food or a source of collective identity.

References

Adams, P. C. (1992). Television as gathering place. *Annals of the Association of American Geographers*, 82(1): 117–135.
Adams, P. C. (2005). *The Boundless Self: Communication in Physical and Virtual Spaces*. Syracuse, NY: Syracuse University Press.
Adams, P. C. (2010). A taxonomy for communication geography. *Progress in Human Geography*, 35(1): 37–57.
Adams, P. C. (2013). Communication in virtual worlds. In M. Grimshaw (Ed.) *Oxford Handbook of Virtuality* (pp. 239–253). Oxford UK & New York: Oxford University Press.
Adams, P. C., & Jansson, A. (2012). Communication geography: A bridge between disciplines. *Communication Theory*, 22(3): 299–318.
Agnew, J. A., & Duncan, J. S. (eds.) (1989). *The Power of Place: Bringing Together Geographical and Sociological Imaginations*. Oxford and New York: Routledge. Retrieved from www.eblib.com.
Albright, J. (2016). The #Election2016 Micro-Propaganda Machine. Online file at: https://medium.com/@d1gi/the-election2016-micro-propaganda-machine-383449cc1fba#.idanl6i8z, accessed 2017-1-15.
Andrejevic, M. (2014). The infinite debt of surveillance in the digital economy. In A. Jansson & M. Christensen (Eds.), *Media, Surveillance and Identity: Social Perspectives* (pp. 91–108). New York: Peter Lang.
Bessi, A. (2016). Personality traits and echo chambers on Facebook. *Computers in Human Behavior*, 65: 319–324.
Bhabha, H. K. (1994). *The Location of Culture*. London and New York: Routledge.
Certeau, M. D. (1988). *The Practice of Everyday Life*. Trans. S. Rendall. Berkeley: University of California Press.
Christophers, B. (2009). *Envisioning Media Power: On Capital and Geographies of Television*. Lanham, MD: Lexington Books.

Cohen, M. Z., & Omery, A., (1994). Schools of phenomenology: Implications for research. In J. M. Morse (Ed.), *Critical Issues in Qualitative Research Methods* (pp. 136–153). Thousand Oaks, CA: Sage.

Cosgrove, D. (2001). *Apollo's Eye: A Cartographic Genealogy of the Earth in the Western Imagination*. Baltimore, MD: Johns Hopkins University Press.

Cresswell, T. (2014). *Place: An Introduction*. New York: John Wiley & Sons.

Cupples, J., & Glynn, K. (2013). Postdevelopment television? Cultural citizenship and the mediation of Africa in contemporary TV drama. *Annals of the Association of American Geographers*, 103(4): 1003–1021.

Deleuze, G. (1966). *Bergsonism*. Trans. Hugh Tomlinson and Barbara Habberjam. New York: Zone, 1991.

Deleuze, G. (1992). Postscript on the societies of control. *October* 59: 3–7.

del Vicario, M., Zollo, F., Caldarelli, G., Scala, A., & Quattrociocchi, W. (2016). *The Anatomy of Brexit Debate on Facebook*. asXiv preprint arXiv:1610.06809.

Dodge, M., & Kitchin, R. (2005). Code and the transduction of space. *Annals of the Association of American Geographers*, 95(1): 162–180.

Doyle, T., & Veranas, J. (2014). Public anonymity and the connected world. *Ethics and Information Technology*, 16: 207–218.

Ekström, M., Fornäs, J., Jansson, A., & Jerslev, A. (2016). Three tasks for mediatization research: contributions to an open agenda. *Media, Culture & Society*, 38(7): 1090–1108.

Flaxman, S., Goel, S., & Rao, J. (2016). Filter bubbles, echo chambers, and online news consumption. *Public Opinion Quarterly*, 80: 298–320.

Gaffney, C. T. (2010). *Temples of the Earthbound Gods: Stadiums in the Cultural Landscapes of Rio de Janeiro and Buenos Aires*. Austin: University of Texas Press.

Gandy, M. (2003). Landscapes of deliquescence in Michelangelo Antonioni's red desert. *Transactions of the Institute of British Geographers*, 28(2): 218–237.

García Canclini, N. (1995). *Hybrid Cultures: Strategies for Entering and Leaving Modernity*. Trans. C. L. Chiappari, & S. L. López. Minneapolis and London: University of Minnesota Press.

Giddens, A. (1984). *The Constitution of Society: Outline of the Theory of Structuration*. Berkeley: University of California Press.

Goodchild, M. F. (2007). Citizens as sensors: The world of volunteered geography. *GeoJournal*, 69(4): 211–221.

Gorman, S. P., & Kulkarni, R., (2004). Spatial small worlds: New geographic patterns for an information economy. *Environment and Planning B: Planning and Design*, 31(2): 273–296.

Gould, P., (1991). Dynamic structures of geographic space. In S. D. Brunn & T. R. Leinbach (Eds.) *Collapsing Space and Time: Geographic Aspects of Communication and Information* (pp. 3–30). London and New York: Routledge.

Graham, S. D. N. (2005). Software-sorted geographies. *Progress in Human Geography*, 29(5): 562–580.

Graham, M., Hogan, B. Straumann R. K., & Medhat, A. (2014). Uneven geographies of user-generated information: Patterns of increasing informational poverty, *Annals of the Association of American Geographers*, 104:4: 746–764.

Haraway, D. J. (1985). A manifesto for cyborgs: science, technology, and socialist feminism in the 1980s. *Socialist Review*, 80: 65–108.
Heidegger, M. (1962). *Being and Time*. Translated by J. Macquarrie & E. Robinson. London: SCM Press.
Howard, P. N., & Hussain, M. M. (2013). *Democracy's Fourth Wave? Digital Media and the Arab Spring*. Oxford: Oxford University Press.
Humphreys, L. (2014). Mobile social networks and surveillance. In A. Jansson & M. Christensen, (Eds.), *Media, Surveillance and Identity: Social Perspectives* (pp. 109–126). New York: Peter Lang.
Jackson, P. (2008). Thai semicolonial hybridities: Bhabha and García Canclini in dialogue on oower and ultural blending. *Asian Studies Review*, 32: 147–170.
Jacobson, S., Myung, E., & Johnson, S. L. (2016). Open media or echo chamber: The use of links in audience discussions on the Facebook Pages of partisan news organizations. *Information, Communication & Society*, 19(7): 875–891.
Jansson, A. (2013). Mediatization and social space: Reconstructing mediatization for the transmedia age. *Communication Theory*, 23(3): 279–296.
Jaquet-Chiffelle, D.-O., Benoist, E., Haenni, R., Wenger, F., & Zwingelberg, H. (2009). Virtual persons and identities. In K. Rannenberg, D. Royer, & A. Deuker, (Eds.), *The Future of Identity in the Information Society: Challenges and Opportunities* (pp. 75–91). Dordrecht, Netherlands: Springer.
Jessop, B., Brenner, B., & Jones, M. (2008). Theorizing socio-spatial relations. *Environment and Planning D: Society and Space*, 26: 389–401.
Jones, M. (2009). Phase space: Geography, relational thinking, and beyond. *Progress in Human Geography*, 33(4): 487–506.
Jones, R., & Merriman, P. (2009). Hot, banal and everyday nationalism: Bilingual road signs in Wales. *Political Geography*, 28(3): 164–173.
Kitchin, R., & Dodge, M., (2011). *Code/Space: Software and Everyday Life*. Cambridge, MA: MIT Press.
Latour, B. (1987). *Science in Action: How to Follow Scientists and Engineers through Society*. Cambridge, MA: Harvard University Press.
Latour, B. (1993). *We Have Never Been Modern*. Cambridge, MA: Harvard University Press.
Liben-Nowell, D., Novak, J., Kumar, R., Raghavan, P., & Tomkins, A., (2005). Geographic routing in social networks. *Proceedings of the National Academy of Sciences of the United States of America*, 102(33): 11623–11628.
Lofland, L. (1973). *A World of Strangers*. New York: Basic Books.
Longhurst, R. (2013). Using Skype to mother: Bodies, emotions, visuality, and screens. *Environment and Planning D: Society and Space*, 31(4): 664–679.
Lukinbeal C. (2012). "On Location" filming in San Diego County from 1985–2005: How a cinematic landscape is formed through incorporative tasks and represented through mapped inscriptions. *Annals of the Association of American Geographers*, 102(1): 171–190.
Lulka, D. (2009). The residual humanism of hybridity: retaining a sense of the earth. *Transactions of the Institute of British Geographers*, NS 34: 378–393.
Malecki, E. J., & Wei, H., (2009). A wired world: the evolving geography of submarine cables and the shift to Asia. *Annals of the Association of American Geographers*, 99(2): 360–382.

Marwick, A. (2012). The public domain: surveillance in everyday life. *Surveillance and Society*, 9(4): 378–393.
Massey, D. (1991). A global sense of place. *Marxism Today*, 38: 24–29.
Massey, D. (2004). Geographies of responsibility. *Geografiska Annaler: Series B, Human Geography*, 86B(1): 5–18.
Mitchell, W. J. (1995). *City of Bits: Space, Place, and the Infobahn*. Cambridge, MA: MIT Press.
Mitchell, D., & Heynen, N. (2009). The geography of survival and the right to the city: speculations on surveillance, legal innovation, and the criminalization of intervention. *Urban Geography*, 30(6): 611–632.
Montjoye, Y. A. de, Hidalgo, C. A., Verleysen, M., & Blondel, V. D. (2013). Unique in the crowd: The privacy bounds of human mobility. *Scientific Reports*, 3 (1376): 1–5.
Morley, D. (1986). *Family Television: Cultural Power and Domestic Leisure*. London: Comedia Publishing Group.
Nissenbaum, H. (2010). *Privacy in Context: Technology, Policy, and the Integrity of Social Life*. Stanford, California: Stanford Law Books.
Pariser, E. (2011). *The Filter Bubble: How the New Personalized Web is Changing What We Read and How We Think*. London: Penguin.
Pickles, J. (Ed.) (1995). *Ground Truth: The Social Implications of Geographic Information Systems*. New York: Guilford Press.
Pinkerton, A., Young, S., & Dodds, K. (2011). Weapons of mass communication: The securitization of social networking sites. *Political Geography*, 30: 115–117.
Pratt, G., & Johnston, C. (2007). Turning theatre into law, and other spaces of politics. *Cultural Geographies*, 14(1): 92–113.
Quattrociocchi, W., Scala, A., & Sunstein, C. R. (2016). *Echo Chambers on Facebook*. Discussion Paper No. 877. Cambridge, MA: Harvard Law School.
Ratti, C., Sobolevsky, S., Calabrese, F., Andris, C., Reades, J., Martino, M., Claxton, R., & Strogatz, S. H. (2010). Redrawing the map of Great Britain from a network of human interactions. *PloS One*, 5(12): e14248.
Rose, G. (2016a). *Visual Methodologies: An Introduction to Researching with Visual Materials*. London: Sage.
Rose, G. (2016b). Rethinking the geographies of cultural 'objects' through digital technologies: interface, network and friction. *Progress in Human Geography*, 40(3): 334–351.
Rutenberg, J. (2016). Media's next challenge: Overcoming the threat of fake news. *New York Times* (Nov. 6, 2016). Online file at: www.nytimes.com/2016/11/07/business/media/medias-next-challenge-overcoming-the-threat-of-fake-news.html?_r=0, accessed 2017-1-15.
Sack, R. D. (1980). *Conceptions of Space in Social Thought: A Geographic Perspective*. Minneapolis: University of Minnesota Press.
Shaw, R. (2014). Beyond night-time economy: affective atmospheres of the urban night. *Geoforum* 51(1): 87–95.
Shaw, I. G. R., & Warf, B. (2009). Worlds of affect: Virtual geographies of video games. *Environment and Planning A* 41(6): 1332–1343.
Sheller, M. (2004). Mobile publics: beyond the network perspective. *Environment and Planning D: Society and Space*, 22(1): 39–52.

Sheller, M., & Urry, J. (Eds.) (2006). *Mobile Technologies of the City*. London and New York: Routledge.

Shields, R. (2006). Virtualities. *Theory, Culture & Society*, 23(2–3): 284–286.

Silverman, C., & Alexander, L. (2016). How teens in the Balkans are duping Trump supporters with fake news. *BuzzFeed News* (Nov. 4, 2016). Online file at www.buzzfeed.com/craigsilverman/how-macedonia-became-a-global-hub-for-pro-trump-misinfo?utm_term=.ikLvXqxzX#.cryVr0ABr, accessed 2017-1-8.

Summers, N. (2014). New tinder security flaw exposed users' exact locations for months. *Bloomberg Businessweek*. February 19, 2014. www.businessweek.com/articles/2014-02-19/new-tinder-security-flaw-exposed-users-exact-locations-for-months.

Sunstein, C. R. (2007). *Republic.com 2.0*. Princeton and Oxford: Princeton University Press.

Tuan, Y. F. (1977). *Space and Place: The Perspective of Experience*. Minneapolis, MN: University of Minnesota Press.

Tuan, Y. F. (1982). *Segmented Worlds and Self: A Study of Group Life and Individual Consciousness*. Minneapolis, MN: University of Minnesota Press.

Tuan, Y. F. (1996). *Cosmos and Hearth: A Cosmopolite's Viewpoint*. Minneapolis, MN: University of Minnesota Press.

Tufekci, Z. (2013). "Not this one": Social movements, the attention economy, and microcelebrity networked activism. *American Behavioral Scientist*, 57(7): 848–870.

Turkle, S. (1995). *Life on the Screen: Identity in the Age of the Internet*. New York: Simon and Schuster.

Warf, B. (2012). *Global Geographies of the Internet*. Dordrecht, The Netherlands: Springer Science & Business Media.

Warf, B., & Sui, D. (2010). From GIS to neogeography: Ontological implications and theories of truth. *Annals of GIS*, 16(4): 197–209.

Warner, M. (2002). Publics and counterpublics. *Public Culture*, 14(1): 49–90.

Zook, M. (2008). *The Geography of the Internet Industry: Venture Capital, Dot-Coms, and Local Knowledge*. New York: John Wiley & Sons.

Zook, M., Dodge, M., Aoyama, Y., & Townsend, A. (2004). New digital geographies: Information, communication and place. In S. D. Brunn, S. L. Cutter, & J. W. Harrington (Eds.), *Geography and Technology* (pp. 155–176). Dordrecht, Netherlands: Kluwer Academic Publishers.

4 Space, Place and Circulation
Three Conceptual Lenses into the Spatialities of Media Production Practices

Helen Morgan Parmett and Scott Rodgers

Introduction

Where is the locus of contemporary media production? We can no longer simply direct our attention towards once-reliable places, such as newsrooms, studios, film sets or editing suites. While these locations still matter, their naturalization as *the* sites of media production cannot today be taken for granted. Such locales rely on closely associating specific production practices and discrete mediums, when media convergence has brought technological transformations weakening medium specificity. Such locales also tend to involve seeing the 'products' of media narrowly, as specific types of content. As Lash and Lury (2007) point out, in recent decades cultural production has increasingly been extended into the mediation of material commodities themselves (e.g. via branding) beyond their representation. Even for more 'traditional' forms of media, production is increasingly layered and dispersed. Through transformations similar to what Deleuze (1995) called emergent 'societies of control', media production has become notably deinstitutionalized: television productions involve various constellations of project teams; films frequently entail an international division of labour; work in the creative industries is characterized by promiscuity and precarity in employment, rather than stable careers; virtually all content producers, from journalists to musicians, must navigate and distribute their work through the commercial network spaces of Google, Facebook, Apple, Amazon and others.

What counts as media production, and its attendant geographies, has therefore become less certain and identifiable. There is not only a far blurrier distinction between production and consumption, but between what is or is not a media product. One of the more prominent tropes in this context is that almost everyone can be a media producer, resulting in new participatory media cultures (e.g. Jenkins, 2006; Bruns, 2008) and new spaces of media production. However, media production has not simply dissolved into a flattened landscape where everyone is a contributor with equal power. Media environments instead retain marked power asymmetries, not just in content production, but also in the design, operation and ownership of new media forms, commodities, devices, data, platforms and infrastructures. There remain meaningful distinctions between, for example, a Facebook engineer designing a facial recognition tool and users relying on such functionalities. Facebook users, dispersed across an enormous range of localized situations and performing a range of media practices (e.g. editing, organizing and sharing images), are in at least some sense its producers because their actions add to its content. Yet the engineer produces Facebook differently, and via contrasting environments. She might work from Facebook's expansive campus headquarters in Menlo Park, California, built on a triangular peninsula jutting into drying marshlands on San Francisco Bay. At and through this particular locale, she does more than just add to Facebook's content; she helps establish the technical and cultural conditions of possibility for that content production to take place elsewhere. This example suggests that we are not quite witnessing the disappearance of what was once called 'the media', and the concomitant rise of 'us' (Couldry, 2009, 2015). Rather, we are witnessing a complex reshaping of how media-related professions, organizations and technical platforms attune with, speak to and act on behalf of others. In turn, it suggests that we not only still need to attend to media production in what might be seen as a more traditional sense – i.e. the work of professionals and industries ordinarily understood to be pivotal in making different media possible – but we need to attend to their changing geographies. In this chapter, we want to rethink how we approach the spatialities of media production, empirically, conceptually and politically. Precisely because of their apparent multiplicities, amorphousness and dispersal, there is a need to better research and specify distinct geographies of production and differential expressions, configurations or hierarchies of media power.

We situate our contribution in both the nascent field of geomedia studies and the field of media production studies. The conjunctive term geomedia, the focus of this volume, for us indicates the arrival of a broadly shared *environmental* view of media: a view in which media are seen not as extrinsic representations of or technological influences on spatiality, but rather as intrinsically geographical. Media always already emerge through environments of action; spatiality is always already mediated. Media production studies (e.g. Mayer, Banks, and Caldwell, 2009; Banks, Conor, and Mayer, 2015) is a parallel field that brings together political economy and cultural studies approaches towards understanding 'how media producers make culture, and, in the process, make themselves into particular kinds of workers in modern, mediated societies' (Mayer et al., 2009: 2). Many of the contributions to *Production Studies* (Mayer et al., 2009) – an influential edited collection primarily focused on the film and television industries – are also concerned with spatialities of media production, from the liminal spaces between production and consumption to the complex dispersal of production through transnationalizing media industries. In important respects, 'production studies' is a reaction to the tendency in cultural studies to focus on practices of consumption, assuming 'that the crucial cultural processes are those that transpire within acts of reception' (Straw, 2010: 210), while abandoning the study of production to political economists. Cultural industries researchers such as Pratt (2004) have suggested that this fails to account adequately for not only media and cultural production, but also media production's specific spatialities. That is, the intrinsic relationships between institutionalized cultural-economic activity and their situated material geographies.

Although we build on these existing approaches, our aim is to dedicate more explicit attention to media production spatialities than is usually offered in production studies. While our examples still focus on media understood relatively conventionally, we contend that contemporary media spatialities demand an approach to production that is more open empirically to emergence and transformation and more open conceptually to which domains might count as media 'production'. In order to do so, we turn, alongside other media scholars, to so-called practice theory (e.g. Schatzki, Knorr Cetina, and Von Savingny, 2001). Thinking of media in terms of practices decentres the longstanding trifecta of media scholarship – industry, text and audience – in that it takes a more open-ended and broadly ethnographic approach to the ways in which 'media' come to matter for what actors do and say (see Couldry, 2004; Bräuchler and Postill, 2010). More importantly for our present purposes, the practice turn in media studies invites a spatialized reorientation, de-emphasizing media as discrete 'things' and putting a priority on how media emerge through situated environments of action. This is a crucial reorientation in a context where both media production and consumption unfold through weakened medium specificity and increasingly deinstitutionalized media. It enjoins us to study media production beyond the places in which we expect it to occur (i.e. outside the studio, the newsroom and so forth) and in so doing question where the work of production begins and ends.

The notion of 'practice' has a long history, particularly in anthropology and sociology, yet it has entered media studies relatively recently, arguably gaining prominence after an influential paper by Couldry (2004) was published in *Social Semiotics*, outlining the disciplinary trajectory towards the study of what he terms 'media related practices'. This led to a culmination of sorts in *Theorising Media and Practice* (Bräuchler and Postill, 2010), an anthology that includes a reprint of and responses to Couldry's (2004) essay. Couldry's intervention has been influential, we would suggest, since it crystallizes a longer horizon of work in audience studies that has begun to question what is now often called 'media-centrism' (see Morley, 2009; Moores, 2012): the taken-for-granted analysis of media as discrete symbolic texts or forms, rather than as phenomena embedded into material environments of action. For Couldry (2004: 121), thinking of media in terms of practice radically inverts the media-centric emphasis of media studies, suggesting a focus not on media per se, but on 'what types of things do people do in relation to media? And what types of things do people say in relation to media?' Bräuchler and Postill's (2010) anthology includes a series of empirical responses and challenges to Couldry's essay, including some chapters (e.g. Ardèvol, Roig, San Cornelio, Pagès, and Alsina, 2010; Greenhalgh, 2010) that address certain aspects of production practices. Yet, however helpful, these considerations of media production practices remain too scattered – and often too anchored onto theorizations of media audiences, use or consumption – to lead us towards a practice-oriented understanding of media production spatialities.

Like cultural studies more generally, then, there is also a consumptionist bias in the application of practice theory in media studies. Even as the everyday practices of media audiences (or users) have proven a fruitful ground for thinking about media practices, production has often been treated as 'generally a rationalized work practice' (Couldry, 2004: 126), more suited to political economy perspectives. What we offer here is a response to this apparent blind spot, which we unfold through three progressively linked conceptual lenses. These suggest we think of media production spatialities as: (1) specific cultures of practice within *circulatory* processes, rather than unidirectional points of origin; (2) a radically contextualized habitus that both makes and inhabits *place*; and (3) practices that are positioned and orientated towards dispersed field *spaces* of production, which are both social and technical. In proposing these three lenses, we seek neither to offer a grand practice theory of media production nor to posit absolute geographical categories. We are not implying, for instance, a stark distinction between place and space. Instead, following writers like Massey (e.g. 1994) and Appadurai (e.g. 1995), as well as the editors of this volume, we are proposing *relational* ontologies and epistemologies towards understanding the changing spatialities of media production practices.

Unfolding Three Lenses into Media Production Spatialities

Media Production as Cultures of Circulation

It is for understandable reasons that Hall's (1980) well-known encoding/decoding model has come to be primarily seen as an assertion regarding the agency of media audiences or users. Its emphasis on linguistic theory offered a potent response to the dominance of media effects approaches, opening the way for empirical 'audience studies' – notably Morley's (1980) research on the *Nationwide* television audience – and eventually, the 'ethnographic turn' in audience research (see Moores, 1993). It is also worth recalling that Hall's larger critique was linear models of communication, those modelled on unidirectional travel of a message between sender and receiver. Inspired by Marx's thinking on commodity production, Hall suggested it was more useful to think about media as forms moving through connected yet relatively autonomous practices, which together form a 'complex structure of dominance' (1980: 117). Such 'moments' in the circulation of media forms are not part of a closed loop but are instead situated in differentiated worlds. So, just as audiences decode media content not in isolation but based on prior knowledge, the conditions of their situated milieus and so on, media producers do their 'encoding' work in ways that fundamentally respond and attune to the complexities of the discursive, social, cultural and political worlds they inhabit.

This kind of open-ended analysis of how media are encountered, used and produced is now well developed in cultural studies of media consumption. Gitelman (2006: 62–64), for example, offers a rich historical account of how women and other users were in many respects responsible for 'making' the early phonograph. They encouraged its eventual development into the 'first nonprint mass medium' (Gitelman, 2006: 59) – read-only devices dedicated to domestic amusement – even though entrepreneurial inventors like Thomas Edison proposed them as read-write tools for business communications. Recognizing that 'making' plays with terminology normally associated with production, Gitelman proposes the more neutral term of 'define' across contexts of production and consumption. This is not so much to reject distinctions made between such contexts, but rather to avoid seeing the former as active and the latter reactive. There are examples in production studies that mirror Gitelman's work, notably Caldwell (2008), to whom we will return later. What is important to note at this point, however, is that cultural studies of media consumption not only trade in more flexible distinctions between production and consumption; they also suggest a different image of the spatial trajectories or mobilities of media forms. If, broadly following Hall (1980), we understand media as moving through interconnected yet situationally autonomous practices, which both 'produce' and 'receive', then an implicitly one-way sender-message-receiver model is unsustainable for notional production and consumption alike. Instead, media forms move through different milieus with varying degrees of multidirectionality, concentration and dispersal.

This alternative lens for thinking about the spatial trajectories of media has been recently named by Straw (2009) as the 'circulatory turn'. The idea of a circulatory turn draws inspiration from Lee and LiPuma's (2002) influential essay on 'cultures of circulation'. For Lee and LiPuma, cultural anthropologies of globalization too often rely on a transmission view of circulation, in which commodities, artefacts, ideas and bodies are imagined as travelling from one geographical point to another. Yet the spatialities of circulation, for Lee and LiPuma, are better understood in performative terms, as involving distributed communities of practice through which forms are mobilized, reproduced, abstracted and evaluated. They suggest that any circulating form – media-related examples could be a magazine, anime franchise or social networking service – presupposes differentiated communities of practice, and conversely, these communities variably enact the form. This would suggest, borrowing Warner's (2002: 67) description of publicness, that media forms be characterized by varying degrees of 'chicken-and-egg circularity'. Media forms are best seen as circulating through, and being reciprocally implicated in, the uneven reproduction of social and cultural life, rather than being created by producers and then transmitted to consumers (see also Bødker, 2016).

Thinking about media in terms of circulation depends on what Straw (2009: 23) calls an anti-interpretive view of media. Instead of interpreting the social from within a media form's content, emphasis is placed on how media forms occupy and move through different social settings, including those associated with 'production'. This first invites a somewhat different analysis of media power. Media production, in this view, is not primarily analysed or evaluated as an originary process transducing, for example, broader discourses into specific media forms, which are then sent out into the world. Rather, media production is seen as expressing power in how, as a specific community of practice, it attunes to, and inherits, the complex prior circulation of a media form, to which it should be seen as partly subjugated (see also Rodgers, 2014: 80–81). On this view, media production practices can still be understood as influentially mediating individual media objects within a 'circular, tightly bound' (Barnett, 2007, cited in Straw, 2009: 27) form of circulation (e.g. producing a television series for a cult fan base); however, our attention is drawn as well to how communities of production practices, in particular, also involve more reflexive understandings of their media as a form scattered and dispersed over time and space.

As may be clear, there are clear overlaps between the circulatory turn and the turn to theorizing media as practice, particularly in its emphasis on how circulating forms are recursively performed into existence. Practice theories offer a similar anti-interpretative intervention to the circulatory turn, though in this case vis-à-vis societal norms and rules. Rather than being posited as a priori or transcendental, practice theories see social norms and rules as recursively produced through action, or through what people and things do (for an overview, see Schatzki et al., 2001). Often grounded in ethnographic methodologies, practice theories examine the dynamic relationships of social structure and individual agency and how these relationships both unfold through the body – as a disciplined, disciplining and resistant agential subject – and through shared languages and tacit knowledge (Rouse, 2006). Approaching media production through practice theory means treating media production not as an a priori domain, but as a recursive practical accomplishment (Ross, 2014). Understanding the spatialities of media production, in turn, should start by positioning such sites as participating in the complex circulation of a media form – participation that may express power but should not be seen a point of origin. Having situated production practices within the circulation of media forms, we now further flesh out how such cultures become contextualized as specific media-related habitus in place.

Media Production in Place

Media and communication technologies have long been associated with the eradication of place and space: the 'annihilation of space by time' (e.g. Harvey, 1989); the rise of 'despatialized simultaneity' (Thompson, 1995); and the proliferation of 'non-places' (Augé, 1995). The practice turn in media studies, however, invites a concomitant respatialization of media. In moving away from thinking of media as discrete 'things', the practice turn conceives of media as aspects within ensembles of action. For writers such as Moores (2012), such a 'non-media centric' orientation involves not only new attention to space, but specifically to the concept of place.

The conceptualization of 'place' has a complex intellectual history. It is associated with phenomenological perspectives – close kin to theories of practice – that see inhabiting place as inherent to all practical action. Place, frequently described in terms of individual perception and emotional attachment, is often assumed to be the subjective experience of objective physical space. The priority phenomenological perspectives put on place, however, is more accurately an attempt to sidestep a subject-object dualism. It affirms the existence of spaces beyond immediate perception yet focuses on how such spaces emerge in place, or through action (Tuan, 1977; Malpas, 2012). Massey's (1994) well-known 'relational' conceptualization of place builds on these perspectives, while offering a more politically attuned response to phenomenological tendencies to romanticize place as 'rooted', often with dangerous and reactionary consequences (illustrated by Martin Heidegger's Nazism). For Massey, places are reflexive, constantly changing assemblages of interwoven, translocal forces. Moores (2012) brings these perspectives together in one of the more detailed considerations of media and place, albeit one primarily focussed on practices of use. He argues against an extrinsic view of media affecting place (e.g. producing 'placelessness', cf. Relph, 1976), instead arguing that media are inherent to how we inhabit and make our place in the world.

How, then, do practices of media production inhabit and make place? Addressing this question is not only conceptually important; it is a growing empirical imperative. Media and cultural production are increasingly described through rhetoric valorizing the significance of place. For example, creative industries are often explained through their ties to particular neighbourhoods and spatialized lifestyles (Pratt, 2004); quality television is associated with the 'authenticity' of place produced by on-location filming (Morgan Parmett, 2016); and emergent 'hyperlocal' media are identified as the antidote to the placelessness of the mainstream (Hess and Waller, 2015). A problem with political economy or industrial perspectives is not just that they overemphasize the rationalized and standardized aspects of media production practices, but that their contact with place is resultantly highly instrumental, figured, often, as the imposition of formulas that leave marks on particular places. As Landman (2009) argues, however, even large-scale globalized media industries, such as those based in the US, have to negotiate with and account for the localized settings they encounter, where creative collaboration results in more than simply 'offshored' U.S. productions controlled at a distance. In this case and in others, there is a clear need to more radically contextualize media production in place.

An important first step is to consider the embodiment of different production practices in place. Here we turn to Pierre Bourdieu's (1990) theory of practice and particularly the concept of habitus, which has received significant attention in media and cultural studies (e.g. Hesmondhalgh, 2006; Born, 2010; Jansson, 2013). For Bourdieu (1990: 53), habitus refers to:

> systems of durable, transposable dispositions, structured structures predisposed to function as structuring structures, that is, as principles which generate and organize practices and representations that can be objectively adapted to their outcomes without presupposing a conscious aiming at ends or an express mastery of the operations necessary in order to attain them...they can be collectively orchestrated without being the product of the organizing action of a conductor.

Without ruling out the possibility of conscious or strategic action, Bourdieu emphasizes a deeper foundation of tacit, embodied, nonrepresentational knowledge. His aim is not merely to provide a way to describe commonsensical activities but to argue that power primarily emerges through the practicing body. Habitus attends to how all practical action is at once structured by learned, accumulated and internalized dispositions and structuring in its enactment. It is a key concept for theorizing place (e.g. Casey, 2001), inspired in particular by Bourdieu's (1990: 271–283) discussion of ethnographic fieldwork on the Kabyle people of northern Algeria. Kabyle homes, for Bourdieu, differentially order and situate bodily comportments, expressing and structuring the social values and practices of Kabyle culture (see Cresswell, 2002). The concept of habitus suggests that practices of media production are more than collections of shared routines; such practices are the expression of relatively durable dispositions to the world. In this way, media production habitus are structured by and structure place: they express immanent relationships between learned dispositions and the arrangement and perception of specific environments (cf. Casey, 2001).

While the situatedness of media production practices in place are not identical to that of Kabyle culture in the home, a common feature is the production of particular kinds of localities. For Appadurai (1995), localities are sites that make social action and space itself socially meaningful. Media production practices are both a product of localized conditions and partake in producing the meaning and spatiality of the locality. At the same time, localities are defined through bounding; they are made meaningful through *not* being another locality. This is particularly important for understanding media production places, which tend to operate through a tacit understanding that they are distinct from nonproduction sites (they are 'special'; see Couldry, 2000). This is most clearly recognizable, of course, in durable places of media production, those 'specific domains of action and value' (Rose, 1996: 143) set apart for the cultivation of specific kinds of media conduct. A film shoot on a street, for example, constructs a boundary around the shoot, demarcating what is in the shot and part of the production from what is not. This kind of boundary making is constitutive of places of film production, enjoining bodies to comport themselves in accordance with the expectations, knowledges and cultures of filmmaking. Or consider, for example, 'the newsroom' – a place so apparently permanent that it is as often used to refer to journalistic culture in general as any locale of news production in particular. Newsrooms emerge as powerful places of media production through the recursive performances of bodies, objects and technologies associated with the organized practice of editing (Rodgers, 2014). While the newsroom is fundamentally oriented to an externalized world beyond, it involves folding in or collating that world into the taking-place of production work and its habitus.

However, if the spatialities of media production are increasingly layered and dispersed, their attendant forms of place making are likely to be ever more fissive, momentary, mobile and contested; perhaps requiring constant ritual maintenance, the invention of new rituals, or new forms of routinization that help to render such places meaningful and distinct. The rising ubiquity of on-location filming is one example. It may be tempting to see such developments as rendering places into mere Hollywood film backlots. On-location filming practices can involve a relatively invasive introduction of distinctly filmic dispositions, not to mention material heft (e.g. large trucks, abundant personnel and technical equipment), to a wide range of settings. Yet on-location filming practices also involve a negotiation of location. Not only contending with the navigation of a particular city's streets, but also its accumulated histories and material textures. Since such new mobilities of filming are, in part, predicated on the search for cheaper places to film, they also demand more flexible practical attunement and adaptability to different locales. Such attunement takes on even more novel shape when localities are mobilized more directly into a production culture. In recent U.S. television series such as *The Wire*, *Treme* and *Portlandia*, for example, specific localities in Baltimore, New Orleans and Portland are invited to partly 'play themselves' (see Morgan Parmett, 2014). These approaches not only indicate the shifting ways certain genres of media production inhabit and make place; they also appear to be encouraging localities at various scales to pursue such media productions and anticipate their practicalities, as part of post-industrial economic development, business and branding strategies.

Media production practices also make place through the inhabitation of settings beyond those in which a particular form is directly enacted. In the more dispersed digital media industries, for example, writers such as Ross (2003) and Neff (2005) note the importance of parties, drinking and socializing – embodied forms of place making that, we suggest, can be vital to the recursive formation of a particular media-worker habitus. As Neff (2005: 150) argues, in New York's Silicon Alley, parties 'make industries from otherwise disparate actors … [who hear] the 'noise' of the industry at these events'. In a similar vein, Turner (2009) suggests the week-long Burning Man festival in Nevada's Black Rock Desert constitutes an important 'infrastructural' support for (what we would term) the habitus of Silicon Valley entrepreneurs. Through this exceptional, geographically isolated occasion, participants are invited temporarily to act out 'a utopian world driven by the pursuit of self-realization, project engineering and communication' (p. 91). These examples remind us that media production practices make place not just via the direct production of their forms, but also through reflexive awareness of their more scattered and dispersed manifestations (cf. Barnett, 2007). To expand on this reflexivity, we now turn from the places of media production towards its spaces.

Media Production in Space

Central to John Caldwell's seminal *Production Culture* (Caldwell, 2008) – a book based on a decade of field research on LA-based film and video workers – is the contention that, if we want to understand how media production workers come to understand their own worlds of work, we should attend to their 'industrial reflexivity', or the workplace stories and narratives they tell each other and the broader world. While Caldwell was also interested in production's physical locations, his main concern was how such places involve inhabiting the broader 'space' of a production culture. Such reflexive spaces can be found in workplace narratives, but they are not mere subjective constructions: they are the traced realities of a shared world of media production practice, held in common, yet geographically dispersed and stretched across time. Caldwell's analysis of industrial reflexivity in media production cultures reminds us of the importance of attending to what Schatzki (2002: 242–243) calls integrative practices. While all manner of dispersed, embodied actions – for example, walking, listening or driving – are specific situated practices, understanding an organized field of media production means attending to how such dispersed actions are integrated and made intelligible by more abstract, normative and commonly shared ends, orientations and emotions. Such shared practical worlds make it possible for different types of media to become what Wenger (1998) termed 'communities of practice', often exceeding localized or physicalized spatialities.

With the notion of habitus, we conceptualized media production as relatively durable embodied practices, radically contextualized in place. Caldwell's (2008) account reminds us however that media production cultures not only inhabit and make place, but also endure and cohere across space. Here we can turn to another of the main concepts in Bourdieu's (1990) theory of practice: that of 'fields', a concept that like habitus, has been important to media studies. For Bourdieu, fields are not just shared spaces of self-reflexive orientation; they are the conditions of possibility for embodied, improvised practices (i.e. habitus). The field position of any given actor, for Bourdieu, is constituted by his accumulation of various forms of capital – social, cultural, economic – and the value these are accorded in a given field. So the stakes related to a field of media production are played like a game, though it is important to emphasize that having a tacit feel for such field games emerges through embodied practice, or habitus. The concept of field draws attention in particular to what Bourdieu (1984) calls classificatory practices. In relation to media production, the analysis of such practices has perhaps been best developed in journalism studies (e.g. Benson and Neveu, 2005; Markham, 2011). Through a wide range of embodied dispositions – for example, intuition, seriousness, humour or misanthropy – journalists distinguish themselves from those in other fields, including other fields of media production. At the same time, they tacitly mark out their positions against others within the journalistic field; classifying others and in the process classifying themselves (cf. Bourdieu, 1984: 466).

As might already be evident, fields are not physical but *social* spaces, which might at first seem problematic for our interest in spatiality. In empirical work, fields are often plotted into the same 'two-dimensional conceptual arrangement of people, objects, tastes and dispositions' (Cresswell, 2002: 380) seen as X–Y axes throughout *Distinction*, probably Bourdieu's best-known book (Bourdieu, 1984). For some, the apparently anaemic geographies of the field concept underscore a broader problem: Bourdieu's reductive view of spatiality. Entrikin (2001: 695), for example, suggests that the concept of habitus seems to eliminate place, rendering it into a mere 'material cipher of the social', the embodiment of field spaces. These limitations are often connected to a latent structuralism. For Born (2010), Bourdieu's coupling of habitus and field presents a model of cultural production overly focused on durable structure and structuring and unable to account for transformation. Despite Bourdieu's avowed intention of surpassing the subject-object or practice-structure divides, many argue he simply repeats those dualisms (e.g. Berard, 2005).

Yet there remain clear merits to field thinking, particularly if the concept is extricated from an inflexible bond with Bourdieu's full-blown 'field theory' and deployed, as Postill (2015) suggests, in a slightly more open-ended way. The notion of field provides a way of thinking about space as experienced through practical action, not only materially but also figuratively and symbolically (Malpas, 2012: 232). Hage (2011) evocatively describes fields as embodying a 'social physics'. They are akin to force fields, exerting a kind of social gravity that acts on agents and is experienced and earnestly acted upon as the 'objective' world that an agent inhabits. This acknowledges geographical space but simultaneously speaks about temporal space. As Butler (1999) suggests, fields appear through a set of presuppositions and predispositions reproduced over time through 'performative interpellations'. Media production practices, in other words, not only inhabit and make place, but also are positioned in and orient towards a symbolic and material space of possibility.

In certain respects, Caldwell's (2008) notion of 'industrial reflexivity' already captures some of the specifically *social* dimensions of media production fields, sensitizing us to think about how production workers develop understandings of their own field and their position in it. Less well understood are how media production practices involve positioning in and orientation towards increasingly complex material, and specifically *technical*, spaces. As Sterne (2003) suggests, technologies are crystallizations of particular forms of organized practice; they are not so much things, but as Heidegger (1977) argues, an 'enframing' of action. Sterne's argument in this context is that scholars should accordingly resist the conceptualization of technology types prior to studying their practical enactment. We would agree but add that it is nevertheless important to account for the proliferation of technical agency around a wide range of media production activities. Contemporary media production practices – certainly in advanced capitalist economies, but to varying degrees globally – involve inhabiting a computational world. That is, encountering field spaces of technical devices, applications, tools, platforms, standards and infrastructures. These are spaces filled with automation, the 'secondary agency' of software and computational systems (Mackenzie, 2006; Kitchin and Dodge, 2011) – agency that is only partly perceived or authorized via media production practices situated in place (Rodgers, 2015). Yet at the same time, such digital and networked spaces are the subject of growing reflexive awareness, knowledge and political problematization, for media producers and users alike (see Couldry, Fotopoulou, and Dickens, 2016; Beer, 2017).

These emergent computational field spaces of media production practices both add new layers of 'productive' agency, and erode some of the autonomy that previously existed between different fields. For example, we might think about the growing importance of software applications for virtually all media work. As Manovich (2013) argues, even though computers are not new technologies, what is relatively new is the widespread use of software applications for authoring or consuming creative content. Through software, computers have become 'remediation machines' simulating once-noncomputational media practices such as typewriting, editing or image manipulation. A media practice such as postproduction, for example, was once highly specialized and largely internalized within the field of film or television. Now, however, postproduction makes use of the same software applications used in many other creative fields, such as video game development or interior design. These applications, moreover, share properties, functionalities and tools with many unrelated software applications, such as cut and paste, file storage or view control (see Manovich, 2013). The use of standardized software applications, in other words, invites new forms of translocal convergence amongst different fields of media production.

Another instance of such emergent and convergent computational field spaces are what van Dijck (2013) describes as 'connective media'. Google, Facebook, Apple and Amazon are not merely big commercial media companies, van Dijck argues, but inter-operable platform spaces increasingly taking on the shape of 'walled gardens'. They are very difficult, if not impossible, for media producers to work around, whether amateur or professional. If the occupants of media production fields can be labelled cultural intermediaries (cf. Bourdieu, 1984), their work has been fundamentally complicated by the arrival of cultural *infomediaries* (Morris, 2015), which automatically gather and interpret data of user preferences and behaviour. Performing professionalized media production practices, then, increasingly involves working within and orienting towards technical field spaces that demand and impose new regimes governing the visibility or appearance of their media forms, content, brands and organizations.

Conclusion

We have proposed space, place and circulation as different ways of seeing the 'where' of media production. These lenses are intended not as absolute geographical categories, but rather as relational ontologies and epistemologies for exploring, investigating and critiquing the spatialities of media production practices. Media production, we suggest, should be seen as cultures of *circulation.* We must avoid an implicit image of production as originary sites for the unidirectional transmission of media content or forms. Such situated cultures of circulation can thus be understood as durable forms of practical habitus, which inherently entail particular forms of *place,* or place making. At the same time, such localized activities in place also belong to, and endure as, more dispersed field *spaces* of media production, spaces that include social rules, resources and narratives, but also technical ecologies of applications, tools, platforms, standards and infrastructures.

We are at a moment when what counts as media production is elusive. Where media products begin or end is increasingly ambiguous, as are distinctions between producers and consumers. In the face of this, we have insisted to some extent on enduring attention towards relatively conventional or ordinary understandings of media production. This is because, as our relatively extensive use of Pierre Bourdieu's theory of practice underscores, we have devoted particular attention to a critique of media production as a form of power. Yet our use of Bourdieu has been qualified. In particular, we have sought to counter his deterministic tendencies, emphasizing instead the emergence, transformation, contingency and uncertainty of all media practices, including those seen as production-related. We have suggested that we 'find' the power of media production practices within circulatory trajectories that are multidirectional, concentrated and dispersed – rather than assuming they reside at the beginning of a unidirectional process. While production practices can powerfully define localities, their place making is always bound up with, for example, the institutions, cultures and material textures that compose a specific milieu. While production practices do crystallize relatively powerful media fields, this is best understood by closely examining situated enactments of orientation and positioning as they relate to a wide range of interwoven social and technical field spaces.

Our analysis in these respects has not just hinged on contemporary developments. The fixity typically accorded to familiar production places (e.g. newsrooms, studios, film sets, editing suites, etc.) has perhaps always been a kind of illusion. On a conceptual level, the apparent amorphousness of production may not be so new, or quite the break often suggested. Thinking of media as a recursive practical accomplishment (Ross, 2014) invites us to attend to production as always-already involved in the performance of media forms, the making and remaking of particular places and localities and the constituting and reconstituting of industrial and technical field spaces. We hope the practice-centred lenses outlined here provide news ways of approaching the increasingly layered, fissive and dispersed spatialities of contemporary media production. We hope too that it offers the potential to revisit media production histories, with new ways into their circulatory processes, places and spaces.

References

Appadurai, A. (1995). The production of locality. In R. Fardon (Ed.), *Counterworks: Managing the Diversity of Knowledge* (pp. 208–229). London: Routledge.

Ardèvol, E., Roig, A., San Cornelio, G., Pagès, R., & Alsina, P. (2010). Playful practices: theorising 'new media' cultural production. In B. Bräuchler & J. Postill (Eds.), *Theorising Media and Practice* (pp. 259–279). New York: Berghahn Books.

Augé, M. (1995). *Non-places: Introduction to an Anthropology of Supermodernity*. London: Verso.

Banks, M., Conor, B., Mayer, V. (Eds.). (2015). *Production Studies, the Sequel! Cultural Studies of Global Media Industries*. New York: Routledge.

Barnett, C. (2007). Convening publics: the parasitical spaces of public action. In K. R. Cox, M. Low, & J. Robinson (Eds.), *The Handbook of Political Geography* (pp. 403–417). London: Routledge.

Beer, D. (2017). The social power of algorithms. *Information, Communication and Society*, 20(1): 1–13.

Benson, R., & Neveu, E. (Eds.). (2005). *Bourdieu and the Journalistic Field*. Cambridge: Polity Press.

Berard, T. J. (2005). Rethinking practices and structures. *Philosophy of the Social Sciences*, 35(2): 196–230.

Bødker, H. (2016). Stuart Hall's encoding/decoding model and the circulation of journalism in the digital landscape. *Critical Studies in Media Communication*, 33(5): 409–423.

Born, G. (2010). The social and the aesthetic: For a post-Bourdieuian theory of cultural production. *Cultural Sociology*, 4(2): 171–208.

Bourdieu, P. (1984). *Distinction: A Social Critique of the Judgment of Taste*. London: Routledge.

Bourdieu, P. (1990). *The Logic of Practice*. Stanford, CA: Stanford University Press.

Bräuchler, B., & Postill, J. (Eds.). (2010). *Theorising Media and Practice*. Oxford: Berghahn Books.

Bruns, A. (2008). *Blogs, Wikipedia, Second life, and Beyond: From Production to Produsage*. New York: Peter Lang.

Butler, J. (1999). Performativity's social magic. In R. Schusterman (Ed.) *Bourdieu: A Critical Reader* (pp. 113–128). Oxford: Wiley-Blackwell.

Caldwell, J. T. (2008). *Production Culture: Industrial Reflexivity and Critical Practice in Film and Television*. Durham, NC: Duke University Press.

Casey, E. S. (2001). Between geography and philosophy: What does it mean to be in the place-world? *Annals of the Association of American Geographers*, 91(4): 683–693.

Couldry, N. (2000). *The Place of Media Power: Pilgrims and Witnesses of the Media Age*. New York: Routledge.

Couldry, N. (2004). Theorising media as practice. *Social Semiotics*, 14(2): 115–132.

Couldry, N. (2009). Does 'the media' have a future? *European Journal of Communication*, 24(4): 437–449.

Couldry, N. (2015). The myth of 'us': Digital networks, political change and the production of collectivity. *Information, Communication and Society*, 18(6): 608–626.

Couldry, N., Fotopoulou, A., & Dickens, L. (2016). Real social analytics: A contribution towards a phenomenology of a digital world. *British Journal of Sociology*, 67(1): 118–137.

Cresswell, T. (2002). Bourdieu's geographies: In memoriam. *Environment and Planning D: Society and Space*, 20(4): 379–382.

Deleuze, G. (1995). *Negotiations, 1972–1990*. New York: Columbia University Press.

Entrikin, J. N. (2001). Hiding places. *Annals of the Association of American Geographers*, 91(4): 694–697.

Gitelman, L. (2006). *Always Already New: Media, History, and the Data of Culture*. Cambridge, MA: MIT Press.

Greenhalgh, C. (2010). Cinematography and camera crew: Practice, process and procedure. In B. Bräuchler & J. Postill (Eds.), *Theorising Media and Practice* (pp. 303–324). Oxford: Berghahn Books.

Hage, G. (2011). Social gravity: Pierre Bourdieu's phenomenological social physics. In G. Hage & E. Kowal (Eds.), *Force, Movement, Intensity: The Newtonian Imagination in the Social Sciences* (pp. 80–92). Melbourne: Melbourne University Press.

Hall, S. (1980). Encoding/decoding. In S. Hall, D. Hobson, A. Lowe, & P. Willis (Eds.), *Culture, Media, Language: Working Papers in Cultural Studies, 1972–1979* (pp. 128–138). London: Hutchinson.

Harvey, D. (1989). *The Condition of Postmodernity: An Enquiry into the Conditions of Cultural Change*. Oxford: Wiley-Blackwell.

Heidegger, M. (1977). *The Question Concerning Technology and Other Essays*. New York: Harper.

Hesmondhalgh, D. (2006). Bourdieu, the media and cultural production. *Media, Culture and Society*, 28(2): 211–231.

Hess, K., & Waller, L. (2015). Hip to be hyper: The subculture of excessively local news. *Digital Journalism*, 4(2): 1–18.

Jansson, A. (2013). A second birth? Cosmopolitan media ethnography and Bourdieu's reflexive sociology. *International Journal of Cultural Studies*, 16(2): 135–150.

Jenkins, H. (2006). *Convergence Culture: Where Old and New Media Collide*. New York: New York University Press.

Kitchin, R., & Dodge, M. (2011). *Code/Space: Software and Everyday Life*. Cambridge, MA: MIT Press.

Landman, J. (2009). Not in Kansas anymore: Transnational collaboration in television science fiction. In V. Mayer, M. J. Banks, & J. T. Caldwell (Eds.), *Production Studies: Cultural Studies of Media Industries* (pp. 140–153). New York: Routledge.
Lash, S., & Lury, C. (2007). *Global Culture Industry: The Mediation of Things*. Cambridge: Polity Press.
Lee, B., & LiPuma, E. (2002). Cultures of circulation: The imaginations of modernity. *Public culture*, 14(1): 191–213.
Malpas, J. (2012). Putting space in place: Philosophical topography and relational geography. *Environment and Planning D: Society and Space*, 30(2): 226–242.
Mackenzie, A. (2006). *Cutting Code: Software and Sociality*. New York: Peter Lang.
Manovich, L. (2013). *Software Takes Command*. New York: Bloomsbury.
Markham, T. (2011). *The Politics of War Reporting: Authority, Authenticity and Morality*. Manchester: Manchester University Press.
Massey, D. (1994). *Space, Place and Gender*. Minneapolis: University of Minnesota Press.
Mayer, V., Banks, M. J., & Caldwell, J. T. (Eds.). (2009). *Production Studies: Cultural Studies of Media Industries*. New York: Routledge.
Moores, S. (1993). *Interpreting Audiences: The Ethnography of Media Consumption*. London: Sage.
Moores, S. (2012). *Media, Place and Mobility*. Basingstoke: Palgrave Macmillan.
Morgan Parmett, H. (2014). Media as a spatial practice: Treme and the production of the media neighbourhood. *Continuum*, 28(3): 286–299.
Morgan Parmett, H. (2016). It's HBO: Passionate engagement, TV branding, and tourism in the postbroadcast era. *Communication and Critical/Cultural Studies*, 13(1): 3–22.
Morley, D. (1980). *The Nationwide Audience: Structure and Decoding*. London: British Film Institute.
Morley, D. (2009). For a materialist, non-media-centric media studies. *Television & New Media*, 10(1): 114–116.
Morris, J. W. (2015). Curation by code: Infomediaries and the data mining of taste. *European Journal of Cultural Studies*, 18(4–5): 446–463.
Neff, G. (2005). The changing place of cultural production: The location of social networks in a digital media industry. *Annals of the American Academy of Political and Social Science*, 597(1): 134–152.
Postill, J. (2015). Fields: Dynamic configurations of practices, games and socialities. In V. Amit (Ed.), *Thinking through Sociality: An Anthropological Interrogation of Key Concepts* (pp. 47–68). New York: Berghahn Books.
Pratt, A. C. (2004). The cultural economy: A call for spatialized 'production of culture' perspectives. *International Journal of Cultural Studies*, 7(1): 117–128.
Relph, E. (1976). *Place and Placelessness*. London: Pion.
Rodgers, S. (2014). The architectures of media power: Editing, the newsroom, and urban public space. *Space and Culture*, 17(1): 69–84.
Rodgers, S. (2015). Foreign objects? Web content management systems, journalistic cultures and the ontology of software. *Journalism: Theory, Practice and Criticism*, 16(1): 10–26.

Rose, N. (1996). Identity, genealogy, history. In S. Hall & P. Du Gay (Eds.), *Questions of Cultural Identity* (pp. 128–149). London: Sage.

Ross, A. (2003). *No-collar: The Humane Workplace and Its Hidden Costs.* New York: Basic Books.

Ross, P. (2014). Were producers and audiences ever separate? Conceptualizing media production as social situation. *Television & New Media*, 15(2): 157–174.

Rouse, J. (2006). Practice theory. In S. Turner & M. Risjord (Eds.) *Handbook of the Philosophy of Science: Volume 15* (pp. 499–540). Amsterdam: Elsevier.

Schatzki, T. R. (2002). *The Site of the Social: A Philosophical Account of the Constitution of Social Life and Change.* University Park: Penn State University Press.

Schatzki, T. R., Knorr Cetina, K., & Von Savingny, E. (Eds.). (2001). *The Practice Turn in Contemporary Theory.* London: Routledge.

Sterne, J. (2003). Bourdieu, technique and technology. *Cultural Studies*, 17(3/4): 367–389.

Straw, W. (2009). The circulatory turn. In B. Crow, M. Longford, & K. Sawchuk (Eds.), *The Wireless Spectrum: The Politics, Practices and Poetics of Mobile Media* (pp. 17–28). Toronto: University of Toronto Press.

Straw, W. (2010). Cultural production and the generative matrix: A response to Georgina Born. *Cultural Sociology*, 4(2): 209–216.

Thompson, J. B. (1995). *The Media and Modernity: A Social Theory of the Media.* Cambridge: Polity Press.

Tuan, Y.-F. (1977). *Space and Place: The Perspective of Experience,* Minneapolis: University of Minnesota Press.

Turner, F. (2009). Burning man at Google: A cultural infrastructure for new media production. *New Media & Society*, 11(1–2): 73–94.

van Dijck, J. (2013). *The Culture of Connectivity: A Critical History of Social Media.* Oxford: Oxford University Press.

Warner, M. (2002). *Publics and Counterpublics.* New York: Zone Books.

Wenger, E. (1998). *Communities of Practice: Learning, Meaning, and Identity.* Cambridge: Cambridge University Press.

5 Media, Materiality, Mobility
Understanding Geomedia as Infrastructure Spaces

Mimi Sheller

Introduction

The material turn in both media studies and mobilities research has begun to highlight geoecological and spatial questions surrounding media infrastructures. Both of these fields feed into an emerging 'geomedia' approach that engages not just horizontal spatiality but also vertical geographies: from the deep sea, through ocean and land surfaces and up to the aerial spaces of aviation, low earth-orbiting satellites and geostationary orbits (Parks and Starosielski, 2015; Graham, 2016; Paglen, 2016). The idea of the field of geomedia studies is, first, that media are always grounded in material or physical arrangements of matter in particular contexts, such that 'world wide' systems including the Internet or mobile telephony take very different forms in specific locations. Second, there is a planetary scale at which such infrastructures work; it consists of the geoecologies of media systems that span an entire vertical geography of planetary urbanization, from deep-sea cables to outer space and from micro relations to macro. Third, there is a geopolitical dimension to the production and uneven consumption of such infrastructural spaces and their dispositions; it includes the extraction of minerals and metals and the production, consumption and circulation of energy and waste.

The emerging field of geomedia studies concerns all three of these aspects of geography, geoecology and geopolitics of media. It seeks to 'establish a bridge between geographical research and media and communication studies' by addressing 'the complex interplay between various technologies and forms of media, the geographical conditions of media use (in the broadest sense, involving all scales from the household to the planet and beyond), and the observed and inferred consequences of media use'.[1] Critical studies of media infrastructure, for example, highlight in particular how 'global' media take multiple and hybrid forms including 'the different ways they are imagined and engaged with by publics around the world, their local effects, and what human beings experience when a network fails' (Larkin, 2013; Parks and Starosielski, 2015). Insofar as networked infrastructures of mobility and communication are imagined, extended, contested and appropriated, this chapter will consider how the new mobilities paradigm can contribute to geomedia studies.

Critical mobilities research brings out the materialities of media embedded in everyday physical constellations of mobility and communication (for example, the assemblage of phones, vehicles, roads, satellites, cables, cell towers, power grids, container ships, etc.) and the narratives or logics that hold such cultural-material assemblages together. These materialist approaches to media and mobilities link systems of communication back to the geo-ecologies and global political economies that shape sea, earth and sky space including the deeper time of media archaeologies based on oil, carbon, ocean currents, and the mining of metals. Geomedia therefore refers in its first sense to a critical cultural materialist approach to these infrastructural spaces of mediated mobilities. Drawing on theories of 'infrastructuring' as an active practice (Star, 1999; Star and Bowker, 2002), materialist approaches to media (Packer and Wiley, 2012; Parks and Starosielski, 2015), critical logistics studies (Cowen, 2014; Easterling, 2015) and critical mobilities theory (Hannam, Sheller, and Urry, 2006; Sheller and Urry, 2006a, 2006b; Adey, Bissell, Hannam, Merriman, and Sheller, 2014), I want to argue for an approach to geomedia that: (a) excavates the underlying materiality of media affordances and infrastructural dispositions; (b) brings into focus the horizontal and vertical geographies of mediated mobilities that span planetary scales and dynamic localizations of media and (c) brings to the political foreground various kinds of uneven topologies, turbulence, disruptions, differential speeds and frictions that at the same time offer handles for resistance, channels for alternative mobilities and media and frequencies for potential interruption or redeployment.

As John Urry and I argued in our introduction to *Mobile Technologies of the City* (2006c) over a decade ago, the mobility systems that constitute urbanism 'include ticketing and licensing [of drivers], oil and petroleum supply, electricity and water supply, addresses and postal systems, road safety and public safety protocols, station interchanges, web sites, money transfer, luggage storage, air traffic control, barcodes, bridges, time-tables, CCTV surveillance and so on' (Sheller and Urry, 2006c: 5–6). Some of these systems engage physical infrastructure, while others concern informational systems; some involve moving things like bodies, vehicles, oil or water, while others involve moving things like data, code and images. We argued that these physical and informational mobility systems are tightly coupled into complex new configurations, such that mobility systems are more complicated, interdependent and dependent on computers and software; media and communication are deeply embedded into specific physical and material contexts.

We understood those contexts as spanning local and global scales, and fitting into the conceptualization that has since emerged of a 'planetary urbanization' that connects global cities to distant networked sites of resource extraction and waste disposal (Brenner and Schmid, 2015) but also to sites of leisure, tourism and 'places to play' that put space into play in various ways (Sheller and Urry, 2004). This sense of planetary infrastructure as a matrix for mediatized processes has been enriched especially by anthropologists working on ethnographies of media in diverse places, such as Nigeria (Larkin, 2008), the Caribbean (Horst, 2013), Mongolia or Zambia (Parks, 2015a, 2015b). This horizontal diversity of media infrastructure spaces and cultural practices is also complemented by emerging work on vertical geographies of media. As Trevor Paglen puts it,

> human infrastructures and activities also inhabit a vertical axis, from deep sea mining and undersea cables to outer, and even arguably interstellar, space. As others have observed, different topologies of development, politics, urbanism, and the production of space emerge when we begin to consider the vertical dimensions of human world-making.
> (cf. Weizman, 2007; Graham and Hewitt, 2012; Graham, 2016; Paglen, 2016: n.p.)

This suggests the importance of understanding media as embedded in deep geoecologies that are assembled with components that are underground, under the sea, in the air and in space, as well as on land, inside buildings and even inside our bodies.

From these various contributions to the study of media, materiality and mobilities, we are arriving at a thicker description of geomedia, with rich local and geographical detail. In the following sections I will first extend these ideas by seeding them with recent approaches to 'infrastructure space' (Cowen, 2014; Easterling, 2015) as a good way to examine the co-dependent entanglement of materializations of media, mobilities and energy and their interplay with geography, geoecologies and geopolitics. Then I will turn to the question of mobility justice and explore how it might inform contemporary geographies of media infrastructures with greater attention to the politics of uneven mobilities (Cresswell, 2006, 2010; Adey, 2009) and the uneven materialities of media infrastructure spaces and practices. I especially consider how a materialist approach to geomedia as mobile infrastructure space can contribute to new critical understandings of unevenly mediated spatial relations, especially those that come to the foreground after breakdowns, disruptions and natural disasters.

Materializing Media, Mobilities and Energy

We can think of any historical period as involving specific assemblages of human mobility and transport of goods (logistics), media infrastructures (such as telegraph, radio or satellite communication) and energy circulation to support these routings (i.e. the current infrastructure for liquid hydrocarbons and electric generation) (Deleuze and Guattari, 1988). Access to energy and the minerals and metals that make up transportation and communication systems are a crucial dimension of uneven mobilities and unequal media materialities. The potentials for mobility and communication are grounded in the source of energy for transportation and telecommunication, its destination and means of transport and who uses most of it. Kinetic elites are increasingly monopolizing control over energy, water and mineral rights, using their offshore financial power (Urry, 2014) to control global resources that are becoming increasingly scarce. Uneven mobilities are therefore geoecological at their root, as well as geopolitical. They are also geomediated. They are made up of flows of information, data and imagery (Parks, 2012) and they rely on mediations of power, connectivity and control for their legitimation. As Larkin (2013) observes, infrastructures serve not only a technical function (moving water, electricity or data), but also have a poetics that operates via fantasy, desire and speculative investments in the future plans of states or corporations.

Energy is consumed by vehicles, buildings and communication networks, but we can also think of these material objects and infrastructures as temporary embodiments of energy: energy turned into processed metals and combined with other materials (such as cement or glass) used in the construction of particular kinds of energy/object assemblages (e.g., coal-fired steam trains and iron railways, oil-based internal combustion engines and roadways, aluminium MacBook Airs and satellite, Wi-Fi and 4G cell systems). There is a raw material basis to energy, transport and communication infrastructures, which shapes and is shaped by geographies of social relations, lived practices and meanings. Control over energy involves transferring it into particular objects and moving it through various distribution networks. This infrastructure then supports particular materializations of energy and information that become routinized in the ways people use and access matter in all its forms, such that material cultures embed energy and information in forms that become taken for granted or invisible (Sheller, 2014b).

We can refer to such assemblages of matter, energy, practices and meanings as an *energy culture* that is embedded in ongoing processes of mobilizing, energizing, making and doing. The origins of our contemporary energy culture lie in the late nineteenth century. The combination of electricity and electrochemical production of metals, called the second industrialization, brought lighter transport systems, new capabilities for aerial mobility and ultimately space travel and satellite communication systems – a shift from heavy to light modernity. As I argue in *Aluminum Dreams: The Making of Light Modernity* (Sheller, 2014a), control over such mobility resources also ensures military supremacy, because bombers, armoured vehicles, weapons, missiles, unmanned aerial vehicles and satellite guidance systems all rely on primary metals like aluminium and nickel, while communication systems need silicon and rare earth metals like cobalt and tungsten. Materials and metals are assembled into weapons, satellite guidance systems and vehicles, which in turn need the global flow of oil and gas through pipelines and tankers and logistics hubs to fuel them.

Caren Kaplan moreover points out that historically the drive for 'air power' afforded huge military advantages to those who controlled the 'cosmic view' from aerial vision technologies, so that military air power is closely tied to modes of visualization and surveillance (Kaplan, 2006). These geomediated mobilities shaped the military logics and dispositions of contemporary infrastructure spaces and therefore contributed to producing the unsustainability of energy usage and ecosystem destruction associated with contemporary forms of life. However, few advocates of 'sustainable' technological transitions fully explore how energy cultures are embedded in emerging technologies and systems that are crucial to military strategy or how everyday artefacts, infrastructures and the routines they support arise out of industries that are closely allied with military research and development, from satellites and the Internet to drones and decentralized energy storage systems. This kind of geomedia is grounded in military control over land, sea and air and ultimately over all infrastructure spaces that distribute circulation across such geoecological spatiotemporal affordances. Yet in most cases this geoecological and geopolitical underpinning of infrastructure space remains in the background, except perhaps during war, when what Paul Virilio calls 'dromoscopy' becomes a crucial mediation of speed (Virilio, 1986, 2005).

This is a point emphasized by science and technology studies of 'infrastructuring' as an active process, with electricity being the foundational example (Hughes, 1983, 1989; Guy and Shove, 2000). 'It is the sheer familiarity of energy use, and its deep embeddedness in taken for granted patterns of everyday life' that make it so hard for us to "see" the energy embodied in objects' (Guy and Shove, 2000: 5) – and I would add in communication infrastructures and media. Studies of large-scale sociotechnical transitions suggest that such social orderings do change over time, however slowly, and will change in the future (Dudley, Geels, and Kemp, 2011). Transition theory has been criticized for not paying enough attention to power relations and to the cultural processes in which technology is situated. We could also add that there is a need to integrate media studies into our understanding of such materialities. This attention to infrastructuring as an active yet hidden material-cultural process has been extended in recent work on the infrastructures that enable both physical and informational mobilities, including the laying of undersea cables and pipelines (McCormack,

2014; Starosielski, 2015), the energy consumed by servers and data centres (Farman, 2010; Holt and Vonderau, 2015), the material geography of satellite transmission and cables connecting the Internet (Parks, 2012; Parks and Starosielski, 2015) and more broadly the forms of what Easterling (2015) calls 'infrastructure space'.

Easterling describes the 'political character of infrastructure space' based on 'accidental, covert, or stubborn forms of power' that hide in its folds (2015: 73). Infrastructure space is not mere background but takes active forms, she argues, through the organization of components into dynamic mechanisms including multipliers, switches/remotes, wiring/topology and interplay/governor. The car, for example, is a multiplier that determines the shape of the road, highway, suburb, housing forms and exurban development. The elevator is a multiplier that shapes the vertical densities of cities. The cell phone is also a multiplier that can expand dimensionally without a point-to-point centralized network. A highway interchange, a dam and a landing point for an undersea cable are all examples of 'switches' that control flows (Easterling, 2015: 74–75). An interplay of many different active forms of multipliers and switches forms a complex topology of infrastructure space. This gives us a way to think of geomedia as taking specific active forms, with particular 'dispositions', which Easterling describes as 'the character of an organization that results from the circulation of these active forms within it' (2015: 73). What then is the disposition of contemporary global systems of geomedia?

It became increasingly clear in the period identified with 'globalization' that mobility regimes assembled around particular infrastructures require constant high amounts of energy to be consumed in producing round-the-clock transport of people, just-in-time delivery of goods and energized communications and logistics networks. As this global energy infrastructure expanded in the 1980s, the problems of speed and its spatial effects became increasingly central to theories of capitalism in the 1990s. David Harvey's analysis of 'time-space compression' and just-in-time logistics (Harvey, 2006), which drew on Marx's vision of the 'annihilation of space by time', and concepts such as 'fast capitalism' (Agger, 1989) and 'liquid modernity' (Bauman, 2000), diagnosed the social problems associated with the speeding up and lightness of late modernity in various ways. Speed and acceleration were central to Paul Virilio's theory of dromologic society (Virilio, 1986). These theorists linked acceleration in technologies of physical and informational mobility not only to shifting forms of capitalist modernity, but also to wider cultural shifts in everyday life and subjectivity (see also Lash and Urry, 1994). Thus there was a particular disposition to the new infrastructure spaces of liquid modernity, to paraphrase Easterling and Larkin, that poetically valorised narratives of speed, acceleration, liquidity and openness even as they politically entrenched infrastructural multipliers, switches and topologies that supported highly uneven access to mobilized and mediatized geographies.

Many people today live 'mobile lives' dependent on such stretched but striated spatiotemporalities (Elliott and Urry, 2010). Mobility depends on what Elliott and Urry call 'network capital' and the possession of capacities and potentials for movement (understood as 'motility' [Kaufmann and Montulet, 2008] – the capacity to appropriate mobility potentials). They describe network capital as a combination of capacities to be mobile, including appropriate documents, money and qualifications; access to networks at a distance; physical capacities for movement; location-free information and contact points; access to communication devices and secure meeting places; access to vehicles and infrastructures and time and other resources for coordination (Elliott and Urry, 2010: 10–11). There is an uneven distribution of these capacities for potential movement in relation to the surrounding physical, social and political affordances for movement. Thus, while there were grand narratives of acceleration, liquidity, mobility and opening associated with these late twentieth-century transformations, we could argue that at an infrastructural level there were quite different dispositions of unequal access, software sorting and remote control built into the new materialities of circulation and spatializations of mobile mediality (Wood and Graham, 2006).

Logistics, or ('the management of the movement of *stuff*'), is one core system of mobility that concerns the infrastructure of global movement of goods, minerals, metals and fuels and the imaginaries and symbolic meanings that drive such organizations of space and time. Deborah Cowen's recent work on logistics rationalities shows that logistics have undergone profound changes since World War II, becoming a driving force of military strategy and tactics, as well as in corporate practices for the global organization of trade (Cowen, 2014). With the rise of the shipping container, the computer and satellite communications to manage logistics, new forms of systems thinking came to the fore, reshaping labour relations, landscapes and forms of security. But we can also think of these highly networked just-in-time logistics systems as new geographies of mediation, dependent on new media of communication and hence as new geomedia. These emergent geomedia are connected to geopolitics because they depend on military power over land, sea and air and the securing of unregulated 'offshore' spaces for banking, factories, tourism, luxury consumption and waste (Urry, 2014; Easterling, 2015).

If infrastructural approaches to media, critical logistics studies and mobilities research have all contributed to this vision of geomedia as a geopolitical infrastructure space, the last element I want to draw in concerns media archaeologies and their relation to ecologies. As the field of software studies insists, information technologies and so-called virtual media also always have a materiality, which is likewise a 'deep time' that is energy-dependent. Like the theorists of verticality such as Graham or Paglen, Jussi Parikka calls for:

> a more geologically oriented notion of depth of media that is interested in truly deep times – of thousands, millions, billions of years and in depth of the earth; A media excavation into the mineral and raw material basis of technological development, through which to present some media historical arguments as to how one might adopt a material perspective in terms of ecological temporality.[2]

If 'the materiality of information technology starts from the soil, and underground' – in metals such as cobalt and gallium, tantalum and germanium, bauxite and aluminium – we find ourselves in a 'double bind that relates media technologies to ecological issues; on the one hand, acting as raw material for the actual hardware, from cables to cell phones; on the other hand, as an important epistemological framework' (Parikka, 2012).

Historically grounded material perspectives on mediated mobilities and mobile medialities, therefore, involve both ontological and epistemological frameworks. They concern both what exists and how we understand it to work. To develop a critical geomedia approach, in sum, first we need to take account of the wider geopolitical and geoecological context of infrastructure spaces and their dispositions. Second, we need to excavate deeper underground histories of resource extraction, mining and metals production, in order to better understand the transnational material and political basis of contemporary built environments and media geographies. And lastly, we need to recognize the possible counter-geographies of geomedia through which advocates of mobility justice can challenge the kinetic elite, the security state and the military-logistical epistemologies driving resource extraction and climate destruction. Each of these dimensions involves not only a politics of infrastructure space, but also a poetics of representational practices and meanings through which it is advanced and legitimated.

In the following section, I want to turn more specifically to questions of mobility justice, especially as played out within post-disaster situations of disrupted infrastructure spaces and their uneven topologies of geomedia. While 'everyday' situations are just as important, sometimes more extreme events can help reveal some of the usually hidden actions of infrastructural space, including their repair and maintenance in the face of disruption (Graham and Thrift, 2007; Graham, 2009).

Mobility Justice, Uneven Mobilities and Contested Geomedia

The new mobilities paradigm argues that the orchestrated movement of people, goods and information via streets, rails, air space, oceans, fiber-optic cables, cell towers, servers and satellites of the world depend on the infrastructures, 'moorings' and mobility regimes that channel and regulate entry and exit, speed and wait-times, mobilizations and demobilizations. We can think of mobilities in relation to the concept of 'technoscape', derived from Appadurai (1996), which Urry and I described as 'contemporary landscapes...shot through with technological elements which enroll people, space, and the elements connecting people and spaces, into socio-technical assemblages – especially the transportational technologies, such as roads, rail, subways and airports, but also the informational technologies such as signs, schedules, surveillance systems, radio signals, and mobile telephony' (Sheller and Urry, 2006c: 9). People and information, bodies and data, move through these technoscapes, layered with informational augmentation and trailing data shadows, which increasingly include biometric and locational data in a transductive 'code/space' (Wood and Graham, 2006; Dodge and Kitchin, 2011).

Within that understanding, mobilities research is also very concerned with critically addressing normative issues of mobility justice and mobility capabilities (Cook and Butz, 2015, forthcoming; Sheller, forthcoming). Since the publication of 'The New Mobilities Paradigm' (Sheller and Urry, 2006a) 12 years ago, and the launch of the journal *Mobilities* with the editorial introduction on 'Mobilities, Immobilities and Moorings' (Hannam et al., 2006), my own work has focussed on themes of uneven mobility, inequality and power. However, over this decade it has also become clearer that we need both a deeper historicizing of mobilities research in terms of (neo)colonial histories and global geographies and a deeper ecologizing of the material resource bases of mobility and mobile media in extractive industries and energy flows (Sheller, 2014). By bringing together studies of migration, transportation, infrastructure, transnationalism, mobile communications, imaginative travel and tourism and geo-ecologies of resource extraction, new approaches to mobility are especially able to highlight the relation between local and global 'power-geometries' (Massey, 1993), bringing into view the 'cartographies of power' informing all kinds of movement, circulation and dwelling. Thus mobilities research is always imbued with normative questions of unequal access and mobility capabilities that can help us better understand the uneven effects of geomedia topologies and their uneven mobilities.

What do we mean by 'uneven mobilities'? To use the categories that serve to organize the recent *Routledge Handbook of Mobilities Research*, the unevenness of mobility may take the form of uneven *qualities* of experience, uneven access to *infrastructure*, uneven *materialities*, uneven *subjects* of mobility and uneven *events* or temporalities of stopping, going, passing, pausing and waiting (Adey et al., 2014). Uneven mobility, therefore, refers to a terrain for movement in which there are divergent pathways, differential access or partial connectivity; second, it refers to means or modes of movement that have a greater or lesser degree of ease, comfort, flexibility and safety; third, to an experience of movement with more or less friction, noise, speed or turbulence and fourth, to the spatial patterns and control architectures that govern such relations of mobility and immobility, speed and slowness, comfort and discomfort. These uneven terrains bring sociotechnical infrastructures to the social and political foreground, for they depend on not only the design of the built environment but also the social practices in which delay, exclusion, turbulence, blockage and disruption are an everyday experience for those who must dwell in and move through marginalized infrastructure spaces seeking livelihoods, passage and asylum.

If 'motility' can be defined as 'the manner in which an individual or group appropriates the field of possibilities relative to movement and uses them' (Kaufmann and Montulet, 2008: 45), one can begin to conceptualize how kinetic elites appropriate not just land and capital, but also communication networks, all kinds of infrastructure supported by data flows and the associated possibilities or potentials for movement and communication. As populations find themselves vulnerable to a changing climate and threatened with loss of access to water, energy or food, issues of security will increasingly come to the fore – including the potential for political unrest and state securitization brought on by climate change and associated urban disasters and disruptions (Graham, 2009). As mobility becomes rationed or far more highly priced due to the politics surrounding the unsustainability of current mobility systems, the inequalities of network capital will be thrown into sharper relief.

For example, as a site 'imbued with power and control,' Peter Adey suggests, 'the airport is now a surveillance machine – an assemblage where webs of technology and information combine' (2009: 1375). Such surveillance often works via automated systems of algorithmic detection and invisible sorting (Wood and Graham, 2006). These infrastructures are tightly coupled with biopolitical governmentalities of bodies (passports, biometric data, digital photography, backscatter X-rays). In *Aerial Life* (Adey, 2010), Adey shows how these mediations have their roots in colonial power relations, including histories of population management, spatial differentiation and bio-politics, linking together early twentieth-century aerial survey methods (developed in places like Northern Rhodesia, Palestine, British Guiana and Borneo) and airport biometrics as used today, as two instances of an 'aerial gaze.' The use of biometrics in airport security already puts in place ways of coupling human bodies with vast data sets of interconnected information, in which the security apparatus treats humans as vectors of potential threat. If geomedia can be understood as key infrastructure spaces for the assembling (and disassembling) of such control systems of global mobility, then these infrastructures such as airport checkpoints will increasingly be a locus of social and political struggle (Parks, 2007; Sheller, 2010, 2015, forthcoming).

Constellations of global and local mobility and communication exhibit various kinds of uneven topologies, turbulence, disruptions, differential speeds and frictions, which, however, offer handles, channels and frequencies for interruption 'from below' or we might say from beside and within. Only with awareness of the injustices of dominant mobility regimes will people be in a position to challenge them with what Graham (2009) calls 'counter-geographies' that might put technologies of mobility and communication in the service of antimilitary urbanism, or perhaps deurbanization. What can we learn from breakdowns in such infrastructures of mobility and communication, taking post-disaster humanitarian responses as a situation *in extremis*? What kinds of social and material practices allow some to remain highly connected even in the midst of general disconnection – moving through the same physical topographies but connected to different Hertzian topologies? How do uneven media infrastructures jump spaces, scales and subjects? If subaltern publics have already appropriated infrastructural possibilities, how might these be refashioned and built on to strengthen and democratize existing modes of social and political action?

Elsewhere I have argued that natural disasters bring to the fore the astounding interdependence and fragility of the complex mobility systems and infrastructural moorings that make up contemporary transnational geographies (Sheller, 2013). Cities and entire islands suffering catastrophic events are illustrative of how the dynamic intertwining of transportation, communication, provisioning and scheduling systems can rapidly unravel, and along with them civic order, markets and everyday life (as seen earlier in Haiti's extremely destructive 2010 earthquake, but most recently in the disruption and destruction of roads, bridges, homes, communication and entire towns and villages in the southwest of Haiti by Hurricane Matthew in October 2016). In the face of large-scale mobility systems failure, we see laid bare the institutional scaffolding and regulatory regimes that govern the spatialization of particular territories, including all the gaps and uneven distributions of social rights and 'network capital' that leave some groups most vulnerable to harm. Natural disasters demobilize and remobilize. They strike at mobility systems but also engender their own unique mobilities (and immobilities) as people seek to flee the onset of an impending catastrophe, to get resituated in its bewildering aftermath, or to locate their dispersed families, food, water and shelter. Infrastructures of geomedia are one important component of such post-disaster struggles for survival.

At the same time, emergency responders, relief workers and armed peacekeepers and soldiers begin to move into the affected area and take control of infrastructures of mobility such as roads, airports, ports and communication networks. Given the already splintered provision of infrastructure in less developed countries and their cities, collapsing mobility systems are likely to have very different effects on the wealthy and the poor, on urban and rural populations, and on lighter elites and darker masses. This is one of the uneven topologies of infrastructural multipliers and switches that support the mobilities and connectivity of kinetic elites while slowing racialized and class-differentiated subalterns. Those with high network capital are able to appropriate their own potential for mobility whether to flee disaster or to come to the rescue; those with low network capital are usually caught in a vortex of displacement, temporary shelter and containment within the disaster zone. An approach highlighting mobility (in)justice in post-disaster situations focuses our attention on who is able to exercise rights to mobility and who is not capable of mobility within particular situations and infrastructure spaces.

Based on my own research in post-earthquake Haiti (Sheller, 2013, 2015), I have argued that there is an *islanding effect* in which mobility regimes in postdisaster situations bring highly motile foreign responders and assistance to some of the affected population, while holding the 'internally displaced' in place, in an ongoing process of marginalization, serial displacement and containment – as if they were marooned on an island of misery, even while surrounded by the coming and going of well-equipped frequent flyers. Distant images are taken from low-earth orbiting satellites, from the stationary GeoEye and from aerial reconnaissance missions and posted in various formats on the Internet, while those on the ground can barely find out what is happening. Yet the very same logistical efforts that enact postdisaster recovery simultaneously produce disconnections and diminish capabilities for mobility for people affected by the earthquake if they are not included in decision-making processes and supported in access to communication networks. There is a connected mobility for kinetic elites (including journalists, humanitarians and eventually researchers) travelling within the disconnected infrastructural spaces of the disaster-affected region, alongside diminished network capital for those they purport to help. My argument is that these dispositions of infrastructural space helped reinforce this uneven terrain of geomedia, although the multiplier effect of cell phones combined with the innovation of mobile money could have been drawn on to disperse aid more widely across an improvised infrastructure.

A geomedia perspective empowers us not only to ask questions about the relation between the transnational mobilities and media infrastructures of humanitarian action as compared to those of local, situated access, but also to show how the rebuilding of infrastructural spaces often deepens uneven geographies. These critical approaches can be applied to other situations of infrastructure building, and more generally 'development', which often involve external funding of infrastructure spaces such as roads, ports, energy generation, etc. Who is connected?

Who benefits? What are the multipliers and switches that structure the topology of infrastructure spaces? Is there any reason to be optimistic about the possibility for 'hacking' or appropriating infrastructures (Easterling, 2015) that might be bent towards greater social justice? I do not propose to answer these questions here but merely to suggest some of the directions of inquiry opened up by the field of geomedia studies.

Conclusion

In conclusion, I have sought in this article to show how the material turn in both media studies and mobilities research supports a turn towards geomedia studies as a critical approach to infrastructure space and the planetary geographies of media infrastructures. I have suggested how histories of mobilities and media reveal their relation to military power and the dispositions of logistics, which in turn inform the political character of all infrastructure space as well as the poetics of its narratives, representations and legitimations of power. By tracing connections between infrastructures of media, mobility and energy, I have sought to show how cultural-materialist approaches to geomedia open up new kinds of questions and critical perspectives. Finally, I have traced these critical perspectives through the example of postearthquake Haiti, briefly sketching some of the connections and disconnections across infrastructures of media and mobility, such as the 'islanding effect'.

This approach draws on theories of 'infrastructuring' as an active practice, materialist approaches to media, critical logistics studies and critical mobilities theory, and through this transdisciplinarity it also calls for new mixed methodologies that can grasp a wide terrain of action while being immersed in locally grounded relations of power. It is advanced by a combination of ethnographies of media practice and local media infrastructures, geographies of infrastructure and logistics, archaeologies of media and materials used in its production and transdisciplinary mobile sociology, all of which shed new light on spaces, temporalities and mobilities in mediatized worlds.

Finally, I have called for a normative dimension to such work, by paying attention to issues of power, justice and inequality. I believe that a critically engaged geomedia studies can help bridge various kinds of political concerns and social movements, revolving around challenging colonial and neocolonial relations of power, promoting racial, ethnic and gender equality, promoting indigenous rights movements and self-determination and fighting for environmental and climate justice. Until we have a better model for understanding the complex spatial connections between these issues at the level of infrastructure space, we will not be able to grasp the deep roots that connect media and mobilities as materializations of uneven worlds.

Notes

1 From the description of the proposed new journal of *Geomedia Studies*, editors André Jansson and Paul C. Adams.
2 Jussi Parikka, *A Call for an Alternative Deep Time of the Media*, 28 September 2012, http://jussiparikka.net/2012/09/28/a-call-for-an-alternative-deep-time-of-the-media/ (accessed 30 September 2012). And see Parikka (2012).

References

Adey, P. (2009). Facing airport security: Affect, biopolitics and the preemptive securitization of the mobile body. *Environment and Planning D: Soceity and Space*, 27: 274–295.
Adey, P. (2010). *Aerial Life: Spaces, Mobilities, Affects*. Chichester: Wiley-Blackwell.
Adey, P., Bissell, D., Hannam, K., Merriman, P., & Sheller, M. (Eds.). (2014). *The Routledge Handbook of Mobilities*. London: Routledge.
Agger, B. (1989). *Fast Capitalism*. Bloomington: University of Illinois Press.
Appadurai, A. (1996). *Modernity at Large: Cultural Dimensions of Globalization*. Minneapolis: University of Minnesota Press.
Bauman, Z. (2000). *Liquid Modernity*. Cambridge: Polity.
Brenner, N., & Schmid, C. (2015). Towards a new epistemology of the urban? *City*, 19(2–3): 151–182.
Cook, N., & Butz, D. (2015). Mobility justice in the context of disaster. *Mobilities*. Online publication date: 2-Jun-2015.
Cook, N., & Butz, D. (Eds.) (forthcoming) *Mobilities, Mobility Justice and Social Justice*. London and New York: Routledge.
Cresswell, T. (2006). *On the Move: Mobility in the Modern Western World*. London: Routledge.
Cresswell, T. (2010). Towards a politics of mobility, *Environment and Planning D: Society and Space*, 28(1): 17–31.
Cowen, D. (2014). *The Deadly Life of Logistics: Mapping Violence in Global Trade*. Minneapolis: University of Minnesota Press.
Deleuze, G., & Guattari, F. (1988). *A Thousand Plateaus*. Trans. Brian Massumi. Minneapolis, MN: University of Minnesota Press.
Dodge, M., & Kitchin, R. (2011). *Code/Space: Software and Everday Life*. Cambridge: MIT Press.
Dudley, G., Geels, F., & Kemp, R. (Eds.) (2011). *Automobility in Transition? A Socio-Technical Analysis of Sustainable Transport*. London and New York: Routledge.
Easterling, K. (2015). *Extrastatecraft: The Power of Infrastructure Space*. New York: Verso.
Elliott, A., & Urry, J. (2010). *Mobile Lives*. New York and London: Routledge.
Farman, J. (2010). Mapping the digital empire: Google earth and the process of postmodern cartography, *New Media and Society*, 12(6): 869–888.
Graham, S. (Ed.) (2009). *Disrupted Cities: When Infrastructure Fails*. New York and London: Routledge.
Graham, S. (2016). *Vertical: The City from Satellites to Bunkers*. London and New York: Verso.
Graham, S., & Hewitt, L. (2012). Getting off the ground: On the politics of urban verticality, *Progress in Human Geography*, 37(1): 72–92.

Graham, S., & Thrift, N. (2007). Out of order: Understanding repair and maintenance. *Theory, Culture and Society*, 24 (3): 1–25.

Guy, S., & Shove, E. (2000). *A Sociology of Energy, Buildings and the Environment: Constructing Knowledge, Designing Practice*. London: Routledge.

Hannam, K., Sheller, M., & Urry, J. (2006). Mobilities, immobilities, and moorings. *Mobilities*, 1(1): 1–22.

Harvey, D. (2006). *Spaces of global capitalism: Towards a theory of uneven geographical development*. London and New York: Verso.

Holt, J., & Vonderau, P. (2015). 'Where the internet lives': Date centers as cloud infrastructure. In L. Parks & N. Starosielski (Eds.), *Signal Traffic: Critical Studies of Media Infrastructures* (pp. 71–93), Chicago: University of Illinois Press.

Horst, H. (2013). The infrastructures of mobile media: Towards a future research agenda. *Mobile Media and Communication*, 1(1): 147–152.

Hughes, T. P. (1983). *Networks of Power: Electrification in Western Society, 1880–1930*. Baltimore: John Hopkins University Press.

Hughes, T. P. (1989). Evolution of large technological systems, In W. E. Bijker, T. P. Hughes, & T. J. Pinch (Eds.), *The Social Construction of Technological Systems: New Directions in the Sociology and History of Technology* (pp. 51–82). Cambridge, MA; London: The MIT Press.

Kaplan, C. (2006). Mobility and war: The cosmic view' of air power. *Environment and Planning A*, 38: 395–407.

Kaufmann, V., & Montulet, B. (2008). Between social and spatial mobilities: The issue of social fluidity. In W. Canzler, V. Kaufmann, & S. Kesselring (Eds.) *Tracing Mobilities: Towards a Cosmopolitan Perspective* (pp. 37–56). Farnham and Burlington: Ashgate.

Larkin, B. (2008). *Signal and Noise: Media, Infrastructure, and Urban Culture in Nigeria*. Durham: Duke University Press.

Larkin, B. (2013). The politics and poetics of infrastructure. *Annual Review of Anthropology*, 42: 327–343.

Lash, S., & Urry, J. (1994). *Economies of Signs and Space*. London: Sage.

Massey, D. (1993). Power-geometry and a progressive sense of place. In J. Bird, B. Curtis, T. Putnam, G. Robertson, & L. Tickner (Eds.) *Mapping the Futures: Local Cultures, Global Change*. Routledge, London.

McCormack, D. (2014). Pipes and cables. In P. Adey, D. Bissell, K. Hannam, P. Merriman, & M. Sheller (Eds.) *The Routledge Handbook of Mobilities Research* (pp. 225–232). London and New York: Routledge.

Packer, J., & Wiley, S. C. (Eds.) (2012). *Communication Matters: Materialist Approaches to Media, Mobility and Networks*. London and New York: Routeldge.

Paglen, T. (2016). Some sketches on vertical geographies, *E-flux Architecture*, Accessed 10/07/2016 at www.e-flux.com/architecture/superhumanity/68726/some-sketches-on-vertical-geographies/.

Parikka, J. (2012). *What is Media Archaeology?* London: Polity.

Parks, L. (2007). Points of departure: The culture of US airport screening, *Journal of Visual Culture*, 6(2): 183–200.

Parks, L. (2012). *Down to Earth: Satellite Technologies, Industries and Cultures*. New Brunswick, NJ: Rutgers University Press.

Parks, L. (2015a). Walking phone workers. In P. Adey, D. Bissell, K. Hannam, P. Merriman, & M. Sheller (Eds.), *The Routledge Handbook of Mobilities*. New York: Routledge.

Parks, L. (2015b). Water, energy, access: Materializing the internet in rural Zambia. In L. Parks and N. Starosielski (Eds.), *Signal Traffic: Critical Studies of Media Infrastructures*. Chicago: University of Illinois Press.

Parks, L., & Starosielski, N. (Eds.) (2015). *Signal Traffic: Critical Studies of Media Infrastructures*. Chicago: University of Illinois Press.

Sheller, M. (2010). Air mobilities on the US-Caribbean border: Open skies and closed gates. *The Communication Review*, 13(4): 269–288.

Sheller, M. (2013). The Islanding effect: Post-disaster mobility systems and humanitarian logistics in Haiti. *Cultural Geographies*, 20(2): 185–204.

Sheller, M. (2014a). *Aluminum Dreams: The Making of Light Modernity*. Cambridge: MIT Press.

Sheller, M. (2014b). Global energy cultures of speed and lightness: Materials, mobilities and transnational power. *SI Theory, Culture and Society: Energizing Society*, 31(5): 127–154.

Sheller, M. (2015). Connected mobility in a disconnected world: Contested infrastructure in post-disaster contexts, In Mei-Po Kwan (Ed.), Annals *of the Association of American Geographers*, SI on Geographies of Mobility.

Sheller, M. (forthcoming). *Mobility Justice*.

Sheller, M., & Urry, J. (Eds.) (2004). *Tourism Mobilities: Places to Play, Places in Play*. London and New York: Routledge.

Sheller, M., & Urry, J. (2006a). The new mobilities paradigm. *Environment and Planning A*, 38(2): 207–226.

Sheller, M., & Urry, J. (Eds.) (2006b). Mobilities and materialities, special issue of *Environment and Planning A*, 38(2).

Sheller, M., & Urry, J. (Eds.) (2006c). *Mobile Technologies of the City*. Routledge, London and New York).

Star, S. L. (1999). The ethnography of infrastructure. *American Behavioral Scientist*, 43(3): 377–391.

Star, S., & Bowker, G (2002). How to infrastructure. In L. Lievrouw & S. Livingstone (Eds.), *The Handbook of New Media* (pp. 151–162). London: Sage.

Starosielski, N. (2015). Fixed flow: Undersea cables as media infrastructure. In L. Parks & N. Starosielski (Eds.), *Signal Traffic: Critical Studies of Media Infrastructures* (pp. 53–70), Chicago: University of Illinois Press.

Urry, J. (2014). *Offshoring*. London: Polity.

Virilio, P. (1986). *Speed and Politics*. Trans. M. Polizzotti. New York: Semiotext(e). First published as *Vitesse et politique*, 1977.

Virilio, P. (2005). *Negative horizon: An essay on dromoscopy*. Trans. M. Degener. London and New York: Continuum.

Weizman, E. (2007). *Hollow Land*. London: Verso.

Wood, D., & Graham, S. (2006). Permeable boundaries in the software-sorted society: Surveillance and the differentiation of mobility. In: M. Sheller & J. Urry (Eds.) *Mobile Technologies of the City* (pp. 177–191). London and New York: Routledge.

Part II
Geomedia Spaces

6 Look Inside™

Corporate Visions of the Smart City

Gillian Rose

In recent years, the 'smart city' has become a global phenomenon. A smart city is a city that harvests big digital data, usually from sensors embedded in its built environment and from smartphones; that data is then put to various uses. The data can generate economic growth, for example, by allowing innovative new product design; it can enhance environmental sustainability by managing the more efficient use of resources like water, energy and transport; and it can also support more open forms of city government by enabling greater citizen participation (Hollands, 2008; Kitchin, 2014; Goodspeed, 2015). Those, at least, are the claims made on behalf of smart cities by their advocates, and it is thus perhaps no surprise that smartness is central to how many cities are planning for the future. A recent survey suggested that 90% of European cities with a population of more than 500,000 have a smart initiative underway (European Union, 2014: 9), and the UK government estimates that the global market in smart products will be worth $400 billion by 2020 (Department for Business, Innovation and Skills, 2013: 3).

The development of a city as smart involves much more than its digital infrastructure, however (Rossi, 2015). Recent scholarship has identified several other key components of smart-city making, including the making of smart urban policy (Bakıcı, Almirall, and Wareham, 2013; Cosgrave, Doody, and Walt, 2014; Rabari and Storper, 2015), efforts to engage 'smart citizens' (Gabrys, 2014; Vanolo, 2016) and wide-ranging discourses about the advantages or disadvantages of smart forms of urbanism (Söderström, Paasche, and Klauser 2014; Vanolo, 2014).

Digital images of various kinds are central to all these aspects of a smart city (McNeill, 2016; Vanolo, 2016). Still images (photographs and computer generated) and moving images (video and animations) are created in order to picture smart cities in a variety of ways, sometimes photorealistic, sometimes graphic or diagrammatic, sometimes cartographic. Sometimes these are atmospheric, and sometimes they are pedagogic or evidentiary. Sometimes they illustrate what a smart city looks like; often they market smart city events and products. Graphics explaining smart processes appear in policy documents, at smart expos and at citizen engagement events. The interface of a smart smartphone app is visual. The screens arrayed in a smart city operations centre like Rio de Janeiro's show a wide range of images, from CCTV camera feeds to Key Performance Indicator 'traffic lights' (Luque-Ayala and Marvin, 2016; McNeill, 2016), as do the data feeds offered by online, open access, smart city data dashboards (Kitchin, Lauriault, and McArdle, 2015; Mattern, 2016b). It is perhaps hardly surprising then that one of the leading suppliers of smart-city technology used the phrase 'Look Inside™' for several years, as its advertising strapline: visuals and visuality are at the core of smart city activity.[1]

These images have not been given much attention by scholars of the smart city, however, with the exception of the screens in Rio de Janeiro's IBM Operations Centre (see Figure 6.1). IBM partnered with Rio in 2010, after the consequences of a catastrophic landslide threatened the city's credibility as the host of the football world cup in 2014 and the Olympics in 2016 (Goodspeed, 2015; Luque-Ayala and Marvin, 2016; McNeill, 2016). The Rio Operations Centre has become perhaps the iconic image of the smart city, its walls and tables of screens encouraging claims that the smart city is the latest manifestation of panoptic surveillance (see for example McNeill, 2016). However, this focus on the Rio centre's screens to the exclusion of all other forms of visualising smart cities obscures the much wider field of smart imagery and the diverse ways it is imbricated in smart-city life. As digital files, these images circulate through many media and materialize in many different forms: in Twitter feeds, on Expo stands, in websites and on Facebook channels, in pdfs and as printed ephemera,

Figure 6.1 IBM's Operations Centre in Rio de Janeiro © Andres Luque-Ayala and Simon Marvin.

in newspaper reports and academic papers, in exhibition spaces and operation centres, gathering to them different forms of engagement in different contexts. Luque-Ayala and Marvin (2016) emphasize that the Rio Operations Centre is also deeply involved in circuits of mass and social media. This broader digital visual field suggests that smart-city imagery is diverse, generated by many actors and encountered in range of sociospatial contexts.

None of that population of smart city images simply reveals what the smart city is, however. Just as with other figures of the digital present such as the 'cloud' and the 'network', visualization techniques play an important part in their production (Munster, 2013; Amoore, 2016; Mattern, 2016a). This chapter will argue that smart cities are brought into existence through their imagery in two ways. First, the smart city must be *represented*. Data is at the core of a smart city, but that data is invisible. Wi-Fi signals and chip circuitry are not visible to the human eye, and so they must be made visible in the urban scene somehow. They are made visible both by existing ways of seeing and representing cities and by the technologies used to create images of smartness; and in being represented smart is also constituted. The smart city is also constituted by its imagery in a second sense. This is because operationalizing the smart city in real time is itself a highly visualized practice. The smart city – its data but also its streets, its buildings, its infrastructure, its inhabitants – is visualized in order to be managed. To the extent that this is enacted in smart-city images, those images become not only representational but also *operative* (McQuire, 2016: 5). That is, they not only picture the smart city, they also enact it by operating directly on the viewer in ways that are not pictorial.

This chapter will explore this claim in relation to one smart-city image, of a particular kind: the promotional videos made by the large corporations who want to sell their smart-city products. While a smart city can in principle take many forms, much smart-city discourse is generated by large software corporations hoping to sell their products to city authorities, and understanding these powerful accounts of smart cities is thus an important part of understanding smart itself (Söderström et al., 2014). In recent years, such corporations have all developed active social media profiles, including Facebook pages, Twitter feeds and YouTube channels. These platforms have become important sites for the enactment of textual and visual discourse about smart. This chapter investigates how smart cities appear on just one of these platforms; it is based on an analysis of 21 YouTube videos by seven US and European companies who deal in smart products: IBM, Microsoft, Intel, Cisco, Siemens, Thales and Vinci.[2]

Most videos mention the name of the company that made them at some point in their voiceovers or interviews. However, in several, the only mention made of the relevant corporation is in the opening and closing credits, and in some there isn't even that. Moreover, almost none of them have a specific product to sell; an IBM video is the sole exception, giving viewers a screen-by-screen walk-through of IBM's Internet of Things demonstrator platform. The rest of these videos seem to be selling the *idea* of the smart city: literally, they offer a vision of what a smart city is and what a smart city does.[3] They offer enthusiastic accounts of smart cities and the wonderful futures that they can bring; the videos are visually attractive, with their cities bathed in sunshine or dazzling at night; graphics are cute[4] and many of these videos are pedagogic, carefully explaining how that future will work. The videos are not simply advertisements, then. Taken as a group, moreover, they offer a remarkably coherent vision of the urban future that awaits the adopters of smart technology. This chapter will elaborate that vision first by discussing how these videos represent the smart city and second by exploring how they operationalize the smart city for the viewers of the videos.

Representing the Smart City: Crowds/Data/System

The videos discussed by this chapter are all between 3 and 5 minutes long. Six are animated graphics (one each from Intel, Thales and Vinci and three from IBM), 14 are based on film footage, and one – an elaborate and often photorealistic digital animation by Siemens called *FutureLife* – is a hybrid of the two. The five videos made by IBM for its Smarter Cities campaign in 2010 are almost entirely a combination of film footage of cities interspersed with talking-head interviews, but the other film-based videos are all made more recently and take advantage of advances in animated graphic design software to include explanatory onscreen text and digital animations of various kinds (Manovich, 2013). Twelve have voice-overs, and all have music. This section begins its discussion where many of the videos also begin: with representational images of the built urban environment in smart cities.

The starting point for many of the videos is urban population growth: six videos mention it in their opening seconds. Urban growth is both taken for granted and presented as a 'challenge' because it generates what in IBM's *Living City* video are described as 'multiple problem spaces'. These problems all have smart solutions; if there is no smart solution, the video does not show the problem. Problems are variously named in the videos but fall into five broad categories. The first are environmental, including water supply, air quality and (not very often) climate change. Sometimes the problem is public safety, specifically safety in the face of traffic accidents or extreme weather events. Efficient energy distribution is another problem area. 'Smart citizens' are also mentioned, particularly the need to ensure their quality of life, education and healthcare. The problem category that occurs most often is transport. There are two related emphases here: making travel around cities easier for workers and residents and coordinating different modes of transport.

Visually, 17 of the videos begin with an aerial view of a city: the camera tracks a plane landing, flies above a city or zooms into the city from a God's-eye view of the globe in space. In IBM's video on Rio, the filmed zoom into the city is intercut with a digital 3D model of a city landscape in which the buildings grow before our eyes, while in IBM's animation *Smarter Cities* the buildings slide up to fill the image; in Microsoft's *CityNext Partners* animation they fall from the sky. In the videos that are mostly film-based, the camera plunges from on high right into footage of crowded streets. The viewer sees busy public spaces, roads full of cars and buses, crowds on train platforms and in shopping centres and markets. The overall impression given by all the videos is immediately one of spaces full of buildings, people and traffic (smart cities have no suburbs, apparently, and only the Thales video and Siemens's *Future Life* animation show domestic spaces).

This emphasis on urban crowds and crowded spaces is particularly clear in the film-based videos; it is one of the most striking ways people are represented in the smart city. The human in smart cities is represented as a mass, an 'agglomeration' (Halpern, 2015: 4). The mass has other characteristics, too. Most obviously, it is shown as a mobile mass. These humans are always on the move; given the importance of traffic management to visions of smart cities, people are shown using many forms of transport – cars, buses, bicycles, trains, pushchairs and, in the Thales animation, a wheelchair – and if not driving, pedalling or being transported, they are walking. The only time humans seem to pause in this endless movement is when they are waiting for some form of transport to arrive – which is consistently figured as one of the problems a smart city will overcome.

If the population of a smart city appears to be a mobile mass of bodies, these videos also suggest other shared characteristics. These are quite specific and produced by the requirement that the problems pictured in these videos must have a smart solution. So, it appears that these bodies use water and electricity and that they need education when young and healthcare when old. None of them does manual labour (factories are not filmed and are represented in the animated graphics by robotic arms next to conveyor belts). The workplace most often pictured is that of the smart city operations centre, which nine of the 21 videos show. The few other people shown at work in these videos also stare at screens, in offices or sometimes in the cabs of cars or buses. Lots of people in those crowded streets and squares are pictured and filmed using smartphones, though, and, less often, tablets and laptops. These bodies, then, very often have a digital prosthesis.

These prostheses are pictured as both transmitting and receiving data. Data is visualized as something that travels to and from a device; in the film-based videos it is made visible by overlaying animated digital imagery onto filmed footage. Data transmission is shown most often by moving geometric patterns of pale, glowing light. Concentric circles pulse from their source points. Lines of dots, dashes or bars of data flow to and from devices. Or the now-conventional symbol for a wireless connection, a cone of parallel lines, is animated and beams data outward. Data never travels by underground cables or distant servers in these videos, but pulses smoothly through the air of the city like multiple heartbeats. The pulse of data is echoed in one of the kinds of music that accompanies these videos. Many have a cutesy, plinky-plonky soundtrack that maintains a simple repetitive rhythm throughout the video: it can be heard as the aural equivalent of those regularly pulsing data emissions. (A few videos use a different kind of sound track entirely. An uplifting orchestral score, often building up to minor climaxes, suggests not the regular heartbeat of data flows but rather the grandness of the urban future being revealed by the video.) Data is thus represented both visually and aurally in these videos, as both the ongoing everydayness of smart cities and as part of their trajectory towards new urban futures.

Luminescent, flowing data is visually similar to an image found in every one of the 17 film-based videos of the crowded city: streams of traffic at dusk or at night, their headlights also flowing through the dark. Human traffic mobility thus looks very similar to the glowing stream of data that these videos picture. Visual parallels are also made between crowds of people and data populations. Crowds are often filmed from above and/or speeded up, so that individuals are not visible; in Thales' animation, the individual members of a crowd seen from above are moving dots in a 3D model of urban space. These videos thus suggest that the urban crowd is equivalent to data flow.

Other objects also generate data in these smart cities. The videos show cars and buses sending out location data, sensors monitoring and transmitting air quality data and river water levels, rubbish bins signalling when they are full, parking spaces signalling to cars. All the videos use animated graphics to visualize what happens to this transmitted data. These graphics are either intercut with filmed footage or overlaid on top of it. They show data's seamless flow from the urban crowd of devices to platforms, through which it flows again as it is integrated and analysed (the voice-overs tell us), before being put to use by a range of applications that generate various outcomes, from traffic alerts on roadside screens to a product being shipped to a retail outlet, by sending signals back to other devices. The video voice-overs also emphasize the integration of data and communication among different devices, sites and purposes.

This data flow is pictured in a very stylized form in the animations. Several emphasize the integration of sites and devices that emit data by picturing them as nodes in a network connected by straight lines. This is a familiar visual device of the 'contemporary connectionist imaginary'

(Munster, 2013: 1), and in these videos it often resembles a map of a star constellation (or 'the universe of data', according to *Smart Data* by Siemens), with bright lines and hubs shining against deep blue backgrounds (there is a lot of blue in the digital parts of these videos). The nodes in these networks are usually icons representing humans, technological devices, data or sectors. Like the visual similarities between traffic flow and data flow and the crowd and data, the visual language of the network renders things equivalent, this time by showing them as connected component parts of the smart city.

Other animations that track the flow of data show its route as lines that move smoothly through a series of platforms and their applications represented as boxes, sometimes with icons that indicate an app's sector. This abstract visual language of lines and boxes clearly draws on the conventions of systems theory (though IBM's *IoT Made Simple* also has echoes of electrical circuit notation). This is not surprising since the notion of the smart city emerges from efforts in the 1960s to use computers to solve urban problems (Goodspeed, 2015; Halpern, 2015). These efforts often drew on cybernetic understandings of feedback loops in systems, and these systems were visualized precisely as boxes connected by directional lines (Goodspeed, 2015: 82). IBM's Smarter Cities initiative was explicitly driven by understanding a smart city as what Intel's Internet of Things animation also calls a 'system of systems', and each of its 5 Smarter City videos emphasizes the benefits of integrating different (data) systems: weather with traffic or energy demand with energy supply.[5]

In these videos, then, crowds of things generate data, are connected by data streams and are on the move like data moves, smoothly flowing, interconnected and converging visually into a smart urbanism of integrated systems. But, despite the corporate invitation to Look Inside™, the viewer is not able to see these smart city processes. These animations do not show data or code. These remain invisible; they are translated into graphics in the animations: in Intel's own Internet of Things animation, data analytics is represented by graphs, bar charts and pie charts on a laptop screen. Instead, what these videos show, through an abstract visual language of lines, boxes and icons, is the smart city as a crowd of things generating data smoothly integrated in a networked system.

Operative Images of the Smart City: Flow/ Integrate/Transform

The previous section suggested that the human inhabitants of the smart city are transformed in these videos' vision into data streams. Indeed, as soon as Microsoft's *CityNext Partners* animation has represented urban growth with buildings falling from the sky, it shows four, stylized, brightly coloured human figures in a row; a magnifying glass then moves over them, turning the figures under its lens into rows of white and grey zeros and ones, which then turn into blue circles that stream away into the cloud (pictured as white and grey clouds). The image of the human being translated into data has generated several critiques of the smart city. Who owns that data, and what rights to privacy regulate that ownership? What forms of surveillance and control might that data enable (Kitchin, 2014)? If humans require digital prostheses to become a citizen of the smart city, what happens to those who do not have them (Gabrys, 2014)? Does the conversion of the human into the digital lose something of the essential creativity of the human and of the city (Greenfield, 2013)?

The smart-city videos under discussion offer little in response to these concerns beyond a few assurances that the data flows will be secure. Indeed, they imply a technocratic form of smart-city governance in which certain kinds of leaders are visualized as individuals able to manage the urban crowd through data analytics rather than, say, democratic debate. Ten of the film-footage-based videos have talking-head interviews – usually several – and three of the animations follow an identified smart-city individual. All the filmed interviews, with one exception, are with officials or elected representatives of city councils who have adopted smart technologies, senior employees of the corporation making the video or (rarely and only in IBM's series of five smarter city videos) with leaders of campaign groups. All are given their names and job titles onscreen. One animation – IBM's *How It Works: Smarter Cities* – also shows a named smart city official, 'Kathy', an operations centre manager dealing with a hurricane as it approaches 'Supercity'. The two other videos that name individuals are animations focussed on smart-city residents: one has a car malfunction in IBM's *How It Works: Internet of Things*, and Vinci's names a pedestrian, two car drivers and a wheelchair user. The unnamed user of Brisbane's Citizen Engagement Pod, filmed by Cisco, best seems to summarize smart's imagined interaction between the crowd and its smart-city government however; he is using the Pod's screen interface to ask about a dog licence. This is citizen engagement with the smart city via information transfer, not debate.

This section will suggest that the image of the smart-city citizen, transmitting data and receiving it via an interface, in fact articulates a second way in which the videos' visuality is productive. It will do so by discussing how these 21 videos are not only representational, but also operative. That is, they not only picture the smart city, its crowd and its managers, they also enact it by operating directly on the viewer in ways that are not pictorial but rather organizational. Their effects reside not only in what they picture but how it is pictured; the spatial and temporal organization of their visuality is also the geometry and rhythm of the smart city.

Farocki (2004: 17) defines operative images as 'images that do not represent an object but rather are part of an operation'. Basing his discussion on the cameras attached to guided missiles in the first Gulf War, he argues that operative images are made neither to entertain nor to inform; rather, they are taken to monitor processes that cannot usually be observed by the human eye. On that definition, these videos are not straightforwardly operative images, since, as the chapter has already implied, they are designed to be visually pleasing if not actually entertaining; they all also explain how a smart city works using interviews, voice-overs and text boxes as well as their visuals. As the previous section suggested, though, they do show something that cannot be seen by the human eye – data flows – and Farocki's (2004) discussion remains useful for thinking about these videos as also more than representational. His comment that operative images appeal to viewers because we are weary of the 'day-to-day practice of re-mythologising quotidian life' (Farocki, 2004: 18) certainly suggests that the all-too-familiar slick production values of these videos may not be their only effect. This section pursues that suggestion and discusses how these videos also enact in their spatial and temporal organization the data-driven vision through which the smart city is operationalized.

The previous section emphasized that the smart city is represented as constantly on the move. People, trains, cars, planes, data and humans are always shown as mobile. The videos also enact this mobility. Their point of view – the position from which the video's camera sees – is rarely stationary. It zooms in and out and pans backwards and forwards and up and down; the camera focusses steadily during talking-head interviews, but otherwise it usually moves through the streets and the air of the smart city, tracking crowds and traffic. This mobility is emphasized in the temporal rhythm of the film-based videos, which often speed up footage of traffic and crowds to emphasize their flow.

As these things move in the smart city, they transform. Data is integrated, smart citizens alter their travel routes depending on real-time traffic alerts, hospitals employ staff to better match patient needs, smart designers alter products according to data generated by their embedded sensors. This emphasis on integration and transformation is also articulated through the visual structure of the videos. They are constantly morphing from one form of visual content to the next.[6] This is less the case in the film-based videos, but even in these, film is frequently overlaid with animated graphics that are often shown appearing gradually: they may be glowing lines highlighting a connected building's structure, as in Intel's film-based video on San Jose, emanating a general air of 'digitalness', or they might be icons extending from shop awnings into the street in Cisco's Brisbane. One of the most striking examples of this transformation of filmed footage into digital graphic is in Siemens's *FutureLife* animation, where a photorealist, aerial view of New York

106 *Gillian Rose*

skyscrapers begins to glow and then dissolves entirely into the luminescent holograph of the city, Siemen's version of the smart-city operations centre (see Figures 6.2 and 6.3). *FutureLife* also enacts another kind of visual transformation. As well as occupying a continuous flow of points of view through all heights and angles, blending one into the next, it also smoothly transitions between four of the most important visual techniques for designing and planning cities: maps (with glowing datastreams, of course), models, panoramas and aerial photographs. These different visual genres are all smoothly assimilated into the animation's smart city vision.

Indeed, all the animations enact a constant visual fluidity. Elements in animated scenes constantly transition from one thing to another. To give just one example, from IBM's Internet of Things animation, a blue screen has three circular icons in a row, which the voice-over explains stand for sensors, the cloud platform and devices. They are linked by a moving horizontal dotted line. The line fades, the circles move from a row to a column while changing colours and graphic content, and text appears beside each one listing 'Collect and Secure Data', 'Run

Figure 6.2 New York Dissolves into Data in Siemens's *FutureLife* Animation
©The ISO Organisation 2012.

Figure 6.3 Siemens's City Cockpit, Visualised in Their *FutureLife* Animation
©The ISO Organisation 2012.

Analytics' and 'Gain Real-Time Insights' as the advantages of the Internet of Things. As the voice-over mentions 'timely business decisions', they move to the right, and a stopwatch icon zooms up into the screen on the left. The clock then disappears upwards and the three circles disappear downwards. This takes around 11 seconds. Transitions between animation scenes are also very often not jump cuts but swipes, or an icon will move, taking the point of view with it, into a new field to be filled with visual content.

Such visual flows and transitions – while not impossible with analogue animation methods – have become much easier to create with digital visualization software, and the overlay of graphics with filmed footage (exemplified most fully by *FutureLife*) has become immensely more sophisticated, enabling what Elsaesser (2013: 237) identifies as 'the malleability, scalability, fluidity, or curvature of digital images'. Indeed, the constant visual changeability in these smart-city videos suggests that there is a recursive relation between the digitality they represent and the digitality they visually operationalize. The different elements of the videos – film, text, graphics – are themselves formed by 'the dynamic relation between data and data' in digital visualization software packages (Manovich, 2013; Hoelzl and Marie, 2014: 266); the luminescent glow of smart-city data and the transformations between points of view and visual genres they exhibit are themselves written in code. The visuality of the videos themselves thus articulates what the videos represent as the spatial and temporal organization of the smart city: both are mobile, integrated and transformative. To use Hoelzl and Marie's (2014: 266) distinction, the videos represent not only *tableaus* of smartness but also an 'algorithmic configuration of a database in the form of a programmable *view*'.

When these videos are watched, then, they both represent the smart city and enact its operative visuality. In this recursive visual field, watching is also entrained into smart visualities as the videos both address and constitute their viewers. Thus, the videos assume the same specific human audiences they *represent*. Many of them speak directly to the embodied humans they constitute as the leaders of the smart city: city officials and technology experts (Intel invites them to 'drive and accelerate the Internet of Things' in yet another reference to mobility and speed). A couple have also managed to reach the smart city's crowds: both Intel's *What Does the Internet of Things Mean?* and IBM's *How It Works: The Internet of Things* had around a quarter of a million views each by September 2016. However, many of these videos also entrain their viewers into *operationalizing* smartness as they watch. Ten videos use split screens, in an echo of the smart operation centre's banks of screens with multiple feeds. Ten of the newer videos also turn the screen of the video into a screen in a smart-city operations centre, or vice versa: that is, instead of watching a picture of a smart-city screen, the screen on

108 *Gillian Rose*

which the video is being watched is itself transformed into a smart-city operations centre screen. In these moments, a different kind of watching, with a different sort of viewer, is enacted. These transitions from image (of a screen) to screen do precisely what smart does: visualize the city (as) data. This returns us to another quality of operative images as defined by Farocki (2004): operative images are made by machines, for machines, while aiming at the human eye. So there is also a sense in which, mirroring its own dynamic animation in its own digital language, these videos show the smart city *to itself*. They are feedback loops through which data visualizations endlessly circulate, showing themselves to themselves, their viewers human no more.

Conclusions

In terms of how they 'look inside' the smart city, the 21 videos discussed in this chapter share a very similar vision. As representations visualizing the smart city, they argue that urban growth is causing a range of problems for which there are smart digital solutions, based on the transmission and integration of data. Some individual humans are identified, as smart leaders, but smart-city populations are otherwise undifferentiated crowds of bodies with screens that have specific needs (for water and electricity) and, like other devices in the smart city, use digital technology to generate data and receive information. All these component parts of the smart city are seamlessly integrated into a constantly flowing urban data stream, which composes systems of systems. This is the representational content of these videos.

More could be said about these videos and their representations. The relationship between their technological solutionism and the gendering of smart cities deserves closer scrutiny, for example. Explanation, advocacy and leadership of smart cities in these videos are overwhelming male. The second in IBM's series of five videos manages to interview two women, an IBM Local Government Executive and the Director of Strategy of NHS England. Of the nine other videos containing filmed talking-head interviews (usually several), three interview no women at all (Intel and IBM) and six have just one (with IBM using the same female executive in three of these). Of the 12 videos with voice-overs, eight are voiced by men. Some of the more recent videos feature women centrally (there's Microsoft's smart-city operations manager in the 2014 animation, and Siemens's 2015 *Smart Solutions for Smart Cities* is mostly a 2½-minute monologue by the female CEO in Spain). Nonetheless, in these videos smart cities are mostly explained, designed and led by men and may thus focus on what are constituted as masculine concerns. There's that disinterest in domestic spaces, for example, and many smart-city animations display very conventional gendered stereotypes: only figures with ponytails and skirts push pushchairs or shop for clothes; the only child in *FutureLife*'s domestic spaces is pictured being held by a woman, and Thales's smart citizen only appears to sleep in his house, leaving work with a group of mates in the evening to go to a stadium sports event (and see Rommes, Oost, and Oudshoorn, 1999; Strengers, 2014). The videos' assumption that a smart city's 'problem areas' can be solved by data analytics may also be a masculinist fantasy.

Another context about which more could be said is the wider visual culture in which these videos are embedded. The chapter has said nothing about the production, circulation and audiencing of these videos (Rose, Degen, and Melhuish, 2014; Rose, 2016a, 2016b). Even granting its limited focus on their visual content, there is a range of visual traditions referenced by the videos and not discussed here: histories of picturing cities as systems and as utopias (Dunn, Cureton, and Pollastri, 2014; Halpern, 2015) and various conventions of contemporary visual culture, including PowerPoint and computer games. The cutesy graphic style adopted by most of the animations discussed here is a style that can be found in wide array of smart-city visualizations and beyond; other aspects of these videos are part of contemporary visual culture more generally. The chapter has commented, for example, on the frequent speeding up of things in these videos, including traffic and crowds. Microsoft's 2016 video, *CityNext Partners*, maintains a particularly fast tempo throughout its 2 minutes 6 seconds, as do IBM's two *How It Works* videos, released in late 2014 and early 2015. The chapter suggests that this reflects the flow of data – often emphasized as happening in 'real time', but it also corresponds to a description of contemporary 'unruly media', exemplified by music videos and often hosted on YouTube, that emphasizes their speed and intensity (Vernallis, 2013).

The chapter has also argued that the videos are not only representational but also operative. Their operative qualities seem particularly important to emphasize. It is clear that, as representations, the videos are highly selective visions, very different from what Kitchin (2014) warns will without doubt be the reality of 'buggy, brittle and hackable' smart cities. Indeed, their representational qualities are easy to critique. As Farocki (2014) notes, everyday life is continually remythologized, not least by the digital production and postproduction of a very wide range of imagery; image makers of all kinds, from IBM's advertising agency to teenage selfie takers, know that images are glamourized, and the inhabitants of city streets learn how to ignore the blandishments of digital screens (Krajina, 2014). Critiques based on the representationalism of these images are thus perhaps beside the point. That is, *how* the videos 'look inside' the smart city may be more significant than *what* they show of such cities. As the second section of this chapter argued, these videos should also be seen as enacting the operation of smartness in their visual form. If smart cities are about the transmission, integration and transformation of data, these videos most exemplify smart in their own constant flow, morphing, glow and transitioning. Critique then should perhaps focus less on what they represent and more on their particular 'distribution of the sensible' (Rancière, 2006) and who and what it allows to be visible and to speak. On the one hand, these videos clearly suggest that data speaks to urban leaders, who speak in turn about how data enables them to better manage their cities. On the other, as operative images, these videos suggest that in smart cities, only data can be seen and heard.

Notes

1. Intel's 'Look Inside' campaign was launched in 2013, later shifting to 'Experience What's Inside'. *Advertising Age* reported in early 2016 that a new Intel video was focussing on 'Amazing Human Experiences': http://adage.com/article/cmo-strategy/intel-spent-a-year-campaign/302188/. Accessed 19 September 2016.
2. The 21 videos were selected using a variety of criteria. All are hosted on YouTube. IBM, Microsoft, Cisco and Siemens were identified in 2016 as the top four companies supplying smart-city technology (Navigant, 2016), and 7 videos were found on their YouTube channels. YouTube was also searched using relevant terms, which located ten more videos from those companies and also videos from Intel, Thales and Vinci. The 21 videos include 9 from IBM, 2 each from Microsoft and Intel, 3 each from Cisco and Siemens, and 1 from Thales and Vinci. They were viewed repeatedly in order to identify their shared thematic and formal qualities.
3. Suggesting that these videos are not advertisements for smart city products does not mean that they are not complicit with the commodification of urban space. Indeed, their clean cities, airy skies and translucent data flows might be seen as yet another example of the 'urban fetish' and its 'apparent aesthetic disconnection from all the old, dirty, unsafe and "ugly" networks' (Kaika and Swyngedouw, 2000, p. 135).
4. Halpern (2015, p. 7) also remarks on 'cuteness' as part of the smart city.
5. These abstract, system-based visions of smart cities – pictured in all these videos using animations – sit somewhat uneasily with the recognition that 'your city is unique' (as Microsoft's *CityNext* video says). A third of these 21 videos mention specific places: 6 film-based videos show smart city initiatives in specific cities and Microsoft's *CityNext Partners* animation lists a large number of cities. None of these places is represented as unique, however. Rather, the videos imply that what works in Hamburg, say, or San Jose, would also work in other cities with the same problem, and CityNext Partners simply drop the appropriate smart icon (for a security system or a healthcare system) onto a named city's location.
6. The older IBM videos are the exception here. They have a much more film-like structure, with very few animations and no overlays.

References

Amoore, L. (2016). Cloud geographies: Computing, data, sovereignty. *Progress in Human Geography*, 0309132516662147.
Bakıcı, T., Almirall, E., & Wareham, J. (2013). A smart city initiative: the case of Barcelona. *Journal of the Knowledge Economy*, 4(2): 135–148.

Cosgrave, E., Doody, L., & Walt, N. (2014). *Delivering the Smart City: Governing Cities in the Digital Age*. Arup, Liveable Cities, UCL, and the Smart Cities Expo.

Department for Business, Innovation and Skills. (2013). *Smart Cities: Background Paper* (No. BIS/13//1209). London: Department for Business, Innovation and Skills. Retrieved from www.gov.uk/government/publications/smart-cities-background-paper.

Dunn, N., Cureton, P., & Pollastri, S. (2014). *A Visual History of the Future* (Working Paper). London: Foresight, Government Office for Science. Retrieved from www.gov.uk/government/publications/future-cities-a-visual-history-of-the-future.

Elsaesser, T. (2013). The "return" of 3-D: on some of the logics and genealogies of the image in the twenty-first century. *Critical Inquiry*, 39(2): 217–246.

European Union. (2014). *Mapping Smart Cities in the EU* (Policy Department A: Economic and Scientific Policy No. IP/A/ITRE/ST/2013–02). Brussels: European Union. Retrieved from www.europarl.europa.eu/studies.

Farocki, H. (2004). Phantom images. *Public*, 29: 12–22.

Gabrys, J. (2014). Programming environments: Environmentality and citizen sensing in the smart city. *Environment and Planning D: Society and Space*, 32(1): 30–48.

Goodspeed, R. (2015). Smart cities: Moving beyond urban cybernetics to tackle wicked problems. *Cambridge Journal of Regions, Economy and Society*, 8(1): 79–92.

Greenfield, A. (2013). *Against the Smart City*. London: Do Projects.

Halpern, O. (2015). *Beautiful Data: A History of Vision and Reason Since 1945*. Durham NC: Duke University Press. Retrieved from http://read.dukeupress.edu/content/beautiful-data.

Hoelzl, I., & Marie, R. (2014). Google street view: Navigating the operative image. *Visual Studies*, 29(3): 261–271.

Hollands, R. G. (2008). Will the real smart city please stand up? *City*, 12(3): 303–320.

Kaika, M., & Swyngedouw, E. (2000). Fetishizing the modern city: The phantasmagoria of urban technological networks. *International Journal of Urban and Regional Research*, 24(1): 120–138.

Kitchin, R. (2014). The real-time city? Big data and smart urbanism. *GeoJournal*, 79(1): 1–14.

Kitchin, R., Lauriault, T. P., & McArdle, G. (2015). Knowing and governing cities through urban indicators, city benchmarking and real-time dashboards. *Regional Studies, Regional Science*, 2(1): 6–28.

Krajina, Z. (2014). *Negotiating the Mediated City: Everyday Encounters with Public Screens*. London: Routledge.

Luque-Ayala, A., & Marvin, S. (2016). The maintenance of urban circulation: An operational logic of infrastructural control. *Environment and Planning D: Society and Space*, 34(2): 191–208.

Manovich, L. (2013). *Software Takes Command*. London: Bloomsbury. Retrieved from available open access at http://issuu.com/bloomsburypublishing/docs/9781623566722_web.

Mattern, S. (2016a). Cloud and field: On the resurgence of "field guides" in a networked age. *Places Journal*, (August). Retrieved from https://placesjournal.org/article/cloud-and-field/.

Mattern, S. (2016b). Interfacing urban intelligence. In R. Kitchin & S.-Y. Perng (Eds.), *Code and the City* (pp. 49–60). Abingdon: Routledge.
McNeill, D. (2016). IBM and the visual formation of smart cities. In S. Marvin, A. Luque-Ayala, & C. McFarlane (Eds.), *Smart Urbanism: Utopian Vision or False Dawn?* (pp. 34–51). Abingdon: Routledge.
McQuire, S. (2016). *Geomedia: Networked Cities and the Future of Public Space.* Cambridge: Polity Press.
Munster, A. (2013). *An Aesthesia of Networks: Conjunctive Experience in Art and Technology.* Cambridge MA: MIT Press.
Navigant. (2016, February). *Navigant Research Leaderboard Report: Smart City Suppliers.* Retrieved from www.navigantresearch.com/research/navigant-research-leaderboard-report-smart-city-suppliers.
Rabari, C., & Storper, M. (2015). The digital skin of cities: Urban theory and research in the age of the sensored and metered city, ubiquitous computing and big data. *Cambridge Journal of Regions, Economy and Society*, 8(1): 27–42.
Rancière, J. (2006). *The Politics of Aesthetics: The Distribution of the Sensible.* (G. Rockhill, Trans.). London: Continuum.
Rommes, E., Oost, E. V., & Oudshoorn, N. (1999). Gender in the design of the Digital City of Amsterdam. *Information, Communication & Society*, 2(4): 476–495.
Rose, G. (2016a). Rethinking the geographies of cultural "objects" through digital technologies: Interface, network and friction. *Progress in Human Geography*, 40(3): 334–351.
Rose, G. (2016b). *Visual Methodologies: An Introduction to Researching with Visual Materials* (fourth). London: Sage.
Rose, G., Degen, M., & Melhuish, C. (2014). Networks, interfaces, and computer-generated images: learning from digital visualisations of urban redevelopment projects. *Environment and Planning D: Society and Space*, 32(3): 386–403.
Rossi, U. (2015). The variegated economics and the potential politics of the smart city. *Territory, Politics, Governance*, 0(0): 1–17.
Söderström, O., Paasche, T., & Klauser, F. (2014). Smart cities as corporate storytelling. *City*, 18(3): 307–320.
Strengers, Y. (2014, August). Smart energy in everyday life: Are you designing for resource man? *ACM Interactions*, 21(4): 24–31.
Vanolo, A. (2014). Smartmentality: the smart city as disciplinary strategy. *Urban Studies*, 51(5): 883–898.
Vanolo, A. (2016). Is there anyone out there? The place and role of citizens in tomorrow's smart cities. *Futures*, 82(September): 26–36.
Vernallis, C. (2013). *Unruly Media: YouTube, Music Video, and the New Digital Cinema.* New York: Oxford University Press.

Videos

All videos accessed on 14 September 2016.

Cisco (2014), The Internet of Everything Transforms Hamburg into a Smart Connected City, www.youtube.com/watch?v=FoEPlE8Pg71.

Cisco (2014), Cisco Connected Transportation and Smart Cities, www.youtube.com/watch?v=x6WfZlETbx4.

Cisco (2014), Brisbane: A City with an Internet of Everything Digital Agenda, www.youtube.com/watch?v=nELVe_Y9p7s&index=51&list=PLFT-9JpKjRT-BO06vEUTM7I91AZ7_-I8XI.

IBM (2016), IoT Made Simple with IBM Watson IoT Platform, www.youtube.com/watch?v=o0kc1Xe6ltQ.

IBM (2015), How It Works: The Internet of Things, www.youtube.com/watch?v=QSIPNhOiMoE.

IBM (2014), How It Works: Smarter Cities, www.youtube.com/watch?v=yJVK25wWvbE.

IBM (2011), IBM Helps Rio Become a Smarter City, www.youtube.com/watch?v=vuBBGYFonXM.

IBM (2010), Smarter Cities: Introducing the Smarter City, www.youtube.com/watch?v=_6b_ztbpRaw.

IBM, (2010), Smarter Cities: The Living City, www.youtube.com/watch?v=LzgPKlAAkwY.

IBM, (2010), Smarter Cities: Powering the City, www.youtube.com/watch?v=lQ0RupXt_8U.

IBM, (2010), Smarter Cities: Cities in Motion, www.youtube.com/watch?v=0Rb_uVezA5U.

IBM, (2010), Smarter Cities: Developing the City, www.youtube.com/watch?v=fZyBGDiRPL4.

Intel (2014), Intel IoT – What Does the Internet of Things Mean? www.youtube.com/watch?v=Q3ur8wzzhBU.

Intel (2014), Smart Cities USA: San Jose, CA, www.youtube.com/watch?v=1Pxuk_SLUdI.

Microsoft (2016), Microsoft CityNext, www.youtube.com/watch?v=e0RFjGiSBgQ.

Microsoft (2016), Microsoft CityNext Partners with Cities Worldwide, www.youtube.com/watch?v=QJtlQTEHWZg.

Siemens (2015), Smart Solutions for Smart Cities, www.youtube.com/watch?v=2XS_zcbahjc.

Siemens (2014), Siemens Smart Data, www.youtube.com/watch?v=ZxoO-DvHQRw.

Siemens (2013), FutureLife, www.youtube.com/watch?v=zuPIyqUc9oA.

Thales (2012), SMART CITY: The Interconnected City: Improving the Quality of Life of its Citizens, www.youtube.com/watch?v=qvGuw2zZ3qc.

Vinci (2015), What is a Smart City? www.youtube.com/watch?v=Br5aJa6MkBc.

7 'The Sounds of Silence' – Writing Urban Spaces

Tindra Thor

Introduction

This is a story about everyday art and everyday urban spaces. It is a story about everyday experiences in urban space and a sensorial story about the ephemeral voices and experiences that only transiently touch and mark urban spaces. It is a story about urban 'sounds of silence'.

Painting graffiti is traditionally referred to as an act of *writing* (see, e.g, Castleman, 1982; Almqvist and Hagelin, 2005). 'Writing' does not, however, refer to mere inscription of letters on a surface but to the full performance of the making of graffiti (as in Cooper and Chalfant, 1984; Macdonald, 2001; Jacobson and Barenthin Lindblad, 2003; Kimvall, 2014). Identifying graffiti as writing signifies an emphasis on the writing of letters. Although graffiti cannot (always) be reduced to simple writing of letters, letters are very central to graffiti culture. This fundamentally makes graffiti an *urban form of communication*. While graffiti is not always easily decoded, short inscriptions in the form of names or messages at least potentially speak to everyone able to read short messages. For those unable to, graffiti speaks (sometimes very loudly) through its form, style, colours, size and/or placement.

These writings are ever-present phenomena in everyday urban life. Although rather scarce in many cities, they are almost always there somewhere. When walking through urban spaces you encounter graffiti everywhere in the form of tags, throw-ups, stickers and similar expressions. Graffiti cultures are in many ways about what is referred to as *getting up*. Getting up means gaining *fame* – admiration, respect or maybe even envy of primarily other writers. According to Craig Castleman, getting up is 'the prime directive in graffiti' (1982: 19). Writings can draw attention to the skills of the writer, to a societal issue or just make someone laugh. However, graffiti writing and getting up are usually endeavours of 'preaching to the choir'. Graffiti communicates to already initiated people – either other writers or graffiti fans. Nancy Macdonald (2001) describes graffiti as being 'urban white noise' to most people without familiarity with graffiti culture (1). She continues:

> [Graffiti] flirts in the public eye, [...] revealing all and yet revealing absolutely nothing. We are unaware that the city walls are alive with its social drama.

In that sense, graffiti is both an 'up in your face' urban art and something that takes place in silences that create a *communicative space of in-betweenness*. It speaks at the same time it does not. It is potentially communicative to basically everyone who can see; at the same time, it often requires some kind of graffiti literacy. It sounds and speaks but is incomprehensible to most people. Graffiti is, consequently, simultaneously an urban 'sound' and 'silence'.

Graffiti is in-between not only communicatively, but also spatially and institutionally. In Stockholm where zero tolerance was practiced against graffiti until October 2014, and where there are few spaces designated for legal graffiti, writers are rarely seen. They move from the visible into the invisible and the shadows, leaving their footprints and marks before moving back into the visible and the light at the same time, as they are, in a way, always visible. Furthermore, some build their own walls, without building permits, creating grey zones in spatial and legal terms. As such, graffiti writing takes and occupies place, *as well as create places* into something new; in-between places sometimes noticed by others and sometimes just passed through.

Graffiti is also institutionally in-between. As pointed out by art historian Jakob Kimvall (2014), graffiti is not a stable concept but rather discursively formed in different spatiotemporal moments where it is constructed as artwork and/or crime. It is an aesthetic practice that performs (and creates) an art space in-between institutionalized and non-institutionalized art and design. It is an expression seen on benches, walls and toilets that is just as likely to appear on cell phone covers and in logotypes as in art galleries. Furthermore, it is in-between in relation to the very concept of art, because of the question: Is graffiti art or vandalism?

In this chapter, I intend to explore these communicative, spatial and institutional in-between emplacements of graffiti in conversation with Gilles Deleuze and Félix Guattari's concept of *nomadology* (1986). Through ethnographic fieldwork, I have explored how Swedish graffiti writers relate to these in-betweennesses. Related to in-betweenness is the intervening character of graffiti. By intervening, I refer to the moments when graffiti functions as disturbances of the hegemonies of the urban. This will entail a focus on what the makers consider themselves to be intervening in, why they are doing it, how they regard the city and how/ if they envision other alternatives. This chapter is thus an ethnographic exploration of how makers of graffiti are (de)territorializing urban space through aesthetic and spatial interventions in Stockholm.

Graffiti as Spatial and Aesthetic Politics

'[...] a vision softly creeping, left its seeds as I was sleeping'.
(Simon, 1964)

Until October 2014, Stockholm practiced a zero-tolerance policy on graffiti and street art. Zero tolerance in Stockholm is, like in New York, an example of policy implementation of 'broken windows' theory (Wilson and Kelling, 1982). In short, the theory states that, for example, broken windows need to be fixed immediately in a neighbourhood, otherwise people will stop picking up after their dogs and litter in general, and the neighbourhood will soon become completely degenerated. The zero-tolerance policy in Stockholm therefore encompassed a sanitation warranty stating that all graffiti will be sanitized within 24 hours, following the logic that one tag will breed more. Although zero tolerance was eliminated following the national elections in September 2014, the consequences for graffiti are still unclear. Stockholm has gotten its first legal wall open for painting graffiti in Södermalm, the southern part of Stockholm, and there are several initiatives for more open walls. In other parts of the city, these initiatives have had less impact or been outvoted.

Anti-graffiti policies and graffiti practices can be understood as fights over public space and who has 'the right to the city' (Lefebvre, 1996). Different practices aim to form different kinds of urbanities. Cultural scientist Catharina Thörn describes this as a fight over the aestheticization of public space, a fight that has become increasingly important as strong marketing powers have great economical interest in making a commercially attractive city (Thörn, 2005). Urban hegemony orders urban discourse and the urban landscape; in the contemporary urban landscape the economic forces, the owners of the means of production, own the right to the formation of the urban landscape. Accordingly, what is not desirable or does not fit into the normative idea of how the urban should look or function runs the risk of being labelled malignant or threatening.

With reference to sociologist Zygmunt Bauman, Thörn describes how cities create different initiatives in order to 'clean up the social dirt in the cities', where 'dirt' is understood as inadequate consumers – the poor, the homeless, the beggars (Thörn, 2005: 172). As pointed out by anthropologist Mary Douglas, dirt is something that is 'in the eye of the beholder', and dirt 'is essentially disorder' (2002: 2). Consequently, that which challenges hegemonic ideas of 'social order' risks becoming 'social dirt'. Dirt is the reminder of dysfunctional environmental, social, cultural and economical politics and therefore (aimed to be) kept in marginalized and delimited spaces. It exists 'below the threshold at which visibility begins' (de Certeau, 1984: 93).

In a similar manner, graffiti becomes an urban dirtiness, a 'visual pollution', by representing another idea of the how the urban could be aestheticized (Thörn, 2005: 174). Graffiti thereby challenges the hegemonic idea of the urban – the commercialized urban – through presenting a counter-narrative where the urban is potentially characterized by visual expressions and spaces that cannot, or should not, be bought or sold. As such, graffiti becomes a kind of 'space hacking' (Dodge and Kitchin, 2006) and bears the potential of constituting new relations between the everyday and the political (García Canclini, 1995). Accordingly, graffiti as counter hegemonic performance bears potential rewritings and reimaginings of urban space. Consequently, writing graffiti can be considered *performing a spatial and aesthetic politics*.

Nomadology and Graffiti in-Between

'[W]ithin the sound of silence'.

(Simon, 1964)

I have chosen to conceptualize this in-between space as what Gilles Deleuze and Félix Guattari (1986) refer to as *smooth space* created by nomadic performances and subjectivities. Deleuze and Guattari (2013) present the concept of *nomadology* in *A Thousand Plateaus* with the interconnected idea of the *war machine* and its smooth space. According to Deleuze and Guattari, the space of the state is striated. Striated space is made by, and it enables only, rules and movement in the same manner as in a game of chess. Not only do the rules of the game decide which moves are possible, these possibilities are also entangled with the squares, the 'geography' of the chessboard. Movement can only happen within the drawn squares and according to a pregiven set of movements.

The space of the war machine, on the other hand, is smooth. This space follows a different logic than striated space. Following the logic of striated space, one move from point A to point B; following the nomadic logic of the war machine, there is no A or B. Points are rather made in movement; subjects are created *situationally* in the smooth space of exteriority (Deleuze and Guattari, 1986: 3). The nomad can thus be regarded as a smooth becoming and a *situational consequence* of moving according to the nonrules of the exteriority. Such movement could be walking without the purpose of going from one point to another, just walking for the sake of walking or taking the subway for the sake of taking the subway. These movements are experiences in themselves rather than transportation.

In graffiti culture, trains have a special kind of status and have been referred to as 'subway art' (Cooper and Chalfant, 1984). The train is the canvas that moves. The train puts you and your name on public display. This not only means that writers seek the train to paint, they also ride 'along the line' to look at paintings, their own as well as others. They engage in nomadic explorations without specific beginnings or ends.

Central to the notion of the war machine is that it is inherently an exteriority of the state. The state can never have or be a war machine in or by itself but 'only appropriate one in the form of a military institution, one that will always cause it problems' (Deleuze and Guattari, 1986: 7). This means that the state will always try to appropriate a war machine. There are (at least) two things at play in such appropriations. First, the state can be in need of one. Second, and I would suggest, more important, is that the state by appropriating a war machine aims to take its exteriority out of the equation. It is, however, not possible to discipline the war machine completely since it will always have the nature of exteriority (Deleuze and Guattari, 1986: 13).

Key to this line of thinking is the notion of *potential*. There is always the potential for something else to happen (see Amin and Thrift, 2002; Harvey, 2008; Deleuze and Guattari, 2013). The war machine, for example, is a subversive force with the creative potential of challenging the rules and designs of striated spaces. Every day we create spaces through movements and actions – we perform spaces. We reperform spaces every day compiling them into a sedentary spaces of layered practices. We engage in what Deleuze and Guattari would call different forms of *territorializing*. Territorializing refers to the act of affecting 'milieus and rhythms', marking them and putting them into an assemblage (Deleuze and Guattari, 2013: 366; 585–586). Every time something makes a different mark on the territorialized, that space is deterritorialized. Deterritorialization is 'the movement by which "one" leaves the territory. It is the operation of the line of flight' (Deleuze and Guattari, 2013: 591). It makes a different mark on the territorialized. Here lies the potential. The potentials of smooth space can always create a break in striated spaces, and thereby the potential of something different is always present. The potential of nomadic space and practice is not a normative perspective on the outcome. As Deleuze and Guattari note, the smooth space of the war machine is not better than the striated, just different (Deleuze and Guattari, 1986: 13). 'Smooth spaces are not in themselves liberatory' (Deleuze and Guattari, 2013: 581). Potentials may well result in the recognition of either fascist or anti-fascist graffiti, for example. Stressing potential is rather stressing the temporal quality of what might be become, since 'the struggle is changed and displaced' (Deleuze and Guattari, 2013) in smooth spaces.

Given the spatial and aesthetic counter-narratives raised by graffiti, graffiti can be conceptualized as reterritorializing performances. They constantly reterritorialize urban space and create potentials of including otherness, difference and multiplicity. Rosi Braidotti describes the nomadic body as 'a threshold of transformations' (2011: 25). Consequently, there is a potential for spatial, aesthetic and political transformations connected to the nomad and de- and reterritorializing practices. Braidotti further writes that central to nomadic thought is the importance of interlinking critique and creation (2011: 6). Nomadic practices consequently involve actively critiquing and producing other concepts or alternatives. This is also of interest here since focus of this text is exploring practices that are fundamentally creative and the ideas and ideologies behind these practices that are the alternatives.

Exploring and Sensing Graffiti in-Between

'In restless dreams I walked alone'.
(Paul Simon, 'The Sound of Silence')

The activities involved in this ethnographic exploration are primarily interviewing: reimagined as place-making events (Massey, 2005; Pink, 2015: 73–85); and go-alongs (Kusenbach, 2003), i.e. I have accompanied and interviewed people while they have been painting. As graffiti is the focus of the study, and considering *tags* are prominent features of graffiti culture, I have chosen to reimagine the go-alongs as *tag-alongs*. Tag-along is not only used as a play on words to signify the specific practice studied, it is also used to emphasize my own active participation in and influence on, not only the interviews as events, but also, by extension, the cultural and social context. Although I have not co-performed actual graffiti writing with the participants, I do nonetheless consider the tag-along as co-performative act for mainly two reasons; first, because it marks that *culture is regarded as performance*; and second, because it highlights *the ethnographic praxis as performative* (cf. Conquergood, 2013: 16–22).

The study encompasses 20 interviews and/or tag-alongs with 18 men and 2 women aged between 15 and 53. All the participants have been rendered anonymous. When referred to in the text they are presented by a pseudonym and age. The collection of participants was made by snowballing in three different 'snowballs'. To clarify, I contacted three potential participants through different channels: personal contacts, Instagram, and official homepages and snowballed from these different points in order to get variation in the material. Obviously, there is a substantial gender bias in the material. I would however argue that this is representative of the environment. All participants have regular jobs and/or attend some kind of education (upper secondary school/university/independent adult education colleges). Several work as full-time artists, and others work as teachers, in television, in IT, etc. None of them lives 'under the radar'. Some of them have families and relationships and lead, in many ways, regular lives. In that respect the group shows, as in criminologist David Shannon's (2003) study on youths involved in graffiti, a 'substantial degree of variation' (95). What assembles the group is the act of graffiti. This is also points to the in-betweenness of graffiti. People move in and out of 'becoming-writer', i.e. the becoming is situationally determined. 'The writer' can in that sense be conceptualized as a *performed situation*.

Methodologically, this study can best be described as an 'ethnography of the senses' as described by Sarah Pink (2015). According to Pink, the researcher's emplaced, experiencing and knowing body is central to sensory ethnography and is what creates the ethnographic place. Pink describes that she started using her own sensory values as a reference point for reflecting on the situated experiences of the participants in her study (61). Pink further describes that this self-reflecting process does not take place before fieldwork but rather during. This is important because although the present entails repetitions of the past, these repetitions are not identical to what came before. The past becomes as much in the present. This means that the difficulties in preparing for an interview, for example, have to do not only with the fact that you are interacting with another living creature whose desires and beliefs you know little about. It also has to do with the fact that your own desires and beliefs are becoming in that same moment. The difficulties in preparing for fieldwork thus also have to do with the difficulties in preparing yourself for encountering yourself. Thus, it is as important to reflect on and accounting for your experiences as those you are trying to explore.

According to Pink (2015), an ethnography of the senses is a way of accounting for space/place, sound, images and tacit experiences and not just observation. Following this argument, participant observation means experiencing, sensing and reflecting on the performative moments of the researcher and the participants. Working with and through the senses is thus a strategy for getting at the complexities of the field. It is accounting for moments of experience and for the embodied conclusions. This also entails a reflexive writing of the self 'into and through the ethnographic text, isolating that space where memory, history, performance and meaning intersect' (Denzin, 2013: 22). The role of the researcher is in that sense impossible to detach from the ethnographic moments. Emphasizing and giving primacy to the role of the researcher is also a way of accounting for the sensory experiences and the sensory dimensions of 'place as event' (Massey, 2005).

I am not a graffiti writer myself. In my teens, I was however very fascinated by graffiti, by the playfulness and the stories behind the writings, although they were completely unknown to me, and thrilled by encountering something familiar, yet unknown. When I started writing my dissertation on graffiti (and street art[1]), I gained a whole new understanding of these phenomena. Not only did I start to comprehend more about how they were emplaced, but researching graffiti also changed me in ways I did not expect. One of these changes concerned the way I move in a city. I am a fairly tall person who has always used the full longitude of myself to move fast through the city. I would call myself a typical busy city walker. Although I still sometimes favour high speed, as the busy city person I am, my work has made me value moving through city space while experiencing the movement and the space I move through. For me, the spaces in-between my points have become essential for me to understand, experience and acquire sensory experiences of graffiti for myself.

Adrift walking has in that sense become a way for me to experience other people's nomadic movements through the city and to form my own sensory understanding of paths previously unknown to me. The idea of this kind of walking is inspired by Michel de Certeau's descriptions of walking the city in *The Practice of Everyday Life* (1984) and Walter Benjamin's idea of the *flâneur* (1999). The purposes of these walks were, in the spirit of nomadology, only to walk and to follow prospective traces in the form of tags, stickers or other kinds of visual expressions encompassed by my research interest.

Absolutely fundamental in this respect is *co-performative curiosity*. When exploring graffiti, or street art for that matter, it becomes clear that it is often found in hidden places, which partially is a consequence of the practice being a crime, but it can also be considered a consequence of the artist's spatial curiosity where the writer or artist is exploring and playing with less visible spaces (see Figure 7.1). Co-performing curiosity thus becomes a way of exploring a specific cultural performative trait through a performative ethnographic praxis.

Writing Critique

'And the people bowed and prayed
To the neon god they made'.

(Simon, 1964)

When talking about graffiti as presenting an alternative urban aesthetic, one might ask, *what are they opposing and intervening in*? There is one very prominent theme articulated by the participants in the study, and that is articulating graffiti as anticapitalist critique. It is articulated as an intervention in the logic of neoliberalism, marketization, ownership and a commodified public space. This critique directly coincides with the critique formulated by, for example, the Situationists International (see, e.g, Debord, 1987; Henri Lefebvre, 1991; David Harvey, 2008).

Central to the Situationist understanding of urban experience is that it has become increasingly commodified. As put by David Harvey, 'We live, after all, in a world in which the rights of private property and the profit rate trump all other notions of rights' (2008: 23). Experiencing the city has become an experience of commodities. Everywhere one walks; there are advertisements, stores, moving billboards, etc. Should you choose to pick up your always-connected smartphone you will be bombarded with targeted ads and offers. If you go into a store and buy something, the cashier might ask you to leave your email address, so that

Figure 7.1 Fingers in ventilator, London, November 2015. Photograph: Tindra Thor.

the store can offer exclusive deals. Your connected physical presence in the city has become almost completely absorbed by your ability or disability to consume goods and services.

This also becomes clear, as there are few examples of cities actively opposing advertising in public space. There is the rare example of São Paulo that banned public advertising in 2006 through the Lei Cidade Limpa (*clean city law*), but in most cities it is everywhere, completely dominating urban experience. Not only are commercialized spaces a dominating trait of the contemporary city, advertisements are also designed to draw attention *to* them and *from* other phenomena potentially competing for the spectator's attention. If people look at tags, or any other kind of noncommercialized expression, they are consequently not looking at the ad designed to make them buy something. It was not until I looked through my pictures that I realized there are ads in them that I never took notice of when taking the picture, which is obvious in the pictures because of the ads' peripheral position in them. It was only later, when actively looking at the spatial context in the images, that I realized 7–11 probably wanted me to buy a bratwurst rather than take a picture of the tag beside the ad (see Figure 7.2. In this picture, the tag becomes a war machine that presents an alternative way of viewing and creating the urban that actively challenges the commodified urban.

Counter to the idea that the urban can be bought, graffiti voices the opinion that the city belongs to the people living in it, situating this narrative in relation to the idea of 'the right to the city' (Lefebvre, 1996). Graffiti accordingly deterritorializes the commercialized urban space, creating a potential for a reimagining of that space, even if only ephemerally.

Figure 7.2 Tag, Stockholm, October 2014. Photograph: Tindra Thor.

> Imagine someone goes to New York, stand in the middle of Times Square and like 'aaah, I'm in Times Square, woah'. [...] What is Times Square, really? It's a fucking intersection. But what makes Times Square so awesome is the advertising. [...] It's not just regular signs, but it rolls and it's like, 'Buy this, buy this!' all the time. And really, nobody has chosen it to be there. [...] But it's legal! [...] Then people just 'yeah, but this is great' [...] Most people are, unfortunately, stupid.
>
> (Daroush, 36)

Experiencing graffiti in the urban space is described by the participants as a completely opposite experience from experiencing advertising in the bought and commodified public space. Graffiti is articulated as something free and available for everyone to see. Furthermore, it is articulated as exposing the power plays of the urban.

> [Graffiti] also exposes certain aspects of society today, power hierarchies that exist. [...] it's a very subversive art form.
>
> (Alexis, 22)

Graffiti consequently gets the function of critiquing power, critiquing the striated state space through subversive acts that follow another logic – the nomadic logic. It is subversive in the way that it not only undermines the commodified urban space; it also challenges it by taking it without asking or paying for it, and, in some ways also reclaims public space to the people living there.

The freedom of not having to pay is thus a value within graffiti culture. This also becomes evident in stories about stealing; something several of the participants describe as the way they went about getting paint when they were younger:

> You know in a class, there's always this tall person, like in 8th grade was taller than everyone else. And he looked like older. He used to borrow his dad's work pants and then he had a winter jacket. And like we went in there and asked about all kinds of stuff. Our job was to entertain the salesmen while he filled that jacket [...] with cans. And then, since he had the pants and it was a hardware store, he looked like... And we were kids! You know? When we came in there, it was like 'what the fuck are they doing there?' In a hardware store. Not so common that like 15 or 14 year-olds walk into a hardware store. But he looked like he belonged there! And yeah, it was like, he stole the cans and then we went and found a wall and just painted it.
>
> (Daroush, 36)

These kinds of stories are fairly common; kids without money stealing as basically the only option if they wish to paint. I do however want to state that my understanding of Swedish graffiti culture today is that stealing paint, or 'racking' (Kimvall, 2014: 208), is unusual.

I would argue that today the act of stealing paint is something that exceeds a nostalgic youth story. Stealing has symbolic value within the culture, reinforced and reproduced by the nostalgia of 'back in the day' stories. The contemporary discursive construction of a hard-core graffiti writer is one who steals his/her cans and paints nothing but trains. I am not suggesting that there are no writers who steal paint today. Rather I am suggesting that whether writers actually steal paint or not is secondary to the fact that this symbolic ideal (a discursive *myth*) regulates and almost *ritually* reproduces graffiti culture.

The other contemporary dimension of stealing is ideological, that making graffiti should be free of charge. 'They steal everything they do because it's supposed to be a free thing for them' (Alexis, 22). Thus, what might have started out as a youth prank or only option among teen writers has turned out to be a political action and symbolic ideal reinforced by the stories creating and forming the cultural practice.

This theme materializes as a basic ideal of freedom. It suggests that art should be free and people should be free to do their art. 'When you do graffiti you realize that ownership is bizarre and that there are so many inhibited by it' (Fredrik, 29). Graffiti becomes a way out, a way for the artists to create a *line of flight* (Deleuze and Guattari, 2013) from the structures of striated space and a tactic (cf. de Certeau, 1984) for opposing and deterritorializing space.

Participants also express the opinion that graffiti is not made for somewhere other than the city. It is supposed to be there. Changing the place changes the visual expression and makes the graffiti something it should not be.

ME: Why can't you paint on a canvas at home then?
MARCUS (29): How fucking boring could you be? [] I sound like super negative when I say that but I've never made a graffiti painting on a canvas, but when I see people who do that, I feel like it's the most boring thing ever.

Assuming that graffiti on a canvas is boring, what is it that makes it fun and exciting? As made clear in the quote above, it is not only the visual expression. If the fun and excitement lied only in making the visual expression, the canvas would have been an adequate substitute for the wall. The place of writing is thus equally important. A canvas puts graffiti in the 'wrong' place. The canvas also confines the visual expression in terms of size. The canvas puts graffiti in a square, within a striated space. Furthermore, considering graffiti as part of an exteriority of smooth space, it can never be entirely limited to the striated space. Although it may appear in such space, it still has the nature of exteriority. As Aleks, 27, said:

ALEKS: Say in some weird imaginary world that it would be 100 per cent legal to paint graffiti everywhere, then it doesn't matter anymore.
ME: What is it that doesn't matter?
ALEKS: Because then you're not taking any risk. The risk is gone. Then anyone can go to [the Central Station] and paint a killer painting. Then it doesn't matter. Then it's just like 'yeah yeah, you had the time. I didn't because I was at work.' You know? It doesn't work. [...] If you did something illegal, then you still took your place in the public. Forcefully if you want to see it that way. And that is the thing, really.

Aleks thus expresses that graffiti is connected to risk taking and spatial appropriation. Furthermore, he suggests that graffiti matters when it is made in public in spite of being illegal. Part of what makes graffiti matter is that it is illegal, that it voices something different and subverts public space and the institutions of the state.

Creating Other Pictures

'The words of the prophets are written on the subway walls
    And tenement halls'.
(Simon, 1964)

The above words voice the same concerns and thoughts that the participants in this study voice. The composer, Paul Simon, was recently on a talk show aired in Sweden and Norway where he raised a similar concern. He told that he had been asked to perform one of his songs at a political event, and that artists often are asked to perform at political conventions and events in order to have the artists 'shine on them'. But, Simon said, when it comes to politics and political choices, people in power stop listening to what the artists have to say, even though many artists actually bring some valuable perspectives to the table (Skavlan, 2016).

The participants in this study express similar opinions. Graffiti is in this narrative a deterritorializing event there to disturb both what is articulated as, an otherwise conform and homogenous urban environment, and quotidian urban territorializations of urban dwellers.

You know that large building next to the mall at [...] Stureplan. They usually have a billboard [...] They smash it up across the whole wall. [...] Or like, in the subway, you know when they take the entire outside of a train and paste like '3G' on it. Then it's like, that's ok. And you know, people are just like 'yes, here comes the train on time.' They do not even REACT to the fact that, there's advertising across the whole train! (Daroush, 36)

In this narrative, urban dwellers are described as kind of asleep (see Figure 7.3), rocked by the familiarity of safe and nonthreatening visual expressions that, without us noticing, alienate us more and more from what is around us, perhaps even people (cf. Lefebvre, 1991; Benjamin, 1999).

As expressed by Daroush above, the familiarity of the commercials and adverts is so embedded in everyday urban life that people moving through the urban neither reflect on the dominance of advertising in the urban nor envision alternatives. The lack of alternative expressions in the city is furthermore articulated as sterile, boring or cold. One participant said that: 'They have succeeded quite well in Stockholm to create a sterile city. [...] Stockholm in general has become a rather cold and depressing city' (Andreas, 40).

This aversion against the sterile, meaning lack of different visualities, is a recurring theme in the material. One participant described it as scary and kind of creepy. In this narrative, the sterile signifies the dead, or the sleeping, the nonliving and expresses an aversion to what could be described as a kind of *zombification of society* where the general urban dwellers are articulated as too numb to see each other, reflect upon their environment, or perhaps even their lives.

Figure 7.3 Sleep, Stockholm, November 2014. Photograph: Tindra Thor.

For several graffiti writers, this is where graffiti comes in: to wake the sleepers. Painting is thus articulated as the deterritorializing event aimed to shake people out of dormancy. This does not mean that graffiti aims to get people in general to appreciate or like it. The aim of 'waking' people might rather be reached by painting something controversial or ugly. The point is to get people to think and thereby *awaken a spatial and aesthetical potential*, to deterritorialize space that can, potentially, be reterritorialized.

> Many think it's about destroying, but it's about creating something different, to make something else.
>
> (Alexis, 22)

This 'something else' is, in short, diversity. It is intended to bring visual diversity to urban life and tell stories that have not been heard before. It is about diversifying public spaces with something other than ads with smiling women with flowing hair inside lit-up ad boxes. It is about reaching out to people and whispering that there are other images to see, other things to do, other battles to fight.

It also means creating something else in terms of art as an institution. If people want to see art they will probably go to a gallery or a museum. When you put art outside on the street people will encounter it differently. There is the element of surprise, and in the name of getting people's reaction this element carries some potential.

> I wanted to meet people on the street who haven't put on their 'culture glasses', who weren't prepared to encounter the art
>
> (Johan[2])

When putting art on the street, the art becomes available in the sense that people are not expected to comment on it, as they might be in a gallery. When art appears on the street it can, consequently, be described as a democratized form of art, available and free of charge. From another point of view it is however anything but free of charge. Graffiti is not, as previously discussed, entirely available, and for the untrained eye sometimes almost impossible to decode. But, as expressed by the participants, it is not always a matter of making the spectators understand or like what they see. Rather the participants express how they do it to 'tease' people (Peter, 41) or to be a 'provocateur' (Oscar, 23). Consequently, doing what the participants do is, as with other kinds of art, a matter of creating difference and affects.

Outro

In this chapter, I have suggested that *writing graffiti* can be considered *performing a spatial and aesthetic politics*. In terms of urban communication, aesthetic and space 'becoming-graffiti' is fundamentally subversive and exterior. Because of its in-betweenness, I have suggested *'the writer'* be regarded a *performative situation*. 'The writer' clearly challenges the urban hegemony, both in terms of subverting formal state institutions through committing illegal acts and by aestheticizing the urban differently. This chapter has shown how almost mythical narratives work as re-enforcements of the idea that graffiti should be, and maybe needs to be, free in economic, spatial and/or aesthetic terms.

Graffiti challenges the idea of who can speak in public, urban spaces and who has access to them. Connected to the ideal of freedom, the participants voice the concern that the contemporary urban only is available to commercial powers, placing graffiti as a subversive, anticapitalistic performance that presents visual diversity to the urban. Through these subversive acts, graffiti consequently creates in-between spaces through deterritorializing dominant communication, spatiality and aesthetization, in and of the urban. It is in-between through its simultaneous invisible/visible (non)communicative character; ephemeral, fluid, and mobile place makings; renegotiations of urban aesthetic and situationally determined becomings.

Further considering the in-betweennesses of graffiti from the point of Deleuze and Guattari, graffiti put in a gallery could be regarded as deterritorialized (i.e. recreating the meanings of graffiti and putting it into a striated space). On the other hand, considering graffiti's central character of war machine and exteriority articulated in this chapter, completely disciplining graffiti seems virtually impossible. Graffiti has and needs to have the creative and, as expressed by one participant, sometimes violent force of a war machine for it to be graffiti. This exteriority is what creates ruptures and in-between potentials in the urban through, in the words of Deleuze and Guattari, changing and displacing struggle. The in-betweennesses are thus simultaneously fluid, mobile, situationally determined, and created forcefully.

Graffiti is a noisy sound *in*, what the participants describe as, urban silence. It is uncomfortable, provoking and teasing. This character of exteriority is, accordingly, part of what fundamentally makes graffiti into graffiti. It is this intervening exteriority that exposes politicizations of urban space and creates in-betweennesses where political struggles and reimaginings of the urban become possible.

Notes

1 Graffiti is sometimes described as 'art on the street' and thereby used synonymously with 'street art', as in Andersson (2006). I would however argue that street art is a phenomenon separate from graffiti, both as discursive formation, as noted by Kimvall (2014), and in terms of aesthetic and communicative objectives (see Thor, forthcoming).
2 Age unknown.

References

Almqvist, B., & Hagelin, E. (2005). *Writers United : Historien om WUFC - Ett svenskt graffiticrew: The Story About WUFC - A Swedish Graffiti Crew*. (M. Thomson, Trans.). Årsta: Dokument.

Amin, A., & Thrift, N. (2002). *Cities: Reimagining the Urban*. Malden: Polity.

Andersson, C. (2006). *Rådjur och raketer: Gatukonst som estetisk produktion och kreativ praktik i det offentliga rummet*. Stockholm: HLS förlag.

Benjamin, W. (1999). *The Arcades Project*. (R. Tiedemann, Ed., H. Eiland & K. McLaughlin, Trans.). Cambridge, MA; Belknap Press.

Braidotti, R. (2011). *Nomadic Theory: The Portable Rosi Braidotti*. New York; Columbia University Press.

Castleman, C. (1982). *Getting Up: Subway Graffiti in New York*. Cambridge, MA: MIT Press.

Conquergood, D. (2013). *Cultural Struggles : Performance, Ethnography, Praxis*. (E. P. Johnson, Ed.). Ann Arbor: University of Michigan Press.

Cooper, M., & Chalfant, H. (1984). *Subway Art*. London: Thames & Hudson.

Debord, G. (1987). *Society of the Spectacle*. (K. Knabb, Trans.). London: Rebel Press.

de Certeau, M. (1984). *The Practice of Everyday Life. Vol. 1, The Practice of Everyday Life*. Berkeley: University of California Press.

Deleuze, G., & Guattari, F. (1986). *Nomadology: The War Machine*. Edinburgh : AK Press.

Deleuze, G., & Guattari, F. (2013). *A Thousand Plateaus: Capitalism and Schizophrenia*. London: Bloomsbury Academic.

Denzin, N. K. (2013). *Interpretive Autoethnography* (2nd edition). Los Angeles: SAGE Publications, Inc.

Dodge, M., & Kitchin, R. (2006, March). *Exposing the Secret City: Urban Exploration as 'Space Hacking'*. Geography Departmental Seminar.

Douglas, M. (2002). *Purity and Danger: An Analysis of Concept of Pollution and Taboo*. London: Routledge.

García Canclini, N. (1995). *Hybrid Cultures [Elektronisk resurs] Strategies for Entering and Leaving Modernity*. Minneapolis, MN: University of Minnesota Press.

Harvey, D. (2008). The right to the city. *New Left Review*, 53: 23–40.

Jacobson, M., & Barenthin Lindblad, T. (2003). *Overground: 9 nordiska graffitimålare: 9 Scandinavian Graffiti Writers*. (M. Thomson, Trans.). Stockholm: Dokument.

Kimvall, J. (2014). *The G-word: Virtuosity and Violation, Negotiating and Transforming Graffiti*. Årsta: Dokument Press.

Kusenbach, M. (2003). Street phenomenology the go-along as ethnographic research tool. *Ethnography*, 4(3): 455–485.

Lefebvre, H. (1991). *Critique of Everyday Life. Vol. 1, Introduction*. London: Verso.

Lefebvre, H. (1996). *Writings on Cities*. (E. Kofman & E. Lebas, Trans.). Cambridge, MA: Blackwell.

Macdonald, N. (2001). *The Graffiti Subculture: Youth, Masculinity and Identity*. London and New York, Basingstoke: Palgrave.

Massey, D. B. (2005). *For Space*. London: SAGE.

The History of Location Production in San Diego

While San Diego's most memorable starring roles include the movies *Some Like It Hot* (1959), *Top Gun* (1986) and perhaps *Anchorman* (2004), it is depicted far more frequently in television shows and movies. The rise of San Diego as a television production centre can be traced to the San Diego Film Commission established by Mayor Pete Wilson in 1974 in response to the city's loss of the ABC television series *HarryO*. *HarryO* was the first television series to be fully filmed in San Diego. While the series ran on ABC from 1974 to 1976, it left San Diego for Long Beach after only 13 weeks of shooting; its tenure was cut short by cost overruns induced by political red tape and a union rule of that era requiring all extras for the show be drawn from Los Angeles (Hellman, 1981). Mayor Wilson saw the departure of *HarryO* as a lost opportunity and created the film commission to help lure productions to and keep productions in San Diego.

The late 1970s and early 1980s brought a few feature films to the area, most notably *Scavenger Hunt* (1979) with Tony Randall and Roddy McDowell and *The Stunt Man* (1980) with Peter O'Toole and Barbara Hershey. For the most part, San Diego remained an occasional site for film and television production with projects coming to shoot individual scenes or establishing shots of local icons (Sea World, The Zoo, Del Coronado Hotel, etc.) and then heading back to Los Angeles for a majority of the project. In 1980, the CBS television series, *Simon and Simon*, came to film in San Diego where the narrative was set. Just like *Harry-O* before it, however, *Simon and Simon* was forced to move to Los Angeles after its first year of production due to high costs. Whereas *Harry-O* changed its narrative so that the show would reflect a private eye working in Los Angeles, *Simon and Simon* retained San Diego as its narrative setting. Thus, though *Simon and Simon* maintained a longstanding set on the 3rd floor of the Keating Building in downtown (Figure 8.1), the entire production was not based in San Diego. As Anderson (1998), the Film Commissioner at the time explains, '[The script] read here, they came here, but they did not live and work here'.

1970s–1980s: Identity Conflict of a Not-Quite Cinematic City

From these anecdotes, we start to see that San Diego became a cinematic city not because it was economically advantageous for productions to do so, but because the city actively marketed itself as such. San Diego, like many other cities, has sought economic development via film production by making the claim that it is can 'double' for other locations around the United States and the world rather than for its ability to 'play' itself in the movies. The downside of promoting a location

136 Chris Lukinbeal and Laura Sharp

Figure 8.1 The Keating building. (Picture by Bernard Gagnon, wikimedia.org.)

in such a manner is that San Diego has to fight to retain its cinematic status and valuation within Hollywood's film industry. In the 1980s, for example, San Diego battled against 'nondescript California' to retain its image as the backdrop for *Simon and Simon*. The city ultimately lost this fight when Kim Lemasters, a CBS program executive, deemed San Diego not 'sexy' enough and accused it of lacking in the 'cinematic values' that viewers would find desirable (Boyer, 1982: 1). Anderson (2000), the former Film Commissioner for San Diego, explains the problem thus,

> I think we all know that San Francisco, New York, Paris, a lot of cities have a specific character to their design and you can just look at their skyline and look at a picture without seeing it and know, all of us know it without ever having traveled [there], we just identify a *very specific look to the city*. I don't think San Diego, and I know that some people will differ with me on this, but I think *San Diego doesn't have a specific look* as far as movie people and storytelling goes. It can look like a lot of different places which means it has diversity, that's what is good business-wise for us in the film industry.
> [emphasis added]

Because so few films are written to play San Diego, Anderson (2005) later argued, 'writers have a hard time identifying what we are as a location and how that connects to the storyline'. This is the disadvantage of selling a location as 'anywhere' because *anywhere else* can come along with better financial incentives and take the next production away.

However, San Diego has played itself in some movies and television shows. Hosting one of the largest Naval bases in the United States, San Diego often plays itself in military narratives like *Gomer Pyle* (1964–1969), *The Boys in Company C* (1978), *Top Gun* (1986) and *Antwone Fisher* (2002) (Figure 8.2). The hippie meets disco beach culture of the 1970s plays prominently in films like *Almost Famous* (2000) and *Anchorman 1 and 2* (2004, 2013). In 2000, Steven Soderbergh directed the Oscar-winning film *Traffic,* which focussed on San Diego's role in the illegal drug trade between Mexico and the US. Finally, detective series like *Simon and Simon* (1981–1989) and *Harry-O* (just the first season in 1974) used the streets of San Diego as their setting.

Figure 8.2 Jim Nabors (right) and Frank Sutton (left) in *Gomer Pyle,* which premiered in 1964. (Picture from public domain, wikimedia.org.)

The 1990s: Becoming Televisual

In 1991, San Diego's future as a cinematic city began to look up when the city's first independent production facility, Stu Segall Productions, established itself at 4705 Ruffin Road in the Kearney Mesa neighbourhood. As of 2016, Stu Segall Productions was one of the largest independent film and television production studios in the United States consisting of 10 sound stages on a 20-acre backlot. Stu Segall specializes in television production and has produced over 1,000 hours of primetime television series. With an annual budget of over $50 million dollars, according to Anderson Stu Segall has 'helped put the city on the map for television and movie production' and 'pumped $700 million into the local economy and created hundreds of jobs since his studio opened in 1991'. Stu Segall Productions became so busy that they created the Studio Diner just outside the studio to provide employees with a place to eat. In 1998, Stu Segall Productions' opened Baja Norte Studios in Tijuana, Mexico, and focussed on the production of Spanish-language television shows.

The fact that San Diego was the third largest producer of television shows in the nation during the 1990s is directly related to Stu Segall Productions (Lukinbeal, 1998, 2004). Television series, more than any other type of film production (features, television movies, commercials), offer the most stable, long-term investment for a regional economy. While television series often have limited budgets in comparison to blockbuster feature films, they have much longer shooting schedules that enable employees to expect and retain work for an extended period. Segall's first television series, *Silk Stalkings* (1991–1998), was perhaps its most stable and long-lasting show. While big stars were occasionally flown in from Los Angeles, most of the 'below the line' labour, or all the employees on a production crew other than the stars, director, screenwriter and producer, were hired locally. Furthermore, up until 2003, Stu Segall used nonunionized employees to keep television productions costs down (McCurdy, 2005).

Stu Segall Productions has a typical annual production cycle: shooting television series during the fall and winter and shooting television movies and feature films during the summer. The continuous nature of television production promotes the establishment of regional infrastructure and a skilled labour force that can help spur further industrial agglomeration. When Segall first moved to San Diego, he took over a refrigerator warehouse. If you were to drive down Ruffin Road, you'd hardly notice its presence, but as McCurdy (2014) explains, this operation has grown into a 'studio system. He has created his own studio system. ... I mean when you walk on his property now ... it's like being on the backlot'.

The studio's presence in the area encouraged further studio development. While film production services are located throughout San Diego County, the industrial centre of film production is in the Kearney Mesa area, with *Stu Segall Productions* on Ruffin Road, *Western Video* on Watson Road, *Multi-Image* and *Four Square Productions* on Complex Drive and the independent television station, KUSI, on Viewridge Avenue. Anderson (2000) suggests that the close proximity to the city of San Diego's auxiliary airport, Montgomery Field, also plays a role in the location of this industrial centre in Kearney Mesa. The airport allows film companies to fly in helicopters and light planes with special stars and actors. Located near the middle of the metropolitan area along major freeway arterials, the industrial centre has easy access and limited travel time to location-production (or on-location) sites.

Situating San Diego within North America's Film Production Market

In a series of papers, Storper and Christopherson (1985, 1987; Christopherson and Storper, 1986, 1989; Storper, 1989; Christopherson, 1996) described the North American film production industry as consisting of developed centres (New York City and Los Angeles), second-order centres, edge centres and occasional sites. They based their analysis on the changes occurring in the film industry from the 1950s through the 1980s as the industry transitioned from a Fordist production model to one based on flexible specialization. Under Fordism production was done by vertically integrated companies under one roof and if needed that company would send a crew to shoot on location for creative reasons. The shift between Fordism and flexible specialization occurred when companies were vertically disintegrated, with parts of their business such as their extensive real estate holdings used for backlots, were sold off, before being reintegrated into mammoth multinational entertainment corporations (Lukinbeal, 2002). Vital to the optimization of profits under flexible specialization was a reliance on the decentralization of production. Decentralization allowed the industry to become more flexible regarding how different projects were put together via a mixing of major film studios (the majors), major independent producers (mini-majors), other independent productions and specialized subcontractors within a single project or as needed for a project. It became more specialized regarding the different kinds of services that subcontracted firms provided within the process of a production. While the developed centres (Los Angeles and New York City) are the focus of the North American film industry, other types of centres and sites now compete for the 'variable flow of production', or those productions that rely on financing from developed centres but are produced elsewhere because they can be made cheaper (Lukinbeal, 2004: 311). According to Lukinbeal (2004: 311), the variable flow of production 'refers to the effect of flexible specialization on the location market. That is, with flexible specialization, locations outside of Los

Angeles have to compete for a set number of productions' that are made outside of Los Angeles.

The economic logic of Storper and Christopherson's (1985) model explained the geography of film production in North American quite well at the time it was written; the model is now problematic and dated. What they could not have predicted was the rise of monetary incentive programs that dramatically increased the variable flow of production and quickened the pace of runaway production or those productions that leave developed production centres primarily for economic reasons though occasionally for aesthetic reasons (Monitor Company and the Screen Actors Guild, 1999). While developed centres and occasional sites are still relevant, the distinction between second-order centres and edge centres holds less value. Storper and Christopherson (1985) note that second-order centres are alternatives for production by major studios and are primarily focussed on the local or regional market of television and commercial production. In contrast, edge centres compete with second-order centres and occasional sites for the variable flow of production. Edge centres have the advantage, however, of being proximate to the developed centres, easing logistics and reducing transportation costs (Lukinbeal, 2004).

Situating San Diego

In the 1990s San Diego, Vancouver and North Carolina were the largest producers of television series and television movies outside of Los Angeles. Because of its tax incentives, a favourable exchange rate and the benefit of being in the same time zone as Los Angeles, Vancouver rose to stardom in the 1990s. In contrast, San Diego's level of production can primarily be attributed to Stu Segall Productions. Production data for the period of 1985 through 2005 from the San Diego Film Commission reveals that Stu Segall Productions accounted for 75% of all filmed activity, 98% of television shows, 41% of television movies and 5% of feature films.

Due to its proximity to Los Angeles, San Diego is more likely to get a higher percentage of occasional productions and second-unit productions that come to film for short periods of time and return to Los Angeles for postproduction work. In this market niche, San Diego competes for productions with other western centres like Vancouver and New Mexico, as well as with other markets that offer a generic beachscape (Los Angeles, Florida and Hawaii). Proximity to Los Angeles is both positive and negative. As Anderson (2005), the San Diego Film Commissioner, suggests, 'through the eyes of the camera San Diego looks a lot like Los Angeles'. Because the look of a place plays a large role in site selection, this means that there must be a significant reason for a producer to want to film in San Diego rather than Los Angeles. Compounding this problem is that, although it is closer to Los Angeles than any other regional market, San Diego is outside of the film 'zone', a 30-mile radius centred on Beverly and La Cienega Boulevards in Los Angeles. This zone, established by an agreement in the 1960s of the International Theater and Stage Employees, the Screen Actor's Guild and the Teamsters, represents the area outside of which per diem has to be paid for six days of shooting, with Sundays off (Storper and Christopherson, 1985; Lukinbeal, 2004). The zone, therefore, limits the amount of time a Los Angeles-based crew will work in San Diego by adding costs that would otherwise not be accrued if the production stayed in Los Angeles. Because of this, a full union production that needs to shoot in San Diego will venture there for a set number of days and then return to Los Angeles to wrap up shooting and other production work.

Mr. Wrong (1996) provides a classic example of how a feature film with a full union crew will conduct its location production activity in San Diego. While the narrative for this feature takes place in San Diego, the film only shot two weeks on location and returned to Los Angeles for the final ten weeks of shooting. McCurdy (1998), the former Director of Features for the San Diego Film Commission, explains,

> that whole feature did not stay here. It was a full union crew, they were already paying hotel and per diem, so it was already an additional cost for them to bring the crew here. I could save them money on some level because there's no permit fee and we tried to get location fees at a very reasonable rate and it would save money compared to LA. But that project would not stay here for the full three months of filming because it was financially just not the right thing to do. So they came here for two weeks and then went back to LA, shot more on location in LA and then built their long-standing sets and did some stage work also.

Four Factors that Influence Where Filming Occurs

While a regional structure of production centres exists in North America, it does so only through the ongoing actions of individuals involved in the film industry. Within a regional production centre, individual actions and business decisions play a significant role in determining which locations will be filmed. When it comes to deciding where to film within a regional market, four items come into play: the production's budget, the locational looks afforded by a place, cooperation with those at the location and the personal preferences of those making the production. These four items constitute what it means when we reference a city as a backlot.

Production Budget

Perhaps the most important item in determining what locations are filmed and not filmed is the overall budget of a particular production. Most locations incur a cost to film, either in terms of a location fee for use or through insurance and security costs. Because of this, a production's budget plays a large role in the total number of sites used in a production. The locational needs of a feature film can differ quite substantially from a television series. In San Diego over the period of 1985 to 2005, the average number of locations used for television shows was five, eight for feature films and ten for television movies, which is considerably lower than a standard big-budget production filmed in Los Angeles, which can use over 50 locations per production. The reason television series do not use as many sites as movies is threefold: the duration of production is shorter, the budget constraints are greater and fewer sites are needed to fulfil the narrative requirements. However, we could not find a direct relationship among the type of production, the amount of money spent and the number of sites used. Television shows and movies have smaller crews than studio-based feature films and often use fee-free public locations or private property that does not require a large location fee.

A typical profile of TV movies and series, according to Anderson (2005), is that they are on a 'hurry/rush' schedule – 'they're into locations that are easier to get in and out of'. Often, local television productions will return to locations where they have had a favourable experience. On the other hand, with larger union-based feature films it's very expensive to move. McCurdy (2005) explains the expenses of moving base camp thus: 'How long does it take to travel from one space to another when you're a traveling circus?' With most productions, especially the large features, companies want to limit the number of moves by choosing versatile locations. Consequently, finding a location that can be depicted as a jail, a library and a museum all in one building, makes for a content producer. Locations that require a lot of 'dressing' or preparatory work will not be as desirable as those that require little preparation. In short, locations need to be easily accessible, versatile and low maintenance (Anderson, 2000).

Location's Look

Geographic diversity is a key factor in attracting filmmakers to a region. Site selection is a series of negotiations through which different individuals attempt to match the look of a script's narrative to a physical locational counterpart. Consequently, the first thing the commission does when a filmmaker is interested in San Diego is to ask for a script and come up with a series of locations that would be suitable for a narrative. McCurdy (1998) notes the most important element in the job is,

> the conversations we have with the producer and our awareness of trying to match the 'look.' In other words ... if the script calls for a police station I know that doesn't mean I go to the San Diego Police Department headquarters down on 13th street. I make recommendations that match the look of what is typically a government institutional building that I know is always accessible for filming. We can't go into the San Diego Police Department and film. Most often it is difficult to go into a business that is operating five days a week or, in that case, seven days a week. So if a script calls for a police station, exterior establishing shot, I will most often recommend the County Administration Building on Harbor Drive. Because the County is very film friendly, offers that as a location, public properties like that are fee-free locations, so we're already saving the producer a dollar amount, and it has that governmental look to it. So it matches the look, it's a budget consideration, and I know it's accessible. So that's a lot of what, what we do, I think matching the look is a crucial point because it doesn't have anything to do with the reality. (Figure 8.3)

Locations are catalogued by their look and accessibility to filming rather than by their actual function in everyday social practice. For example, the representation of a police station in cinematic space does not mean that a police station was used to produce that image. Filmmaking empties a location of its everyday narratives and functions and replaces them with fictional characters and storylines. Location production sites are created on a daily basis in San Diego, which in turn reproduces San Diego's cinematic

Figure 8.3 San Diego County Administration Building. Photograph: Chris Lukinbeal.

landscape. At each site, the absolute location is important primarily for business decisions and budgetary considerations. On the other hand, architectural characteristics, ambiance and a location's look are of primary importance in the production of cinematic space. The link between the material space and the space that appears on screen is established primarily through a site's sense of place or architectural characteristics.

Cooperation

Cooperation is a large part of what the film commission provides to the production industry. Cooperation refers to the amount of assistance a filmmaker can draw upon when filming on location. It can also refer to the ability of the film commission to resolve issues that arise during the production process. The lack of cooperation between the producers of *HarryO* and the City of San Diego led to the formation of the film commission. It could also be argued that it was mainly due to cooperation that San Diego has a large percentage of its current production. In the late 1980s, Stu Segall was looking for a location to set up a studio. Anderson (1998) explains, 'Stu was interested in Vancouver because he had an episodic TV show [*Silk Stalkings*] with a very tight budget'. Cathy put together a package that included location sites and buildings that could work as soundstages and even addressed personal concerns such as where good schools and houses were located. Of particular importance was that Cathy created a special permitting process for episodic television whereby Stu Segall could obtain permission to shoot at local properties in a single day. Because of this interaction, Stu Segall moved to San Diego rather than Vancouver.

While good cooperation between members of industry and the film commission encourages production, the commission must also cooperate with community and neighbourhood groups to address their concerns over filming. Community involvement in the site-selection process typically becomes an issue when a community experiences a high rate of filming, referred to as 'neighborhood burnout'. When this occurs, residents become annoyed with constantly seeing large semi-trucks blocking roadways and taking up parking. Film crews can also be noisy and disturb the everyday sense of place in a community. The communities in San Diego that have experienced high rates of film activity include the Gas Lamp Quarter, Mission Hills, Ocean Beach, Coronado, Rancho Santa Fe and La Jolla (Figure 8.4).

Personal Preference

In an industry as fluid and flexible as film production, all factors of site selection can be overridden by personal preferences. As a San Diego-based film producer Schlotter (1999) explains, 'when it comes to

Figure 8.4 Editorial about Overfilming in the La Jolla Neighbourhood. (*La Jolla Light*, May 18, 1995, editorial page.)

deciding where to shoot the most important factor is the producer's ego'. Schlotter claims that producers want to be the first to discover a place or property. At the other end of the spectrum, you can have location managers and scouts developing a repertoire of favourite places they know are easily accessed and where they have formed a good relationship with the property owners to ensure that they can keep filming there in the future. Thus, within a regional market, site selection can be significantly shaped by the personal preference of producers, location managers, scouts, communities and others. Sometimes the best planning, cooperation and budgetary incentives are overridden by personal preference:

> These are people we are working with, and sometimes the producer may spring something like, 'my family lives in Seattle, so we're going to go,' and throw everything else out even though you have everything working. There's something that is unscientific about a personal preference.
>
> (Anderson, 2005)

Personal preference can also refer to the effect that filming in isolated locations (i.e. locations far away from Los Angeles) can have on a film crew. For example, San Diego often competes with Florida for productions requiring beachscapes. McCurdy (2000) notes, 'I've seen it played both ways, I had the production leave Orlando and look for another city because they haven't had the best experience there because they're so isolated. When they're in Orlando, it's a matter of morale, and the crew's not happy. That's an important consideration'.

When it comes to filming on private property, a filmmaker must obtain permission to shoot at that site from the home or business owner. Homeowners typically receive financial compensation for the use of their property. While business owners also receive compensation, there are other considerations. Of all the private businesses filmed in San Diego, most (except hotels) are small business owners.[2] In general, it is easier to get permission to film at a small business rather than at large businesses like retail chain stores, discount warehouses, grocery chain stores and department stores. This is mainly because these larger businesses do not see the benefit of closing down for the day even if costs are covered because closure might impact their regular customer base (Maier, 1994). This means that representations of the service industry may have an undue emphasis on independent ownership and small locally run stores rather than on chain retail stores like Wal-Mart, Lucky, Sears, Montgomery Wards, etc.

Conclusion

In this chapter, we have examined the concept of city as backlot through the lens of on-location filming markets in North America and, more specifically, the role that San Diego plays within these markets. Using San Diego as an example of market forces, we first examined the history of film production in San Diego and showed how localized politics in the 1970s–1980s forced television series to leave San Diego for Los Angeles simply because it was too expensive to film in the city. However, with increased televisual production from the 1990s to present due to the rise of cable television, San Diego was able to capture a share of this production. This feat can primarily be attributed to Stu Segall Productions, which established one of the country's largest independent film and television studios in the Kearney Mesa neighbourhood of San Diego. Stu Segall Productions was able to overcome past political and economic barriers experienced by other television shows by (a) working with the San Diego Film Commission to create a fast and efficient film-permitting process and (b) establishing a studio that allowed for the agglomeration of a skilled labour force and infrastructure to support ongoing production. The relative location of the studio within San Diego also continues to play an important role for the production company because it is situated near a small airport (Montgomery Field) where 'above the line' people could be brought in quickly and with minimal disruption to their daily lives in Los Angeles.

Stu Segall Productions, like the De Laurentiis Company in Wilmington North Carolina and possibly other independent production companies in North American, fundamentally changed the location production market described by Storper and Christopherson in 1985 as constituting developed production centres, second-order centres, edge centres and occasional sites. Before the establishment of independent producers, film production was mainly done in Los Angeles and New York City with second-order centres producing regional televisual productions. Edge centres functioned as nearby places for first- and second-unit shooting by developed production centres. Occasional sites where just that: occasionally used because of the narrative needs of a script. With the increase in televisual productions in the 1990s, independent production companies like Stu Segall were well situated to take on this kind of work because they were *flexible* in terms of what they could produce and when they could produce it and *specialized* in terms of being well outfitted with a skilled labour base and infrastructural investment.

The beginning of what MacDonald (2011: 164) has called 'the race to the bottom' began in the late 1990s when Vancouver offered the earliest and lucrative tax incentives to lure film and television productions. In the early 2000s, if you turned on the television in the United States and wondered where a television show was filmed you could have simply guessed Vancouver and been right more often than not. Tax incentives fundamentally changed the location production industry as American states, Canadian Provinces and other countries began competing to be the next north, south, east or west Hollywood. The *variable flow of production* (Lukinbeal, 2004), or the amount of production that occurs outside of the developed centres in North America, has risen dramatically since the late 1990s. Just consider that in 2013 California tied for second with Canada for the total number of feature films produced from Hollywood funding. Who was number one that year? Louisiana, where film incentives included a 30% tax reduction on qualified local spending 'including the payroll for residents and nonresidents, and 5% additional for residents' payroll' (FilmLA, 2014: 9).

State subsidies for the products of transnational corporations present reasons for concern about 'market distortion' (Christopherson and Rightor, 2010: 349). Christopherson and Rightor (2010) point out that 'the broader economic impact of film subsidies have been carried out rarely, if ever' and that information to be able to do such studies are 'rarely, if ever, made publicly available'. They go on to point out that studies by state fiscal officers show that film tax incentives have a negative impact on a state's revenue and that there is an efficacy issue as to who pays for these incentives. Most filming and expenditures occur in major cities that reap the reward of the incentives while producing tax revenue deficits that have to be covered by all residents of the state. So it appears that Hollywood is in a new Golden Age of production, one in which 'the worldwide taxpayer-funded production financing 'gold rush' in entertainment media is still on' (Christopherson and Rightor, 2010: 349).

In addition to this economic framework, several ground-level factors affect which locations are filmed within a regional film market for a given production, which we sought to illuminate in the third section of this chapter. These factors include the production's budget, the issue of a location's look, the need for cooperation within film-production practices and finally how personal preference can influence and overthrow all site-selection decisions. A production's budget not only defines which location production market will be used but also affects the number of locations used and the distance those sites are from the production's home base. After these questions are dealt with, the location's look comes into play. Sites that have a versatility of looks add production value by enabling them to be used for different scenes in a narrative and thereby lowering production costs because a crew does not need to relocate as frequently during shooting. Nearly all regional location production markets will tout their versatility and ability to play 'anywhere USA', but this has become less of a selling point and more of an expectation. Cooperation can occur during a number of different transactions when filming on location occurs. In San Diego, and in most regional location production markets, cooperation among a producer, the local film commission, local skill based film production crews and people living in film-saturated neighbourhoods is crucial to the successful completion and revenue generation of a product. Personal preference refers to when a producer, or other 'above the line' talent, makes a request as to where filmmaking will occur.

Hollywood has become a globalized geographical menagerie driven by transnational corporations that create films subsidized by global citizens through tax rebates then sell these citizens a fictional glitz and glam to perpetuate these subsidies. While San Diego garnered a foothold in the industry via Stu Segall Productions, further agglomeration has not occurred, and the demise of the film commission in 2013 following city budget cuts is telling: while the sale of glamour may sometimes work, when it comes to budgeting a city's balance sheets, a working film commission is expendable. In an era of regional competition, San Diego has been fortunate to become the location of an independent production company. San Diego is not, however, trying to lure new filmmaking through the use of tax incentives that are being offered by many other cities and states.

Notes

1 The lead author served as an intern for the San Diego Film Commission between 1997 and 2000. Film commissions are significant sources of information about location production because they often function as a confluence

of industry personnel and the locations and location owners. The San Diego Film Commission acted as the liaison between the city, county and port district and anyone shooting a film in these areas. Coordination is necessary because in order to shoot on location, a permit for each location is required. This permit shows that the production company has insurance and security, is in compliance with regulations stipulated by the jurisdiction and is willing and able to mitigate any problems that arise. During his time as intern, Chris Lukinbeal reviewed all production notes surrounding past and current television shows and movies, created a digital database of locations, visited and photographed locations and attended several shoots. The four categories identified in this chapter – the production's budget; a location's look; cooperation between production crew and local industry workers and residents and personal preference of decision makers – arose from these daily practices and interviews with the film commissioners at that time and subsequently over the years. The film commissioners discussed in this chapter were chosen because they oversaw permitting for all television and feature films during the time of this research.

2 Hotels, especially the Hilton and Marriott, are used frequently as film sites. Unlike other large businesses, these locations can offer space for filming and still maintain their daily business activities.

References

Albrecht, D. (1993). Backlot America: The impact of film and television on architecture. In N. Covert (Ed.), *Architecture on Screen* (pp. xxi–xxv). Program for Art and Film, a joint venture of the Metropolitan Museum of Art and the J. Paul Getty Trust.

Anderson, C. (16 December 1998). *Personal Interview.* Former Film Commissioner/CEO, San Diego Film Commission.

Anderson, C. (10 July 2000). *Personal Interview.* Former Film Commissioner/CEO, San Diego Film Commission.

Anderson, C. (20 June 2005). *Personal Interview.* Former Film Commissioner/CEO, San Diego Film Commission.

Bordwell, D., Staiger, J., & Thompson, K. (1985). *The Classic Hollyzvood Cinema: Filmn Styles and Mode of Production to 1960.* London: Routledge and Kegan Paul.

Boyer, P. (August 18 1982). San Diego rises up against CBS. *Los Angeles Times* VI (Calendar), 1–6.

Buchmann, A., Moore, K., & Fisher, D. (2010). Experiencing film tourism: Authenticity and fellowship, *Annals of Tourism Research*, 37(1): 229–248.

Christopherson, S. (1996). Flexibility and adaptation in industrial relations: The exceptional case of the U.S. media entertainment industries. In Lois S. Gray & Ronald L. Seeber (Eds.), *Under the Stars: Essays on Labor Relations* (pp. 86–113). Cornell University Press: Ithaca.

Christopherson, S., & Storper, M. (1986). The city as studio; the World as Back Lot: The impact of vertical disintegration on the location of the Motion Picture Industry. *Environment and Planning D: Society and Space*, 4: 305–320.

Christopherson, S., & Storper, M. (1989). The effects of flexible specialization on industrial politics and the labor market: The motion picture industry. *Industrial and Labor Relations Review*, 42(3): 331–347.

Christopherson, Susan. And Rightor, Ned. 2010. The Creative Economy as "Big Business": Evaluating State Strategies to Lure Filmmakers. *Journal or Planning Education and Research* 29(3): 336–352.

Clarke, D. (1997). *The Cinematic City*. New York: Routledge.

FilmLA. (2014). *Feature Film Production Report*. www.filmla.com/data_reports.php. Last accessed 7/21/2016.

Fletchall, A., Lukinbeal, C., & McHugh, K. (2012). *Place, Television and the Real Orange County*. Stuttgart: Steiner-Verlag.

Hellman, M. (1981). *Television in San Diego*. The San Diego Union Tribune, 9/20/1981, section E-1.

Kim, S. (2012). Audience involvement and film tourism experiences: Emotional places, emotion experiences. *Tourism Management*, 33: 387–396.

Lukinbeal, C. (1998). Reel-to-real urban geographies: The top five cinematic cities in North America. *California Geographer*, 38: 64–77.

Lukinbeal, C. (2002). Teaching historical geographies of American film production. *Journal of Geography*, 101: 250–260.

Lukinbeal, C. (2004). The rise of regional film production centers in North America, 1984–1997. *GeoJournal*, 59 (4): 307–321.

Lukinbeal, C. (2012). On location filming in San Diego County from 1985–2005: How a cinematic landscape is formed through incorporative tasks and represented through mapped inscriptions. *Annals of the Association of American Geographers*, 102(1): 171–190.

MacDonald, A. 2011. Down the Rabbit Hole: The Madness of State Film Incentives as a "Solution" to Runaway Production. *University of Pennsylvania Journal of Business Law* 14(1): 85–165.

Maier, R. (1994). *Location Scouting and Management Handbook: Television, Film Still Photography*. Boston: Focal Press.

Matthews, V. (2010). Set appeal: Film space and urban redevelopment. *Social and Cultural Geography*, 11(2): 171–190.

McCurdy, K. (16 December 1998). *Personal Interview*. Former Director of Features, San Diego Film Commission.

McCurdy, K. (10 July 2000). *Personal Interview*. Former Director of Features, San Diego Film Commission.

McCurdy, K. (20 June 2005). *Personal Interview*. Former Director of Features, San Diego Film Commission.

McCurdy, K. (12 June 2014). *Personal Interview*. Former Director of Features, San Diego Film Commission.

Miller, T., Covil, N., McMurria, J., Maxwell, R., & Wang, T. (2005). *Global Hollywood 2*. London: BFI Publishing.

Monitor Company and the Public Affairs Coalition of the Alliance of Motion Picture and Television Producers. (1994). *The Economic Impact of Motion Picture, Television and Commercial Production in California*.

Monitor Company and the Screen Actor's Guild. (1999). *U.S. Runaway Film and Television Production Study Report*. www.sag.com/releases.html#DGA/SAG.

Nevada Film Office. (2016). www.nevadafilm.com/.

Rybczynski, W. (1995). *City Life: Urban Expectations in a New World*. New York: Scribner.

Schlotter, W. (March, 1999). *Personal interview with this San Diego based film producer and former director of the San Diego Film Commission.*

Shiel, M., & Fitzmaurice, T. (Eds.) (2001) *Cinema and the City: Film and Urban Societies in a Global Context.* Oxford: Blackwell Publishers.

Sorkin, M. (1992). *Variations on a Theme Park: The New American City and the End of Public Space*, New York: Hill and Wang.

Stenger, J. (2001). Return to Oz: The Hollywood redevelopment project, or film history as urban renewal. In M. Shiel & T. Fitzmaurice (Eds.), *Cinema and the City: Film and Urban Societies in Urban Contexts* (pp. 59–72). Oxford: Blackwell Publishing.

Storper, M. (1989). The transition to flexible specialization in the US film industry: External economies, the division of labour, and the crossing of industrial divides. *Cambridge Journal of Economics*, 13, 273–305.

Storper, M., & Christopherson, S. (1985). *The Changing Organization and Location of the Motion Picture Industry.* Research Report R854, Graduate School of Architecture and Urban Planning, University of California, Los Angeles.

Storper, M., & Christopherson, S. (1987). Flexible specialization and regional industrial agglomeration: The case of the US. motion picture industry. *Annals of the Association of American Geographers*, 77(1): 104–117.

Symon, E. V., & Gianopoulos, A. (2016). *5 Tricks You Learn Finding Background Locations for Movies.* Retrieved May 1, 2016, from www.cracked.com/personal-experiences-1988-im-location-scout-breaking-bad-better-call-saul.html.

Widmer, R. March (1999). *Personal Interview.* Former Director of Commercials at the San Diego Film Commission.

9 Unimaginable Homes
Negotiating Ageism through Media Use

Kristian Møller and Maja Klausen

Introduction

The mediatization of culture and society has a profound impact on later life. As societies are ageing (Wilson, 2001) older people now constitute the fastest growing group in the population of developed societies. In combination herewith, older people are the fastest growing segment of Internet users as well as users of social media and smartphones (Eurostat, 2015). The proliferation of digital media technologies thus affects how the elderly person experiences, structures and gives meaning to everyday life. Older people structure and live postretirement life with and in media in a variety of ways and face different types of age-related economic, social and/or cultural exclusion while doing so (Givskov and Deuze, 2016: 2). Within research on ageing and information and communications technologies (ICTs) there has been a call to 'gray the cyborgs' (Joyce and Mamo, 2006) and concepts such as 'silver surfers' (Choudrie, Grey, and Tsitsianis, 2010) and 'technogenarians' (Joyce and Loe, 2010) point to a field of research that combines gerontological questions, that is questions regarding ageing and old age, with investigations of how media and technologies influence and potentially transform both life in the third and fourth age and hegemonic representations and discourses about the process of ageing and old age. Therefore, as technologies play an increasing role in the everyday life experience of the senior person, there is a growing need for research that examines how elderly people amplify, reappropriate or resist cultural assumptions about old age in their everyday life with media.

With the analyses put forth in this chapter we wish to grasp the complex and diverse ways in which the elderly person's life with technology takes shape in order to centre the diversity in the lived experience of older people in new media environments, as called for by Givskov and Deuze (2016: 2; see also Higgs and Gilleard, 2006; Higgs and Formosa, 2013). In doing so we contribute to and place the study of nonnormative lives within the growing fields geomediatization studies (Fast, Jansson, Tesfahuney, Ryan Bengtsson and Lindell, this volume) and media gerontology.

Unimaginable Homes 153

We ask: how do elderly people practice their mediatized homes? Which roles do media play in constituting and disturbing the *flows of bodies* into the home? We understand flows of bodies as the continuous introduction of outside others into the mediatized home space of the elderly person. Moreover: how do dominant categorizations of elderly media users intersect with and shape the home-making practices of different groups of marginalized elderly? We answer these questions by looking at two marginalized groups: elderly who are disenfranchised and live alone and elderly who are sexually minorities living in nonmonogamous relationships.

The chapter opens with a brief presentation of our empirical material, method and analytical strategy. We then present the theoretical framing of the homes of 'in-between' identities, which draws from the fields of critical mediatization theory and cultural gerontology and employs a critical approach to and definition of intimacy. Within this framework, we present both the chapter's notion of home as permeated by flows of bodies, as well as the categories of ageing ('silver surfer' and 'the daddy') with which our participants are confronted when using media. The following analysis falls into two parts: first, we explore flows of bodies in the mediatized homes of our two participant groups. We look at how feelings of dependence relate to hook-up app use and the experience of depending on so-called 'warm experts'[1] when using media. Second, we analyse how the categories of the 'silver surfer' and the 'daddy' shape media use, call out the ageing body and participate in the making of the mediatized home space. We conclude by returning to the research questions and making explicit how researching flows of bodies that in many ways inhabit homes of the in-between contributes to both gerontological and geomediatization research agendas.

Two Intersections of Ageing, Sexuality and Relationship Status

The empirical material consists of semistructured and ethnographic interviews (Spradley, 1979) with six participants. Three of them represent gay male relationships of men in their 50s and 60s, all with relatively high media competences. Out of the other three participants, two female and one male, the one woman has lived alone for many years after her mother, with whom she resided, passed away. She has never lived with a spouse or partner. The other two are widowed from straight relationships. The two women have low media competences and the man's is relatively low. All three of these participants have low incomes (live on their pension) and reside in subsidized housing complexes in the southwest of Copenhagen, an area marked by high unemployment rates and relatively low living standards. Names and other identifying details are changed in order to protect the participants' privacy. The interviews with the gay men were conducted by Kristian Møller from January to March 2014, and the interviews with the straight men and women by Maja Klausen from October to December 2016. All of the participants are white.

The gay participants are markedly younger than the straight participants. We do not approach experiences of aging and ageism as clearly comparable from person to person, but rather as meaningful in relation to the cultures and identities in which age-marked bodies are involved. Research has shown that gay men more often than straight men are marked as old.[2] While our gay participants are relatively young, in their 50s, they are still to a large degree affected by ageing discourse. Generally, we take an intersectional (Lykke, 2003) approach to aging and ageism, which requires that we understand the way age is made meaningful in relation to a number of other power symmetries, such as race, gender and sexuality. The degree to which age serves as something one orients oneself towards and the meanings that are assigned to age are thus not universal, but must be interrogated in relation to the intersecting identity positions available to the subject. In this chapter, intersections of sexuality and relationship status are explored.

The participants Dennis (50) and Jeff (50) are Brits living together in Copenhagen. They have a nonmonogamous relationship and use computer-mediated-communication (CMC), particularly hook-up apps, to establish contacts with gay men with whom they have sex separately. This is relatively new to them, and Dennis (with whom the interview was performed) has recently gone through a phase of learning and adapting to the social codes of hook-up app use.

Finn (62) and Tom (61) are Brits living together outside Brighton, UK. They have a nonmonogamous relationship. They are both technologically adept, especially Tom who for many years has used CMC to establish and maintain relationships with gay men around the world, sometimes including sex. Their media biography is exemplified by Tom's already engaging in video chat around 2000 using the ICQ application. During the interview, a number of hook-up apps (Grindr, Scruff, Growlr), a dating website (bear411.com) and communication services (ICQ, Skype) are mentioned.

Berit (77) lives alone in her flat in the south-west of Copenhagen. Her husband passed away seven years ago. In her life as a widow, she has taken over the financial part of the housekeeping formerly done by her husband. She has a son who in the role of a 'warm expert' assists her in computer- and smartphone-related matters. Berit's son has given her an iPad and taught her its essential use: amongst other things how to transfer money and pay bills online. Using her iPad and smartphone, the latter also a gift from her son, is accompanied by unease as she feels unsafe about which information could be accessed by a third party. Berit's media biography is thus to a large extend written through her relation to her son as a warm expert.

This is also the case with the other female participant, Maren (84). She has never been married or lived with a partner/spouse. She lives in the flat in which she was born; she has lived there alone, since her mother passed away many years ago. A niece has given her a used computer, but Maren prefers to keep it stowed away in a closet when not being used. She uses it only for online banking purposes. A range of different warm experts have helped her with the computer, amongst others a nephew and Kitt, who is employed by the local community centre and runs the 'IT-hjaelpen' (the IT-help), where anyone can book a session of one and a half hours for free and receive private IT-support. Maren talks about the frustrations related to using the computer and her dependence on warm experts in order to be able to perform simple tasks.

Kurt (83) lives in an allotment shed he built himself in the south-west of Copenhagen. His wife passed away several years ago. Kurt has had many different jobs, including janitor and taxi driver. In the beginning of the '80s he owned a second-hand bookshop with his wife, and in the late '80s he bought his first computer as he wanted to do the accounting himself. He taught himself to use the computer and has become a warm expert amongst his elderly friends and neighbours. During the interview, he mentions computer software, problems with his two partially functioning smartphones and the 3G network and talks about how he keeps his computer virus free.

Homes and Identities of the In-Between

The chapter brings together materials that reflect vastly different experiences of ageing and belonging in relation to both the *mediatized homes* and the *identity categories* available to persons marked as old. This facilitates an analysis of how hegemony privileges and casts out different body-technology assemblages.

'Home' is in everyday as well as academic understandings often associated with a sense of safety, rootedness, joy, privacy, togetherness, recognition and control (Zingmark, Norberg, and Sandman, 1995). With regards to media and the home, domestication theory marks the home as a source of ontological security, something the introduction of digital and mobile media disrupts in new ways. Within mediatization theory, recognizing the *mobilization* of computer mediated communication among intimates, it has been argued that the home is 'more than ever an important signifier of media technologies and their implications for society' (Peil and Röser, 2014: 234). While media respond to the mobilization of communication practices and the new perforations of the home *space*, less attention has been given to the normative structures that are ascribed to the concept of 'the home' itself. Recent work by Jansson (2015, 2016) seems to respond to such blind spots in the mediatization framework. Jansson uses Williams' work to clarify that his critical mediatization theory acknowledges the operation of hegemonic and counter-hegemonic 'structures of feeling' in any given mediatized area of life (2015, 2016: 14). The homes we examine are in many ways spaces of the in-between, as their multidimensional materialities are configured in a landscape that does not readily accommodate them.

A home space is always already practiced, permeated and disturbed by bodies. Drawing from domestication theory, we centre media as significant in the material and symbolic construction of the home. From a geomediatization perspective (Fast et al., 2017), we examine homes as *experiences of belonging* (Møller and Nebeling Petersen, 2017) deeply dependent on media. Thus, we look at how the experience of belonging is negotiated through flows of bodies in relation to both media as objects and media as environments. However, in taking a critical approach, we explore how flows of bodies are integral to different kinds of homes, including those that do not conform to the ideal of the perfectly bounded space privileged through heteronormativity. Such homes are often cast as without capacity for intimacy. This particular attention is drawn from Berlant's work on intimacy (see Berlant, 1998; Berlant and Warner, 1998) that understands intimacy as the affective modus through which certain kinds of closeness are naturalized. Intimacy is an affective force with which normalization occurs, with very real consequences for those 'outside intimacy':

> only one plot counts as 'life' (first comes love, then...)? Those who don't or can't find their way in that story—the queers, the single, the something else—can become so easily unimaginable, even often to themselves.
>
> (Berlant, 1998: 286)

Berlant succinctly expresses how ideas of intimacy are served up as 'plot points' or scripts for how a life can be lived in a socially imaginable or acceptable way. As will be shown, our research participants are on the verge of being imaginable within hegemonic scripts of home making.

In the second part of the analysis, the marginalized home making of our participants is further explored by examining which identity categories are (un)available to their age-marked bodies. How are these categories navigated? How do media participate in this? Cultural gerontologists criticize the neoliberal paradigm of 'successful ageing' (Katz, 2001), a paradigm that serves as a counterpart to the decline discourses depicting old people as frail, technologically illiterate and dependent (Loe, 2010). Successful ageing portrays old people as fit, health-conscious and agile consumers. While such a representation allows for a more optimistic depiction of old age than that of decline, it has also been criticized for reinforcing a dichotomy between 'good ageing' and 'bad ageing' (Holstein, 2011: 235) and thus imposing new norms that discipline older bodies in particular ways. In the vein of cultural gerontology, we examine these conflicting 'bipolar' cultural imageries through which many old people negotiate their social identities.

In relation to ageing and media use, we examine the 'plot point' expressed in the notions of the 'silver surfer' and 'the daddy'. In our heterogeneous empirical material, both categories hover over the aged-marked bodies with their different promises of making them imaginable to hegemony. They both serve as figures in relation to which the ageing of the subject is measured. Thus, both operate in direct relation to the successful ageing discourse. The silver surfer is culturally constructed as an 'object of desire' (Berlant, 2006), a cluster or category of potentialities to be pursued and performed by the subject. Within gay culture, the ageing man can become an object of desire through the 'daddy' figure, which is a sexual category that fetishizes the aged body subject. The analysis section 'Silver Surfers and Daddies: Objects of Desire' will explore how media use navigates the available categories, ultimately producing a mediatized home space of the in-between.

Flows of Bodies in the Mediatized Home

Feeling Independent with and from Hook-up Apps

Both gay couples in the material are competent users of the hook-up apps that facilitate how warm bodies for friendship and sex become available. These media competences are central to their relationships and homes, as their nonmonogamous relationships require such a flow to feel right. They leverage their media competences in different ways to control which bodies are included into their mediatized home. This difference is reflected in various notions of independence, which we will now unpack.

To Dennis, the separation of sex from the relationship with his partner has made him acutely aware of how independence and sociality are interrelated for him:

> [I]t's only over the last 10 years I'm starting to get used to being on my own and being independent and things like that, because I'm always better around people than when I'm on my own.

Needing to find sex elsewhere threatens Dennis' sense of independence but also requires that he take on a social role that he craves. He needs to be able to become recognizable as a sexual subject online for him to get his sexual needs met. Initially he had problems with successfully establishing contacts online: 'I was nobody's flavour when I first started. I didn't get a hook up for, I think, the first three months'. Dennis experiences that he tends to speak in ways that are not rewarded in the communicative cultures of the hook-up apps he uses. In other words, he lacks the media competences it takes to become a sexual subject within this particular media framework. Sex is not part of the home sphere, as signalled by his saying that 'the rule is it doesn't get in the way of my partner's and my relationship'. In turn, the privacy of the home is dependent on their being able to become sexual subjects within a mediatized gay sex culture.

Dennis has low hook-up app competences, which he feels when interacting with potential sexual partners online. One hook-up app interaction in particular marks his ascent into sexual media literacy:

> He picked up on the fact that I was new, even though I was older he knew I haven't done this before. We actually joked about it afterwards, saying he 'popped my Grindr cherry' and that sort of thing.

His lack of competences is remedied by simply interacting with people more adept than he. Dennis takes on the role of the enterprising self and eventually understands and is able to use the coded and condensed chat language, exemplified in his use of smileys with a sex partner to signal sexual intent: 'I know what the winky smiley means now. …He would just winky smile, means he's up for it'.

While Dennis and his partner must be able to use hook-up apps individually, Finn and Tom use digital media together, in order to forge emotional ties with others. This is clear from the way they talk about a neighbour who is in the 'nearby' section of the hook-up app with whom they chat everyday:

> We send voice messages to one another … He gets worried if he doesn't hear from us by a certain time as we do the same with him. We always say 'good morning' to each other and we always say 'good night'. …

Through this they 'draw in' the neighbour to their sense of home, with variations in his availability becoming a source of both joy and anxiety. His mediated body flows into the home space and becomes a meaningful body to which joy and anxiety are attached, in other words, it is domesticated.

On a practical level, Tom and Finn pool their resources. Reflecting a traditional specialization of competences within the home, Tom manages the apps and reaches out while Finn takes a backseat. On Tom 'chatting away on his phone and messaging like mad', Finn says: 'If I'm not happy about some of the conversation, I will tell him so if that person is not … as sincere as I think he should be'. Their sense of home is built not around a sense of independently developed skills to engage with a public, but to large extent on being able to sort out the people online who are 'insincere.' Independence to them comes from successfully managing the incoming flow of bodies from the hook-up apps in a way that makes sure that the potential friends and lovers are 'sincere'. Insincere others are those looking only for sex and gossip, something, Tom says that 'gays are very good at'. Such an independence script reflects that they are constructing a 'chosen family script' of caring, intimate others. The way they 'vet' subjects online to participate in their home is a practice historically contingent on the gay liberation movement's work to foster alternative kinship models for those excluded from the heteronormative home (Weston, 1991).

Dependence, Warm Experts and Stupid Machines

Maren has no children but has contact with nieces and nephews who all live in other parts of Denmark and abroad. She says that her nieces and nephews gave her one of their old computers a few years back. Meanwhile, she would have preferred not having 'that filth' in her home, despite actually having acquired some elementary media competences and occasionally uses the computer for online banking purposes. Talking about her earlier work life, Maren tells how those 'stupid machines' entered her work place, replacing face-to-face encounters and the opportunity to 'have a nice little talk over the phone' with co-workers. Moreover, having to use the computer in her work life made her feel as if she 'didn't really do anything: "We liked doing it manually much better. It gave us the impression that we really got something done"'. In her private life Maren has chosen to keep the computer offered to her making it part of her media repertoire. Maren's lacking media competences have put her into contact with a range of different warm experts. She tells of a nephew who taught her the essentials of online banking and continues:

> But he [the nephew] is dead and gone now. He helped me out in the beginning. But I have to admit, I only have Kitt to go to now. I also knew a young man who lived over there [pointing to the street]. He was an IT-man, but he simply doesn't have the time to help.

Maren has thus had to actively seek out and find access potential warm experts. This differs from Berit. While she also depends on a warm expert to manage her mediatized home space, she has a son to whom she always turns with computer-related problems. Berit finds that communicating digitally with authorities, which became mandatory in Denmark in 2014, is 'extremely confusing'; she feels 'safer' receiving mail from municipalities, hospitals, etc., by snail mail. She would prefer not having to ask for assistance and during the interview she came up with the idea of a 'digital care worker' assisting elderly with technology in their homes on a weekly basis: 'I do have a son, but he can't take over 100%. He has a job to do as well'.

It is in relation to this (changing) line of warm experts that Maren's and Berit's mediatized homes are assembled. The dependence of this home space on warm experts does not easily accommodate normative notions of homeliness and its close connections to independence and privacy. The warm expert is an outside other who provides a sense of safety, albeit a vague one, leading to a precarious set of media competencies. This perforated home space has the capacities to disturb and enable experiences of belonging for Maren and Berit: The loss of independence, i.e. the need for the assistance from warm experts when using digital technology, combined with having those 'stupid machines' as part of their material media home, disturbs the home as a resource of ontological security. However, through the warm experts, both women are enabled to appropriate technologies that makes their mediatized home space an ambiguous space of opportunity, marked by feelings of anxiety and inadequacy. This plays into Berlant's point about the contradictory desires marking the intimacy of daily life: 'people want to be both overwhelmed and omnipotent, caring and aggressive, known and incognito' (1998: 285). We see how these contradictory desires emerge through a body-technology assemblage that relates the body to a younger more media-competent body.

Silver Surfers and Daddies: Objects of Desire

Now we turn to the categories of the silver surfer and the daddy and explore how they function as objects of desire in different empirical cases. We explore how ageism works through these categories by supplying an ever-narrowing space of identification for age-marked bodies. Further we explore how media is integral to the navigation in this ageist landscape of opportunities.

The Silver Surfer

The notion of the silver surfer (Cody, Dunn, Hoppin, and Wendt, 1999; Choudrie et al., 2010) imagines the older media user as tech-savvy, playfully appropriating and exploring the potentials of media and the Internet. The silver surfer (the aged but technologically skilful subject) is in keeping with neoliberal ideas supporting individual entrepreneurialism and the 'enterprising of the self' (Foucault, 1994). In our context, the enterprising self is an ageing body subject who in an entrepreneurial manner has taken it upon himself to obtain and maintain the skills required for managing life as an individual within mediatized society. Rose (2006) underscores, according to Stage (2015: 113), how biopolitics today has come to centre a new and primarily individually managed focus on controlling and optimising the individual biology. Stage (2015) also points to this change and notes that health-management in neoliberal times has become an individual responsibility and that even the terminally ill in an entrepreneurial vein are expected to 'make the best of the situation' (Stage, 2015: 112). We view the silver surfer as part of this societal framework: As an object of desire it comes to discipline the old body, as the latter strives to age successfully by interacting (relatively) skilfully with digital technologies. In the following, focus is placed on how the participants are implicitly interpellated through the image of the silver surfer and how it works as an object of desire disciplining the subject.

Occasionally Berit uses the iPad to read about antiquities, a hobby of hers, or to look up health-related issues and possible side effects from her prescribed medicine. When her son gave Berit the iPad, he told her: 'You have to get at it, mum', since she at that point still had not used the Internet. Berit continues: 'I'm thinking: Oh no! Oh no! Oh no! I didn't want to do this at all. Not at all'. Moreover, Berit is encouraged to simply 'play' with the iPad by her son:

> Then he says… Well, when something strange pops up [on the iPad], I tell him I can't remember how I got there, and then he just says: 'No, but now you just sit and play with it, mum, then it'll be fine, you'll see'. He just says: 'now you just sit and play with it, mum'.

'Playing' with technology, however, is not a mode of appropriation available to Berit, as she finds it challenging to use and is nervous about causing irreparable damage by 'clicking' on notifications, etc. In this sense, communication with her son interpellates Berit through the hegemonic ideals linked to the category of the silver surfer. This also is the case for Maren. During the interview with Maren talks about when she was offered an old computer by a couple of her nieces and nephews:

> Because they wanted me to write down on this computer… about my parents and the family background. And I did not do this. … Well, a little bit, but not much. Because it doesn't interest me at all. But now I have been given it. … I use it for online banking only.

Digital technology has thus found its way underhandedly into Maren's home. Implicated in this offering was a script denoting her younger relatives' imagined use on her behalf: That she would enjoy writing down the family's history on the computer. This script affords a positive attitude towards (digital) technology as well as a desire to use it for more than necessities.

Returning to Berit, it is assumed that she naturally has a desire to 'get at it'; to master the technology and use it in her everyday life. In the slipstream of the successful ageing discourse, opting out of a life with and through digital technologies and the possibilities commonly associated with the Internet, comes to be associated with neglect and thus with a (nonacceptable) acceptance of the decline linked to growing old in the competing discourse. We thus hold that successful ageing problematically implies the individual's pursuance of not only good health but also good media competences. Media then become a potential framework reinforcing antiageing discourses as well as the dichotomy of 'good' vs 'bad ageing'. Accordingly, media use becomes yet another arena wherein the old body can either shine or fail.

Since Kurt bought his first computer in the late '80s, he has tried to keep up and maintain his media competences. He enjoys helping other elderly people with computer-related problems and calls them his 'students'. He tells how he helped one of those students file for a tax deduction online, a problem Kitt couldn't solve: 'Kitt couldn't handle that, but I could'. And later in the interview:

KURT: And then every time Anette has problems she just gives me a ring and says: 'It's [the computer] doing this and this. What do I do?' Then I just tell her which buttons to click and turn on and off. It's because it hasn't read the programmes right.
INTERVIEWER: So you give her a hand with computer-related problems?
KURT: Oh yes. I also do that with one who's living out here, who's called Frits. [...] Lives right down there [pointing]. And when he has problems with something he just drops by. And then that's done with.
INTERVIEWER: Are there anyone else who helps out like that?
KURT: No, it's primarily me...
INTERVIEWER: How often does someone drop by?
KURT: Well, very often...
INTERVIEWER: Ok. Are you happy about... this role?
KURT: Well, yes, yes I am. It's very nice to have company.

Kurt has become a warm expert in his neighbourhood. He enjoys that his media competences allow his mediatized home space to be perforated and turned into a node in a network of other (aged) bodies and technologies. Kurt's media biography, how he taught himself to use a computer and his role as a warm expert, play into his ideas about home and how he practises his mediatized home space. This space is practised through and around his digital technologies (his *Medion* computer, that he bought in the discount supermarket *Aldi* and his two partially functioning smartphones (see Figure 9.1)) as well as through the affective meetings amongst bodies and technologies. Moreover, the use of these technologies is described by Kurt, as effortless: 'And then that's done with'. Kurt's sense of independence in relation to media use and the key role this plays during the interview, where he also

Figure 9.1 Kurt with His Two Smartphones (one in butterfly cover). Photographed by Maja Klausen.

shows his computer and some of its antivirus software, is important, because it confirms the aged, but technologically skilful, body as an object of desire. However, as an ideal born within the successful ageing discourse, the silver surfer category operates through privileging not only a certain set of media competences but also a certain lifestyle and economy available to the middle classes and up. Accordingly, this category is only partially within reach for Kurt; He may have some of the competences required, but his lifestyle and economy are not compatible with these ideals. In this manner, he only accommodates the silver surfer category partially; he is in a marginal position between 'good' and 'bad' ageing.

Daddy Figures

In gay (online) sex culture the notion of 'tribes' provides a complex set of sexualized identifications that go well beyond simple sexual positions of 'top' and 'bottom'. In hook-up apps, targeted gay men are reproduced and configured in different ways (see Figure 9.2). The user can mark his interest in one or more of these, mark himself as inhabiting a figure and

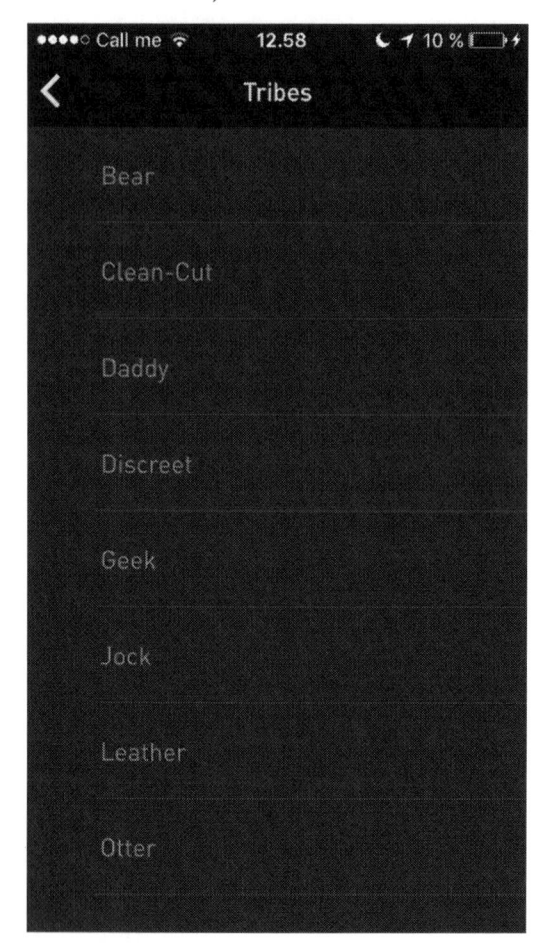

Figure 9.2 Screenshot of Subset of the 'Tribes' Available in the Grindr App Interface, Including Bear and Daddy.

search for other. Each tribe centres on a set of characteristics relating to a number of factors, for example, body composition, amount of hair, sexual roles, fetishes and, in this context most interestingly, age. While a number of categories are not available to bodies that are socially marked as old (for example, 'twink', a young, thin, man with only little body hair) some do accommodate ageing (such as 'bear', a hairy, heavy-set and normatively masculine man). 'Daddy' is another tribe that draws on the hegemonic daddy-son relationship that the 'daddy' figure plays on and sexualizes into an authoritarian and caring relationship between a younger and an older gay man. Thus, taking on or inhabiting the 'daddy' figure is a way for the aged body to become an object of desire, in a way that centres and sexualizes certain kinds of ageing.

Unimaginable Homes 165

At first, Dennis spoke about the daddy and bear categories as being unavailable to him: 'I don't fit a certain look, that is generally in the gay community called a "daddy" or a "bear". I'm neither one or the other. So I have a tendency not to get anyone'. Here the tribes are implicitly ageist, as those accommodating older men are not functional for him. Later, however, Dennis laments that he is 'being called a "daddy" all the time', and goes into details about the sexual attention he does get: 'There are people as young as 18 trying to hook up with me and I find that really disturbing, to be honest'. These movements speak to his ambivalence about the fact that in his early 50s he is construed and in turn fetishized as 'old' in the gay hook-up apps. This marking is a diminishing of sexual categories available to him, while it presents clear opportunities to become sexually imaginable in other ways. He has deeply ambivalent feelings about the age gap as a gateway to sexual encounters: 'there's something really depressing about picking them up at the playground. [laughs] But he's very charming, and he's a very nice boy…'. While ambivalent, Dennis chooses a pragmatic and opportunistic course by engaging with the 'boy' through the very specific set of opportunities that taking on the daddy category makes possible.

Finn and Tom also experience being marked as old in their hook-up app interactions. Tom tells: 'I've had people saying to me: "Oh, you're too old"'. He positions himself as not differentiating between 'age, colour, race, nothing' thus placing the ageism directed at him within a broader system of oppression that he opposes.

Finn and Tom bring up another 'daddy figure' as part of the problems, which they face when interacting in online gay spaces, namely that of the 'sugar daddy': 'A lot of young people seeing an older grey-bearded, greying-haired guy automatically think, "Oh, is that a wallet?" You know, a sugar daddy'. They feel the differentiation that comes from them being construed as old is wrong and reject what they experience as an invitation to monetize the emotional and sexual relationship to younger men. Here, the normative notion of successful ageing works to mark the older person as economically resourceful. This glimmer of opportunity is rejected, and one strategy to keep it from disturbing their sense of self and home is to be very cautious when anything remotely relating to money is brought up in chats with strangers online. Thus, when a man asks: 'Oh, what do you do for a living?' Tom answers with the vague and ambiguously hostile: 'I work hard.' Again, we see that the private sphere of trust is available to a certain subset of others, and is gate kept through careful vetting in order to make clear their intentions. Younger men's centring of their age results in Finn and Tom excluding them.

Both they and Dennis are uncomfortable with the specific and limited ways in which ageing bodies become imaginable subjects in the hook-up apps that they dependent on. But where Dennis engages with this range of opportunities and to a certain degree leverages them to become an object of desire, Finn and Tom reject these ageing figures. Dennis is deeply invested in becoming sexually imaginable in the perceived online community of hook-up apps, as his sense of home indirectly depends on this kind of independence. On the other hand, Finn and Tom have created a sense of home that is so disintegrated from the public sex cultures they face online that they are able to downright reject engaging with ageist discourse and subjection.

Conclusion

In this chapter, we have inverted the gaze from looking at the ageing body itself, and the capacities (or lack thereof) afforded it, and instead looked at the flows of bodies surrounding it. We have found that the mediatized homes of our participants are constructed in relation to flows of bodies introduced into the home either by way of media communication technologies or as warm experts providing assistance with such technologies. The potential of the media to build and disturb the home spaces is negotiated through flows of potentially sexualized bodies in the case of the coupled, gay men, or warm experts in the case of the disenfranchised men and women living alone.

Through this approach it has come into clear focus how age-marked bodies are subject to and must navigate a number of media-reinforced categories. We approach the research participants' sense of home as always already compromised, to better understand how the specific ways in which such disturbances operate and are controlled. Concretely we have located such disturbances in what we call 'flows of bodies'. With this analytical construct, we see how our research participants maintain a sense of home in the midst of quite intense flows of bodies entering their privatized home spaces, while at the same dealing with questions of independence and ageism.

In the second part we have explored how ageism works through the narrowing of categories available to the ageing subjects. Specifically our participants are confronted with expectations and (limited) possibilities of the 'silver surfer' for the one group and the 'daddy' category for the other. We find that these categories are positioned as objects of desire, or in other words, something the ageing person must negotiate to become imaginable. We explore how ageism works through these categories by supplying an ever-narrowing space of identification for age-marked bodies. Though these categories operate in different hegemonic spaces, we see that all of our research participants are subjected to them in different ways. A range of negotiations can be seen in both groups of participants: while some try to accommodate the categories and the ideals implied herein, others resist or use them in ambivalent ways, while others yet again are rejected entirely by the categories.

We have focussed on two spaces of the in-between that in different ways resist dominant categorizations. We see that age-marked lives are indeed lived in-between spaces that are arranged in ways that cannot accommodate them, thus making them unimaginable. As we draw from critical intimacy theory, we find the notions of public and private in many ways are impossible to keep separate. This in turn intensifies the precarity of the homes of our participants as they from the outset are marked as homes of the in-between.

By bringing together very different populations of age-marked bodies, we have shown how media participate in the distribution of scripts that work in relation to both hegemonic and counter-hegemonic cultures. In answering the question posed by Jansson: 'How does it feel to live with mediatization?' (2016: 15), we see above all how all of the participants acknowledge the indispensability of media in their lives and to different degrees take on the entrepreneurial role required of them. It is with ambivalence that they continue to construct their mediatized home spaces under precarious, age-related circumstances.

The new direction of geomediatization studies (Fast et al., this volume) opens a pathway for media scholars to engage with cultural gerontological questions regarding life on the margin, while supplying the latter with a framework for understanding how media participate in the construction of a (limited) space of opportunity for the elderly person.

Acknowledgements

Part of this research is funded by the Velux Foundations and is part of the project 'Ageing and old age in the media and elderly people's media use' led by Associate Professor Christa Lykke Christensen, University of Copenhagen.

Notes

1 The concept 'warm expert' is coined by Bakardjieva and describes 'a close friend or relative who possess relatively advanced knowledge of computer networks and personal familiarity with the novice user's situation and interests' (2011: 74).
2 Being marked as old is of course intimately tied to one's age, but research shows that the sex culture in which one participates explains profound variations in the valuation of ageing. Regarding the question of ageism being relevant to gay men younger than 65, it has been documented that most gay men in their 50s living with HIV/AIDS experience age-related stigma (Emlet, 2006: 781). It seems reasonable to assume that such stigma in some way operate across serostatuses. A study of online personal ads shows that men seeking men (MSM) are much more inclined to indicate an age preference than men seeking women (MSW) (Kaufman, 2003: 229). Further, both older and younger men are marked as preferred from people outside their age group. Thus, among MSM who are white (mirroring the ethnicity of this chapter's participant), those under the age of 30 are six times more likely to prefer older men; those over 40 are 2.5 times more likely to prefer younger men, than the MSW (Kaufman, 2003: 231). Thus, for gay men age simply

matters quite a lot, thus making it reasonable to assume that the question of ageism is relevant to people below the 65 age cut that is often used to delineate 'old age'.

References

Bakardjieva, M. (2011). The Internet in everyday life: Exploring the tenets and contributions of diverse approaches. *The Handbook of Internet Studies*, 11: 59–82.
Berlant, L. (1998). Intimacy: A special issue. *Critical Inquiry*, 24(2): 281–286.
Berlant, L. (2006). Cruel optimism. *Differences*, 17(3): 20–36.
Berlant, L., & Warner, M. (1998). Sex in public. *Critical Inquiry*, 24(2): 547.
Choudrie, J., Grey, S., & Tsitsianis, N. (2010). Evaluating the digital divide: the Silver Surfer's perspective. Electronic government, *An International Journal*, 7(2): 148–167.
Cody, M. J., Dunn, D., Hoppin, S., & Wendt, P. (1999). Silver surfers: Training and evaluating Internet use among older adult learners. *Communication Education*, 48(4): 269–286.
Emlet, C. A. (2006). You're awfully old to have this disease: Experiences of stigma and ageism in adults 50 years and older living with HIV/AIDS. *The Gerontologist*, 46(6): 781–790.
Eurostat (2015). *People in the EU-Statistics on an Ageing Society: Eurostat Publication.* Available at: http://goo.gl/0Fx8q3.
Fast, K., Jansson, A., Tesfahuney, M., Ryan Bengtsson, L., & Lindell, J. (2018). Introduction to geomedia studies. In K. Fast, A. Jansson, M. Tesfahuney, L. Ryan Bengtsson, & J. Lindell (Eds.), *Geomedia Studies; Spaces and Mobilities of Mediatized Worlds*. London: Routledge 2018.
Foucault, M. (1994). *Viljen til Viden. Seksualitetens historie 1.* Frederiksberg: Det lille forlag.
Givskov, C., & Deuze, M. (2016). Researching new media and social diversity in later life. *New Media & Society*, 1–14.
Higgs, P., & Formosa, M. (2013). The changing significance of social class in later life. In P. Higgs & M. Formosa (Eds.), *Social Class in Later Life* (pp. 169–182). Bristol, England: Policy Press.
Higgs, P., & Gilleard, C. (2006). Departing the margins: Social class and later life in a second modernity. *Journal of Sociology*, 42(3): 219–241.
Holstein, M. (2011). Cultural ideals, ethics, and agelessness: A critical perspective on the third age. In D. Carr & K. Komp (Eds.), *Gerontology in the Era of the Third Age* (pp. 225–243). New York: Springer.
Jansson, A. (2015). Using Bourdieu in critical mediatization research: communicational doxa and osmotic pressures in the field of UN organizations. *MedieKultur: Journal of Media and Communication Research*, 31(58): 13–29.
Jansson, A. (2016). Mediatization is Ordinary : A Cultural Materialist View of Mediatization. In *ICA conference* (pp. 1–31).
Joyce, K., & Loe, M. (2010). A sociological approach to ageing, technology and health. *Sociology of Health and Illness*, 32(2): 171–180.

Joyce, K., & Mamo, L. (2006). Graying the cyborg: New directions in feminist analyses of ageing, science and technology. In T. Calasanti & K. Slevin (Eds.), *Age Matters: Realigning Feminist Thinking.* New York: Routledge.

Kaufman, G. (2003). Is Ageism alive in date selection among men? Age requests among gay and straight men in Internet personal ads. *The Journal of Men's Studies*, 11: 225–235.

Katz, S. (2001). Growing older without aging? Positive aging, anti-ageism, and anti-aging. *Generations*, 25(4): 27.

Loe, M. (2010). Doing it my way: old women, technology and wellbeing. *Sociology of Health and Illness*, 32(2): 319–334.

Lykke, N. (2003). Intersektionalitet-ett användbart begrepp för genusforskningen? *Kvinnovetenskaplig tidskrift*, 1: 47–57.

Møller, K., & Nebeling Petersen, M. (2017). Bleeding boundaries: Domesticating gay hook-up apps. In R. Andreassen, K. Harrison, M. Nebeling, & T. Raun (Eds.), *New Media – New Intimacies: Connectivities, Relationalities, Proximities.* London: Routledge.

Peil, C., & Röser, J. (2014). The meaning of home in the context of digitization, mobilization and mediatization. In A. Hepp & F. Krotz (Eds.), *Mediatized Worlds.* Palgrave Macmillan.

Rose, N. (2006). *The Politics of Life: The Politics of Life Itself: Biomedicine, Power, and Subjectivity in the Twenty-First Century* (pp. 41–76). Princeton, NJ: Princeton University Press

Spradley, J. P. (1979). *The Ethnographic Interview.* Belmont: Wadsworth.

Stage, C. (2015). Sygdom på sociale medier. *K&K-Kultur og Klasse*, 43(120): 103–124.

Weston, K. (1991). *Families We Choose: Lesbians, Gays, Kinship.* New York: Columbia University Press.

Wilson, C. (2001). On the scale of global demographic convergence 1950–2000. *Population and Development Review*, 27(1): 155–171.

Zingmark, K., Norberg, A., & Sandman, P. O. (1995). The experience of being at home throughout the life span. Investigation of persons aged from 2 to 102. *The International Journal of Aging and Human Development*, 41(1): 47–62.

… Part III
Geomedia Mobilities

10 Mobilism in Translation
Putting a New Research Paradigm to the Test

Maren Hartmann

This chapter has two main aims: it first introduces a new theoretical concept – mobilism (a combination of mobilities and mobile media research) – and second, it aims to translate this concept into a possible empirical application. The example used for this translation process is media use in the context of homelessness. The starting point is the following combination of ideas or remarks from other studies: first, Emma Jackson's description of the homeless as 'fixed in mobility' (2012); second, Peter Adey's claim that 'to move is to be political' (2010: 131) and third Tim Cresswell's reminder that 'mobility was not invented by the mobile phone' (2012: 646). Taken together, they underline that there is mobility in homelessness, but also a tension to other kinds of mobilities. At the same time, this field is always embedded in questions of social inequality. However, anyone turning to media use to find answers to inequality needs be cautious. Equality was not invented by the mobile phone either. Overall, the chapter aims to show how this complex empirical (and moral) field offers interesting theoretical insights for the growing field of geomedia studies.

The Mobility/Mobilities Turn

The mobility (or rather mobilities) turn in the social sciences is not a new phenomenon. It was explicitly pronounced as such in the second half of this century's first decade, but some of the questions underlying the mobilities turn were already asked a few years prior. Hence, Scott Lash and John Urry stated already in 1994: 'modern society is a society on the move' (252). Urry followed this up with a claim for sociology beyond societies (2000) and later – together with Mimi Sheller – the often-cited call for a new mobilities paradigm (Sheller and Urry, 2006).[1] Hence the mobilities turn (Cresswell, 2011; Faist, 2013), as it has been called, is a call to question not only the development of the world, but also its academic treatment. This is partly a question of methods (Law and Urry, 2005) or, more appropriately, of mobile methods (Büscher and Urry, 2009).[2]

The main claim of the mobilities paradigm is, first, a quantitative shift to more movement, which is closely related to a perceptive shift. In the mobilities concept, physical movement,[3] its representations and (shared) meanings as well as its embodied practice come together (e.g. Cresswell, 2010, 2012). They are also historically specific. Immobilities – both forced and desired – are an intricate part of mobilities. A discussion of mobilities therefore always includes the question of the capacity for movement as well as 'the way in which entities access and appropriate the capacity for socio-spatial mobility according to their circumstances' (Kaufmann, Bergman, and Joye, 2004: 750). This capacity has been called motility (Kaufmann et al., 2004). There is hence a tension between mobility and immobility as well as between the capacity and the actuality of movement. Both these tensions hint at the fact that mobility is not equally distributed. Some aspects of social mobility are closely linked to the question of physical immobilities, especially in times when social status is increasingly related to the question of motility. As Doreen Massey stated some years ago: 'Differential mobility can weaken the leverage of the already weak' (1994: 150). However, communicative mobilities further complicate the field.

One particular area, in which yet another tension has come to the forefront – that between desired and forced mobilities in their diverse forms (as well as consequences) – is the field of transnationalism, migration and diaspora studies (e.g. Levitt and Jaworsky, 2007; Faist, Fauser, and Reisenauer, 2013), sometimes extended to cosmopolitan studies (e.g. Christensen and Jansson, 2015). The interaction between this academic field and the mobilities paradigm has only recently begun to become more widespread.[4] Faist (2013) additionally underlines that this potential cooperation needs additional work, especially with regard to uncovering the political assumptions around mobilities as well as the mechanisms of (re)production of inequalities. The related question of communication and media's role in relation to transnational/transcultural communication has also been widely discussed, opening yet more avenues through which to regard mobilities (e.g. Hepp, 2015), emphasizing, amongst others, the quality of such mobilities and assemblages (as well as their interruptions – see Georgiou, 2010: 17).

All of the above are reflected in Urry's definition of mobilities, which includes not only the corporeal travel of people and the physical movement of objects, but also virtual, communicative and imaginative travel (2007: 47). This emphasis on communication aspects underlines that mobility (or mobilities) is a concept that not only lends itself to be included in the core concepts of media and communication research, but that, vice versa, communication concepts should equally be included in its further conceptualization. A next step will therefore be to take some of the core concepts from mobile communication research and add them to the equation.

'Mobility was Not Invented by the Mobile Phone': Mobility and Media

Cresswell's above-mentioned remark that 'mobility was not invented by the mobile phone' (2012: 646) provides one of the best summaries of the relationship between mobility and media. Mobility is an old phenomenon – one that changes and transcends, one that has gained in importance and in quantity, but one that has always existed. The mobile phone, on the other hand, is still fairly new. The first mobile phone might have existed in laboratories and experimental fields in the 1970s (with the first mobile phone to go on sale in 1984), but it only became more widely used in the 1990s. Hence while the mobile phone has gone through radical changes since then (both in its communicative possibilities and in its uptake), it did not invent mobility. It has enhanced the possibility to communicate while on the move, which also implies that it is possible to work, to organize, to be entertained (or to entertain) and much more while moving. Thus, mobility has changed – as have the more sedentary aspects of life. The relationship between mobility and mobile media is an intricate one: mobile media actually sustain mobility, since all the aforementioned actions are now more easily doable in movement. At the same time, the general spread of digital, personalized media – which are often mobile media in terms the devices – allow certain fixities, since many things can now be done virtually that before would have afforded physical movement.

There is a clear interconnection between these phenomena: hence mobility is differently possible with mobile media (from the reliance on Google Maps to GPS-organized car rental services or an indication where wheelchair-friendly cafes can be found as well as the possibility to send mails while on the go), while mobile media become more complex (and potentially more interesting) when they are actually used in mobility, while they are indeed often used in non-or only marginally mobile situations as well.[5] In order to understand these contexts better, both mobility and mobile media research could learn from each other. All the more astonishing that for a long time, mobile media research did not explicitly address the question (and theory) of mobility while mobilities research has always mentioned mobile media (and included them in their research), but has nonetheless also tended to ignore many of the theoretical and empirical insights gained in mobile media research.[6] This is beginning to change (conferences like Geomedia or journals such as *Mobile media & communication* (MMC) are cases in point). As always, there are exceptions to the rule (notable exceptions include e.g. Morley, 2000; Hjorth, 2009, esp. chp. 2; Moores, 2012; Adey et al., 2013; Goggin and Hjorth, 2014; de Souza e Silva and Sheller, 2015a). Not surprisingly, however, the claim for a closer collaboration between the two fields has been stated quite clearly by prominent scholars in the field. Adriana de Souza e Silva and Sheller thus write:

> More importantly, it is no longer possible today to develop scholarship within mobility studies without being in dialogue with mobile communication and locative media scholars ... Mobile communication and locative media scholars will also benefit from incorporating mobilities theoretical frameworks in their approaches to studying mobile technologies, including a stronger spatial dimension. ...
> (de Souza e Silva and Sheller, 2015b: 6)

And in the same year Rowan Wilken and Gerard Goggin emphasize that 'the dynamic aspect of mobility' is increasingly important in research on portable media, since our 'everyday engagements' with these devices cannot be separated from our 'movement through space and time' (Wilken and Goggin, 2015: 7 – see discussion below). They further claim that (some) mobile media research helps to address questions of attentiveness, i.e. of our levels of engagement with the media as well as with our environment. This includes theorizing the body and its relationship with the technologies, i.e. expanding the understanding of a user (Wilken and Goggin, 2015). At the same, our understanding of the technologies needs to be broadened and, building on this, the above needs to be slightly differentiated. While many aspects of the devices are indeed embedded in movement through time and space, Hjorth's (2009) claim that the mobile phone is primarily a 'domestic technology', which might 'have physically left home', but nonetheless 'psychologically still resides and connects users to a sense of place and home', partly because 'ideas of locality (...) and place are still, if not more, enduring' (Hjorth, 2009: 59), still resonates. Plus, use takes place in rather stable environments (e.g. in the household). This already underlines that everydayness and dynamism are not congruent. This distinction between the ideas surrounding the technologies and their actual uses is very helpful. Nevertheless, as we have moved towards even-more personalized convergent and locative media, our notions of home and location have changed even more than before. Hence, these central theoretical building blocks necessarily need to be updated in the move towards a timely and appropriate research framework.

Let us briefly return to the question of motility. In some cases, mobile media enable mobilities; sometimes, however, they impose these. The same applies to fixities. An increasing mediatization of society also leads to these technologies becoming the norm. Staying in control of one's life increasingly implies the use of mobile media. If businesses and organisations, for example, are now beginning to implement rules as to when they are meant to be available online (or rather, when not – see recent legislation in France[7]), this is at the same time an indication of the widespread normalization (and expectation) of use. Nonuse as a general principle thereby becomes problematic, while a media diet is the privileged version of nonuse. Such aspects always apply even more to already marginalized populations, such as the homeless.

So far, then, the combination of mobile media and mobilities research has offered us a chance to readdress the question of space (particularly location and the notion of home) and movement in relation to mobile media use, while also emphasizing the importance of the body, the technologies (and services) and the question of shifting attentiveness. The latter in particular is embedded in the (potential) change of the social world that mobile media and their appropriations bring about. More specific concepts help to describe these changes further. While some of these concepts are not 'hot off the press', they nonetheless provide important insights, especially in their overlaps. What can be found here is an emphasis on the reorganization of social presence, one of humanity's fundamental social arrangement. While Kenneth Gergen labelled this shift the 'absent presence' (2002), Christian Licoppe called it the 'connected presence' (2004). The latter was taken one step further by Stephen Groening when he called it the 'connected isolation' (Groening, 2008). However, while Groening and Licoppe share a term, the overall assessment of the changes is shared more between Gergen and Groening.

Groening tries to show the embeddedness of such social processes in the wider social world rather than in technology. He underlines that while certain forms of communication are desired and enabled with mobile technologies, it also allows us to shield ourselves from other communication acts – those that we want less. In his view, this enables us to isolate ourselves from the unwanted while increasing the possibilities for those kinds of communication we want. Gergen's argument is similarly divided between the good and the bad – his division is along the lines of particular technologies, though (the other media vs the cellular phone). Gergen describes the absent presence as the 'diverted or divided consciousness invited by communication technology, and most particularly the mobile telephone' (2002: 227). He manages to develop a rather bleak and pessimistic assessment of the role of the media in and for the social (the absent presence as the downfall of our face-to-face communication culture) but then turns it around to hail the cellular phone as providing a totally different kind of absent presence that returns us to our traditional values (he uses these words). Licoppe, on the other hand, speaks of 'a continuous pattern of mediated interactions that combine into 'connected relationships', in which the boundaries between absence and presence eventually get blurred' (2004: 136). His account is less judgemental and focussed not so much on individual technologies, but rather on our interactions. This focus – plus the tension between two poles – is what characterizes the often-quoted notion of 'networked individualism', which was proclaimed the dominant social form by Rainie and

Wellman (2012). Overall, these concepts serve to show that bipolarities are less common, but rather that these poles appear in many different combinations and on scales that many users can easily use. The social is hence not disappearing but is experiencing massive differentiation.

The latter can also be seen in Joachim Höflich's work; he has shown in several different studies that these more complicated communication relationships afford new rules. His concept of the triadic communication relationship (2005, 2013), in which the social relationship ((wo)man – (wo)man) is extended to include either the machine or a virtual/absent (wo)man, is increasingly complicated. Overall, these shifts in social presence imply (or rather require) more reflexivity on the users' side but also lead to a change in social norms and expectations. Similarly, Ling (2008) outlined early on that digital media could be seen as an attempt to return to or rather recuperate earlier kinds of intimacies and thereby define these as community-enhancing technologies. He assigns the mobile phone or rather the therein-based interaction, for example, a high potential for intimacy and a high socioemotional value. Overall, these concepts underline the complex relationship between technology and the social but also underline that changes in communication have wider repercussions. Taking such conceptual hints from mobile media studies enrich the debates around mobilities.

'To Move Is to be Political'? Defining Mobilism

The concept that tries to bring together the above-mentioned frameworks is called 'mobilism'. This concept combines the aforementioned focus on mobilities with a focus on mobile media use and thereby provides a (new) perspective. Despite its emphasis on (mobile) media, mobilism follows and develops a non-media-centric view (cf. Morley, 2009).

As such, it should contribute to – rather than contradict – the mobilities paradigm. It carries certain ontological and epistemological assumptions and via these re-emphasises particular aspects in the existing framework. Next to combining these existing research strands then, the mobilism perspective adds a new emphasis on the need for both mobilisation and momentum for mobilities and motilities, thereby addressing the tension between change and stability in the social. This is similar to the emphasis on critical mobilities, i.e. those mobilities that interrupt current flows (Cresswell, 2014).[8] One could argue that through this move, the perspective begins to become an ideology or at least shows normative tendencies. However, as a perspective it rather aims at focussing the overall mobilities framework more clearly. In line with other criticisms (e.g. Fallov, Jørgensen, and Knudsen, 2013), this perspective aims at indicating the hindrances to mobilities more clearly, while underlining the differentiated nature of the developments of mobilities.

The (felt) need for the mobilism focus stems from certain observations:

a   Despite all differentiated and critical engagements with mobilities, the term itself implies a progression of sorts. Hence, the works engaging with the hindrances to mobilities (both on the social and more basic material level) often label themselves accordingly (such as the above-mentioned critical mobilities, the question of stillness, or so-called marginal mobilities). The active resistances, the alternatives and simply the more stable aspects in life or in human development as well as the interplay between change and stability are all highly important aspects of mobilities and often feature as such. The mobilism term, however, is meant to enable a move away from the add-on-terminology to include mobilities and immobilities in one term that is potentially less bipolar.
b   One subaspect emphasized in particular in the mobilism concept is the question of the beginning of movement, i.e. every individual or group needs to be motivated and/or mobilized in order to participate in mobilities (whether the mobilization is intrinsic or extrinsic). The mobilization applies to nonhuman aspects as well.
c   Similarly, the movement needs to continue, i.e. it needs to gain a certain momentum in order to become visible, leave traces, lead to somewhere or something. This momentum needs to be added to both definition and empirical projects.
d   Last, but not least, the question of the mediated and communicative nature of mobilities is central to the new framework (see above), always trying to follow a non-media-centric approach.

In the following, I will return to some of these aspects, but for reasons of clarity and length, by far not all. I will also briefly outline where the inspiration for the mobilism concept came from, i.e. the roots of the mobilism term and concept, in the next section. In the case study presented here, the fourth aspect – the communicative aspect of mobilities coupled with the question of motility and immobilities – will be focussed on.

The Term Mobilism

Mobilism stems from several sources, with more or less clear-cut inspirations. It combines geotectonics with theoretical input from history (France) and cultural theory (Japan) as well as more applied design theory (US-French). The term mobilism appears directly in three out of these four. Let me therefore begin with the least explicitly related: Fernand Braudel and his take on history.

Braudel has often been quoted for his criticism of historical research as being too focussed on the event rather than long-term, less prominent developments. He alternatively introduces the often-quoted term 'longue duree' (1995/1972) for those developments over time (in contrast to the event and mid-term history). He chose a particular region (the Mediterranean) to show how the environment (geography, geology, climate, etc.) especially plays a major role in how certain areas develop. This environmental emphasis is then further extended in relation to communication networks and the human development therein, but the emphasis is on the given structures. Hence history is clearly embedded in many other processes, some of which are easily changeable, others less so. The same 'caution' can be used in relation to assumptions concerning mobilities. These, too, are not equally spread, not equally adaptable or applicable to everyone and everywhere. Hence, aspects of Braudel's work help to emphasize these diversities in speeds of mobilities. These different speeds also imply differing directions of movement (and development). This clearly relates to other theories of speed (Virilio, 2007) and acceleration (Rosa, 2013). However, neither shares the emphasis on the longue duree, particularly in relation to material aspects and thereby also on developments that partly withstand the normalization of speed.

The aspect of directions is more clearly visible in the geotectonic reference. This refers the actual origin of the term 'mobilism'. Mobilism is part and result of a long-term debate in Earth science, also called the continental drift debate (for a summary of these developments see Frankel, 2012). At the heart of the controversy was Alfred Wegener, who began publishing on the topic in 1912. He claimed in his theory of the continental drift that the continents are not fixed (this is the basis for the opposite theory of fixism), but that they move on the Earth's surface (Frankel, 2012). He also claimed that today's continents emerged from one large one, which broke into smaller pieces. An important implication of his mobilism idea is that the continents are still moving today. One consequence of this development (which is now an accepted and further developed theory) is that these movements occur in different directions (drifting towards, pulling away from or rubbing against each other). This also has to do with the different materials that the Earth's parts consist of.

If I summarize this approach in lay terms, it indicates (a) that movement rather than a fixed state is the norm, (b) that this movement takes place in different directions and at different speeds (a relative stability is definitely one possible state therein, but not a standard) and (c) that these movements can cause frictions or more but also provide a potential for new developments. All of this is here taken as part of the basic understanding of mobilism in our context as well. Movement is taking place, but in different directions and at different speeds – which can be a cause for friction on all kinds of levels. While Braudel emphasizes the question of time and speed as well as the material conditions, the geotectonic notion of mobilism adds an emphasis on movement, on direction and friction.

How does this now relate to culture and/or communication? The link was made by two different people in the same period (2005–2006). Neither, however, seemed to know each other nor did they refer to geotectonic references (or Braudel for that matter). Both, however, used the term mobilism to refer to a similar phenomenon. In Japanese communication and media scholar Kenichi Fujimoto's research, the term mobilism is enriched through the addition of the term 'nagara', (while-doing-something-else), which 'refers to the state of multitasking separately, in parallel, and asynchronously while walking, moving, or playing' (2006: 80). Hence, multitasking in motion is one of the two aspects Fujimoto sees in combination, with mobilism emphasizing 'broader cultural and social dimensions such as malleability, fluctuation, and mobilization' (2006). Fujimoto uses this to differentiate mobilism from mobilities, which he declares to be much less bounded (by culture, geography, etc.). In contrast, I would like to develop mobilism as the wider framework that includes mobilities but opens up the array of their nature, their speed and direction. At the same time, Fujimoto's emphasis on the limits to these processes is an important one.

For Fujimoto, mobilism serves as the context within which the nagara development is embedded. This becomes clearer when we turn to Fujimoto's cultural reference to the legend of Sontoku (Kinjiro) Ninomiya (1787–1856), who he describes as a national role model. According to the legend, Sontoku Ninomiya read as a boy while collecting firewood, showing his eagerness for education. This reading-in-movement, according to Fujimoto, can be found again in young women's engagements with their mobile phones while walking (he sees it as a particular twist in history, however). This brief reference underlines the cultural embeddedness of actual developments, that are, however, rarely taken over in a straightforward and direct line. The phenomenon Fujimoto concretely refers to – young people's mobile phone culture in movement (in the late 1990s and early 2000s) – neatly combines mobility and mobile media use. At the same time, the mobilism framework as briefly outlined by Fujimoto additionally emphasizes similar aspects as Braudel and the Wegener reference have shown: there are historical-cultural forerunners that can (and should) be considered that influence the current cultural form. Additionally, Fujimoto emphasizes that developments take place at different speeds and in different directions.

Last but not least, the work of Eric Adigard, a French designer based in the US, further helps to add new aspects, while re-emphasizing those just mentioned. Adigard edited a visual essay on the theme of mobilism in 2005, which was a preliminary publication for his installation in the Lisbon Biennale later in the same year, which was entitled Catalysts! Engage. The resulting mobilism website (http://madxs.com/mobilism) first offered a mobile phone screen, which had three buttons: one for the aforementioned Biennale installation (The Culture of Engagement), one for M-A-D, the interdisciplinary design agency (m-a-d.com/about) of which Adigard is a part and one for a visual essay about 'ten thoughts on the desktop', which he wrote with John Alderman, a creative director and content strategist. The core for the here-developed mobilism-concept then is the installation at the Biennale, in which Adigard provides a brief but clear-cut definition of what mobilism stands for: 'Mobilism = (Mobile media + Mobilization) × Momentum' (2005).[9] This is more removed from the other emphases stated until now, albeit Fujimoto also mentioned mobilization (for him, however, mobilization primarily refers to movements with mobile in action in the streets in a 'quasi-military' style – 2006: 86). For Adigard, as far as one can tell from the small written piece in which this line is embedded, mobilization (next to the momentum) is a key aspect for mobile media's chance for impact. It basically signifies that media and ideas come together and are recognized.

I interpret the formula, taken with the other references already mentioned, to signify the importance of both particular moments and a certain wider recognition coming together, before mobilities and mobile media actually change something. Put differently, mobilism first implies a scepticism concerning any revolutionary rhetoric, while at the same time emphasizing that these processes can (and must) be helped along. They offer a notion of agency, while allowing the unpredictable to shine through. Sometimes, all the conditions seem right for mobilities to emerge, but they do not come together in recognizable movement (of people, ideas, things) in the end. Hence, there is a tension between the different ideas/concepts used here. If movement – however slow and potentially near stable it might be (see Braudel) and whatever traces of the past it might contain (see Fujimoto) – is the norm (see geotectonics), mobilization and momentum as triggers for social impact bring in a less 'automatic' aspect. What they help to ask, however, and to emphasize, is the visibility and therefore traceability (and copyability) of such movement. If we take Adigard (and actually 'tune him down' a bit), this is the additional emphasis provided.

With this brief turn to the momentum element that Adigard throws into the equation, a decision concerning the term momentum's usage becomes unavoidable. The original Latin term refers to the length of a movement, while in English, momentum refers to what in other languages is called the impulse. Physically, the impulse is the mechanical movement of a physical object. This movement, the momentum or impulse, is greater the faster and heavier something is. Colloquially, however, momentum refers to the right moment, to the impulse that might be over soon. Political movements, for example, need a certain momentum before they gather speed and the number of supporters increases so that the movement gains visibility and therefore possible impact. Mobile media themselves can sometimes provide the momentum for mobilities. This could be quite literally – as in the tendency to share (and compare) one's results from running apps, establishing a communicative culture around the use of the app and the related physical movement. While mobile media are not always as directly involved in the provision of a certain momentum, they are often an important element of the momentum in the mobilism 'formula'.

The latter now adds up to the following: mobilism as a concept combines mobilities with a (nonexclusionary) emphasis on mobile media, embedded in wider social and cultural contexts. It uses the question of mobilization (individual and collective) and momentum, to ask about the relationship to social mobility and the role of these and other kinds of hindrances/resistances to mobilities to overall address the question of the speed and direction of social change in relation to media change. One of the difficulties in this combination (apart from the number of aspects just mentioned) is that related cultural values are shifting (and need to be questioned), but this is a complex process. Hence when Cresswell states that 'in some ways, of course, the mobilities turn is a result of a dissatisfaction with the valorization of forms of stillness – rootedness and the sedentary' (2012: 648)[10] and mobilism begins to re-emphasize the importance of e.g. the sedentary for our understanding of the speed and direction of change, then the valorisation is an important, but never straightforward aspect. Important to understand is that here the valorisation given in discourses as well as quotidian actions needs to be understood – but not necessarily validated.

These numerous proclamations are of only theoretical substance as of yet. In order to begin to translate the concept into an empirically applicable one, I will try in the remaining pages to apply the proclaimed concept to a specific empirical field: media use of the homeless.

Translating a Concept

The chapter will now begin to define a possible application of the theoretical construct. In principle, this kind of application could be found in countless areas, applied to a great number of phenomena. The path chosen here, however, combines a version of 'marginal mobility' (Kalcic, Juntunen, and Rogelja, 2013) with (potentially) marginal mobile media usage. The term 'marginal' refers here to the homeless population in Berlin. They have been chosen because they provide a particular challenge for the question of mobilization and momentum and thereby help to assess how far the framework is actually applicable.[11] They are seen to provide an extreme within the possible array of mobile lives: they often combine social immobility and little communicative mobility (something to be explored) with a somewhat constant physical mobility (at least one with atypical moorings), often within a rather limited geographical area. This is also a combination of visibility and invisibility rarely found elsewhere (constantly watched, but not seen).

184 *Maren Hartmann*

Before we dive into this particular field, it should be stressed again that the focus on homelessness and (mobile) media use is only one of many possible 'translations' and that it will be necessary to cover several of these in the long run in order to see how far the mobilism construct holds and/or where it needs to be amended. For the time being, it is primarily a perspective and the work has been mostly theoretical.[12]

'Fixed in Mobility': Homelessness and Media Use

Homelessness is a hypermobile state of being, which at the same time often excludes many mobilities (not only but especially social mobilities). As Jackson (2012) put it so well, many homeless people are 'fixed in mobility', often actually moving less than other people (Parker and Dykema, 2013). They are also 'without abode', living a nonsedentarist lifestyle, thereby appearing more mobile.[13] While some have actively chosen to live this way, many would rather change this situation – or they are no longer in a state of articulating such wishes thanks to long histories of drug abuse, mental illness or similar states of being. The vast range of choice and nonchoice cannot be taken into account here; rather I side with a lot of the literature that assumes that homelessness is a social problem that can at least be lessened (in terms of numbers, but also simply in terms of the level of exclusion). One of the questions here is whether part of the solution (and only ever a part) can be the provision of and the explanation of digital and/or mobile media.

Why is homelessness a neverending topic? Homelessness (or rooflessness in particular)[14] is generally seen to represent the lowest end of deprivation. In a report on homelessness amongst migrating populations in Europe (European Commission, 2014), for example, the following differentiation was made: poverty is defined as referring primarily to material deprivation, while social exclusion adds nonparticipation to the equation. Destitution, according to this definition, is additionally characterized through limited control over one's life, while homelessness is seen to be the ultimate form of deprivation: next to the destitute state (material deprivation, nonparticipation, lack of control), the homeless are additionally lacking a roof over their heads.

This range of exclusion levels is similarly represented in Peter Somerville's differentiation between levels of security in the homeless population. Somerville actually explored the meaning of home in the context of homelessness (Somerville, 1992). Therein, he differentiated between physical, physiological, emotional, territorial, ontological, spatial and spiritual senses of security (see Figure 10.1). While the ontological actually includes many aspects and can most easily be related to media use (see Hartmann, 2014), the differentiation of all of these senses of security helps to underline the networked and differentiated nature of deprivation. The media, as will be argued below, can strengthen some,

Key Signifier	General connotation	Sense of Security	In relation to: Self	In relation to: Others
Shelter	Materiality	Physical	Protection	Roofing
Hearth	Warmth	Physiological	Relaxation	Homeliness
Heart	Love	Emotional	Happiness	Stability
Privacy	Control	Territorial	Possession	Exclusion
Roots	Source of Identity	Ontological	Sense	Reference
Abode	Place	Spatial	Rest	Living/Sleeping Space
Paradise	Ideality	Spiritual	Bliss	Non-existence

Figure 10.1 Taken from Somerville (1992: 533).

but by far not all, of these senses of security or aspects of deprivation as mentioned above (especially the nonparticipation and lack of control).

As Andreas Hepp, Peter Lunt and I have argued, exclusion is increasingly taking place on the level of the (non)participation in the communicative construction of reality (2015). This can be seen in the analyses of media images of the homeless, for example, which underlines how much homelessness is also a discursive and therefore a cultural-communicative construction (e.g. Pascale, 2005). In more positive terms, participation in the communicative construction of reality by the homeless can potentially be increased – and thereby their levels of deprivation lessened and the sense of security increased. A word of caution, however, is always necessary in order to avoid a naïve celebration of media technologies, because even digital inclusion can go hand in hand with social exclusion (see Bure, 2005).

Before we relate this back to our concept of mobilism, let me briefly outline where the hope for an increase in participation in the communicative construction stems from. The assumption is based mostly on existing research from the US and other places (Canada, Australia, UK), often on young homeless. Jill Woelfer and David Hendry, for example, suggest, that these young homeless not only organize their everyday lives on the street, but also explore identities and cultivate social ties (Woelfer and Henry, 2012). This supports the idea that networked media, especially mobile media, can in principle aid the homeless individuals 'to define and sustain their own ontological security wherever they happen to be' (Silverstone, 2006: 233), i.e. to build somewhat more stable (albeit always in process) identities and social bonds based thereon. This is particularly true for applications such as social network sites, as another study shows, which states that Facebook 'is a safe space for people experiencing homelessness to share their ideas', since 'no one can get in unless they're invited' (Yost, 2012: 25). This experience of being in control of how they are perceived by others is an extremely important one, since this lack of control is one of the aspects of deprivation experienced in homelessness (see above). It is also an important aspect, usually, of being housed: being able to decide who is let in and who is not. Hence, like nonhomeless youngsters, they connect with different peers online and offline as well as with their families and use 'social networking technology to access a variety of home and street-based social network ties' (Rice, Monro, Barman-Adhikari and Young, 2010). Hence, the action is similar but more unusual for this population, since it requires a much higher effort (Pollio, Batey, Bender, Ferguson and Thompson, 2013: 174). Access is often in public settings with limited time and resources.

An Australian study underlines other content aspects, i.e. the use of digital media for 'the avoidance of isolation, the reduction of boredom, to improve mental health, to reduce health and safety risks, and discover to exit points from homelessness and often, unemployment' (Goodwin-Smith and Myatt, 2013: 10). This study also emphasizes another important point: that even amongst the more connected homeless (in their study, all seventeen participants owned and used mobile phones), Internet access does not take place via the mobile phone. Not only do they not necessarily own a smartphone, but costs are much too high for this kind of use. Ian Goodwin-Smith and Susan Myatt therefore conclude that 'the financial risks linked to using mobile platforms as ICTs are largely prohibitive for homeless people' (2013); nonetheless, the Internet is critical (and mostly done through fixed access points where- and whenever possible, as stated above). In fact, as 'it is increasingly impossible to exit homelessness without accessing the internet, as public and private services increasingly require interaction with an electronic interface' (Goodwin-Smith and Myatt, 2013: 12), this kind of provision of access points to the Internet is seen to be as important as the possibility of owning and maintaining a mobile phone. The two serve different purposes but equally point to the normalization of mobile media use in public life.

Recent research on an Internet café for homeless people in Vienna underlines this even more clearly. This study suggests that the provision of a café environment with a holistic view on people (rather than a problem-focussed approach) provides through its open access to not only the digital technologies but also the social environment around them the necessary starting point for avoiding loneliness. The combination of the social and the educational is the basis of this project's success (Studeny, 2015). Hence, it is important to keep both access varieties – and the different forms of use and appropriation – in mind when designing a study and/or advising policy makers. Last, but not least, content and its presentation are rarely inclusive. Woelfer and Hendry, for example, point out that content needs to be made more suitable for the homeless population in terms of possibilities for pseudonymity, for differentiated identities, etc. (Woelfer and Hendry, 2012).

The ever-recurring emphasis on young people (e.g. Rice et al., 2010) should not be underestimated, since recent research on homeless people in Bremen (Germany) indicated that prior media-use patterns, i.e. biographical traces, are extremely important for the media-use patterns amongst the homeless (Knief, 2016). Research should always put the heterogeneity of 'the homeless' at the forefront. This obvious claim is insofar important, as speaking about homelessness is always already a moral act, often with normative claims about participation attached. The general call for self-reflexivity in (qualitative) research is doubly important in this context.

Overall, the above-mentioned results need to be read with caution. If it is increasingly impossible to exit homelessness without access to the Internet (at least in our Western cultures), this does not imply that access to the Internet guarantees an improvement of the situation, let outline exit options. Not only is the homeless population much too diverse for such assumptions; assuming too much power to any such technology or service has never proven to be correct, regardless of the particular context. Hence, Bure's above-mentioned early warning (Bure, 2005) about the difference between digital and social exclusion needs to be a guiding principle in any research on homelessness and media use. This is also (yet another warning) that the normalization of certain media uses often leaves few alternatives – and thereby reduces rather than expands some social fields, since this kind of mediatization is inescapable.

Despite all these limitations, we can begin to summarize the above to state that digital media, i.e. mobile media, but also Internet services, have a potentially positive role to play in the process of reducing exclusionary processes around homelessness. Access to and training for the use of surveillance-free (social) media accounts and other applications becomes necessary. As Hepp, Lunt and Hartmann argued, it is important to provide opportunities for the homeless to take on an active, constitutive role in communicative figurations (2015). This is an important step in including the homeless in the community – making them visible and audible again.

Returning to Mobilism

One might now ask how (and why) a future study on homelessness in media use, based on the existing studies presented above, should be seen to be a suitable case study for the mobilism concept and mobilism research (and what such study should entail in order to fulfil this role). Above, mobilism was defined as a concept that combines mobilities with a (nonexclusionary) emphasis on mobile media, embedded in wider social and cultural contexts, thereby addressing the question of the speed and direction of social change. Additional emphases include mobilization and momentum, social mobility and hindrances/resistances to mobilities. Especially these latter subconcepts underline the time aspect of mobilities (seen as processes). The geotectonic reference helps to emphasize the incremental and long-term nature of some developments. Taken with questions of motility and immobilities, this helps to introduce questions of the longer-term consequences, for example, of the aforementioned increasing normalization of mobilities and mobile media. Next to the long term, we also have immediate and fast kinds of developments and practices, the more ephemeral (Hartmann, 2016), which can be both applications and/or uses. Mobilism's ontological and epistemological stance includes an emphasis on the differential, unequal and/or graduated nature of mobilities. This relates well to the chosen case study.

Homeless media use is underresearched in Germany, wherefore any such study promises to at least fill a gap. Additionally, Germany (as do many other European countries) provides a rather different social setting and therefore also a different homeless population than those countries that have thus far researched the topic more extensively. Additionally, the opening of some Eastern European borders and the more recent refugee 'crisis' has changed the homeless population (and will continue to change it). This fact begins to also upset or challenge the theoretical underpinning of the research. Movements of people – partly forced, partly not – have provided a new basis for homelessness, but also a different emphasis on media use.[15] One can begin to see traces of recognition of media use as a basic human right, which implies that humanitarian aid will eventually have to include the provision thereof (UNHCR, 2016). While Internet access is increasingly common in homeless shelters in the US, it is fairly unusual to see it in the German context.[16]

These rather factual emphases might sound like answers, but they are actually questions to be posed under the umbrella of mobilism research. The homeless definitely offer a chance to study mobilities, embedded in wider social and cultural contexts (see definition above). Any study on the homeless and their (potential) media use should therefore add a mapping of these mobilities and connect these to the question of media use. Homeless mobilities are nonetheless not easily put into recognizable categories. Research indicates that the homeless actually physically move less than the rest of the population (Parker and Dykema, 2013), while other research points to the relational nature of their mobilities (Kaufman, 2016). High spatial constraints for the homeless' mobilities are often produced in and through sociocultural relations such as stigmatization (Jocoy and Del Casino, 2010). Hence, while the assumption is that the (visibly) homeless represent mobility simply through their rooflessness, this somewhat naïve assumption is based on exactly the before-mentioned valorisation of the sedentary (and the perceived contrast of the sedentary and the moving) that homelessness helps to reconsider. The question-marks outweigh the answers for the time being, especially when these mobilities are combined with media use.

While we started with an emphasis on mobile media – again a somewhat logical step when thinking around mobilities – this has now necessarily broadened to include other kinds of access points and fixed-media uses (see above). This automatically helps to address the question of inclusion and exclusion (and thereby also social mobility as well as hindrances and resistances to mobilities) and the core question of the speed and direction of social change. The mobile media studies' perspective helps to address the question of personalization of media but also asks whether concepts such as the triadic communication relationships, networked individualism and/or connected presence actually play out here in similar or different ways than they do elsewhere. What are the appropriation (domestication) processes taking place in these highly de-personalized and somewhat fragile environments?

So far, most mobilism aspects seem to be relevant for the empirical case (and often seem to gain an extra perspective). The emphases on mobilization and momentum, however, are still not addressed. Again, the empirical case does not lend itself to any easy application or straightforward answer (in fact, it might turn out that these aspects are not core to the mobilism definition after all). The immediate question is who is mobilized – and for what? While research in this field might indeed need to be experimental (e.g. offering access and services to people who were not yet connected and exploring how far usage occurs (and makes sense)), it then becomes interventionist. This again implies at least a certain form of mobilization (mobilizing the research subjects to experiment; mobilizing them to participate). Whether this translates into a momentum that reaches beyond the methodological questions to a more fundamental engagement remains to be seen. Overall, however, mobilism is yet a fragile concept with quite a few question marks attached. It lends itself to study the relationship among homeless, media use and all kinds of movements – and I hope opens up new emphases in geomedia research and mobilities.

Notes

1 If we were to map the influences that shaped the mobilities paradigm, they would be few and far between: theorists and theories such as Simmel, ANT, STS or complexity theory; concepts such as motility or embodiment and wider movements such as social network research, emotional geographies or the spatial all fed into the new paradigm turn (cf. Sheller and Urry, 2006; Urry, 2007).
2 Similar to Cresswell who states that 'a mobile subject demands a mobile method' (2012: 647), the other authors try to develop ways to acknowledge the fluid, the mobile, the sometimes invisible in the research methods at hand.

3 Creswell emphasizes that new bodily mobilities were emerging at the beginning of the 20th century. These include dance, sport, youth movements, etc. (2012: 646).
4 See below for a brief discussion of the relationship between media and communciation studies and the mobilities field.
5 Let us briefly consider, for example, the laptop used at home: this is often moved between the living room and other rooms or maybe used in bed. Other domestic media already allowed such minimal movements (telephones with an extension cord, portable cassette players or radios), while some were usually more stable. The perception of portability has, however, come to the forefront of discourses surrounding these technologies. At the same time, these minimal movements are not exemplary of the rest of the discourse (of freedom, travel, etc.).
6 See e.g. Hannam, Sheller, and Urry (2006) for the limited references to existing studies in the field.
7 www.welt.de/wirtschaft/article160846376/Franzosen-haben-jetzt-das-Recht-auf-Abschalten.html.
8 Many of the predecessors to mobility theories seem to have started from a similar critical standpoint (e.g. Massey, 1994; Harvey, 2008).
9 In a later version, Adigard changed the definition to 'mobilism = mobile media + cultural globalism' (2006), with a footnote stating 'mobilism is the impetus of mobile devices and ideas when they share a single momentum'.
10 Nonetheless – or maybe exactly therefore – Cresswell introduced works on stillness, or on what sounds even more intriguing, 'still/stuck/stopped' (2012: 648).
11 The question of mobilization and momentum, however, is not the key focus in this paper. It will be addressed in subsequent publications. The focus here is more on the general questions of 'translateability' of theory into empirical work.
12 The project trajectory is a typical (?) story of many detours and failed attempts for funding that at the same time provide the basis for further focussing and re-evaluating the original ideas. The empirical focus on homelessness is currently under review (once again) as part of a larger research project.
13 The term lifestyle might sound cynical in this context, at the same time, many homeless chose a different lifestyle to others, i.e. they are clearly not all victims, longing for our kind of 'better life'.
14 The 'European Typology on Homelessness and Housing Exclusion' (ETHOS) differentiates between the roofless (living rough; staying in a night shelter), the houseless (living in accommodation for the homeless or in other kinds of supported accommodation (e.g. women's shelters; immigration accommodation)), the insecure (threat of eviction or violence), the inadequate (unfit housing, overcrowded housing, etc.) (www.feantsa.org/spip.php?article120&lang=en – retrieved on 15/09/2016).
15 Emerging research is beginning to underline the initial impressions that mobile media use is not only very widespread amongst refugees, but on several levels a lifesaving instrument (but also used to store memories, to find people, to translate, to find services, etc. – see e.g. UNHCR, 2016).
16 One exception can be found in a meeting place in Hannover, where media access is mentioned next to cooking and washing facilities: 'In unseren Tagestreffs werden Selbsthilfekräfte und Kontakte gefördert. Darüber hinaus bestehen Dusch-, Koch- und Waschmöglichkeiten zur Grundversorgung. Informationsmaterial und der Zugang zu Medien stehen zur Verfügung'. (www.diakonisches-werk-hannover.de/ueber-uns/abteilungen-ansprechpartner/zentrale-beratungsstelle-wohnungslosenhilfe/.)

References

Adey, P. (2010). *Mobility*. London: Routledge.
Adey, P. et al. (Eds.) (2013). *The Handbook of Mobilities*. London: Routledge.
Adigard, E. (2005). *The Culture of Engagement Exhibit*. Retrieved 14 Sep. 2016. http://madxs.com/mobilism/catalysts/index.html.
Adigard, E. (2006). *Mobilism*. Retrieved 14 Sep. 2016. http://slideplayer.com/slide/2558922/.
Braudel, F. (1995/1972). *The Mediterranean and the Mediterranean World in the Age of Philip II. Vol. 1*. Berkeley: University of California Press.
Büscher, M., & Urry, J. (2009). Mobile methods and the empirical. *European Journal of Social Theory*, 12(1): 99–116.
Bure, C. (2005). Digital inclusion without social inclusion: The consumption of information and communication technologies (ICTs) within homeless subculture in Scotland. *The Journal of Community Informatics*, 1(2): 116–133.
Christensen, M., & Jansson, A. (2015). *Cosmopolitanism and the Media: Cartographies of Change*. London & New York: Palgrave Macmillan.
Cresswell, T. (2010). Towards a politics of mobility. *Environment and Planning D: Society and Space 2010*. 28: 17–31.
Cresswell, T. (2011). Mobilities I: Catching up. *Progress in Human Geography*, 35(4): 550–558.
Cresswell, T. (2012). Mobilities II: Still. *Progress in Human Geography*, 36(5): 645–653.
Cresswell, T. (2014). Mobilities III: Moving On. *Progress in Human Geography*, 38(5): 712–721.
de Souza e Silva, A., & Sheller, M. (Eds.)(2015a). *Mobility and Locative Media: Mobile Communication in Hybrid Spaces*. London: Routledge.
de Souza e Silva, A., & Sheller, M. (2015b). Introduction: moving toward adjacent possibles. In: A. de Souza e Silva & M. Sheller (Eds.), *Mobility and Locative Media: Mobile Communication in Hybrid Spaces* (pp. 1–15). London: Routledge.
European Commission (2014). *Study on Mobility, Migration and Destitution in the European Union*. Final Report. Brussels.
Faist, T. (2013). The mobility turn: A new paradigm for the social sciences? *Ethnic and Racial Studies*, 36(11): 1637–1646.
Faist, T., Fauser, M., & Reisenauer, E. (2013). *Transnational Migration*. Cambridge: Polity.
Fallov, M. A., Jørgensen, A., & Knudsen, L. B. (2013). Mobile forms of belonging. *Mobilities*, 8(4): 467–486.
Frankel, H. R. (2012). *The Continental Drift Controversy. Volume I: Wegener and the Early Debate*. Cambridge: Cambridge University Press.
Fujimoto, K. (2006). The third-stage paradigm: Territory machine from the girls' pager revolution to mobile aesthetics. In M. Ito, D. Okabe, & M. Matsuda (Eds.), *Personal, Portable, Pedestrian: Mobile Phones in Japanese Life* (pp. 77–102). Cambridge, MA: MIT Press.

Georgiou, M. (2010). Identity, space and the media: Thinking through diaspora. *Revue Européenne des Migrations Internationales*, 26(1): 17–35.
Gergen, K. (2002). The challenge of the absent presence. In J. E. Katz & M. Aakhus (Eds.), *Perpetual Contact: Mobile Communication, Private Talk, Public Performance* (pp. 227–241). Cambridge: Cambridge University Press.
Goggin, G. & Hjorth, L. (2014). *The Routledge Companion to Mobile Media*. London: Routledge.
Goodwin-Smith, I. & Myatt, S. (2013). *Homelessness and the Role of Information Technology in Staying Connected*. Report for Anglicare-SA, Australian government.
Groening, S. (2008). *Connected Isolation: Screens, Mobility, and Globalized Media Culture*. Unpublished PhD thesis, University of Minnesota.
Hannam, K., Sheller, M., & Urry, J. (2006). Editorial: Mobilities, immobilities and moorings. *Mobilities*, 1(1): 1–22.
Hartmann, M. (2014). Home is where the heart is? Ontological security and the mediatization of homelessness. In K. Lundby (Ed.), *Mediatization of Communication. Handbooks of Communication*, No. 21 (pp. 641–660). Berlin: De Gruyter Mouton.
Hartmann, M. (2016). Soziale medien, Raum und Zeit'. In M. Taddicken & J. Schmidt (Eds.): *Handbuch Soziale Medien*. Wiesbaden: Springer VS.
Harvey, D. (2008). The right to the city. *New Left Review*. Nr. 53, 23–40.
Hepp, A. (2015). *Transcultural Communication*. Malden: Wiley.
Hepp, A., Lunt, P., & Hartmann, M. (2015). Communicative figurations of the good life: Ambivalences surrounding the mediatization of homelessness and the transnational family. In H. Wang (Ed.), *Communication and The Good Life* (pp. 181–196). Berlin & New York: Peter Lang.
Hjorth, L. (2009). *Mobile Media in the Asia-Pacific*. Abingdon & New York: Routledge.
Höflich, J. R. (2005). An mehreren Orten zugleich. Mobile Kommunikation und soziale Arrangements. In J. Höflich & J. Gebhardt (Eds.), *Mobile Kommunikation. Perspektiven und Forschungsfelder* (pp. 19–41). Frankfurt a.M.: Peter Lang.
Höflich, J. R. (2013). Relationships to social robots: Towards a triadic analysis of media-oriented behavior. *Intervalla*, 1: 35–48.
Jackson, E. (2012). Fixed in mobility: Young homeless people and the city. *International Journal of Urban and Regional Research*, 6(4): 725–741.
Jocoy, C. L. & Del Casino Jr., V. (2010). Homelessness, travel behavior, and the politics of transportation mobilities in long beach, California. *Environment & Planning A*, 42(8): 1943–1963.
Kalcic, S., Juntunen, M., & Rogelja, N. (2013). Marginal mobility: A heuristic tool for comparative study of contemporary mobilities. *Dve domovini*, 38/2013: 7–20.
Kaufman, A. (2016). *Canadian Homeless Mobilities: Relational perspectives on At Home/Chez Soi participants' interurban migrations*. Unpublished MA thesis. Department of Environment and Geography, University of Manitoba, Winnipeg.

Kaufmann, V., Bergman, M. M., & Joye, D. (2004). Motility: Mobility as capital. *International Journal of Urban and Regional Research*, 28(4): 745–756.
Knief, A. (2016). *Zur Mediennutzung einer sozialen Randgruppe. Eine qualitative Befragung von Bremer Obdachlosen.* Unpublished MA-Thesis, University of Bremen, MA Media Culture.
Lash, S., & Urry, J. (1994). *Economies of Signs and Space.* London: Sage.
Law, J., & Urry, J. (2005). Enacting the social. *Economy and Society*, 33(3): 390–410.
Levitt, P., & Jaworsky, B. N. (2007). Transnational migration studies: Past developments and future trends. *Annual Review of Sociology*, 33: 129–156.
Licoppe, C. (2004). Connected presence: The emergence of a new repertoire for managing social relationships in a changing communication technoscape. *Environment and Planning D: Society and Space*, 22(1): 135–156.
Ling, R. (2008) *New Tech, New Ties: How Mobile Communication Is Reshaping Social Cohesion.* Cambridge: MIT Press.
Massey, D. (1994). *Space, Place, and Gender.* Minneapolis: University of Minnesota Press.
Moores, S. (2012). *Media, Place & Mobility.* Houndsmills: Palgrave Macmillan.
Morley, D. (2000). *Home Territories: Media, Mobility and Identity.* London: Routledge.
Morley, D. (2009). For a materialist, non-media-centric media studies. *Television & New Media*, 10(1): 114–116.
Parker, R. D., & Dykema, S. (2013). The reality of homeless mobility and implications for improving care. *J Community Health*, 38(4): 685–689.
Pascale, C.-M. (2005). There's no place like home: The discursive creation of homelessness. *Cultural Studies ↔ Critical Methodologies*, 5(2): 250–268.
Pollio, D. E., Batey, D. S., Bender, K., Ferguson, K., & Thompson, S. (2013). Technology use among emerging adult homeless in two US cities. *Social Work*, 58(2): 173–175.
Rainie, L. & Wellman, B. (2012). *Networked. The New Social Operating System.* Cambridge, MA: MIT Press.
Rice, E., Monro, W., Barman-Adhikari, A., & Young, S. D. (2010). Internet use, social networking, and homeless adolescents' HIV/AIDS risk. *Journal of Adolescent Health*, 47(6): 610–613. (www.ncbi.nlm.nih.gov/pmc/articles/PMC2994071/-accessed 12/09/2013.)
Rosa, H. (2013). *Social Acceleration: A New Theory of Modernity.* New York: Columbia University Press.
Sheller, M., & Urry, J. (2006). The new mobilities paradigm. *Environment and Planning A*, 38(2): 207–226.
Silverstone, R. (2006). Domesticating domestication. Reflections on the life of a concept. In T. Berker, et al. (Eds.), *Domestication of Media and Technology* (pp. 229–248). Basingstoke: Open University Press.
Somerville, P. (1992). Homelessness and the meaning of home: Rooflessness or rootlessness? *International Journal of Urban and Regional Research*, 16(4): 529–539.
Studeny, S. (2015). Internetcafé ZwischenSchritt. Überwindung des "Digital Gap" im Rahmen der Wiener Wohnungslosenhilfe. *Soziales kapital:*

Wissenschaftliches Journal Österreichischer Fachhochschulstudiengänge Soziale Arbeit, 13: 160–172.
UNHCR (2016). *Connecting Refugees. How Internet and Mobile Connectivity can Improve Refugee Well-Being and Transform Humanitarian Action*. Geneva: UNHCR.
Urry, J. (2000). *Sociology Beyond Societies*. London: Sage.
Urry, J. (2007). *Mobilities*. Cambridge: Polity.
Virilio, P. (2007 [1977]). *Speed and Politics*. Los Angeles: Semiotexte.
Wilken, R., & Goggin, G. (2015). Locative media – Definitions, histories, theories. In R. Wilken & G. Goggin (eds.), *Locative Media*. New York & Abingdon: Routledge.
Woelfer, J. P., & Hendry, D. G. (2012). Homeless young people on social network sites. In *Proceedings of the SIGCHI Conference on Human Factors in Computing Systems*. http://vsdesign.org/publications/pdf/p2825-woelfer.pdf, pp. 2825–2834.
Yost, M. (2012). The invisible become visible: An analysis of how people experiencing homelessness use social media. *The Elon Journal of Undergraduate Research in Communications*, 3(2), 21–30.

11 Artists Out of Place
The Invalidation of Network Capital in a Small-Town Cultural Community

André Jansson & Linda Ryan Bengtsson

Introduction

Experiences of foreign cultural environments, far-ranging social networks and media-related skills and resources are conventionally seen as assets in a globalized society. Sheller and Urry (2006) have acknowledged this general development in their claims concerning a 'new mobilities' paradigm within the social sciences. They trace this 'mobility turn' to vast and ongoing changes through which material movements of people and goods have increased alongside the rapid expansion of the Internet and other forms of digital communication networks. As a consequence, the social sciences (including an interdisciplinary area of perspectives) are increasingly 'putting social relations into travel and connecting different forms of transport with complex patterns of social experience conducted through communications at-a-distance' (208). These interdependencies (ontological as well as epistemological) between mobilities and 'the social' imply that issues of power take the centre stage. *Whose* networks and *whose* mobilities count as important, and whose do not? Questions of mobility, 'of too little movement or too much, or of the wrong sort or at the wrong time' (Sheller and Urry, 2006) have become intimately linked to questions of social privilege. Kaufmann (2002) suggests that the ability to control one's own mobility, deciding when to be mobile and when to stay put, what he calls *motility*, is a strong marker of social power in a globalized society. Similarly, Urry (2003) has introduced the term *network capital* as a way of highlighting how the possession of various forms of mobility and communication resources correspond with, and can be turned into, social power.

How are such resources played out in local contexts? What happens when network capital is confronted with placed-based power structures related to, for example, culture, politics or business? In this chapter, we analyse these questions based on an interview study among in-migrating and 'homecoming' artists – who in most cases can be considered rich in both cultural capital and network capital – in a Swedish small town.

Urry's understanding of network capital is grounded in the fact that 'mobilities in themselves do nothing' (2003: 196); what is important are the ways in which mobilities can be used to produce and sustain networks of relations. Network capital, as Urry defines it, 'is the capacity to engender and sustain social relations with those people who are not necessarily proximate and which generates emotional, financial and practical benefit (although this will often entail various objects and technologies or the means of networking)' (197). Network capital is thus related to Bourdieu's notion of *social capital*, which he defines as 'the sum of the resources, actual or virtual, that accrue to an individual or a group by virtue of possessing a durable network of more or less institutionalized relationships of mutual acquaintance and recognition' (Bourdieu and Wacquant, 1992: 119). By comparison, however, network capital signifies more fluid and centrifugal connections with a greater world, which are not reliant on durable and institutionalized forms of recognition. In this respect, network capital differs even more from Putnam's (2000) understanding of social capital, which points to the mutual obligations and reciprocities that keep local neighbourhoods together over time and regulate the social status of different social actors. Urry (2003: 199–200) argues that network capital is a way of problematizing *both* the stability of local communities, bringing into light that the reproduction of seemingly enclosed and sedentary places and cultures is actually dependent on various mobilities and people's capacity to connect with the surrounding world, *and* the idea that trustful and reciprocal relations can only emerge within close-knit communities based on face-to-face relations.

A number of empirical studies have pointed in similar directions. Much-cited examples are Florida's (2002) famous account of the 'creative class', the social significance of 'weak ties' (Granovetter, 1983) within such groups and Wittel's (2001) analyses of 'network sociality' as a key resource among the new middle classes of media and computer-literate people associated with urban culture and communication industries (53). More recently, Jansson and Andersson (Jansson, 2010; Jansson and Andersson, 2012) have analysed the significance of network capital in rural communities in Sweden, arguing that the appropriation of such resources (including e.g. infrastructural networks and mediated global connections) may actually work as a social stabilizer, strengthening local communities and reinforcing people's sense of place. The social impact of network capital is thus relatively open ended and should be studied in relation to particular contexts and geographies.

Still, surprisingly few empirical studies have systematically analysed the significance of network capital in specific contexts. Even fewer have tried to assess its validity within settings marked by the stronghold of local traditions and social capital (in Putnam's understanding). This is surprising for two reasons. First, Urry (2003: 197–198) explicitly

Artists Out of Place 197

operationalizes network capital through the listing of eight constitutive elements, which could be easily identified in empirical research. These eight elements are (in condensed form): (1) appropriate documents, visas, money and qualifications; (2) others at a distance (that is, social relations); (3) movement capacities (bodily as well as intellectual); (4) location-free information and contact points (material as well as mediated); (5) communication devices; (6) appropriate, safe and secure meeting places; (7) access to various means of mobility and communication and (8) time and other resources to manage and coordinate 1–7. It would thus be a relatively easy task to empirically distinguish those who are richer in network capital from those who are poorer in order to estimate how this complex resource is maintained and circulated.

Second, Urry holds that network capital has arisen as a social resource that should, at least in the North, be taken as an equivalent to economic and cultural capital today, as conceived by Bourdieu (1979/1984). Network capital is explicitly elaborated to compensate for Bourdieu's overly static and nationalcentric analysis that, according to Urry (2003: 195), fails to account for the extent to which people's agency is shaped in relation to various mobility complexes today. This far-ranging claim, however, needs to be further substantiated through empirical as well as theoretical studies. Urry does not specify how network capital is related to other forms of capital within a Bourdieusian social space or whether there exists a separate social field where network capital functions as the dominant form of capital (cf. Bourdieu, 1972/1977). One reasonable interpretation of Urry's ideas would be that various forms of mobility and (mediated) networking have become increasingly important assets for the accumulation of social capital – in *both* Putnam's *and* Bourdieu's sense of the term – implying that the mutual relations of recognition that mark out social fields (Bourdieu), as well as the sustainability of place-based communities of trust (Putnam), become dependent on intensified mobilities and connectivities vis-à-vis the surrounding (and ultimately global) world. This development, in turn, might be taken as a sign of the broader meta-process of (geo)mediatization (see Chapter 1 in this volume). But if we are to understand to what extent network capital actually constitutes a separate form of capital and under what conditions it can be converted into other forms of capital, that is, its sociocultural validity, there is no way around concrete fieldwork.

Against this background, in this chapter we set out to examine the status of network capital within a particular local context *and* a particular social field. We want to learn more about whether network capital constitutes a resource that can help social agents transcend geosocial boundaries in order to claim status positions in new settings. Our empirical study concerns independent artists and craftspeople who are active in the provincial municipality of Arvika, Sweden, a small town characterized by a lively cultural scene and strong cultural traditions.

Most of the artists and craftspeople we have interviewed, altogether ten people, possess large amounts of network capital, including considerable media literacy as well as (inter)national professional networks and experiences. Furthermore, in many cases they have a background in other places than Arvika. These agents have thus entered a (more or less) foreign environment where they not only have to play by the rules of the game prescribed by their particular field (in this case the artistic field), but must also obey and/or negotiate the sedimented structures of economic, political and social life that keep the local community together. One might say that while these in-migrants still operate within the same overarching field, they have entered a more peripheral part of it, *as well as* a particular geosocial environment whose capacity to mould social relations may even distort certain taken-for-granted logics of the field. Theoretically, this study allows us to bring together, and problematize, the ideas of Urry, Bourdieu and Putnam and advance a critical geomedia perspective that explicates how the sociomaterial structures of place set limits to and condition the impacts of mediatization (see Chapter 1 in this volume).

The chapter starts out with a presentation of the study and its contexts, which includes a further specification of our research aim. This is followed by an empirically grounded description of Arvika's cultural economy and an estimation of the town's relatively strong reputation among artists and craftspeople in Sweden as well as abroad. By describing what attracts artists and craftspeople to move to, or return to, a small town in a nonurban area, we provide an understanding of the specific geosocial boundaries within the local context of Arvika. In the remaining sections, we present and discuss the results of our study. As mentioned, the informants represent mobile life biographies (in- or return-migration) and attain strong extraregional, sometimes international networks. Yet, their experiences of *placing* their careers in the small-town setting of Arvika are marked by dissonance. They see themselves as valuable to local cultural life and relatively integrated in it; they are, however, prohibited from converting their network capital into other forms of capital. It means that they uphold an ethos that largely corresponds with the predominant, even hegemonic, view of network capital and established relations with the centres of the field (Bourdieu's social capital) as something that 'should count' – but feel that these resources are not recognized by local actors. These findings problematize the notion of network capital as a broadly recognized 'currency' and provide an in-depth view of how the sociomaterial structures of place may repel the transformative forces of mobility and mediated connectivity. We thus conclude that the significance of network capital must be empirically assessed not only in relation to different cultural fields, but also in relation to the place-specific materialization of such fields – what we may call local cultural ecosystems. By way of conclusion, we reflect upon how these place-based mechanisms play into the overarching meta-process of mediatization (Krotz, 2007).

The Study and Its Contexts

In the wake of Florida's (2002) work on the importance of the so-called creative class to economic growth and its need of a creative urban environment, criticism has been launched against the focus on the cosmopolitan city. At the same time, creative industries have come to be regarded as an important resource for economic growth and a desired population increase also, in rural areas (Banks, 2007; Ross, 2008). This development has in turn led to local initiatives to reinforce and advance the art and culture sector, but often such investments have missed the target because they have been modelled on big-city efforts and based on the assumption of 'one-size-fits-all' (Bell and Jayne, 2010). As a consequence, there is a need of a more nuanced and place-specific understanding of the creative sector in nonurban areas (Luckman, Gibson, and Lea, 2009; Waitt and Gibson, 2009; Bell and Jayne, 2010). Many such studies have been conducted recently, showing that *place* is central to how creative entrepreneurs in nonurban areas navigate daily life. Local resources such as venues for exchange and cooperation (Waitt and Gibson, 2013), Internet access and other technological infrastructure (Jansson and Andersson, 2012; Roberts and Townsend, 2015), local politics and access to professional networks affect the possibility of working in a small community (Luckman, 2012; Lysgård, 2016). Bell and Jayne (2010) recognize that creative practice takes place in the interaction of people, place and creativity and suggest that we study this interaction more closely. Luckman (2012) emphasizes the role of place even further, arguing that creative work in nonurban areas occurs in a constant negotiation with place. A place is thus an actor in creative processes and carries its own affordances (Luckman, 2012).

The question we want to explore in this chapter is therefore if (and how) the importance of network capital is formed by place-specific features. These involve *social* features, primarily linked to the political sphere, various power relations and what Putnam terms social capital and *material* features, including economic resources and other material preconditions in the form of geography, infrastructures, venues, premises and technical equipment. Together, they make up the sociomaterial structures of a place. On the basis of interviews with ten artists – mostly homecomers or newcomers to a small Swedish town – we investigate how they relate to and renegotiate their network capital in relation to the sociomaterial structures of place. By pinpointing the formal and informal prerequisites and barriers that affect individual integration in the local context, we probe whether and how existing network capital might be converted into other forms of capital, notably cultural, economic and social capital.

The study was carried out in 2013 in Arvika, a small town situated in a Swedish nonurban area, 400 kilometres to the west of the capital Stockholm, near the Norwegian border. The municipality has a population of 26,000 and, despite its small size, it has several prominent actors in the cultural sector such as an art museum, and galleries, craftsmanship shops and platforms for music and theatre performances. There are many cultural and creative actors of varying prominence. The town is somewhat geographically remote, but there are good communications since it is on the railway line between Stockholm and Oslo and one hour by car from an airport. The digital infrastructure is well developed, and yet the town is struggling to keep its residents. At the rate of industrial closedowns and public service downsizing, job opportunities have been reduced. This is the main reason for the growing faith in the 'creative sector', resorted to and invested in by many towns in Sweden and Europe.

The interviewees, five men and five women, aged 24–65, are artists in the areas of theatre, music, film, literature and/or arts and crafts. Five of them are homecomers, and five have moved in from other cities. Most of them are also engaged in creating, building and developing networks in their respective arts. Six of them were at the time sole traders, and four of them had full-time employment. The informants were identified using snowball sampling (Biermacki and Waldorf, 1981), which we initiated through contacts with the local library staff. Starting out with three informants, we could eventually gather ten people working with different art forms or craftsmanship. The recruitment process continued until saturation was reached in their answers and reasoning. The interviews were conducted in the informants' home/studio or in a café, each taking between 40 and 90 minutes. The interviews involved a semi-structured set of thematically organized questions oriented towards professional practices, relations and experiences.[1]

The Attractions of a Provincial Place

Let us first give a picture of what it is that attracts artists and artisans to a small place like Arvika. The interviewees come from other parts of Sweden or have lived in another town for a long period of their lives. Those who have lived elsewhere, moved from Arvika when they left school to study. The reasons for moving were often linked to the family situation, forming a family or inheriting a property. At the same time, our interviews indicate that the cultural distinction of the place is a decisive factor for Arvika's attractiveness to creative practitioners. Several interviewees mentioned the local network associated with arts and crafts. For the returning artists the network functions as a resource for recreating their social capital. The network and its shared shop provide a chance to make a living, at least partly, on their art, which they claimed is not possible in a city.

> Without Konsthantverk [local community and shop for art and handicraft] I would not have been here now. And the other craftsmen in the district, because they are a network too. I'd not have moved here were it not for these people that I can relate to.
>
> (Respondent 7)

The respondents who did not grow up in Arvika chose to move there for various reasons: a family member got a job in the area or they wanted to raise a family in a smaller place. But the knowledge that Arvika is a place with a lively culture was important, especially the nearby education opportunities and the fact that many in the cultural sector live and work in Arvika.

> My husband at the time had contacts at Ingesund [music college][...] and we knew that Arvika was a bit more exciting than the average backwater. And that many had stayed or moved here.
>
> (Respondent 2)

Many also mentioned other advantages of moving or returning to a smaller community. It is cheaper to live there than in cities, and there are better opportunities for combining studio and residence. In addition, Arvika's communications with several major cities are good compared to other towns and places. Cheap accommodation is also available for temporary cooperation with dancers, musicians or actors required for productions. Many mentioned the closeness to nature, the beautiful surroundings and the stillness as a pleasant environment to work in as well as an inspiration. Escaping the traffic and the reality of distance in big cities was seen as an advantage. The mobility patterns are characterized by push and pull factors typical of counter-urbanization. Residency is the result of an active choice based on the ambition to form a harmonic and creative life (see e.g. Halfacree, 1994; Benson and O'Reilly, 2009; Phillips, 2010; Savage, 2010; Jansson and Andersson, 2012). In the case of Arvika, these patterns are reinforced because of the town's rich cultural opportunities. Many respondents mentioned the traditions established through the Rackstad colony, a group of artists living in Arvika at the turn of the 20th century, which they thought heralded the sense of creativity and appreciation of culture and the value of handicrafts among the residents. One respondent, for example, regarded the local knowledge of art handicraft compared to other parts of Sweden as a great advantage.

> We know a lot about that in Arvika. And we understand the process and know about the work behind an object. I wish it was like that in the whole of Sweden. That would have made a great difference!
>
> (Respondent 7)

Arvika's attractiveness is thus strongly associated with its historical and present cultural setting, which offers a different type of lifestyle to art practitioners than the city does. Previous studies show similar lines of thought (see, e.g. Duxbury and Campbell, 2011; Gibson et al., 2012; Collins, Freebody, and Flew, 2013), in which creative artists refer to previous professional and private networks or identify potentials for networking beyond the basics of being able to afford and practise their art. Summing up, moving to Arvika can be understood as *both* a pragmatic choice (see Luckman, 2012) based on careful deliberation to improve a life situation and an emotional project where the history and identity of the place promise creativity.

The Significance of Network Capital

A common denominator for the respondents is that they have a relatively large amount of network capital, which is evident in having the opportunity to *choose* to move to Arvika and in bringing important resources such as networks and communicative skills. The respondents are active in a number of formal and informal networks linked to their professional areas. The networks, especially the informal ones, are principally national and mostly created through their education. Some also have informal international networks, established through participation in international exhibitions, festivals, conferences, workshops or 'visiting artist residence' abroad. The more formal networks consist of branch-specific associations, often national but also local. These associations disseminate information and arrange seminars, lectures, conferences, etc., thus creating venues. Certain associations can also have a more agent-like role, mediating commissions or inviting artists to exhibitions. The respondents' degree of activity and their roles vary. A critical factor is the distance to the place where the activities take place, which is often the big cities, and participation requires time and money.

> It's more about geographical distance, I would prefer to go to their meetings in person rather than reading the minutes afterwards.
> (Respondent 1)

> It's about physical meetings... As soon as I go to something, a conference or a course, I network, and it always leads to something.
> (Respondent 2)

The interviews provide a good picture of how closely intertwined network capital is with social and cultural capital. The status of these artists within their fields can be understood as the outcome of longer periods of successful strategies of capital conversion and consecration, also involving a willingness to *move and network* in particular, expected but largely unspoken ways. These prescribed ways of networking are dictated from the centre of the field and tend to gravitate towards the centre; agents need to maintain a sense of proximity to the centre even though they are geographically removed from it.

The interviews also testify to the need to *maintain* one's network capital. Compared to cultural capital, often embodied in, and recognized through, qualification titles and artistic skills (see, e.g., Bourdieu, 1983), network capital is a more ephemeral resource based on the interplay between mobility and encounters. It is more up to the individual to ensure that the right connections are in place, what Wellman et al. (2005) call networked individualism (see also Urry, 2003: Ch. 10). Our interviewees emphasized that physical meetings would probably strengthen their roles in the networks and increase their commission, cooperation and exhibition opportunities. They are aware of missing out on exhibitions, concerts and branch contacts and networks in different forms because of their location. Many think that travelling grants would enable them to be more visible in different contexts, which would benefit their work.

Again, this shows how symbolic power geometries are inscribed in the physical landscape, making places like Arvika seem *and feel* more or less 'remote'. Network capital thus comes to the surface as a very material precondition for staying in touch with the symbolic centres of the field. Furthermore, because of the limited access to economic resources for travelling and meeting people in other parts of the country and abroad, media play an indispensable role among these artists. Networks are maintained through mailing lists and social media, mainly Facebook. Many of the formal networks use mailing lists while the informal networks are usually active on Facebook. This enables the linking of formal and informal networks.

> I use Facebook a great deal in my profession. To me Facebook is a means of contact with a professional network. My network then grows, all you have worked with, all course participants who are active around the world. It's an enormous network!
> (Respondent 4)

Under the geosocial pressures of mediatization, that is, the normalized reliance on media to overcome geographical and social distances, media literacy (in a broad sense) emerges as a prerequisite for maintaining network capital. Some of the interviewees have a Facebook page specifically linked to their work where they upload information and marketing. But most of them use Facebook as private persons, adding professional aspects. They do not see any problem with this but regard it as a result of the fact that their friends are in a similar professional area and that their private and professional realms are closely inter-linked (increasingly so because of social media).

A further central arena for extending contacts is the artistically oriented institutions of education in the region. Such institutions serve as meeting-places, providing new knowledge and exchange opportunities with invited guest lecturers from Sweden or abroad, for example. They thus function as venues where social capital can be exchanged into network capital.

> Working at Kyrkerud's Folk High School is being at the centre of art, even if very few have understood that ... For those of us who have worked there it has been a vitalizing experience the whole time.
> (Respondent 4)

The interviewees' pre-established networks, which should here be seen as social capital in the Bourdieusian sense, are important for many different reasons. They are a way of getting inspiration and discussing their own artistic expressions as well as obtaining commissions more or less linked to their work. Especially the informal networks from their student days are important, as these are the most important channels for exhibitions, contacts and finding project partners. Several of them are active in local networks, which are often semi-formal, targeting a specific group such as women or a certain age. Many of the interviewees think that local artists support one another, thus enabling inspiration, discussion and technical material support. They do not compete but cooperate in creating a shared environment conducive to their work.

The interviews thus show that network capital can be reinforced by the social and material structures of place, for example, via institutions and societies that embody and legitimize cultural capital. However, in our study this argument mainly applies to the returning artists that have locally and/or regionally anchored social capital to build on. They may have the right connections (Bourdieu), while being recognized as 'natural members' of the community (Putnam). Several of the homecomers described how they had been positively surprised at how easy it was to be included in the local community and how their works and exhibitions quickly received attention in the local press. However, the interviews also indicate that certain artists are excluded. This applies especially to new arrivals without roots in Arvika or its vicinities.

The Invalidation of Network Capital

The main result of our analysis is that network capital does not function as the bridge to a new cultural community as could be expected. Rather, actors run the risk of being excluded because of their network capital, which may seem paradoxical since the very nature of network capital is about increased mobility opportunities and social connections. In the following, we discuss these exclusion mechanisms, that is, the local invalidation of network capital in three contexts: (1) the cultural community; (2) municipal politics and (3) conflicts between regional and national logics of recognition.

The Cultural Community

As mentioned above, many of the homecomers feel that their reintegration in Arvika has been fairly smooth and has even attracted some public attention. The local community, including local media, takes pride in cultural profiles returning to their hometown. The respondents who were not from Arvika and had made a more uncertain investment in a new hometown described the opposite.

> When I phoned the local newspaper, so [...]. Well, I explained what I did and why I wanted them to come. Said I was new to Arvika and invited them to an exhibition. [...] When I finished the tirade he said, well, who are you? [...] He was fishing for some kind of connection to Värmland or relatives etc. And then there was no interest. So they never turned up.
>
> (Respondent 6)

If you are not from Arvika, it takes a long time to be included in the local art and culture circle. Lack of local connections cannot be easily compensated by network capital or a broader artistic reputation. Such resources may even be counter-productive and lead to active exclusion by the local cultural community. New residents recalled how they had problems finding an available exhibition hall, seldom felt welcome and that the local press did not review their exhibitions of performances. In the interview material, their frustrations and experiences of feeling out of place are expressed in a vocabulary that reproduces the very divide between centre and periphery they set out to overcome. Cultural life in Arvika is classified as 'provincial' (as opposed to professional), 'parochial' and 'closed', that is, as the very opposite to dynamic and globally connected cultural scenes.

> It's difficult to work here. And the provincial does not accept the professional. And it's dangerous to say so, but it's the truth.
>
> (Respondent 4)

> But I think it's pretty parochial. Cultural life is very closed. [...] But, by God, it's not easy to be a cultural artist here. Especially not as a new resident. This is evident. Socially and professionally.
>
> (Respondent 10)

The same social structures that can be supportive to the already included tend to erect barriers for new residents. The mechanisms are similar to those Bourdieu identified in his analyses of cultural fields (see, e.g. 1983), with the difference that what matters in our case is not primarily whether somebody can acquire the right kind of cultural capital to be included in the field. Rather, what matters is whether one originates from, or is connected to, a region or a place. International networks and mobile life biographies, especially when combined with cultural capital and symbolically manifested through, for example, records of previous exhibitions and travel grants, can be perceived as the antithesis of the local community, ultimately as a threat, by the already established actors in a place. This often leads to a form of subtle exclusion, which in turn means that the networks brought by new residents do not benefit the local cultural activities. The situation may seem paradoxical, especially since all the respondents stress the need for external influences to enrich their own productions as well as cultural activities and events in Arvika generally. This very ambition towards more variation and open attitudes runs the risk, however, of further fuelling the local invalidation of network capital.

Municipal Politics

As Arvika is strongly associated with a lively cultural scene, artists expect the municipality to be strategically engaged in cultural politics. However, there is dissonance between the expectations of the arts and culture practitioners and what the municipality actually does. This regards the absence of articulated cultural politics; the municipality's unwillingness to recognize arts professionals and their networks as a local resource and the failure simply to say, 'thanks for nice work'. The municipality has declared the ambition to 'muster for consensus on the value of Arvika's strong brand, in which culture is *value carrying*, thus increasing Arvika's attraction'. The vitality of the town's arts and culture activities is often used in information and marketing; nevertheless, the respondents did not experience a consensus on culture as a 'value carrying' factor in their encounters with politicians and officials. Leading politicians were said to lack interest in visual and performing arts issues. Municipal officials, on the other hand, were seen as accommodating but lacking mandate.

> There is no investment made in the arts and culture sector here. There is arts and culture here because people have chosen to live here and because there are education programmes. But they have missed out on something, it's a huge failure.
>
> (Respondent 2)

> There's a bit of a cultural gloom in Arvika, I'm afraid. The politicians seem to lack insight. There's a rich history to make use of, but it takes money.
>
> (Respondent 8)

The interviewed artists evidently think that the arts and culture scene in Arvika rests on mobile actors with great engagement and many contacts, in line with how Urry (2003) conceives of the mutual interplay between network capital and local communities, but that the politicians do not understand the value of these resources. Several of the artists who moved to Arvika, both homecomers and newcomers, contacted the municipality to find out how the arts and culture sector works and if the municipality offered any kind of support and to inform the municipality about this new available resource. The contacts were great disappointments.

> After the talk I had [...] I'm rather disappointed. [...] When I asked what they could offer, is there any way you can support a newly established artist in Arvika? the answer was really nothing.
>
> (Respondent 8)

> I tried when I moved to Arvika, called the municipality and said: 'Hi, I'm an artist moving to Arvika and I wonder if there are any support programs for me in any way? Is there a studio, or studio support, or do you know of any art community I could contact or...?' All I got was: 'Eh, what? What do you want?'
>
> (Respondent 4)

Several mentioned that they, having been in Arvika for some time, felt needed and serve a function in the local community. They feel that they contribute knowledge of art and culture and inspire further expressions by bringing art into various settings such as the schools and public environments. In other words, they see themselves as a potential bridge between the social life of place and a broader cultural field, whose epicentres are located beyond the regional contexts. They would like their engagement in local culture and its importance to be publicly recognized and their potential to contribute to Arvika's reputation through their cultural *and* network capital to be acknowledged.

> On our part, we think we are ambassadors of Arvika. Self-appointed really. We haven't been asked. [...] But we would be happy if they said: 'this is, you are good ambassadors. You boost Arvika's reputation so this is how we would like to support you.' Then we would be grateful and accept.
>
> (Respondent 9)

The respondents also think that there are commissions or projects in the municipality for which their expertise is ideal but not requested, for example, art for new constructions or renovations, involving local artists in political processes instead of external consultants and buying art and planning cultural events. On the few occasions when they have been asked, there was no reimbursement or it was difficult to get reimbursement. Artists are expected to work for free. The respondents pointed out that while it is not a municipal responsibility to pay artists a salary, a municipality professing to have cultural resources and attractions should favour the activities that create these very attractions. Instead, the municipality is perceived as making it hard for artistic newcomers to be included in the local sphere of art and culture, which undermines the value of the artists' network capital, not to mention their artistic reputation (cultural capital), which in turn affects their ability to make a living as artists.

Conflicts between Regional and National Logics of Recognition

Being an artist and moving to a small town in a nonurban area often means moving from a national to a local cultural context. Our interviews show that it can be difficult to maintain and utilize the networks established at the national level or in a big-city context. The problem involves two aspects: (1) the unwillingness to support art and culture without a specific regional connection or relevance at the regional/local level and (2) the unwillingness to highlight and favour art and culture produced in small places at the national level. These aspects can be seen as two competing logics of recognition, which together foreground the ambivalence of the newcomers' experience of trying to get established in a Swedish small town while trying to achieve (inter)national success and prestige.

As a consequence, the respondents feel that they do not get the attention they deserve at the national level while the regional decision makers do very little to enable broader national attention. One of the respondents described how she managed to get a play she wrote to open on a main stage in Stockholm, but her economic support from the region was cut in half because it did not benefit regional culture when produced elsewhere. She was forced to abandon the project, as it was then not financially viable. The same phenomenon recurs in other interviews; regional support to international conferences, exhibitions and other events are rejected with reference to the nonregional location. The respondents, however, argue that it would be an asset to the region if they were on a wider market displaying regional resources. Since the regional support is so important to the artists, they must adjust to the directives, which restricts their opportunities to expand networks and reach an (inter)national market.

It is impossible to ignore the local and regional levels, as it is very difficult to get national grants. In this respect, several interviewees find that there is a clear bias towards the big city regions, to which the bulk of arts grants is allocated. The Swedish Arts Council never visits, and national grant givers show very little interest. The respondents feel that national organisations have little or no knowledge of their activities and that it is difficult to assert themselves in relation to the more visible artists in the big cities. Being noted involves exhibiting artworks or staging a play on the 'right' stage as well as getting media attention. In both respects, reaching beyond the regional context is difficult even if the artist has established contacts. One of the respondents mentioned that an established art critic in one of the major dailies in Sweden used to have a summer cottage in the vicinity of Arvika, and major events were then covered in the summers. Presently, however, it takes something exceptional to feature in the national media.

The interviews also display frustration with regional and national funding providers' view of art and its role. The respondents think that art has its own value; it should not be conflated with the economic system. It does not follow that the state or municipality has a duty to provide for the artist, but that the public sector has a duty to contribute to the arts.

> The old view that artists should make a living by selling their works is still there. But it's very difficult to do that.
> (Respondent 6)

> The efforts made looking for creative and profitable entrepreneurships that I have seen [...] to which I'm very skeptical. This is the art they are seeking and they can't see that art has a value without profit, or being really sellable.
> (Respondent 8)

The respondents agree that it is impossible for them to live on their art. Deliberate societal efforts and strategies to back up their situation are needed, but public actors have an approach that requires cultural and artistic entrepreneurships to be developed like economically viable companies on market-based terms. This is a basic conflict regarding what art is and how it should be valued. In a situation where the opportunities to get economic support are slim and where the economic viability of being an artist must be built largely on locally established contacts, that is, social capital rather than network capital, it is not surprising that individuals with a nonregional background are particularly frustrated.

They have actively relocated from the city to live on their art but at the expense of greater professional success.

Concluding Discussion: Fractured Trajectories and Accentuated Mediatization

Our interviews with new and homecoming artists in a small town show that a place involves opportunities as well as barriers to converting network capital into other types of resources. To a great extent, our respondents meet the criteria or elements that, according to Urry (2003), characterize network capital. They have established networks, including local as well as international contacts, good relations to regional and extraregional media, access to media technology and infrastructure, not to mention an established audience. However, there are barriers in the form of the subtle social codes of the local community, conflicts between regional and national logics of recognition and the absence of local political support. The distance between centre and periphery is evident at different levels; between the big city and nonurban areas (where the marginalization of the nonurban is notable in the absence of resource allocation and media attention) and between local political potentates and newly arrived art workers (not least regarding the view of art and its role in society).

These complex relationships are, as Luckman (2012) points out, under constant negotiation. Together they form what we might call a local cultural ecosystem that can be affected on one hand by new actors or technologies gaining access, but, on the other hand, by virtue of its established operations and relations between various actors, can make it difficult for newcomers to be included. By extension, this means that local cultural ecosystems may evoke a great deal of friction for the geosocial trajectories of particular groups. In previous research this phenomenon has been acknowledged primarily in relation to international migrants (notably those travelling from South to North), whose professional qualifications are often devalued in their new home countries (see, e.g., Andersson, 2008) and among return migrants who may feel that their internationally acquired experiences and assets are 'out of sync' with the environment they left (see, e.g., Dürrschmidt, 2016). Our analyses have shown that similar, albeit less critical, experiences of devaluation and fractured trajectories can be found among groups who travel shorter distances and traverse less complex borders.

The local invalidation of network capital also holds interesting implications in relation to mediatization. As we have seen from the interviews, media-sustained networks and media-related skills are rarely recognized as important assets in the local cultural community or among politicians and public officials at the local/regional level. What is important to stress, however, is that this negation of network capital does not seem to diminish the significance of various forms of media and mediations. On the contrary, individual actors, in this case the newly settled artists and craftspeople, are forced to rely *even more* on mediated communication and to improve their entrepreneurial and networking skills even further in order to maintain their positions in the cultural field at large. Mediated connectivity becomes a way of compensating for the frictions of the local cultural ecosystem and sustaining relations with the strategic centres of the field. Again, it is possible to draw parallels to more extended forms of migration where media often play a crucial role in enabling individuals and groups to maintain a sense of coherent identity under mobile life conditions (see Madianou and Miller, 2012; Christensen and Jansson, 2015: Ch. 5). Paradoxical as it may seem, our study thus suggests that the local invalidation of network capital reinforces media dependence and accentuates the overarching meta-process of mediatization.

Our findings thus underline that mediatization should be understood as an agglomeration of socially conditioned processes that can only be grasped if we study them in their particular settings and from a nonmediacentric, or socially oriented, perspective (see, e.g., Morley, 2009; Couldry, 2012; Krajina, Moores, and Morley, 2014). In the case at hand, the overarching force of mediatization is experienced, and *felt*, in different ways among the artists depending on whether they have any accumulated social capital in Arvika to fall back upon or not. For those who do not, but rather enter this cultural ecosystem for the first time, the need to stay connected with the 'outside world', and thus to engage in various forms of mediated connectivity, becomes more critical. The ultimate reason is that network capital may work as a resource for exitability and 'trajectory restoration', that is, making it possible for the individual to actually leave Arvika and resettle in a place where the exchangeability of different forms of capital are better in sync with the habitus of the individual. By extension, these results highlight not only the rather anticipated fact that the dynamics of cultural fields alter, as they blend with a host of other social, cultural and economic conditions, depending on geographical location. As Bourdieu puts it, 'the limits of the field are situated at the point where the effects of the field cease' (Bourdieu and Wacquant, 1992: 100). The results also highlight that the social force of mediatization, that is, the growing reliance on media technologies and institutions, should be critically gauged in relation to different kinds of mobility as well as different kinds of geosocial spaces and distances (Jansson, 2017). This is ultimately what critical geomedia studies is about, whether we study elite mobilities, forced labour migration or counter-urbanizing cultural workers.

Note

1 The interview study was carried out by Linda Ryan Bengtsson in 2013 as part of the research project *Rural Networking/Networking the Rural*, led by André Jansson (funding from the The Swedish Research Council Formas, 2009-2013). The current analysis is also associated with the Music Innovation Network Inner Scandinavia project led by Linda Ryan Bengtsson (funded by Interreg/EU 2016-2018).

References

Andersson, M. (2008). The matter of media in transnational everyday life. In I. Rydin. & U. Sjöberg (Eds.) *Mediated Crossroads: Theoretical and Methodological Challenges*. Göteborg: Nordicom.

Banks, M. (2007). *The Politics of Cultural Work*. Basingstoke: Palgrave Macmillan.

Bell, D., & Jayne, M. (2010). The creative countryside: Policy and practice in the UK rural cultural economy. *Journal of Rural Studies*, 26(3): 209-218

Benson, M., & O'Reilly, K. (2009). Migration and the search for a better way of life: A critical exploration of lifestyle migration. *The Sociological Review*, 57(4): 608-625.

Biermacki, P., & Waldorf, D. (1981). Snowball sampling: Problems and techniques of chain referral sampling. *Sociological Methods & Research*, 10: 141-163.

Bourdieu, P. (1972/1977). *Outline of a Theory of Practice*. Cambridge: Cambridge University Press.

Bourdieu, P. (1979/1984). *Distinction: A Social Critique of the Judgement of Taste*. London: Routledge.

Bourdieu, P. (1983). The field of cultural production, or: the economic world reversed, *Poetics*, 12: 311-356.

Bourdieu, P., & Wacquant, L. J. D. (1992). *An Invitation to Reflexive Sociology*. Chicago: University of Chicago Press.

Christensen, M., & Jansson, A. (2015). *Cosmopolitanism and the Media: Cartographies of Change*. Basingstoke: Palgrave Macmillan.

Collis, C., Freebody, S., & Flew, T. (2013). Seeing the outer suburbs: Addressing the urban bias in creative place thinking, *Regional Studies*, 47(2): 148-160

Couldry, N. (2012). *Media, Society, World: Social Theory and Digital Media Practices*. Cambridge: Polity Press.

Dürrschmidt, J. (2016). The irresolvable unease about be-longing: Exploring globalized dynamics of homecoming, *European Journal of Cultural Studies*, 19(5): 495-510.

Duxbury, N., & H. Campbell (2011). Developing and revitalizing rural communities through arts and culture. *Small Cities Imprint*, 3(I): 111-122.

Florida, R. (2002). *The Rise of the Creative Class*. North Melbourne: Pluto Press Australia

Gibson, C., Brennan-Horley C., Laurenson, B., Riggs, N., Warren, A. Gallan, B., & Brown, B. (2012). Cool places, creative places? Community perceptions of cultural vitality in the suburbs. *International Journal of Cultural Studies*, 15(3): 287-302.

Granovetter, M. (1983). The strength of weak ties: A network theory revisited. *Sociological Theory*, 1: 203–233.
Halfacree, K. (1994). The importance of 'the Rural' in the constitution of counterurbanization: Evidence from England in the 1980s. *Sociologica Ruralis*, 34: 164–189.
Jansson, A. (2010). Mediatization, spatial coherence and social sustainability: The role of digital media networks in a Swedish countryside community, *Culture Unbound*, 2: 177–192.
Jansson, A. (2017). *Mediatization and Mobile Lives: A Critical Approach*. London: Routledge.
Jansson, A., & Andersson, M. (2012). Mediatization at the margins: Cosmopolitanism, network capital and spatial transformation in rural Sweden, *Communications*, 37(2): 173–194.
Kaufmann, V. (2002). *Re-thinking Mobility: Contemporary Sociology*. Aldershot: Ashgate.
Krajina, Z., Moores, S., & Morley, D. (2014). Non-media-centric media studies: A cross-generational conversation. *European Journal of Cultural Studies*, 17(6): 682–700.
Krotz, F. (2007). The meta-process of 'mediatization' as a conceptual frame. *Global Media and Communication*, 3(3): 256–260.
Luckman, S. (2012). *Locating Cultural Work: The Politics and Poetics of Rural, Regional and Remote Creativity*. UK: Palgrave and Macmillan.
Luckman, S., Gibson, C., & Lea, T. (2009). Mosquitoes in the mix: How transferable is creative city thinking? *Singapore Journal of Tropical Geography*, 30: 70–85.
Lysgård, H.K. (2016). The 'actual existing' cultural policy and culture-led strategies of rural places and small towns. *Journal of Rural Studies*, 44: 1–11.
Madianou, M., & Miller, D. (2012). *Migration and New Media: Transnational Families and Polymedia*. London: Routledge.
Morley D. (2009). For a materialist, non-media-centric media studies. *Television & New Media*, 10(1): 114–116.
Phillips, M. (2010). Counterurbanisation and rural gentrification: An exploration of the terms. *Population, Space and Place*, 16(6): 539–558.
Putnam, R. (2000). *Bowling Alone: The Collapse and Revival of American Community*. New York: Simon and Schuster.
Roberts, E., & Townsend, T. (2015). The contribution of the creative economy to the resilience of rural communities: Exploring cultural and digital capital. *Sociologia Ruralis*, 56(2): 197–219.
Ross, A. (2008). The new geography of work power to the precarious? *Theory, culture & Society*, 25(7–7): 31–49.
Savage, M. (2010). The politics of elective belonging. *Housing, Theory and Society*, 27(2): 115–135.
Sheller, M., & Urry, J. (2006). The new mobilities paradigm. *Environment and Planning*, 38: 207–226.
Urry, J. (2003). *Mobilities*. Cambridge: Polity Press.
Waitt, G., & Gibson, C. (2009). Creative small cities: Rethinking the Economy in Place. *Urban Studies*, 46(5–6): 1223–1246.

Waitt, G., & Gibson, C. (2013). The spiral gallery: Non-market creativity and belonging in an Australian country town. *Journal of Rural Studies*, 30: 75–85.

Wellman, B., Hogan, B., Berg, K., Boase, J., Jarrasco, J.-A., Côté, R., ... Tran, P. (2005). Connected lives: the project. In P. Purcell (Ed.) *Networked Neighbourhoods*. Berlin: Springer.

Wittel, A. (2001). Toward a network sociality, *Theory, Culture & Society*, 18(6): 51–76.

12 Geographical Imaginations, Politics of Hospitality and the Media in the European Refugee Crisis

Kaarina Nikunen

In 2015, more than 1.3 million refugees and migrants entered Europe in what has been called 'the worst refugee crisis' since the Second World War. While the refugee crisis has more severely affected countries outside Europe, such as Turkey, Lebanon and Jordan, the European imagination has regarded the arrival of refugees as an unexpected and exceptional emergency (UNHCR, 2016). The arrival of large amounts of people has created enormous challenges for European nations to manage the integration processes and overall situation. However, it has also revealed various underlining pressures, values and emotions that shape the European imaginations and sense of responsibility in the face of global events.

The ongoing conflict in Syria, the aftermath of the Arab Spring and continuous unrest in various parts of the African continent have resulted in increasing waves of people moving towards Europe seeking safety and a better future within the borders of the European Union (EU). Over the decades, people have sought refuge and better livelihoods in countries and regions that seem able to offer them. In the imaginations of many, Europe has long held a position as an avenue to new possibilities.

Entering Europe became more complex after the establishment of the Schengen Agreement in 1997. It opened the inner borders of the EU while strengthening the outer borders of Europe, resulting in what has been termed Fortress Europe. While the refugee crisis has made the general public aware of the dangers of crossing borders, these dangers have a long history. Reports of refugee deaths on the borders of Europe were already systematically collected in the 1990s by United for Intercultural Action, an umbrella organization for various nongovernmental organizations. It reported more than 2,000 deaths on the borders of Europe from 1993 to 2000 (Nikunen, 1999; United Against Racism, 2016). It is clear that migrants and refugees hoping to enter Europe often do so in extreme and life-threatening conditions. The camps set up in Melilla and Ceuta in the early 2000s, the Spanish Canary Islands in 2006, Lampedusa, Italy, after the Arab Spring in 2011, Lesbos Island in Greece and the bordering areas of Syria and Turkey in 2015 evidence the hard conditions refugees have faced for years in the border areas of Europe.

The local villages and cities on the coast of the Mediterranean Sea have dealt with migration and the so-called refugee crisis in different ways. In the 1990s, border control was still elementary on the Calabrian coast of Italy. Italy had been a transit country for Europe, so its political leadership had not considered migration to be a burning problem and had not made controlling the border a priority (Menz, 2008). By the late 1990s, other EU nations, especially Germany, started to pressure Italy to tighten its border control to decrease cross-border migration to other countries. In the 2000s, the EU started to financially support new operations to control its external borders.

Local people have witnessed the increase of national and European border controls and the launch of surveillance and rescue initiatives, such as the Nostra Mare and Frontex-led operations (De Genova, 2002; Cuttitta, 2009; Friese, 2012; Horsti, 2012; Musaro, 2017). At the same time, in contrast to the militarization of the border, a politics of hospitality emerged among the locals who witnessed the arrival of refugees and migrants in the region (Friese, 2012; Smith, 2016). The locals' hospitality has drawn attention and wonder in public discussion as something unexpected. This chapter explores the politics of hospitality that emerged in the small southern Italian village of Badolato in Calabria in the 1990s and years later during the refugee crisis 2015. In the 1990s, Badolato suffered from widespread problems throughout Calabria and Southern Italy: high unemployment rates, an ageing population, organized crime and a bleak vision of the future. The local government saw the arrival of more than 800 Kurdish refugees in December 1997 as an opportunity to reinvigorate Badolato by inviting the refugees to stay. This exceptional story soon brought media from all around Italy and Europe to report on these unusual events.

Drawing on the theories of space and place, this research operationalizes the concept of geographical imagination proposed by Harvey (1973/2009); it also looks at the idea of the politics of hospitality to examine how media imaginations shape a region economically, politically and culturally. What happens when hospitality becomes a political tool for survival circulated by the local and global media? In what conditions might such a politics of hospitality emerge, and most importantly, what kind of agency does it offer to refugees and migrants?

This chapter first introduces the key concepts of geographical imagination and the politics of hospitality, followed by a case study of Badolato in southern Italy based on ethnographic research. Finally, it discusses the European refugee crisis of 2015 and the ways in which the politics of hospitality has been appropriated in the crisis. These questions are connected with larger issues of refugee policies in the European imagination: are refugees and migrants threats to Europe's future, values and identity, or is Europe open to change? How do European towns and villages see themselves in the midst of changes? This critical consideration of the concept of geographical imagination shows the possibilities and limitations of imaginations in times of uncertainty and increased mobility.

Geographical Imagination and the Politics of Hospitality

The concept of geographical imagination was first formulated by Harvey (1973/2009: 24) in response to Mills' (1959) concept of sociological imagination, which refers to the ability to grasp history and biography and their relations in society. Harvey (1973/2009: 24) believed that the concept lacked spatial consciousness and introduced the concept of geographical imagination to emphasize the process through which the individual can 'recognize the role of space and place in his own biography' and understand the relations between social structures and space. Geographical imagination highlights the connections among social processes, spatial forms and social justice. The ways in which geographies are imagined have been multiplied and complicated by globalization, global media and digitalization. Local–global ties are actively manufactured; they shape our understanding of ourselves and others and the way we act in the world (Castree, 2004: 139). In the process of change, whose imaginations are at play becomes relevant. To be able to imagine connections between places and people across borders and to perceive opportunities that can be seized despite enormous challenges are crucial for asylum seekers and migrants who are seeking new futures in distant places. The imagination of Europe as a place of opportunity and prosperity provides crucial incentives for migration. Often, these imaginations are formed through media images and narratives, as well as messages and information from relatives, friends and acquaintances already living in Europe (Gillespie et al., 2016). At the same time, the capacity to imagine opportunity and responsibility for change is relevant to the construction of transnational, hospitable places. Here, the connections of media, geographical imagination and politics of hospitality become pertinent.

The chapter pays particular attention to the role of media in the process of geographic imagination, first on the level of representation. To follow Harvey (1989: 287–288), media images and investments in image building have assumed growing importance in cultural and economic practices, as well as in political and social life. In geographical imagination, media publicity holds significant power to define and shape how places are imagined. The media construct notions of places by focussing on particular issues, events and angles (Hanna, 1996; Ellapen, 2007). Through the machinery of news production and particular forms of framing, the media have the power to redefine places as violent, dynamic, dangerous, hopeless or attractive (Gold, 1994). These framings produce the social meanings of a place that can have significant political and material consequences. Especially in moments of change, the identity of a place becomes visible, accentuated and the object of struggle.

The role of media in terms of geographic imagination is not limited to representation of places. In the context of migration, mobile media particularly have increasingly important roles in providing information that can be life saving in dangerous crossings. Examples of mobile maps and technological alarm systems for refugees and migrants (Walsh, 2013; Gillespie et al., 2016). This illustrates the importance of media technologies on migrant routes. These technologies are also used by officials and the media in tracing refugees and migrants on their routes, and thus they are connected with different forms of power (Latonero, 2016). Media is also known to be important for enhancing long-distance social relationships with friends and family, and these possibilities have increased significantly with social media (Gillespie, 2000; Madianou, 2005; Bailey et al., 2007; Leurs, 2015). While media provides possibilities for imagining, connecting and finding information, they also provide voices for people to take part in public debates. Thus, geographic imaginations are made in these debates and discussions concerning everyday life and politics. These aspects are present also in the idea of mediapolis, the global civic space through which we can imagine and realize cosmopolitanism (see also Georgiou, 2013; Smets, 2016).

Another concept relevant here is hospitality. It is widely used in different theoretical contexts, often drawing on Kant's perpetual peace (1795/2003), but for the purposes of this chapter, the work by philosopher Levinas (1981), further developed by Derrida (2000) and Silverstone (2007), offers reference points relevant to geographic imagination. To imagine a place as transnational and open to change is a prerequisite for hospitality in the sense discussed by Levinas (1981) and Derrida (2000). In short, hospitality refers to the obligation to share space with the Other and operates on two levels: ethical and political. The ethical level refers to the individual's moral obligation, whereas the political level refers to the state's obligation to offer shelter to strangers and humanity. Derrida (2000) discusses hospitality in the context of the cosmopolitan rights of asylum seekers in western societies, focussing on the relation between conditional and unconditional hospitality. For Derrida (2000), this tension between unconditional hospitality (an unachievable ideal) and conditional hospitality (limited by various laws and regulations) can disrupt, challenge and open existing practices. Becoming open to others leads to new experiences and insight and consequently to the possibility of threshold for hope (Derrida, 2000, 2001). The politics of hospitality then can be seen as an attempt to create a place that provides such openness towards others – a place that is inclusive and cosmopolitan in its basic premises. Such a place comes close to Massey's (1994: 146–156) idea of a progressive, open place. A mediated version of a progressive, cosmopolitan place is formulated in Silverstone's (2007) idea of a mediapolis. Silverstone (2007: 22), following Hanna Arendt, defines mediapolis as a space of appearance, connection and compassion in the late modern world. It is a space of multiplicity with media narratives, images and interaction where people may come together as publics. Mediapolis, as cosmopolitan technologized space, entails several levels of mediated encounters and imaginations that may promote solidarity or enhance the sense of togetherness. For Silverstone (2007), hospitality is connected to mediapolis and, in this context, it means recognizing the Other's right to be heard and to listen to the Other. Silverstone promotes particularly the idea of unconditional hospitality as the responsibility of the media.

Borden (2015) and Couldry (2012) have criticized Silverstone's concept as too abstract and absolute. It hangs on the idea of universal cosmopolitanism without acknowledging localized and culturally specific practices as part of hospitality (Borden, 2015). Both critics present Aristotelian care ethics as a model for a more practice-based hospitality. In this view, hospitality is understood contextually as part of cultural practices and traditions, not as a separate, individualistic cosmopolitanism. As argued by Borden (2015), the contextualized understanding of hospitality might offer a better analytical tool for understanding the relevance of the politics of hospitality in the context of migration than do calls for unconditional hospitality in the name of universal cosmopolitanism. However, we should not forget that the defence of humanity, especially in times of crisis, is essential, although this understanding might not provide practical means to improve the conditions of vulnerable humans in the best way. The complex implications of the culture of hospitality become clear in empirical research on migration, border areas and reception centres. Anthropologist Friese (2011), who has explored life on the island of Lampedusa, describes how cultures of hospitality become professionalized and institutionalized. These developments, after years of managing the arrival of refugees, have rendered refugees invisible: they have become hidden in the extraterritorial space of transition, in a form of exclusive inclusion (Friese, 2012). Thus, managing refugees, as it becomes institutionalized, creates separate spaces of limited welcome instead of recognition.

In this chapter, these theoretical concepts of geographic imagination and hospitality are explored in two case studies; one situated on the Mediterranean coast in Badolato, Italy, and the other on the Northern fringes of Europe, in Kauhava Finland. This research applies an ethnographic approach to explore the mediated process of geographic imagination in the context of refugee politics in Europe. The aim of ethnographic research is to achieve a holistic understanding of a phenomenon or process. Thus, one must spend months or even years with the research. I follow Marcus' (1986) guidelines on multisited ethnography to identify the relevant sites of the phenomenon studied by following the processes, items, objects and information relevant to the study. Thus, this research utilizes a wide range of sources and methods, from the analysis of media texts and documents to interviews and participatory observation. This is also close to the idea of multilocal fieldwork (Hannerz, 2002) that combines different sources of knowledge to gain an understanding of the processes that shape the phenomenon studied. In this case, the temporal dimension (1997–2016) forms the frame for observing the process and long-term significance of imaginations.[1]

The Hospitality of Badolato

The story of this chapter begins in December 1997 on the old ship *Ararat* carrying 836 passengers from Turkey to Italy. Most passengers were from the Kurdish regions of Turkey and sought asylum in Europe. Many had supported the Kurdish separatist army PKK or were otherwise politically active. However, many were simply on a journey to start new lives in better conditions. Among the passengers were 27-year-old Karzan, 22-year-old Sherim and Nazin, a 23-year-old mother who had left Turkey with her brother and 3-year-old son. Nazin was heading to Germany, where her husband already lived. Communicating across distances was very different in 1997 than in the 21st century. Very few people had their own mobile phones, and Internet access was rarely available free of charge. While travelling, migrants and refugees contacted relatives and friends by making calls through landline pay phones and writing letters to poste restante. Through networks of friends and relatives, many had some kind of image of what life in Europe might entail, how they could prepare for it and what kind of jobs might be available, for instance, in Germany.

On Christmas night, 25 December 1997, the *Ararat* deviated from its route and shipwrecked on the coast of Calabria. The passengers all survived and soon received help from the Coast Guard and the local people. Local volunteers collected dry clothes, blankets and food for the survivors. Soon after the relief operations, Gerardo Mannello, the mayor of Badolato, decided to invite the passengers of the *Ararat* to stay permanently in the village. He wanted to help the refugees and migrants and, at the same time, use the opportunity to revitalize Badolato, a small municipality in Calabria. Badolato had suffered from emigration for years. Many of its medieval stone houses on the hillside looking down at the Mediterranean were deteriorating. The more lively and modern centre, Sea-Badolato, was 10 kilometres away on the coast. The region suffered from high unemployment and poverty and had weak prospects for future growth. In addition, Calabria had a reputation as the stomping grounds for organized crime.

In 1954, the population of the village was 7,000, but by 1998, it had fallen to only 600. Most of the remaining inhabitants were elderly people. The largest wave of emigration took place in 1960s as people moved away, especially to Switzerland. In the 1970s, more than 500,000

Italians lived in Switzerland working in the construction, textiles and machine industries. There, Italians suffered from ethnic discrimination, poor housing conditions and restrictions on residence permits and family unification (Efionayi, Niederberger, and Wanner, 2005). Consequently, many in Badolato had experiences of migration and marginalization in their own family histories. This experience appeared to be relevant to how the locals related to the arriving migrants and refugees.

In 1997, the centre square of Badolato had three cafes, two restaurants and a small grocery store, which flourished mostly in the summertime as tourists and relatives from northern Italy visited. As the village of 600 was suddenly populated with 300 new inhabitants, it was evident that the change would affect the everyday life of the village in many ways. A local cultural association, Pro Badolato, was established to organize cultural events where locals and newcomers could interact and get to know each other in order to avoid conflicts. For example, migrants and locals celebrated the Kurdish New Year, Newroz, in March 1998. The mayor, who represented the Communist party, created a plan to renovate 20 old, deteriorating houses for the arriving asylum seekers. The plan included establishing a new restaurant and a convenience store and creating jobs for social workers and interpreters. Eventually, Badolato was granted 686,000 Euros in federal funding to realize this plan. Renovations provided work for local businesses, which were also granted subsidies for employing asylum seekers. In February 1998, a Kurdish restaurant named after the shipwrecked boat *Ararat* was opened. Karzan and Nazin found work at the restaurant, while Sherim started to work in a tourist shop, selling local goods and souvenirs, close to the town square. All these developments happened within several months of the shipwreck.

The story of Badolato was unusual enough to attract publicity, and reporters from throughout Italy and Europe came to the village to cover the story. The publicity was predominantly positive, which also affected the overall attitude towards the project in the town. The people of Calabria were accustomed to reading headlines associating the region with poverty, crime and social problems, but this time, the region was presented as an exemplar of hospitality and global responsibility. Positive media coverage was so unusual that it became news itself in the local press (*Gazzetta del Sud*, 29 March 1998). In 1998–2001, Badolato received unprecedented attention in the media, and the media coverage became a powerful site of geographic imagination. The news stories from 1998 to 1999 gave a detailed description of Mannello's plans to offer housing to the refugees and to invite them to stay in the village. The Badolato method received attention in a wide range of media, including local, national and international press, from high-prestige national newspapers to women's magazines and the popular press to local political left-wing newspapers. Within this variety of publications, the general tone of the coverage was surprisingly harmonious, indicating a shared sense of enthusiasm for the project. The news stories framed Badolato as a place that could 'set an example' (*Neues Deutschland* 24/25 1998) and offered 'a different model of integration' (*Le Courrier*). These stories carried a sense of hope and optimism, singling out Badolato as an exceptional town with an innovative vision for the future and a true ethic of hospitality. The Badolato method became a successful political concept and was referred to in several stories. Mayor Mannello became the central figure in the press coverage, and the 'miracle of Badolato' was attributed to him as his personal idea. The media attention made Mannello a public name, and he received several awards and honours.

The arrival of refugees and migrants shaped Badolato in many ways. First, the new inhabitants and their languages and traditions brought multiculturalism into the village. Its once-silent streets became lively, filled with children and families. In the cafes surrounding the square, new customers, mostly men who had arrived in the *Ararat*, smoked and talked politics. The offices of Pro Badolato, which handled refugee issues, were constantly crowded with people requesting documents and exchanging news with Daniela, a staff member with the refugee organization CIR (The Italian Refugee Council). The new interest in the town was evident in the streets, as well as the media, as reporters and politicians visited the village. These visitors included then-Interior Minister Giorgio Napolitano, later the president of Italy, who gave his support to the project. His visit was carefully documented by the local press. The visits by politicians and reporters expanded the boundaries of the locality, connecting Badolato to the larger issues of refugee politics in Europe. The new people in the village and the interest in them created a sense of a place open to the world and open to change. This sense of a place was born out of the synergy between the symbolic level of media publicity and the material level of everyday life. Mayor Mannello acknowledged that the media publicity was extremely valuable for him in realizing politics of hospitality (interview 28.07.2011). The support of positive media coverage enabled him to follow through with initiatives that would have otherwise been difficult to achieve. The news media emphasized Mannello's vision and the actions of the village rather than the conditions and struggles of the refugees and migrants in the deteriorating situation in the Mediterranean area.

What did this politics of hospitality mean to the refugees and migrants themselves? Evidently, none of the passengers of the *Ararat* expected the reception they received in Badolato. They were not prepared to be part of 'the miracle' Badolato. Initially, the general atmosphere was full of excitement and optimism. The everyday life of people working in restaurants and shops was devoid of idleness and the frustration of waiting. Sherim and Karzan interacted with locals and tourists and learned the Italian language through these interactions. At the same time, migrants' networks and contacts to Germany and elsewhere in Europe remained important and gave rhythm to their lives. Through phone calls, letters and news, they learned about others' situations and possibilities elsewhere. Nazin, who worked in the Ararat restaurant, talked with her husband on the phone every day. Politically active members of Kurdish associations were in touch with others in different parts of Europe, particularly Belgium and Germany. They took part in television debates about refugees and the Kurdish situation in Italy.

However, the migrants who did not have jobs remained caught in 'the time of suspension and wait' (Capparelli, Lagozzo, and Vitale, 2006: 105). In the living quarters at the local schools, satellite television with Med TV provided leisure entertainment with Kurdish programming. The men who lived at the school premises spent most of their days watching television, playing cards and talking with others in the same situation. Badolato did not offer a particular solution to their situation. Instead, waiting for their asylum decision and documents that would enable them to continue their journey to other European countries seemed to provide the solution. In practice, almost all of the passengers of the *Ararat* were granted asylum in Italy, although the procedure took several months. The bureaucracy and slow process of the documents became the daily topic of conversation in cafes and streets (see also Capparelli et al., 2006). More importantly, the inability of Mannello's plan to provide employment to all refugees became the inherent problem and defect in the politics of hospitality. It did not change the incapacity of the narrow regional economic structure to provide long-lasting employment for its new population. Even if the refugees and migrants were welcome in the village, their future prospects there seemed unrealistic. Even most of those who secured jobs in Badolato left the village to find new possibilities in northern Europe. Their existing networks with friends and family members seemed more significant than the possibility of staying and working in tiny Badolato. By the end of 2000, most migrants who had arrived on the *Ararat* had moved on to northern Italy or northern Europe as the young people of Badolato had done for years before them.

Value of Hospitality

To understand the relevance of the politics of hospitality, it is useful to look at it as part of a longer development. As I returned once again to Badolato in 2011, the refugee situation in Europe had become more difficult since the Arab spring of 2011, with uprisings in Tunisia, Egypt and Libya forcing new waves of refugees and migrants from North Africa to Europe. These developments had little impact in Badolato, which seemed to be declining rather than flourishing. One of the three cafes and the tourist shop had closed. The Kurdish restaurant had changed ownership, and it had been turned into a local Calabrian restaurant. Nazin had moved to Germany with her husband, while Karzan and Sherim had moved to northern Italy. The mayor of Badolato had also changed. The new mayor, Nicola Parretta, lived in Rome and visited the village on weekends. The village still had refugees, organized by a central administration in Rome. Groups of 15 people who had been granted refugee status were sent to Badolato for three-month integration periods. During that time, they were supposed to learn Italian and find work.

The Afghan refugees then living in Badolato did not perceive the village as especially hospitable. Indeed, they felt that the locals were not interested in communicating with refugees or even offering them lifts from the village to the coast (interviews 2–3 August 2011). The local cafe owner recognized the same change in climate. He longed for the interaction and events of late 1990s and described how the village was slowly withering (interview 6 August 2011). This was clear in the evenings as locals and refugees gathered in separate groups in the square.

However, the politics of hospitality was still relevant in the brand of the town. The image of Badolato as an exceptionally hospitable village has found its way into the village's tourist brochures, website and advertising. Real estate agents used the story of the hospitable town to sell and rent houses to foreign tourists. The municipality also promoted several initiatives that utilized its reputation for hospitality. In 1998, a group of local politicians suggested that Badolato receive the Nobel Peace Prize.[2] In 2006, Badolato and the refugee organization CIR applied for the World Habitat prize for a project aimed at improving social housing with innovative solutions. Badolato unsuccessfully applied to be included in UNESCO's World Heritage list. Through such initiatives, Badolato strove to redefine its identity and move away from the reputation as hopeless and marginalized to the image of a unique, globally valuable place (Valaskivi, 2016). The event that drew the most attention nationally was the making of a film based on the story of Badolato by German director Wim Wenders. The short film *Il Volo*, released in 2010, was partly funded by the municipality of Badolato.

In the imagination of the politicians of Badolato, hospitality became a resource, through which the locals strove to redefine their value and assume a position as agents of change, not victims of it. Various materials produced for tourists emphasized hospitality. A local real estate agent explained that a news story in the Swedish newspaper *Dagens industri* helped him close a deal with a Swedish family in the summer of 2011 (interview 29 May 2011). German, Swiss and Danish tourists have also bought houses in the village, and an entire Danish holiday village has been built close to Badolato. The holiday village illustrates the unequal power geometry of globalization (Massey, 1994: 149; Sheller, 2004) that placed people in different social and economic positions. Even if the Danish tourists remain separate from locals, the holiday village itself has benefitted some refugees. A man who arrived in Badolato as an asylum seeker from Ethiopia has found a permanent job as a gardener in the holiday village. When we met in August 2011, he lived with his brother in Badolato and was waiting for his wife to arrive in Italy (interview 5 August 2011).

The refugee issue remains significant currency in local politics. The new mayor Parretta strove to make impacts on the Mediterranean situation by cooperating with other mayors in the region (Riace and Lampedusa). In a joint declaration, the mayors of Badolato, Riace and Lampedusa called for Northern Europe to display solidarity in solving the refugee situation in the Mediterranean region (interview 5 August 2011). The relevance of politics of hospitality becomes clear when comparing Badolato to the other municipalities in the area. For example, in Sant' Anna, a village 100 kilometres from Badolato, asylum seekers are hosted in old warehouses, and the relationships between locals and asylum seekers are tense (Donadio, 2010). The reception centre has been investigated for financial unclarities concerning the daily allowances for asylum seekers. According to investigations by humanitarian organizations, the centre has failed to pay allowances of more than 2 million euros (Consentino and Mezzaroma, 2014; UNHCR, 2016). Compared to this, the appropriated politics of hospitality in Badolato, even if failed, illustrates the incentive to create humane processes of integration. This direction in politics profoundly affected the self-understanding and identity of the town. The locals viewed themselves as heroes and humanitarians in the process – not as victims of the undesired change. This position is relevant to how refugee issues are solved at a local level and shows the power of geographic imagination to shape things on a concrete level.

What was the relevance of politics of hospitality in the lives of Sherim and Karzan? Both moved to northern Italy, close to Milan in the early 2000s. Their decision to stay in Italy was influenced by the fact that they had already learned Italian in Badolato and could find work and interact with locals. Neither had strong relations or networks in other parts of Europe. They are now self-employed, working in their own restaurant. Although they have left Badolato, they still keep in touch with the mayor and Daniela, who worked for the refugee organization CIR. However, the media environment has changed drastically during these years and impacted their possibilities to communicate and maintain social relationships. When they first arrived in Badolato in the late 1990s, communication took place primarily through landline phones and letters. During the 2000s, media technology provided new means of communication through the Internet and mobile phones illustrating the virtual transnationalism of people living in diaspora (Sheller, 2004; Bailey et al., 2007; Eide and Nikunen, 2011). The former mayor Mannello and Daniela with CIR keep in touch with dozens of refugees through Facebook. Sherim and Karzan also use Facebook to keep in touch with the transnational network they developed during their years of refuge.

Their friends include those with whom they travelled to Badolato who have now gone separate ways, relatives from home and new friends they made since settling down in Italy. Facebook offers ways to recreate personal identity by sharing everyday life with others and by showing how life goes on. It also offers possibilities to create past narratives and momentarily gather together around shared memories. Every 25 December, Daniela posts a picture from *Ararat* on her Facebook page, remembering the event that shaped the lives of both the passengers of Ararat and the people of Badolato. Both people living in Badolato and the refugees who arrived in Badolato come together to the page and write comments under the picture. Most comments testify to the unique, life-changing nature of the event and express gratitude to the municipality of Badolato, as Sherim did in 2014: 'thank you for taking us in your hearts'.

The 2015 Refugee Crisis

How should we understand the relevance of the case of Badolato to the European refugee crisis in 2015? Although the scale of the refugees arriving in Europe was very different in 2015 than in the 1990s, movements of hospitality as in Badolato can be seen in different parts of Europe. The response to the newly arrived refugees and migrants in many European cities and towns was initially welcoming. Examples of campaigns to provide water, blankets and food to refugees in parks and railway stations in European cities expressed a sense of solidarity for the plight of refugees arriving from Syria and the Middle East. The local residents on the island of Lesbos and in Lampedusa have received awards for their exceptional humanitarian assistance rescuing and accommodating refugees and migrants arriving by sea (IFRC, 2015; United Nations, 2016). In Greece, the lack of proper management of asylum seekers and migrants has given rise to new forms of anarchist movements to help people in need (Strickland, 2016). From these sentiments of charity and hospitality, several new Europeanwide movements, which also operate on social media, such as Refugees Welcome and Refugees Hospitality Club, have been born.

However, after the initial wave of hospitality, sentiments of fear and chaos started to emerge. In the public sphere, refugees were connected with terrorism, especially after the Paris attacks in October 2015, and with sexual violence after the allegedly organized sexual harassment of women in Cologne on New Year's Eve 2015. These events and their media publicity, along with the growing anti-immigrant movement in European politics, have influenced public opinion and fuelled growing opposition towards refugees (Bachman, 2016). Media coverage has provided cartographic imaginations of refugee crisis in forms of maps, charts and numbers, depicting the inhumanized figures that undermined European borders. The space for the politics of hospitality has become increasingly narrow. The so-called refugee crisis has become a central issue in the EU and seems to threaten core EU values and principles, including the Schengen Agreement, Dublin Treaty and free movement of people. Instead of generating new alternatives to refugee politics, the main focus was managing the masses through increased surveillance and closed borders. On the macro level of European politics, the geographic imagination appears to have reinforced closed nationalism through intensified border control.

Although much of the public focus has been on hostilities and conflict, on the local level, several examples of politics of hospitality can be found. As new reception centres were rapidly established across Europe, many small towns hosted refugees for the first time. In Finland, for instance, the annual number of asylum seekers multiplied from around 6,000 to 32,000 (Migri, 2016). In Kauhava, a small town of 16,000 inhabitants, a reception centre for 300 asylum seekers was established in September 2015 on the premises of a former air force base. The centre at first faced fierce resistance among the locals. The arriving asylum seekers were considered threats to the security of the locals, especially the local girls, who were seen as potential targets of sexual violence. However, after initial resistance, the centre slowly became accepted as part of everyday life in Kauhava.

The Red Cross reception centre was led by a former air force officer, Ilkka Peura, who lived permanently in the area. His vision reflected that of Mannello in Badolato: Peura sought to integrate the asylum seekers into the local community and create jobs through local businesses. His aim was to provide activities and means to improve the living conditions as much as possible for the asylum seekers who had to wait up to eight months for their application decisions. These ideas were exceptional and distinct among reception centres and offered an alternative imagination of how integration processes could be realized. Soon, the Kauhava reception centre had its own laundry, a small weaving factory and a tailor shop. To manage salaries, the centre founded a cooperative to organize employment. The reception centre also had its own ten-member parliament elected through free elections. In June 2016, dozens of asylum seekers were working either in the centre or outside in local businesses and small industries. In many ways, the initiatives to offer jobs to asylum seekers while profiting local businesses in Kauhava were similar to the initiatives in Badolato. The aims were to increase the integration of asylum seekers and to revitalize local business. Instead of treating the asylum seekers as passive victims or masses of travellers passing through, Kauhava provided several activities and employment in local businesses for asylum seekers.

Like Badolato, Kauhava was strongly defined by media publicity. Initially, Kauhava inspired headlines representing local fears and racist commentaries, but a few months after establishing the reception centre, the town was presented as an example of a place that treats asylum seekers well and offers possibilities for the future. Here, the mainstream media constructed the image of a place open to change and capable of responding to the challenges of a global crisis. However, the tone was different on social media. Notably, in the case of Badolato in 1997, publicity was created primarily through mainstream media and local print media, whereas the 2015 refugee crisis was discussed and debated largely on social media. Although social media provides access to multiple perspectives and voices from the margins, it is also characterized by affective, conflictual and propagandist tones. In the case of Kauhava, several online sites, including blogs, tabloids and discussion forums, circulated false rumours of terrorists or bombs on the premises of the reception centre and sexual relations between locals and asylum seekers (Metropoli 18 November 2015; MV 15.5.2016; Suomi24[3]). Such rumours and false information drew on existing prejudices and previous stories to circulate the sentiment of fear. This kind of emotional energy fuels social media and its affective economy (Ahmed, 2004). However, actual encounters with asylum seekers at the local grocery stores and workplaces created necessary counternarratives to the imaginations and circulating narratives of threat. The geographical imagination of Kauhava was formed at the intersection of contradictory images from mainstream media, social media and the material practices of the everyday. It also became part of the larger narrative of the European refugee crisis as local experiences were interpreted and reflected through European developments.

The crucial question in politics of hospitality is how it positions migrants, refugees and asylum seekers. Are they granted agency and political subjectivity? Through the politics of hospitality, do they become invisible and separate from the rest of the community, or are they understood as part of the community, interacting with others? In the case of Badolato, the ideal of hospitality was connected to a shared sense of humanity. However, in practice, it was disconnected from the everyday structures of local economic life; so it could not provide sustainable solutions for the newcomers. It momentarily opened the door of community to the refugees, but in time the divide and sense of difference between the locals and the refugees grew. However, the refugees and migrants who entered Europe through Badolato achieved a fair start in Europe, unlike so many of the asylum seekers who have entered Europe after them. As the case study shows, such experience is relevant to the sense of belonging and citizenship in the long run. The hospitality in Badolato was constructed as the result of locals' exceptional humanitarianism, so they became heroes of the story. The refugees and migrants were cast into the role of grateful, apolitical victims, which is a persistent problem in humanitarian discourse and universal, unconditional hospitality (Ticktin, 2010). In the case of Kauhava, the politics of hospitality was formed in the continuous cross-draft of contradictory ideas and images of what Kauhava should be and how asylum seekers might or might not be part of that future. In this context, the reception centre created space for alternative imaginations of the politics of hospitality by challenging the idea of asylum seekers as passive victims and locals as victims of change. Hospitality was contextual and pragmatic, making use of local businesses. It was formed through the local cultural tapestry without the accent of the cosmopolitan idea of shared humanity. New practices emerged from this politics of hospitality, but it faced continuous resistance and criticism within local social media. Although the asylum seekers were assumed to be active agents, their agency was constantly challenged, suspected and rendered potentially dangerous in social media debates.

Mediated Geographic Imagination

Geographic imagination refers to the capacity to understand the role of a place in social processes, as well as how this role is constructed. The concept refers to the forms and quality of knowledge produced by these imaginations and the ways in which we can form an understanding of the world, power relations, social structures and their material consequences. In the context of the 2015 European refugee crisis, we can make a distinction between macro- and micro-level imaginations. On the macro level of political decision making and media imaginations, Europe appeared to be under attack by an influx of migrants and refugees. The solution imagined was a move away from an open, cosmopolitan Europe towards re-establishment of borders and rise of nationalism. On the micro level of local everyday life, however, there were several examples where ordinary people furthered the imagination of an open, hospitable Europe, welcoming and helping migrants and refugees and creating new forms of help and hospitality while faced with increasing imaginations of fear and hatred.

In this chapter, I have attempted to demonstrate that the media constitute a significant dimension of geographic imagination and the politics of hospitality. The cases point out how media operate on different levels, defining, connecting and providing space for debates in which these imaginations are again circulated and redefined. The ways in which media shape our understanding of the world have consequences for practices and places. The media might enhance a sense of cosmopolitanism, but they can also make the world seem dangerous through representations of fear and chaos. The role of media has changed throughout the years, and clearly it has become more immersive, embodied and mobile. Media travel now along with refugees and migrants all the time and provide new means to communicate across distances as well as gain information. However, the latest media technology does not always guarantee that the imaginations of better future are realistic and realizable.

Mediated imaginations of cosmopolitan place do not necessarily help such imaginations to be realized.

Possibilities to imagine alternatives, rooted in the local cultures, are an essential part of the concept of geographic imagination. Such imagination is also necessary for refugees and migrants to assume agency. As the case studies of this chapter have shown, assuming agency through the politics of hospitality is far from easy. Even if the politics of hospitality consists of benevolent efforts to help, it might undermine the capacity of refugees and migrants to define their own positions and imagine alternative futures from their own perspectives. This reminds us how important spaces of voice, participation and connection are.

Geographic imaginations that are built on universal and technocratic sources of knowledge lack a contextualized understanding of the conditions and situations at stake. As such, they fail to create long-lasting alternatives, sustainable solutions and social change. Therefore, it is necessary that the imagination created through and with media not paint unrealistic utopias or dystopias but focus on the concrete, manifold perspectives rooted in everyday life, building on interaction and solidarity based not on obligation but on a shared understanding of the world in which we live.

Notes

1 I visited Badolato four times between 1998 and 2011. I made the first visits as a journalist covering the story of Badolato and the last visit as a researcher. During my visits, I collected materials through interviews, observation and various statistical, historical and archive materials. These research materials include journalistic interviews that are treated as background information. As well, Mayor Gerardo Mannello provided archive materials, including 106 news stories, 23 images, 67 letters and cards and 37 invitations and honors to the mayor from 1997 to 2003 (see also Nikunen, 2015). Since my last visit, I have kept in contact with the interviewed locals and refugees through email. The names of the interviewed refugees and asylum seekers have been changed to protect their anonymity, but the real names of politicians and officials are used. In addition to the materials from Badolato, the research materials include materials from Kauhava, Finland: interviews, observation, media coverage and statistical and historical documents gathered from June to August 2016.
2 The Mediterranean region sought the Nobel Peace Prize in 2015, when the people of the Island of Lesbos who welcomed more than 30,000 refugees were nominated.
3 http://keskustelu.suomi24.fi/paikkakunnat/etela-pohjanmaa/kauhava Accessed 12.9.2016.

References

Ahmed, S. (2004). *The Cultural Politics of Emotion*. Edinburgh: Edinburgh University Press.

Bachman, B. (2016). *Diminishing Solidarity. The migration Policy.* [Online]. Accessed 12.9.2016. Available from: www.migrationpolicy.org/article/diminishing-solidarity-polish-attitudes-toward-european-migration-and-refugee-crisis.

Bailey, O., Georgiou, M., & Harindranath, R. (Eds.). (2007). *Transnational Lives and the Media: Re-imagining Diaspora*. Basingstoke: Palgrave.

Borden, S. (2015). A virtue ethics critique of Silverstone's media hospitality. *Journal of Media Ethics*, 30(3): 168–185.

Capparelli, A., Lagozzo, M. C., & Vitale, S. (2006). I Kurdi in Calabria: A Badolato comune catanzarese. In *Studi e Richere di Geografia XXIX Unica 2006*. Universita della Calabria. Reggio di Calabria.

Castree, N. (2004). Differential geographies: place, indigenous rights and 'local' resources. *Political Geography*, 23(2004): 133–167.

Couldry, N. (2012). *Media, Society, World. Social Theory and Digital Media Practice*. Cambridge: Polity Press.

Consentino, R. & Mezzaroma, A. (2014) Milioni sulle pelle dei rifugiati. *Il Repubblica* 6.5.2014

Cuttitta, P. (2014). *The Mediterranean Grenzsaum: Migration Controls and Borders in the Strait of Sicily*. [Online]. [Accessed 20 August 2016]. Available from: www.altrodiritto.unifi.it/frontier/storia/grenzsaum.htm.

De Genova, N. (2002). Migrant illegality and deportability in everyday life. *Annual Review of Anthropology*, 31: 419–437.

Derrida, J. (2000). *Of Hospitality. Anne Dofourmantelle invites Jacques Derrida to respond*. Stanford: Stanford University Press.

Derrida, J. (2001). *On Cosmopolitanism and Forgiveness*. London and New York: Routledge.

Donadio, R. (2010). Race riots grip an Italian town, and Mafia is suspected. *New York Times*. [Online]. 10 January. [Accessed 28 March 2012]. Available from: www.nytimes.com/2010/01/11/world/europe/11italy.html?_r=0.

Efionayi, J., Niederberger, M., & Wanner, P. (2005) *Switzerland Faces Common European Challenges*. Migration Policy Institute. [Accessed 18.09.2015]. Available online: www.migrationinformation.org/USfocus/display.cfm?ID=284.

Eide, E., & Nikunen, K. (Eds.) (2011). *Media in Motion: Cultural Complexity and Migration in the Nordic Region*. Farnham: Ashgate.

Ellapen, J. A. (2007). The cinematic township: cinematic representations of the 'township space' and who can claim the rights to representation in post-apartheid South African cinema. *Journal of African Cultural Studies*, 19(1): 113–137.

Friese, H. (2011). Limits of hospitality: Undocumented migration and the local arena. The case of Lampedusa. In M. Bauman & K. Rosenow (Eds.), *Crossings and Controlling Borders. Immigration Policies and Their Impact on Migrants Journeys* (pp. 249–272). Opladen: Budrich Unipress.

Friese, H. (2012). Border economies: Lampedusa and the nascent migration industry. *Shima: The International Journal of Research into Island Cultures*, 6(2): 66–84.

Georgiou, M. (2013) *Media and the City: Cosmopolitanism and Difference*. Polity Global Media and Communication Series. Cambridge: Polity Press.

Gillespie, M. (2000). Transnational communications and diaspora communities. In S. Cottle, (Ed.), *Ethnic minorities and the media: Changing cultural boundaries* (pp. 164–178). Buckingham: Open University Press.

Gillespie, M., Ampofo, L., Cheesman, M., Faith, B., Iliadou, E., Issa, A., ... Sklrparis, D. (2016). *Mapping Refugee Media Journeys: Smartphones and Social Media Networks*. [Online]. Accessed 13.10.2016.

Gold, S. (1994). Locating the message: Place promotion as image communication. In S. Gold & J. Ward (Eds.), *Place Promotion: The Use of Publicity and Marketing to Sell Towns and Regions* (pp. 19–37). Chichester: Wiley.

Hanna, S. (1996). Is it Roslyn or is it Cicely? Representation and the ambiguity of place. *Urban Geography*, 17: 633–649.

Hannerz, U. (2002). Among the foreign correspondents: Reflections on anthropological styles and audiences. *Ethnos*, 67(1): 57–74.

Harcup, T., & O'Neill, D. (2001). What is news? Galtung and Ruge revisited. *Journalism Studies*, 2(2): 261–280.

Harvey, D. (1989). *The Condition of Postmodernity: An Enquiry into the Origins of Cultural Change*. Cambridge: Blackwell.

Harvey, D. (2009) [1973]. *Social Justice and the City*, rev. edn. Athens: University of Georgia Press.

Horsti, K. (2012). Humanitarian discourse legitimating migration control: FRONTEX public communication. In M. Messier, R. Wodak, & R. Schroeder, (Eds.), *Migrations: Interdisciplinary Perspectives* (pp. 297–308). Vienna: Springer Science & Business Media.

IFRC (2015). *Lampedusa Honoured for Its Role in Maintaining the Dignity of Migrants Fleeing Violence*. [Online]. [Accessed 12.9. 2016]. Available from: www.ifrc.org/en/news-and-media/news-stories/europe-central-asia/italy/Lampedusa-honoured-for-role-in-migrant-safety-68025/.

Kant, I. (1795/2003). *Perpetual Peace. A Philosophical Sketch*. Indianapolis: Hackett publishing.

Latonero, M. (2016). *For Refugees, A Digital Path to Europe*. Responsible Dataforum 8.2. 2016. [Accessed 28.12.2016]. Available at: https://responsibledata.io/for-refugees-a-digital-passage-to-europe/.

Leurs, K. (2015) *Digital Passages. Migrant Youth 2.0. Diaspora, Gender & Youth Cultural Intersections*. Amsterdam: Amsterdam University Press.

Levinas, E. (1981). *Otherwise than Being, or, Beyond Essence*. The Hague: Nijhoff.

Madianou, M. (2005). Contested communicative spaces: Rethinking identities, boundaries and the role of the media among Turkish speakers in Greece. *Journal of Ethnic and Migration Studies*, 31(3): 521–541.

Marcus, G. (1986). Contemporary problems of ethnography in the modern world system. In J. Clifford & G. Marcus (Eds.), *Writing Culture* (pp. 165–193). Berkeley: University of California Press.

Massey, D. (1994). *Space, Place and Gender*. Minneapolis: University of Minnesota Press.

Menz, G. (2008). *The Political Economy of Managed Migration: Nonstate Actors, Europeanization, and the Politics of Designing Migration Policies*. Oxford: Oxford University Press.

Migri (2016). [Online]. [Accessed 20 June 2016]. Available from: www.migri.fi/tietoa_virastosta/tilastot/turvapaikka-_ja_pakolaistilastot.

Mills, C. W. (1959). *The Sociological Imagination.* New York: Oxford University Press.

Musaro, P. (2017) Mare Nostrum: the visual politics of a military-humanitarian operation in the Mediterranean Sea. *Media, Culture & Society* 39(1): 11–28.

Nikunen, K. (1999). Euroopan rajoille menehtyy satoja pakolaisia vuosittain. *Helsingin Sanomat* 19.1.1999.

Nikunen, K. (2015). Hopes of hospitality. *International Journal of Cultural Studies*, 19(2): 161–176.

Sheller, M. (2004). Demobilizing and remobilizing the Caribbean. In M. Sheller & J. Urry (Eds.), *Tourism Mobilities: Places to Play, Places in Play* (pp. 13–21). London & New York: Routledge.

Silverstone, R. (2007). *Media and Morality: On the Rise of the Mediapolis.* Cambridge: Polity Press.

Smets, K. (2016). Ethnic media, and the nation state: Kurdish Broadcasting in Turkey and Europe and mediated nationhood. *Media, Culture & Society*, 38(5): 738–754.

Smith, H. (2016). Refugee crisis: How Greeks opened their hearts to strangers. *The Guardian.* [Online]. 13 March 2016 [Accessed 12.9.2016]. Available from: www.theguardian.com/world/2016/mar/12/refugee-crisis-greeks-strangers-migrants.

Strickland, P. (2016). Greek anarchists organise for refugees as 'state fails'. *Al-Jazeera.* [Online]. 16 January 2016. [Accessed 14.6.2016]. Available from: www.aljazeera.com/indepth/features/2016/01/greek-anarchists-organise-refugees-state-fails-160117032251199.html.

Ticktin, M. (2010). From redundancy to recognition: Transnational humanitarianism and the production of non-moderns. In E. Bornstein & P. Redfield (Eds.), *Forces of Compassion: Humanitarianism between Ethics and Politics* (pp. 175–219). Santa Fe: SAR Press.

UNHCR (2016). [Online]. Available from: www.unhcr.org/figures-at-a-glance.html.

United Against Racism. (2016). [Online]. Available from: www.unitedagainstracism.org/wp-content/uploads/2015/06/Listofdeaths22394June15.pdf.

United Nations (2016). *Greek Volunteers Awarded Top UN Humanitarian Honour.* [Online]. Available from: https://refugeesmigrants.un.org/greek-volunteers-awarded-top-un-humanitarian-honour-efforts-migrants-and-refugees.

Valaskivi, K. (2016). *Cool Nations: Media and the Social Imaginary of the Branded Country.* London and New York: Routledge.

Walsh, (2013). Re-mapping the border: geospatial technologies and border activism. *Environment and Planning D: Society and Space*, 31: 969–987.

13 Fast Media
John Tomlinson

The terrain of geomedia studies, within which the chapters of this book in their different ways are located, is in part at least, a landscape that opened out – inevitably as can be seen in retrospect – from the field of globalization studies. Globalization studies, beginning in the 1980s, had grasped the deep grammar of time/space transformation that underlay the dynamics of complex connectivity, interdependence and global flows. It had also begun to identify the particular significance of media systems, institutions and practices in the restructuring of global-cultural time/space. However, it is perhaps fair to say that within the broader analysis of globalization, attention to the media was subordinate to, for the most part, and even subservient to, the compelling logic of political economy. There were of course some valid reasons for not displacing the central role of global capitalism in favour of a media-centric analysis, and the most persuasive analyses insisted on a multicausal approach in which economic, political, cultural and technological factors were seen as acting in concert in the emergence of globalization. However, as the decades have passed it has been increasingly difficult to ignore the degree to which telemediation itself has impacted cultural, economic and political practices and experiences across the globe. It has become clear that media have their own distinct and intrinsic time/space organizing properties – albeit often working in concert with the other dynamics of globalization.

Geomedia studies is emerging as the field of analysis appropriate to this recognition. The shifting of perspective that it entails – away from those set by both 'traditional' media studies and globalization studies – promises new ways of understanding the profound cultural changes we are witnessing. As a student of the cultural aspects of globalization, I have travelled in a similar direction, gradually coming to see that what might be important is not only the increasing *reach* of media across culturally organized space but also other intrinsic meaning-giving properties of telemediation. This is to pose the question of whether there might be quite separate cultural accounts to be given of global media than that which stresses, for obvious example, a uniformity of global cultural experience delivered by media conglomerates or, considered more positively, the opening up of localities to the diversity of ways of being made available through new media technologies (Tomlinson, 1999).

In this chapter, then, I want to focus on the question of speed. Telemediated culture is undoubtedly novel and significant in terms of the experience of *proximity* it affords – drawing global populations, for both good and ill, into common arenas – but it is no less transformative in terms of the *immediacy* it imparts. To grasp the full cultural significance of contemporary global media, then, we need to pay attention not just to its scale and scope, but to its speed. In what follows I will suggest some ways in which this may be approached, beginning with a short account of the place of speed in the constitution of global cultural modernity and moving on from this to broach the question of the affinity between media systems and technologies and the acceleration of modern life.

Speed and Cultural Modernity

The relationship between speed and space in the constitution of global modernity has of course been long recognized. Perhaps the most famous instance of this is Marx's comments in the Grundrisse, on the importance of speed in the expansionist tendencies of capitalism:

> ....the important thing ... is ... the speed – the amount of time – by which the market can be reached. Thus whilst capital must on the one side strive to tear down every spatial barrier to exchange, and to conquer the whole earth for its market, it strives on the other side to annihilate this space with time, i.e. to reduce to a minimum the time spent in motion from one place to another.
> (Marx, 1973: 538–539)

Writing in 1857, Marx was typically prescient in his perception of the key importance of speed in the dynamics of capitalism. However, it is fair to say that he was not the first to recognize the cultural impact of mechanical speed. In fact, Marx's famous phrase 'the annihilation of space by time' first appears in a book called *The Railway Companion* published in 1833. In 1846, Charles Dickens (2002), in *Dombey and Sons*, gives one of the great literary evocations of the ambiguous nature of mechanical modernity in his description of a railway journey on the new line between London and Birmingham. The train's roaring progress between light and darkness – 'mining in through the damp earth, booming on in darkness and heavy air, bursting out again into the sunny day ... spurning everything with its dark breath' – captures the mixture of promised enlightenment and emancipation on the one hand and rapaciousness and confusion on the other.

This tension persists in certain ways in the cultural reception of an accelerating world for at least the next hundred years. Before the 1820s, no one in the world had experienced speeds faster than that of a galloping horse, but by the 1840s steam locomotives were regularly reaching speeds of 60 to 70 miles per hour. An initial fear of these unprecedented speeds quickly gave way to a wide popular enthusiasm for the opportunities for affordable travel offered by the railways. Thus mechanical speed, bound in with both industrialism and capitalism, became assimilated with a dominant cultural narrative stressing the march of progress. There were oppositional voices – John Ruskin, for example, launched invectives against the railway entrepreneurs for their assault on the landscape so that, 'every fool in Bakewell can be at Buxton in half an hour and every fool in Buxton at Bakewell'. But these early environmental protests were in the minority: for the most part the domination of nature by machinery was celebrated as an emancipation. As Emerson persuasively put it, 'Who would live in the stone age or the bronze or the iron…? Who does not prefer the age of steel, of gold, of coal, petroleum, cotton, steam, electricity and the spectroscope?'

So, as the century turns, mechanical speed becomes progressively normalized, and new, more complex, narratives emerge to interpret it. Georg Simmel's 1903 essay 'The Metropolis and Mental Life' (1997) particularly identifies speed as an increase in the pace of life in the great cities, contrasting with the slow habitual rhythm of rural life: 'the rapid crowding of changing images… and the unexpectedness of onrushing impressions'. Aside from academic interest in the phenomenology of speed, it becomes the focus of a new cultural politics.

The year 1909 is somewhat of a watershed here – the year in which Bleriot flew across the English Channel, the Model 'T' Ford started in production, the first Pathé Newsreel appeared, the Indianapolis racetrack opened and Filippo Tommasso Marinetti paid to publish an article on the front page of the French newspaper, *Le Figaro*. This article was the Futurist Manifesto. In it Marinetti says, 'The world's magnificence has been enriched by a new beauty; the beauty of speed. Time and Space died yesterday. We already live in the absolute, because we have created eternal omnipresent speed' (1973) The Futurists were an odd kettle of fish and certainly the most opinionated artistic movement ever to exist: deliberately outrageous, theatrical, often pompous, posturing and with politically naïve and often distinctly Fascist political leanings. The manifesto itself is indeed frequently incendiary in its prose: 'We will glorify war – the world's only hygiene – militarism, patriotism … and scorn for women. …we will destroy the museums, libraries. …we will fight moralism, feminism, every opportunistic or utilitarian cowardice'. However, it is rather difficult to take seriously as a political manifesto: 'Come on! set fire to the library shelves! Turn aside the canals to flood the museums! … Take up your pickaxes, your axes and hammers and wreck, wreck the venerable cities pitilessly'. Marinetti, who liked to describe himself as 'the caffeine of Europe', is perhaps more accurately regarded, as Robert Hughes

(1991) says as a sort of artistic *agent provocateur*. Though frequently rather ridiculous in his posturing, he nonetheless had his finger on the cultural pulse and expresses in much of his work the sheer exuberance and reckless excitement of early modern speed. More than this, he is one of the first to recognize the significance of media technologies in close integration with fast machines within the constitution of the modern lifeworld:

> Those people who today make use of the telegraph, the telephone, the phonograph, the train, the bicycle, the motorcycle, the automobile, the ocean liner, the dirigible, the aeroplane, the cinema, the great newspaper (synthesis of a day in the world's life), do not yet realise that these various means of communication, transportation and information have a decisive influence on their psyches.
> (Marinetti in Tisdall and Bozolla, 1977: 8)

Marinetti, for all his bombast, raises important subthemes in the cultural narrative of technological modernity, particularly in the celebration of the sensual-aesthetic experience to be derived from speed and the link between this and the courting of risk and even violence. Perhaps the figure who most epitomizes the modernist confidence in the value of the acceleration of life is the architect Le Corbusier, whose urban planning philosophy is summed up in his maxim: 'A city made for speed is made for success'.

Le Corbusier's great modernist polemic *l'Urbanisme* is a *tour de force* of singlemindedness. Writing in 1924, Le Corbusier is convinced of the need radically and dramatically to reconstruct the world's great cities – 'the spiritual workshops in which the work of the world is done' – to meet the challenge of 'the machine age'. The crux of this challenge is speed. In the name of speed he is prepared, in the *Voisin plan*, to destroy 600 acres of the historic right bank of Paris from Montmartre to the Seine to provide space for a new high-rise business hub serviced by 'speedways'. To make a city for speed and success means clearing away the clutter of old Paris to allow room for the serious work of the new modern capitalists: 'Men of business'. He writes: 'The rhythm which actuates business is obvious; it is speed and the struggle for speed'.

Le Corbusier's attitude to speed is recorded in a well-known passage describing his experience of the traffic on the Champs Elysées in the autumn of 1924:

> Motors in all directions, going at all speeds. I was overwhelmed, an enthusiastic rapture filled me ... the rapture of power. The simple and ingenuous pleasure of being in the centre of so much power, so much speed. We are part of it. We are part of that race whose dawn is just awakening. We have confidence in this new society, which will in the end arrive at a magnificent expression of its power. We believe in it.
> (Le Corbusier, 1971: 5)

This rhetorical voice of the emerging modernist attitude is in fact more accurate than it may seem. Le Corbusier has sometimes been characterized as a slightly mad lyric visionary hoping to solve the problems of modern urban existence at a stroke by the destruction of the old chaotic unplanned city where people and machines randomly and perplexingly mingle: 'We must kill the streets!' His hyperbolic prose style has invited comparisons with Marinetti, but Le Corbusier explicitly disavowed this comparison: 'This is no dangerous futurism, a sort of literary dynamite flung violently at the spectator' (Le Corbusier, 1971: 178). Indeed, what is most instructive in the example of Le Corbusier's work is his vision as a planner rather than an iconoclast. Despite all the scorn heaped upon the modernist vision by later urban planners, this cluster of ideas and values – scientific reason, progress, organization and planning, energy, industry, entrepreneurship and the harnessing of speed – form the deep grammar of modernism that underlay political-institutional culture for most of the twentieth century and continues in key respects to colour our understanding of the basis of social order in developed societies.

I have spent a fair amount of time sketching the place of speed in the historical constitution of institutional and cultural modernity but so far have said little specifically about media. This is because when we come to consider what I'm going to call 'fast media', a quite new cluster of values, attitudes and cultural imaginings begins to emerge that in certain respects diverges from and even challenges the narrative of modernity that has served for getting on for two centuries.

What are Fast Media?

In one sense, the term is a tautology. Seen as a series of technological developments there really are no slow media. We saw that as early as the 1900s Marinetti could include the media forms of his day amongst fast machines. Le Corbusier describes the 'luminous and radiant offices' of his ideal speed-designed Paris as containing, 'apparatus for abolishing time and space, telephones, cables and wireless'. Since the invention of the telegraph and the telephone, modern media have always been on a trajectory towards increasing speed. The very concept of 'the news' – one of the defining functions of media systems and institutions – is only intelligible as information communicated without delay.

Yet there is a sense in which we can speak of fast media without redundancy. Fast media are media that decisively, dramatically accelerate the pace of everyday life. This is to acknowledge a shift both in the affordances of media technologies, in the forms of consumption that accompany them, and in the broader cultural attitudes and assumptions they have engendered. Media like the radio or the newspaper, throughout most of the twentieth century, can certainly be counted as key aspects of modern societies steadily embracing more and more speed. But these media were still governed of the narrative of speed first inaugurated in the nineteenth century. Although they remain, the world they now inhabit – the world of Twitter, Facebook and Google – is informed by an entirely different set of cultural values.

Given this, it is tempting to broach the shift to fast media through a focus on the typical forms of media technology that characterise twenty-first century culture. Yet we must be careful to avoid making spurious distinctions between old and new media. It doesn't get us far to debate whether – or indeed in what sense – CMC technologies are 'faster' than, say, television. No, fast media are defined by a combination of their technical capacities, the way these capacities are exploited in an institutional environment and the cultural expectations generated in respect of them.

Fast media, then, are better regarded as a set of telemediated practices and experiences that have become routine and taken-for-granted aspects of everyday life in developed societies. They typically include typing, scrolling, clicking and browsing at the computer screen, talking, texting or sending and receiving pictures on a mobile phone, watching television (a medium that in its continuing centrality to media culture effortlessly bridges the flimsy distinction between old and new media) and tapping in PIN codes and conducting transactions on a keypad. Importantly, they are conducted in a political-economic and cultural context that is not entirely of their own making, but rather arises out of broader dynamics in the career of modernity.

But let us now try to put some flesh on these arguments by considering a couple of examples. Neither of these is in itself deeply significant, but they are both I think emblematic of the sort of trajectory of media culture that I'm after here. To underline the point, I have deliberately chosen an example from what some might consider 'old media' television rather than the obvious suspects of CMCs.

The Impatience of the News Ticker

Sometimes called a 'crawler', the news ticker is the moving ribbon you find in what TV people call the 'lower third' of the screen on news channels. Its function is to give you 'breaking news' – news additional to the news you are hearing from the mouths of the announcers. The news ticker has an interesting ancestry in the form of the original news ticker – called The Motograph News Bulletin – an illuminated moving display that was first installed on the front of the New York Times building in Times Square in November 1928.

There is a famous image of this device taken in June 6th, 1944, showing the announcement of the D-Day landings in Normandy. The significant difference between this and the TV news ticker is a matter not of technology but of cultural assumptions. In 1944, the crowd gathered in Times Square is focussing on the news delivered faster than by the newspapers. But in 2016 the TV viewer is simultaneously given the news and some other news to think about. Some people find this irritating and distracting. But what is more interesting is the assumption by the broadcaster that the viewers need/want this extra information – that they aren't satisfied with the linear presentation of a story in a schedule but crave simultaneous trailers and catch ups. This assumption of an impatient, restless media consumer is part of what I mean by fast media. Of course it is an assumption, and it may well be mistaken as is illustrated by my next example.

End-Credit Promotions: The Banal Logic of Viewer Retention

End-credit promotions, or ECPs, refer to the practice of providing the trail of upcoming TV programmes whilst the credits for the current programme are still running. In order to facilitate this, a practice emerged of squeezing the credits down into a corner of the screen making them virtually unreadable and at the same time fading out title music and adding a voice-over describing what is coming next. Now there is a very simple economic rationale for ECPs, and this is to maximize audience retention. Persuading viewers to stay with a channel or to return to it later helps deliver audiences to advertisers (advertising rates are measured in cost per thousand viewers) or in the case of the noncommercial broadcasters like the BBC to sustain viewing figures and thereby justify the license fee.

However, in a rare example of the triumph of public opinion over economic logic, the practice of credits squeezing was ended by the BBC in 2013, partly as a result of survey evidence by the actors union EQUITY that showed a majority of viewers appreciated seeing the credits and were intensely irritated by the practice. But they continued to show ECPs without squeezing the credits and maintained a continuity voice-over. So a partial victory.

Well, as I say, these examples are fairly insignificant in the overall scheme of things, but they are illustrative of a trend in media culture – as in the wider culture – in which the pace of life is constantly ramped up. The way this often presents itself in the media and communications sphere is in terms of a combination of the anticipations of desires and incitements to satisfy these. So think for instance of what is called variously 'behavioural' or 'predictive' or 'anticipatory' browser advertising: that is to say, online adverts for things marketeers think they can sell you, based on your previous shopping or browsing behaviour – the ads that pop up on your browser when you are not necessarily shopping – perhaps just checking the weather forecast. The point for me is not so much the issue of intrusion or nuisance value, but of the relentless accelerating pace set in everyday mediatized experience. There is, of course, a fairly obvious political-economic context to which we can refer all this in what has been called 'fast capitalism'.

Fast Media and Fast Capitalism

The impetus towards increasing speed in the circulation of capital has always been a defining feature of modern industrial capitalist economies. The idea of fast capitalism points us towards something new, a step change in pace facilitated by the integration of media and communications systems into the operations of capitalist production, exchange and indeed culture. In the most general sense, this can be seen as an increase in the intensity, energy and mobility of the capitalist order overall. In its global scope, impatient with various forms of constraint and regulation, contemporary 'turbo-capitalism' looks rather like a recrudescence of the impulses of nineteenth-century free-market liberalism. But what has enabled this are some key shifts in the operation of capitalism. One of the earliest commentators on this, the economist Will Hutton, describes it as follows:

> It's a capitalism that is much harder, more mobile, more ruthless and more certain about what it needs to make it tick. Its overriding objective is to serve the interests of property owners and shareholders, and it has a firm belief ... that all obstacles to its capacity to do that – regulation, trade unions, taxation, public ownership, etc. are unjustified and should be removed. ...It's a very febrile capitalism, but for all that and its short-termism, it has been a very effective transmission agent for the new technologies and for creating the new global industries and markets.
> (Hutton, 2000: 9–11)

Some of these changes in the nature of capitalism relate to the techniques of the production and exchange of actual commodities, particularly those attributable to the connectivity of globalization. These include flexible, global sourcing of materials and components, a global distribution of labour, computer-controlled automation of production processes, web-based work-flow systems, just-in-time delivery logistics and so on. Others are essentially sophistications in the manipulation of the capitalist market. These latter allow, for example, speculation on the future value of commodities ('futures') and, through the increasing use of synthetic instruments collectively known as 'derivatives', financial trading at a high level of abstraction from the actual exchange of commodities.

In what ways is this abstract, mathematically complex, information-sensitive capitalism *fast*? In the first place, it is the near-instantaneous speed of computerized, networked, fund-transfer systems combined with the speed of market intelligence via the Internet that makes the whole business of this sort of high-risk, high-gain speculation possible. In the second place, and as a consequence of the first, these economic practices, though they are parasitic upon the slower pace of 'real' trade flows (and, in the case of futures actually *depend* on this slower pace) are necessarily short-term, super-fast deals, deals that generate their profits in anticipation of value fluctuations in the real world of trade. It is fair to say, then, that what makes contemporary capitalism fast is in large part the deep integration of media and communication into its operation. Fast capitalism then, depends on fast media – in the narrow sense of media technologies that operate at the near instantaneous speeds necessary to support its accumulative proclivities. But it simultaneously generates fast media. This is so in the fairly straightforward sense of providing the economic dynamics necessary for the research, development and commercial exploitation of new media technologies. But it is also true in the more subtle sense that fast capitalism has an impact on the cultural context within which we appropriate these technologies. The remainder of this chapter addresses this question of the broader culture of fast capitalism/fast media.

The Condition of Immediacy

What I am going to suggest is that a media-saturated environment, in concert with the accelerating dynamics of contemporary capitalism and its attendant incitements to consumption, has produced a new cultural condition that contrasts sharply with that of the culture of twentieth-century modernity I sketched in the first part of this discussion. To try to grasp this contrast, I'm going to deploy a general cultural concept that I shall call 'immediacy' (Tomlinson, 2007).

In the cult British film *Withnail and I*, a couple of unemployed London actors find themselves in the unfamiliar surroundings of the small market town Penrith in the Lake District. Following an epic round of lunchtime boozing, they enter a genteel tearoom in search of food. The staff is uneasy – these are not the usual clientele – and their loud, drunken requests for cake are not immediately met. At this point, the eponymous hero Withnail ups his demands: 'We want the finest wines available to humanity; we want them here, and we want them now'. Watching the *hauteur* with which he delivers this unlikely order, we feel there exists in his beer-fuddled imagination at least a faint belief that it might be fulfilled. Instead, the nervous proprietor calls the cops.

The humour of this situation is certainly in the contrast between the slow and ordered world of middle-class/middle-aged rural life and the impatience and audacity of an urban culture in the throes of change. However, immediacy, as I want to understand it, is rather more than this simple demand for instant gratification. Of course, Withnail's demands are not serious ones, but they are troubling to the social order because they represent a sort of *reductio ad absurdem* of a rudimentary human impulse towards the unimpeded gratification of desire that has generally been suppressed within class society. The threat of its dramatic eruption was at the centre of the youth counterculture of the 1960s – when the film is set.

It is a mistake then, I think, to see the desire for instant gratification as a new phenomenon. It has a long history reaching back into the myths of spinning gold from straw. Throughout the modern period, these dreams of overnight riches manifested themselves in get-rich-quick schemes from the 'Railway Mania' of the 1840s to the dot com bubble of the 1990s. But the impetus that drove these was a much more general one – with no link with any particular technological form or regime of capital. Although in some instances it fell towards avarice, it was generally closer to the basic human wish for abundance – for the abolition of want. This impetus to tear down barriers to satisfaction was indeed an integral part of the promise of early modern speed. It belonged to the same cluster of modernist values – progress, efficiency, the conquest of nature by human application and ingenuity.

Immediacy, by contrast, belongs to a new cultural world – one in which the finest wines available to mankind might soon conceivably be delivered to the Penrith Teashop within 30 minutes, by drone, courtesy of Amazon Prime Air. In such a world, it is not far-fetched to imagine that the gap that has existed between desire and its fulfilment – a gap that has, indeed, been the primary lever of human enterprise – has finally in some sense been closed. This is the promise of immediacy.

The adjective 'immediate' from which I coin the noun immediacy has two connected meanings that are relevant to the analysis of fast media. First, in relation to *time*, it means, 'occurring without delay or lapse in time; instant'. This connotes ideas of the acceleration of the pace of life and a culture of instantaneity, adapted and accustomed to the rapid delivery of goods and (particularly) information, and underpinning this, an economy and an associated work and consumption culture geared not just to sustaining but to constantly increasing this tempo of life.

In relation to *space*, it means 'proximate, nearest, close' – implying a sense of directness, of cultural *proximity*. Etymologically this is actually the primary sense: from the Latin 'immediatus' meaning 'not separated'. Immediacy suggests not just an acceleration in culture, but a distinct *quality* to cultural experience. This may be grasped as an increasing routine connectedness both with other people and with the access points (predominantly now, websites) of the institutions that afford and govern global-modern social existence. Daily life becomes increasingly saturated in communicational practices and increasingly dependent on the ubiquitous presence/availability, via electronic media, of informational and human resources. Media are thus (literally) at the centre of immediacy.

This density of communicational connectedness promotes a new kind of intensity in everyday experience, mixing pace and vibrancy with a sense of effortlessness. There is no doubt that, in the relatively affluent sectors of contemporary western society, it has vastly increased the ready availability of material goods, information and entertainment. It has also profoundly transformed everyday social interactions and relations through social media.

But it is not an unmixed blessing. Immediacy also brings an increase in communicational *demands* on the individual and, arguably, a new sense of compulsion and 'drivenness' in life. The condition of immediacy seems to involve a curious mixing of the soft and the hard: of leisure and labour.

A good example of this trend is the creeping encroachment of work activities into home and family time and space. For example, the tendency to send or to pick up work-related emails outside of normal working hours is now widespread (not least amongst academics). How should we regard this? In one sense, it is simply exploitative in extracting more labour time from employees than is contracted. In another, this sort of flexible integration represents a degree of autonomy and flexibility in time use – a relaxation in the clocked discipline of the labour contract of the modern workplace.

One way of approaching this blending of work and home life is to consider how it might fit within E.P. Thompson's classic discussion of 'Time, Work-Discipline and Industrial Capitalism'. In this essay, Thompson compares the 'time orientation' of labour imposed within clock-regulated, Taylorist factory capitalism with the 'task orientation' of a pre-industrial work culture. The demands of work discipline within the capitalist labour contract meant that the worker came to regard his/her labour in terms of the time he/she must spend within the factory, rather than in terms of the intrinsic nature of the task to be performed. This was a sharp contrast with the 'task orientation' of cottage industry, in which, as Thompson says, 'social interaction and labour are intermingled-the working day lengthens or contracts according to the task' (1991: 358). It is not unreasonable to see the reach of mediated work relations into home life as – in some limited degree – a return to task orientation. Social interaction and labour are certainly intermingled, and there is clearly a relaxation of the rigid discipline of the factory system offering the employee more control over when a task is done – if not during the actual working day, than when it can be fit in. Of course the task still *has* to be fit in – and into an increasingly busy, time-scarce (Schor, 1992) everyday existence. So this re-emergence of a form of task orientation does not go so far as to return entire control of labour to the worker. On the other hand there is arguably an experience of softness in this way of working even as it demands and obtains more of us without imposing the harder disciplines of the time clock and the factory whistle.

There is also a certain lightness and softness in the actual exertions and manipulations associated with the use of media and communications technologies – in the acts of typing, clicking, scrolling and texting and the immediacy of the responses these elicit – which in a sense also blur the boundaries of work and play. For what precisely differentiates a work-oriented email from a message sent about, say, a sports fixture or web-research for a work project as opposed to that done to help the children with their homework? Surely little other than, as Thompson puts it, 'a distinction between [the] employer's time and [the worker's] "own" time' (1991: 359). Something with so little actual task differentiation involved that is often hard to maintain.

I don't, however, want to give the impression that the condition of immediacy somehow resolves the alienations of labour by blending them with playfulness. Fast capitalism has lightened its structures and processes, notably by shedding some of its older encumbrances-heavy plant, large permanent and often powerfully unionised workforces. But as Zygmunt Bauman (2005) insists, this has not made modern experience 'light' in the sense of being easy, comfortable and anxiety-free, even for those who are, as it were, the economic winners in capitalist globalization.

What can be said is that the sharp differentiations between the culture of work and the culture of consumer-inflected leisure are blurring as societies emerge from an era in which heavy, labour-intensive industry-dominated and organized daily life into clear-cut time/space regimes. Indeed some have argued that consumption itself has become a form of labour. Teresa Brennan, for instance, claims that consumer practices in fast capitalism involve a significant element of unpaid labour:

> To go online and buy products, or book airline tickets, is to perform delivery work. Such work is squeezed into the time once given to rest and revival. The turn of the century has witnessed a shift in the burden of service labour, from producer to consumer.
>
> (2003: 133)

Such online consumer practices take time and a certain level of skill and are often frustrating. Yet they don't quite seem like 'work' in the way we have become accustomed to viewing it.

As a final example of this mixing of the playful and the industrious, we can consider an emblematic piece of media consumer technology: The Apple Watch. The Apple Watch is marketed as a smart watch – meaning that it not only tells the time but is a sort of wearable computer. It can be used for getting email notifications, as a phone or for texting (although you really need an iPhone as well for this). You can also monitor your heart rate and track your fitness, get directions like a sat-nav, use it to store e-tickets and loyalty cards and as a mobile payment device. Of course, it has at hand the now ubiquitous voice-activated personal assistant Siri. And it's fun! – you can get it in a cute Mickey Mouse clock face.

The marketing tells us that, 'Apple Watch actually understands what time means to you. It helps you be more productive and efficient'. Time is short, and we must make the most of it – hence it is, 'full of features that help you stay active, motivated and connected' …'you can get important information and do things quickly and conveniently right from your wrist-so you never have to put your day on pause'.

It's not unreasonable, then, to describe the Apple Watch as primarily a device to enable mobile, efficient human productivity. Like all fast media, this is an impatient technology, matched to the demands of a busy work – and play – schedule. The marketing for the second generation – Apple Watch Series 2 – tends to stress its physical fitness-monitoring functions: 'See if you've been sitting too much. Track how many steps you've taken and how many calories you've burned. And aim for 30 minutes of exercise, even if it's not all at once'. All good lifestyle advice, but a competitive ethos is never far away from the corporate imagination of everyday life: 'compete to see who can hit their goals first. Receive notifications on your friends' progress and easily respond direct from the notification – whether it's to send encouragement or a little trash talk'. There is even an app to deal efficiently with the stresses of this high-performance lifestyle: the 'Breathe App': 'Stay centred as a beautiful animation and gentle taps guide you through a series of deep breaths. Time to Breathe reminders help you practise mindfulness every day'.

Of course, we should not attach undue significance to the banalities of corporate marketing, and we must remember that consumers appropriate technologies according to their own cultural agendas. Nonetheless, there are clear indications here of the conflation of consumption and productivity that are features of the condition of immediacy.

Legerdemain

We have seen that the condition of immediacy enabled by fast media involves a number of paradoxes, and I'm going to a conclude with a few thoughts on these. To do this I'm going to introduce one last interpretive concept: *legerdemain* – literally a lightness of hand – in English we would say a slight of hand.

In one sense, *legerdemain* refers us to a new set of commonplace bodily practices that are particularly underlined by the lightness of our interaction with new communications technologies: with keyboards, keypads, screens, handsets and remote controls, smart watches. These manipulations are deft and smoothly choreographed into our working (and playing) rhythms, almost seeming less physical operations than gestures. Think of the way in which we can purchase goods simply by *waving* a contactless card – or maybe our Apple Watch – at a payment terminal. This lightness of touch is closely associated with the perception of immediate and ubiquitous access. Things – and particularly people – do often seem to be pretty much immediately available simply by the lightest pressure on a keypad or the wave of a hand. This association of physical lightness and (near) effortlessness in the operation of communications technologies with a tacit assumption of the instant and constant availability of things and people – of a world, as it were, waiting to be accessed – is characteristic of the experience of immediacy.

This perception raises another sense of *legerdemain* – something like an act of conjuring that, whilst seeming effortless and offering delights, nonetheless involves certain concealments and deceptions.

One of these is simply the tendency of media technologies to hide their technical complexities behind a user-friendly interface. (Think of the rather complex set of code that is invoked when you drop a file into the recycling bin). Fast media are examples of what Anthony Giddens once called expert systems (1990), which we depend on and interface with but don't really (most of us) understand.

There are other, more problematic concealments, for example, of the costs and consequences of the immediate satisfaction of consumer desire. For increasingly large sectors of the population within developed economies, there exists a broad assumption that goods and particularly technological advances will simply and continuously be delivered, become affordable, morph from luxuries into necessities. Whatever else may be taking place in our lives, and whatever uncertainties and anxieties are born out of the turbulence of global modernity, the promise of immediacy is that 'stuff arrives'.

There is then arguably a new complacency in consumer culture that matches the insouciant style of contemporary communicational practice. What this also conceals of course is the inescapable material cost of unrestricted consumption growth, in the exploitation, somewhere in the world, of the natural environment and of human labour. In his theory of commodity fetishism, Karl Marx wrote of the concealment of the human economic relations that are present in the commodity form – in goods that appear 'as if by magic'. He would probably have thought of the instant conjuring up of goods, services and indeed people themselves by fast media as the apotheosis of this form of obfuscation.

Fast media, then, in concert with fast capitalism, has played a significant role in the constitution of twenty-first-century global modernity. I have tried to sketch some of the differences that this condition of immediacy has produced from the comparatively stable, ordered, culture of modernity that held sway for most of the twentieth century. It is not, of course, the only dynamic that has been at play here, and in comparison with some of the other social forces unleashed by globalization it may not be the most decisive. However, when considered alongside other aspects of our current cultural condition – for instance the rise of what has been called 'post truth politics' (Davies, 2016) – it begins to look rather more threatening to the broader institutional foundations of the modern world, a world in which the shaping of public opinion by factual information is losing ground to appeals to emotion and personal belief – in which presidents can ignore evidence in favour of gut feeling and conduct diplomacy via twitter feeds – is to say the very least a new and uncertain one – a world away from the political values of earlier modernity. The expectation of immediate solutions to life's contingencies cultivated by fast media seems only likely to add to the popular impatience with the processes of deliberative democracy this portends.

References

Bauman, Z. (2005). *Liquid Life*. Cambridge: Polity.
Brennan, T. (2003). *Globalization and its Terrors: Daily Life in the West*. London: Routledge.
Davies, W. (2016). The Age of Post-Truth Politics. *The New York Times*, Aug 24.
Dickens, C. (2002). *Dombey and Son*. London: Penguin (First published 1848).
Giddens, A. (1990). *The Consequences of Modernity*. Cambridge: Polity.
Hughes, R. (1991). *The Shock of the New*. London: Thames and Hudson.
Hutton, W. (2000). In conversation with Anthony Giddens. In W. Hutton & A. Giddens (Eds.), *On The Edge: Living with Global Capitalism* (pp. 1–51). London: Jonathan Cape.
Le Corbusier (1971). *The City of Tomorrow and its Planning*. London: The Architectural Press. Trans. Frederick Etchells. (First published as *L'Urbanism*, 1924).
Marinetti, F. T. (1973). The founding and Manifesto of futurism. In U. Apollonio (Ed.), *Futurist Manifestos* (pp. 19–24). London: Thames and Hudson. (First published in 1909).
Marx, K. (1973). *Grundrisse*. London: Penguin.
Schor, J. (1992). *The Overworked American: The Unexpected Decline of Leisure*. New York: Basic Books.
Simmel, G. (1997). The metropolis and mental life [1903] Trans. Hans Gerth. In D. Frisby & M. Featherstone (Eds.), *Simmel on Culture* (pp. 174–185). London: Sage.
Tisdall, C., & Bozzolla, A. (1977): *Futurism*. London: Thames and Hudson.
Thompson, E. P. (1991): Time, work discipline and industrial capitalism. In *Customs in Common* (pp. 352–403). London: The Merlin Press. (first published 1967).
Tomlinson, J. (1999). *Globalization and Culture*. Cambridge: Polity.
Tomlinson, J. (2007). *The Culture of Speed*. London: Sage.

14 Afterword: Geomedia
In Praise of Unruly Conjunctions

Scott McQuire

'As beautiful as the chance encounter of a sewing machine and an umbrella on an operating table'.
   Isidore Ducasse (Comte de Lautréamount), *Les Chants de Maldoror* 1868–1869

'Not creating from a place of "Don't fuck it up". But creating from a place of "Fuck it up".'
   Macklemore and Ryan Lewis, *This unruly mess I've made*, 2016

Geomedia is a term that first began to appear in various academic writings a bit under a decade ago. Thielman (2010) set his use of the neologism in a context of broader shifts in both media and geography, adopting 'media geography' as the overarching banner to deal with the interaction between 'locative media and mediated localities'. Lapenta's (2011) article also largely equated geomedia with burgeoning interest in locative media, while my own use of the term (McQuire, 2011), which grew out of earlier work on mediated urbanism (McQuire, 2008), focussed more on intersections between digital media platforms and cultural practices, and, perhaps paradoxically, gave as much emphasis to changes in temporality as to spatial experience. I'm not citing these three articles to privilege them as starting points, as I think questions of origin for any new research orientation are invariably far more complex, but simply to note two things. First, that a certain problematic concerning the way that networked digital media platforms are implicated in reworking the space-time of everyday life became more urgent and insistent around this time, evidenced by the fact that a term such as geomedia suddenly 'made sense' in several different contexts. Second, this problematic was neither entirely new nor properly the province of any one discipline.

This last point should be abundantly clear to anyone who has read the contributions collected here. If one can broadly divide them between those who tend to begin from *media*, in order to understand the diverse relations of media, place and space (for instance, production ethnographies or analysis of representations of existing, imagined or future cities), and those who treat the affordances of contemporary media as part of a broader research paradigm such as mobilities or globalization, there is a much greater diversity in disciplinary affiliations, conceptual frameworks and methodological approaches than such a binary division implies. This is scarcely surprising given that the different contributors enter this debate from a variety of fields including media and communications, journalism, geographical studies and sociology, to name a few.

Of course, starting points remain important. They tend to bring with them accustomed approaches, sets of literature and conceptual armatures and emphases. Is 'geomedia', then, best seen as a new moment in 'media and communication studies'? Or is it a different approach to – or within – geography? Is it more useful for understanding the impact of contemporary media on mobility studies? Or is it better positioned as a constitutive dimension of debates about globalization? If it is something of a cop-out to answer 'all of the above', my caveat is this would only be the case if such an answer obviated the need to revisit and revise existing disciplinary paradigms. All disciplines have their well-travelled routes, as well as their blind spots – even, and perhaps especially in this context, traditional meta-disciplines such as philosophy. (This something I will return to below.) What is striking here is the extent to which the various authors recognize a need to challenge their dominant disciplinary paradigms in order to penetrate salient features of the present. What particularly appeals to me about the essays collected in this book is a preparedness to 'follow the problem', not without disciplinary preconceptions but with a willingness to learn from them *and* to question them. What emerges is a fertile interdisciplinarity that is neither an excuse for lack of rigour nor yet one for a facile discrediting of disciplinary thinking. Geomedia *studies*, as practiced here, is about establishing not a new meta-concept or unified definition but a space of encounter. If this encounter is not as eclectic and deliberately jarring as Lautréamount's *monstrous* image that André Breton seized as emblematic of the surrealist imagination, my test of its validity is closer to Macklemore's sense of the *unruly* as capable of constituting a productive, creative space.[1] What might look 'messy' at first sight is in fact a much needed space for critical and reflexive dialogue within and between disciplines, as a means of generating insights into emergent practices and platforms and thereby thinking their relation to still embryonic theories and experimental methods.

* * * *

Preparedness to 'follow the problem', beginning from different places and, while not necessarily heading towards the same end, generating insights at points of shared concern *en route*, seems particularly important when we are dealing with phenomena that are new: new technologies, new practices, new conjunctions. Given that *new* is such an overburdened and ideology-laden term, not least in media studies, how can we clarify what is 'new' in this field? As I indicated above, the broad problematic of media, space and place has a longer history, defined – as most histories are – as much by significant absences as by what is positively recorded and on record. Nevertheless, the moment in which 'geomedia' percolates to the surface of discourse belongs to a very recent period in which digital media and communication technologies, broadly understood in their coupling with computational systems and networked infrastructure, have been implicated in transformations that are both transversal and multiscalar. Without seeking to position the 'technological' as some kind of autonomous origin, it is important to recognize that the transformations associated with networked digital media now cross into multiple domains simultaneously, reworking social, political, cultural and economic systems and processes, while also penetrating social praxis at micro and macro scales. In short, *geomedia* names changes that are *epochal*. As the contributions here collectively establish, convergent digital platforms are altering dominant paradigms, up to and including the role of the national as the primary 'container' for organizing relations between territory and politics, economics and culture, while simultaneously implicated in the recalibration of intimate relations and psychosocial life.

In what follows, I don't seek to wrap up the concept of geomedia neatly so as to enclose the space of encounter that it seems to be productively opening, but rather to identify three issues I see as critical to the elaboration of this field. These are: (1) the history of thinking 'media' as environment; (2) the key elements peculiar to the condition of 'media' in the present and (3) the implications of these developments for thinking 'media' in the future.

Media as Environment

Media are a somewhat paradoxical object of study. On the one hand, 'media' enable techno-material-symbolic shaping of the social relations of space/time, allowing communication to travel across distance and to persist over time, and, as 'text' and 'archive', to produce a wide range of sociopolitical effects. On the other hand, despite these manifold capacities to recursively shape space, time and subjectivity, 'media' are always grounded. Historically specific material, technical, institutional and cultural instantiations condition the unfolding of different media platforms and the way they afford diverse possibilities for communicative exchange among individuals and groups occupying particular territories. The intersection of these two strands situates what we might call the broad frame of 'geomedia' thinking, establishing a looping pair of questions that can be posed from either direction: how do media platforms impact space and place, understanding both terms as complex and dynamic assemblages of heterogeneous elements, and how do space and place impact media?

This double optic has a longer history, part of which is discussed in some of the contributions here. Rowan Wilken recalls earlier work on media and place that was largely driven by changes in broadcasting undertaken by media scholars including Moores, Silverstone, Couldry and Morley. He also notes the significant contributions of Falkheimer and Jansson (2006) and Adams (2009), characterizing the first as evidence of a 'spatial turn' in media studies and the second in terms of a 'cultural' or 'communicational turn' in geography. These projects are certainly part of the groundswell that I observed above as a formative condition for the emergence of a neologism like 'geomedia' (see also McQuire [2016] for a critical analysis of 'geomedia' in the context of the public space of contemporary cities). Equally formative for me is the earlier work of two scholars not directly mentioned here: Marshall McLuhan and Harold Innis.[2]

In his essay 'The Invisible Environment' (published 50 years ago as I write), McLuhan (1967: 164) argued that the 'environmental' effects of any technology or medium tended to disappear from view and become 'invisible' as it became dominant. In this respect, he contended that the environment established by 'electric' media such as television had receded from consciousness, becoming the taken-for-granted space of thought and social life in 1960s North America. From this perspective, McLuhan (1970: 14) later argued in typically provocative fashion that 'new media' such as television 'are not bridges between man and nature: they are nature'. This understanding supported his well-known disdain for then-dominant forms of media criticism such as content analysis and his advocacy for analysing environmental effects that, he argued, related principally to questions of scale, pattern and rhythm. This framework underpins his famous assertion that the impact of television is less a function of what is 'on' the TV set at any moment than the fact that the TV is 'on' simultaneously in millions of homes spread across what was starting to become a global territory (McLuhan, 1974).

The understanding of technology that informs this stance is not so far from Heidegger's famous characterization of technology as *enframing*; namely, the belief that any dominant technology or medium – and every technology is a medium for McLuhan – tends to constitute a 'total space' for thinking and acting. However, a more direct inspiration for McLuhan in developing his thesis was Harold Innis' account of the 'biases' of different media. Innis argued that media such as stone and paper offered different affordances defined by their differentiated capacities to enable the archiving (preservation over time) and transportation (movement across space) of information. Where *time-biased* media such as imprinted clay tablets, which were durable, but heavy, bulky and difficult to transport 'helped sustain centralised religious forms of tradition', Innis argued that *space-biased* media such as paper favoured more dispersed political and administrative arrangements. In Innis' (1951: 116) account, 'Transportable media favoured the growth of administrative relations across space, thereby facilitating the decentralised growth of secular and political authority'.

McLuhan's audacious move was to transpose Innis' framework into the era of 'electric' media, in the process formulating a series of well-known but often poorly understood provocations concerning the new modes of subjectivity, territoriality, knowledge, commerce and governance that were emerging under the artificial light of television. The limits of McLuhan's work are well-known, particularly his tendency to overestimate the generative effects of 'media', not least by seeming to assume that new technologies dropped wholly formed from the sky. Williams' (1974) scathing critique rendered McLuhan's once-magisterial name unfashionable for several decades, during which time far more nuanced models of understanding the complex interrelations between 'technology' and 'society' emerged. Yet McLuhan's contribution seems important to recall at this moment in which both media infrastructure and the territorial organization of the planet seem to be entering a different phase. This is not simply to repeat a cautionary tale based on the need to avoid technological determinism, as if, by simply naming the problem, we understand its complexity *and* resolve it, but to register a tension or ambiguity that I think remains active in the present.

On the one hand, McLuhan's *environmental* understanding of 'electric' media leads him to prophesy a looming irrelevance of place. A key manifestation of this would be the wholesale dissolution of urban form. In *Understanding Media,* he argued: 'With instant electric technology, the globe itself can never again be more than a village, and the very nature of the city as a form of major dimensions must inevitably dissolve like a fading shot in a movie' (McLuhan, 1974: 366). This logic was shared by many contemporaries, including architect Moore (1967: 38), who asserted: 'In an electronic world where space and location have so little functional meaning, there seems little point in defining cities spatially …'. While this kind of rhetoric proclaiming the looming irrelevance of physical space didn't gain significant traction outside the architectural *avant-garde* in the 1960s, it was revived with a vengeance in the 1990s as 'cyberspace' was persuasively imagined as a parallel world that could somehow be magically separated from the messy materiality of fleshy bodies and lived places. Influential thinkers such as Esther Dyson and her colleagues including futurist Alvin Toffler (1994) saw 'cyberspace' as the final overthrow of materiality, boldly declaring: 'The central event of the 20th century is the overthrow of matter'.

This streak of what can only be called *deep idealism* often attached itself to McLuhan, *in absentia* proclaimed the 'patron-saint' of *Wired* magazine, and frequently called upon to justify the seeming irrelevance of 'bricks' in favour of 'bytes'. However, it would be a mistake to regard this as the sole trajectory of McLuhan's thought. A somewhat different line emerges from his suggestion that 'electric' media elevates *pattern recognition* over older forms of perception and categorization. In 'The Invisible Environment', McLuhan (1967: 163) also notes: 'As data can be processed very rapidly we move literally into the world of pattern recognition, out of the world of mere data classification. One way of putting this is to say that our children today live in a world in which the environment itself is a teaching machine made of electric information'.

This idea of the environment itself being *made of information* takes on a new potency half a century later, as urban space becomes increasingly saturated with information technologies, and the globe is reconstituted as an intensively mediated terrain, criss-crossed by network infrastructure including geostationary satellites and transoceanic submarine cables that afford new scales and rhythms of recursive exchange involving previously inconceivable volumes of data. It also highlights a constitutive tension in much of our thinking concerning media. Media, which have long been understood in terms of their capacity to overcome spatiotemporal limits and thereby to engineer social experiences of displacement, have become increasingly implicated in contemporary place-making practices. This brings me to the second point I want to raise here. If there is a sense in which all media, including print and broadcast platforms, constitute 'environments' to the extent that they become taken-for-granted spaces for thinking and acting, what is distinctive about networked digital media as environment in the present?

Media in the Present

Several characteristics arguably distinguish contemporary media platforms. In terms of thinking the field of geomedia, the most important to my mind are:

- greater diversity in situations of production and use
- new capacities for devices and platforms to use location awareness
- changing temporal patterns of communicative exchanges

The growing pervasiveness of media devices and infrastructure has been widely noted across different disciplines from computing to media and cultural studies to geography, architecture and urbanism. Mobile and embedded media devices, coupled with extended digital networks, mean that contemporary cities in particular have become intensively mediated spaces in which connectivity is seemingly available 'anywhere, anytime'.

If this ubiquity is still somewhat mythical, restricted by a combination of technical and politico-economic factors among others, the departure from earlier eras in which access to platforms such as telephone, television or computer was far more spatially restricted, is marked. This is particularly the case in relation to the appearances and affordances of the city, as the proliferation of mobile devices, embedded screens and computerized signage gives new salience to McLuhan's idea of an 'information environment'.

Greater portability of networked devices that enable both production and consumption of 'content' is tightly coupled with the growing role of location in coordinating communication processes and filtering information resources. The relation between greater access to GPS data for civilian use and the emergence of new devices such as smart phones in driving development of locative media and location-based services, is well known. Given the growing ease and relative low cost of data collection, aggregation and analytics in a convergent digital media environment, there is a heightened capacity to attach information to 'place'. Equally, and as the flipside of the same process, there is greatly enhanced ability to gather place-based information, not only about various forms of media use, but also about a wide range of other social behaviours. These two trajectories are generating new social practices and commercial logics that are now routinely enacted in different settings across the globe. As McCullough (2004: 88) once noted: 'With the spread of positioning systems, which in effect make anyone who carries such a system into a live cursor, the city plan itself becomes a living surface'. The decade since his observation has not only confirmed its relevance, but its gradual extension, as network access extends across new 'frontiers' from previously unconnected continents to the interior of homes boasting smart appliances to airplanes in flight. In conjunction with the ubiquity of devices and connectivity, the era of location-aware media infrastructure supports the extension of a social logic in which the apparently freewheeling mobility of individual users is integrally related to the calculative analytics of mass surveillance.

An equally significant transformation is the 'realtime' temporality of contemporary digital networks. I'm using 'realtime' not in the technical sense of low latency that is privileged by electrical engineers, but as a descriptor for the changing social relations of communication that define the networked present. Of course, 'live' media have a more than century-long history, dating at least from the rollout of telegraphy and telephony. The capacity to orchestrate social simultaneity through 'liveness' comes to play a decisive social and political role in the context of broadcast media platforms such as radio and television and is implicated in powerful experiences of political identification as well as new rituals redefining domestic and cultural life.[3] What changes in the present is the way the distributed architecture of digital networks opens the potential for 'realtime' communication involving multiple senders who are also receivers, supporting novel experiences of social simultaneity. This potential is evident in the new dynamics affecting public assembly in the present, as novel forms of recursive communication and coordination can occur between diverse actors even as events unfold. Heightened capacity for realtime exchange based on recursive 'feedback' alters key valences of social encounter more generally and is arguably becoming a key feature of contemporary sociality (Day and Lury, 2017).

While I recognize the longer history of relations of media, space and place, in my own work I have reserved 'geomedia' to name the condition – characterized by ubiquity, location specificity and capacities for realtime feedback – that contemporary media enter. This new condition points in multiple directions, but I want to raise two that I think are particularly important for future work in this space. The first concerns the centrality of *data*, not only in digital media platforms, but also as the key lubricant of the digital economy and a critical feature in social life more generally. Capacity to generate data and establish proprietary control over core data sets (what Tim O'Reilly (2005) proselytized as the 'new Intel inside' of the web 2.0 era) is the key to market-leading companies such as Google and Facebook. The centrality of data has to be understood at multiple levels, beginning with control over infrastructure and platforms, as Gillian Rose notes here in her astute analysis of the 'smart-city' paradigm. A second level concerns the growing role of algorithmic power in so many domains of everyday life, as 'blackboxed' hardware and software enable smart devices and various search and recommendation systems to filter everything from news to social interactions. A third level concerns the role of large-scale data in enabling both detailed profile building and unprecedented mass surveillance at individual and population levels.

Insofar as a correlate of geomedia is the threshold of 'big data', McLuhan's emphasis on pattern recognition has already achieved a new level of operationality, as capacity to generate and analyse data sets about disparate phenomena from people movement to sites where photographs are being taken or topics that people searching for or talking about at any moment becomes routinized. However, it is important to recognize that capacity to read these streams of data is unevenly distributed, both in terms of access to data sets and in terms of possession of the requisite analytical skills and computational resources. This unevenness has significant implications for future geomedia scholarship, as capacity to conduct independent, critical analysis of fast-growing domains such as social media or smart-city systems is skewed in favour of platform owners and controllers (see Thatcher, 2014). If the need to engage in dialogue across the 'two cultures' famously identified by novelist C.P Snow in his 1959 Rede Lecture has been evident at least since the early twentieth century, this has become increasingly urgent as complex technical platforms become operational in more and more contexts of everyday life. Mobile communication devices, home-entertainment systems, gaming consoles and wearables are all increasingly integrated with other domains such as marketing, credit, transport and logistical systems. In this context, geomedia studies demands a new commitment to *unruly* thinking, predicated on systematic and creative engagement between humanities and social science scholars in fields such as media, geography, cultural studies, sociology and journalism with those working in areas such as computer science and geospatial sciences, but also in areas such as law and public policy. It is only such conjunctions that might enable the new breadth and depth of critical competencies required to respond to the pace and scale of change that defines the present.

Media in the Future

The final point I want to flag here stems from the changing role of media in the everyday lifeworld. As Jansson (2017) has observed, in contemporary life 'there are fewer and fewer space-times that do *not* entail mediation'. This shift has both empirical and ontological consequences. If the former relates to the manifold ways in which mediation and mediatization (as the ritualization of mediated practices into social habitus) reconstitute social practices, the latter suggests the need to reconsider the customary relation between 'media' and all that we have conventionally placed under the heading of 'immediacy'. As a discipline, media studies has been organized by a structured opposition between the primary domain of social experience – which is embodied, face to face, and the domain of full 'presence' – and the mediation of this domain that turns into representations of some kind, records and recordings that are subsequently distributed, consumed, archived and analysed. Clearly, the linear temporality organizing this relation has been troubled for some time, as 'live' broadcast media began to allow the distribution of 'real' events across multiple sites, orchestrating powerful experiences of social simultaneity that eventually bled into paradoxical forms such as 'reality television'. But this disturbance pales in significance as experiences of 'realtime' communication and distributed media production and consumption using voice, text and still and moving images begin to rework so many social situations. The uncertain result are the multiple and varied forms of mediated presence and embodied absence that define the present, as our attention and sense of social 'situation' is routinely reframed by the capacity for one context to be interrupted by another or to overlap with many others.

In the same year that McLuhan published 'The Invisible Environment', Jacques Derrida (1976) noted the closure of the era of Western metaphysics defined by a certain thinking of 'presence'. For Derrida, closure did not amount to *end*, according to the common logic in which one paradigm is simply supplanted by another. Rather, 'closure' signals a threshold when it becomes possible to problematize – and perhaps begin to think differently – key terms and concepts that have governed a certain period. While this shaking of metaphysical foundations has involved diverse forces, media have their stake in this process. Arguably, this has become more visible at a phenomenological level in the contemporary era as more and more everyday activities involve forms of mediation and mediatization, making it more difficult to comprehend 'media' by instituting a binary separation between the apparent 'presence' of face-to-face activity and all the forms of mediation that subsequently ameliorate 'absence'. Part of the difficulty of thinking the new intricacies of the emergent relation between media and immediacy is the long history of neglect of 'media' *within* philosophy (Derrida is an exception).[4]

This is the uncertain space/time we are now thrust into, one in which the embodied and the face to face are neither outside nor beyond media or the 'technological' in general. Such a change has enormously important experiential and political consequences, as the technological domain has assumed new force, rhythm and 'agency' in the digital era. For Bernard Stiegler (1998: 80) – who is arguably the most important interpreter of Derrida in the context of the new digital platforms – the digital constitutes a new type of 'technical object' that is profoundly transformative of the milieu in which it is concretized:

> The technical object [...] becomes concretized by closely conforming to this milieu, but in the same move radically transforms the milieu. This ecological phenomenon may be observed in the informational dimension of present-day technics, where it allows for the development of a generalized performativity (for example, in the apparatuses of live transmission and of data processing in real time, with the fictive inversions engendered therein)—but it is then essentially the human milieu, that is human geography and not physical geography, that is found to be incorporated into a process of concretization that should no longer be thought on the scale of the object, but also not on the scale of the system.

This, then, is the final unruly conjunction the present demands: a media theory that is not mediacentric but emerges from a seriously messy encounter between media and philosophy. Geomedia studies may well offer a fertile space in which such an encounter might begin to be elaborated.

Notes

1 A more academic but less poetic reference would be the advocacy of 'messy' theory and analysis by Law (2004) and ANT more generally.

2 Although the connection to McLuhan is not made explicit in essays here, the environmental aspect of media is mentioned in Parmett and Rodgers' essay and perhaps touched on in Sheller, with her reference to the 'eco-dimension'. Aspects of McLuhan's work (on writing, broadcasting and the 'global village') are discussed in Adams' book.
3 This is a vast terrain, but key thresholds include the affective politics precociously established by the Nazi use of radio in the 1930s (McQuire, 1994), the altered rhythms of home life under the eye of television that Scannell (1996) terms 'dailiness' and the development of new sociocultural rituals dependent on live broadcasting that Dayan and Katz (1992) defined as 'media events'.
4 Kittler (2009: 24) argues: 'More than any other theorists, philosophers forgot to ask which media support their very practice'.

References

Adams, P. (2009). *Geographies of Media and Communication*, Malden MA, Blackwell.
Day, S., & Lury, C. (2017). New technologies of the observer: #BringBack, visualization and disappearance. *Theory, Culture & Society*, ISSN 02632764 (Forthcoming)
Dayan, D., & Katz, E. (1992). *Media Events: The Live Broadcasting of History.* Cambridge, MA: Harvard University Press.
Derrida, J. (1976). *Of Grammatology* (trans. G.C. Spivak) Baltimore: Johns Hopkins University Press. (originally published in French in 1967).
Dyson, E., Gilder, G., Keyworth, J., & Toffler, A. (1994). A magna carta for the knowledge age. New *Perspectives Quarterly*, 11(Fall): 26–37.
Falkheimer, J., & Jansson, A. (Eds.) (2006). *Geographies of Communication: The Spatial Turn in Media Studies*, Göteborg: Nordicom.
Innis, H. (1951). *The Bias of Communication*, Toronto: University of Toronto Press.
Jansson, A. (2017). Critical communication geography: Space, recognition and the dialectic of mediatization In Adams, P., Cupples, J., Glynn, K., Jansson, A., & Moores, S. (Eds.), *Communications/Media/Geographies* (pp. 95–131), London and New York: Routledge.
Kittler, F. (2009). Towards an ontology of media. *Theory, Culture and Society*, 26(2–3): 23–31.
Lapenta, F. (2011). Geomedia: on location-based media, the changing status of collective image production and the emergence of social navigation systems. *Visual Studies*, 26(1): 14–24.
Law, J. (2004). *After Method: Mess in Social Science Research.* London and New York: Routledge.
McCullough, M. (2004). *Digital Ground.* Cambridge, MA: MIT Press.
McLuhan, M. (1967). The invisible environment: The future of an erosion. *Perspecta* 11: 161–167.
McLuhan, M. (1970). *Counter Blast.* London: Rapp and Whiting.
McLuhan, M. (1974). *Understanding Media: The Extensions of Man.* London: Abacus. (first published 1964).
McQuire, S. (1994). The go-for-broke game of history: The camera, the community and the scene of politics. *Arena Journal*, 4: 201–227.

McQuire, S. (2008). *The Media City: Media, Architecture and Urban Space.* Sage.

McQuire, S. (2011). Geomedia, networked culture and participatory public space In R. Hinkel, (Ed.), *Urban Interior: Informal Explorations, Interventions and Occupations* (pp. 113–128), Baunach, Germany: Spurbuchverlag.

McQuire, S. (2016). *Geomedia: Networked Media and the Future of Public Space.* Cambridge: Polity.

Moore, C. (1967). Plug it in Rameses, and see if it lights up. Because we aren't going to keep it unless it works, *Perspecta*, 11: 42–43.

O'Reilly, T. (2005). *What Is Web 2.0? Design Patterns and Business Models for the Next Generation of Software.* Available at www.oreilly.com/pub/a/web2/archive/what-is-web-20.html.

Scannell, P. (1996). *Radio, Television, and Modern Life: A Phenomenological Approach.* Oxford, UK & Cambridge, MA: Blackwell.

Stiegler, B. (1998). *Technics and Time 1. The Fault of Epimetheus* (trans. R. Beardsworth and G. Collins) Stanford: Stanford University Press.

Thatcher, J. (2014). Living on fumes: Digital footprints, data fumes, and the limitations of spatial big data, *International Journal of Communication*, 8: 1765–1783.

Thielman, T. (2010). Locative media and mediated localities: An introduction to media geography, *Aether: The Journal of Mediated Geography*, Va: 1–17.

Williams, R. (1974). *Television: technology and cultural form.* London: Fontana/Collins.

List of Contributors

Paul C. Adams is Professor in the Department of Geography and the Environment at the University of Texas at Austin. He holds a Ph.D. from the University of Wisconsin-Madison (1993). He is the founder of the Media and Communication Specialty Group of the American Association of Geographers. His articles have appeared in *Transactions of the Institute of British Geographers, Progress in Human Geography, Annals of the Association of American Geographers* and other leading journals. His books include *Geographies of Media and Communication*, the *Research Companion to Media Geography* (co-edited with Jim Craine and Jason Dittmer) and *Communications/Media/Geographies* (co-authored with Julie Cupples, Kevin Glynn, André Jansson, and Shaun Moores).

Karin Fast is Senior Lecturer in Media and Communication Studies and one of the Geomedia Research Group coordinators, at Karlstad University, Sweden. Her research interests span topics such as (geo-)mediatization, consumer work/free labour, media discourse, and media industries (e.g. music production and consumption). She has published her work in journals such as *Journal of Computer-Mediated Communication, International Journal of Cultural Studies, European Journal of Cultural Studies,* and *Media Culture and Society, Communication Theory.*

Maren Hartmann is Professor for Communication and Media Sociology at the University of the Arts (UdK) in Berlin. She has held several teaching and research positions in the UK, Belgium and Germany and has been a visiting professor in Denmark and Sweden. Her research focuses primarily on media appropriation in everyday life (especially domestication) and mobile media, but also on cyberculture, the urban as well as mobilities. She is currently co-heading a research project on time and (mobile) media.

André Jansson is Professor of Media and Communication Studies and Director of the Geomedia Research Group at Karlstad University, Sweden. His most recent publications include *Mediatization and Mobile Lives: A Critical Approach* (2018), *Communications/Media/*

Geographies (2017, with P. C Adams, J. Cupples, K. Glynn and S. Moores) and *Cosmopolitanism and the Media: Cartographies of Change* (2015, with M. Christensen).

Maja Klausen, PhD (University of Southern Denmark) is a postdoctoral researcher at the Department of Media, Cognition and Communication, University of Copenhagen. Her research lies within the cross-disciplinary field of media and cultural studies. She applies theories of mediatization, cultural gerontology and critical cultural studies in a combination with ethnographic qualitative mehods. She has examined and written about participation, citizenship, affect and urban space. Recent work has been published in *Space and Culture, Culture Unbound* and *The Journal of Urban Cultural Studies*.

Johan Lindell, previously postdoctoral researcher at Karlstad University, is Senior Lecturer in Media and Communication Studies at the Department of Geography, Media and Communication, Karlstad University. Lindell is a media sociologist seeking to understand class discrepancies related to globalization, mediatization and news media use from a Bourdieusian perspective. Lindell has published his work in, for example, *Distinktion: Journal of Social Theory, Journalism Studies, International Communication Gazette, European Journal of Communication* and *Communication Theory*.

Chris Lukinbeal is an Associate Professor and the Director of Geographic Information Systems Technology programs at the University of Arizona. He as published books on *The Geography of Cinema, Mediated Geographies and Geographies of the Media*, and *Place, Television, and the Real Orange County*. He also has published academic papers and book chapters on topics ranging from representation, media, GIS, remote sensing, cartography, urban geography, mental maps and GIS, landscape studies, and geographic education. He an editor of the book series, *Media Geography at Mainz* and an Associate Editor for the journal *Geohumanities*.

Scott McQuire is Professor of Media and Communications in the School of Culture and Communication at the University of Melbourne, Australia. He is one of the founders of the Research Unit for Public Cultures which fosters interdisciplinary research at the nexus of digital media, art, urbanism, and social theory. Scott has published widely and his books including *Visions of Modernity: Representation, Memory, Time and Space in the Age of the Camera* (1998), *The Media City: Media, Architecture and Urban Space* (2008) and *Geomedia: Networked cities and the future of public space* (2016).

Helen Morgan Parmett is Assistant Professor in the Department of Theatre at the University of Vermont. She received her Ph.D. from the

University of Minnesota in Communication Studies. Her research focuses on relationships between media and urban space, with a particular emphasis on production, television, and sports. Her work is published in journals including *Television & New Media, International Journal of Cultural Studies, Communication and Critical/Cultural Studies, The Journal of Sport and Social Issues*, amongst others. Her book, titled *Down in Treme: Race, Place, and New Orleans on Television,* is forthcoming with Franz Steiner Verlag.

Kristian Møller (PhD, University of Southern Denmark) is a guest lecturer at Roskilde University. Drawing from social geography as well as critical theories of affect and intimacy his dissertation examines how hook-up apps mediatize gay men's social and sexual lives. His recent works have focused on the mediatization of non-monogamy and home making practices in gay relationships, and the specific 'collapses of context' that this entails. Further, his methodology and ethics contributions to critical communication studies, include a 'go-along' method for exploring smartphone use, and a renegotiation of 'boundary work' for practice based internet ethics. Follow @ kristianmj

Kaarina Nikunen is Professor of Media and Communication Research at the University of Tampere. Her areas of expertise include media and migration, emotions and affectivity, solidarity, humanitarianism, gender and social media practices. She is the editor of *Media in Motion: Cultural Complexity and Migration in the Nordic Region* (Ashgate 2011, co-editor Elisabeth Eide) and *Pornification: Sex and Sexuality in Media Culture* (Berg 2007, with Susanna Paasonen and Laura Saarenmaa).

Scott Rodgers is Senior Lecturer in Media Theory at Birkbeck, University of London. His research specializes in the relationships of media and cities and the geographies of communication. Scott also has broad interests in media production practices, digital and networked technologies, journalism, urban politics, philosophies of media and ethnographic methodologies. His publications have appeared in journals such as *Society and Space, International Journal of Cultural Studies, International Journal of Urban and Regional Research, Space and Culture and Journalism: Theory, Practice and Criticism.* With Tim Markham, Scott is co-editor of *Conditions of Mediation: Phenomenological Perspectives on Media* (2017, Peter Lang).

Gillian Rose is Professor of Human Geography at the University of Oxford and a Fellow of the British Academy. She is the author of *Visual Methodologies* (Sage, fourth edition 2016), as well as a number of books and papers on ways of seeing in urban and domestic spaces. Her current research interests focus on contemporary digital visual culture and cities. She is currently investigating how a range of socio-technical practices constitute a place as a 'smart city', with a particular interest in role of visualisations in both representing and operationalising 'smart', from photorealist computer generated images to app interfaces.

Linda Ryan Bengtsson is Senior Lecturer in Media and Communication Studies and coordinator of the Geomedia Research Group at Karlstad University, Sweden. An interdisciplinary researcher with a wide and varied background, her work investigates the relations between creative life, interactivity, media, and place. Her PhD thesis, *Re-negotiating Social Space: Public Art Installations and Interactive Experience*, laid the groundwork for her current projects: Music Innovation Network Inner Scandinavia (MINS), which examines the contemporary music environment and its digital echoes in the border region between Sweden and Norway, and Interactive Place-Based Tourism, which investigates enhanced experiences in digital tourism in the province of Värmland.

Laura Sharp is a PhD Candidate in the School of Geography and Development at the University of Arizona. She has published articles on film geography, montage, and media as practice. Her research brings together science and technology studies, economic geography, and cultural theory to understand the film locations market in Los Angeles, California.

Mimi Sheller, Ph.D., is Professor of Sociology and founding Director of the Center for Mobilities Research and Policy at Drexel University in Philadelphia. She is President of the International Association for the History of Transport, Traffic and Mobility, and founding co-editor of the journal *Mobilities*. She is author or co-editor of ten books, including the forthcoming Mobility Justice (Verso, 2018); *Aluminum Dreams* (MIT Press, 2014); *The Routledge Handbook of Mobilities* (2013); *Mobility and Locative Media* (2014); and *Citizenship from Below* (Duke U.P., 2012). She was awarded the Doctor Honoris Causa from Roskilde University, Denmark (2015) and in the Fall of 2016 was the inaugural Distinguished Visiting Scholar at the Center for Advanced Research in Global Communication at the Annenberg School of Communication, University of Pennsylvania. She has held Visiting Fellowships at the Davis Center for Historical Studies, Princeton University (2008); Media@McGill, Canada (2009); Center for Mobility and Urban Studies, Aalborg University, Denmark (2009); and Penn Humanities Forum, University of Pennsylvania (2010).

Mekonnen Tesfahuney is Professor of Human Geography at the Department of Geography Media and Communication Studies, Karlstad University.

Questions of mobility, power, space and geophilosophy are his research concern. Amongst his latest publications are the anthologies *Privileged Mobilities: Tourism as World Ordering* (Tesfahuney and Schough, 2016) and *The Post-Political City* (Tesfahuney and Ek, 2018).

Tindra Thor is a PhD Candidate in Media-and Communication Studies at Stockholm University. She holds a Master of Science in Political Science (specializing in Politics and Gender), and a BA in History. Her research interests include art as interventions, urban spatial subversions, aesthetic cosmopolitanism and performativity. She is currently working on her dissertation on Stockholm graffiti and street art. Her on-going work is part of the research project "Cosmopolitanism from the Margins: Mediations of Alternate Expressivity" conducted by Professor Miyase Christensen (Stockholm University/Royal Institute of Technology) and Professor André Jansson (Karlstad University). The project is financed by the Swedish Research Council.

John Tomlinson is Professor Emeritus at Nottingham Trent University. His many publications on the themes of globalization, cultural modernity and mediated cultural experience include *Cultural Imperialism* (Continuum 1991), *Globalization and Culture* (Polity 1999) and *The Culture of Speed* (Sage 2007). His books have been extensively translated (eleven languages). He has lectured at many distinguished universities and research institutions across Europe, the United States and East Asia as well as at artistic institutions such as The Bauhaus Institute; Tate Britain and the Festival Filosofia, Modena. Professor Tomlinson has also made presentations and acted as consultant on issues of culture and globalization to international public sector organizations, including UNESCO, The Council of Europe, The Commonwealth Secretariat, and Geneva Centre for Security Policy and NATO Defence College.

Rowan Wilken is Associate Professor in Media and Communication, and Principal Research Fellow in the Technology, Communication and Policy Lab, at RMIT University, Melbourne, Australia. He is the co-editor, with Justin Clemens, of *The Afterlives of Georges Perec* (Edinburgh University Press, 2017), and, with Gerard Goggin, of *Locative Media* (Routledge, 2014) and *Mobile Technology and Place* (Routledge, 2012); he is also the author of *Teletechnologies, Place, and Community* (Routledge, 2011). At present he is completing two books: a research monograph, *Cultural Economies of Locative Media* (Oxford University Press), and a co-edited book, with Gerard Goggin and Heather Horst, *Location Technologies in International Context* (Routledge).

Index

3G 31, 126, 155
4G 24, 31, 82
5G 24, 31
7-11 123
ABC 135

activity-logs 49
actor-networks 49, 53; *see also* ANT
ad-targeting 29
Advertising Age 110n1
advertising: agency 109; industry 29
Africa 44, 215, 223
ageism 152, 154, 160, 165–166, 167–168n2
Airbnb 29, 34
airports 87–89, 139, 146, 200
Aldi 162
Algeria 69
algorithmic: configuration 107; detection 88; modelling 46; power 256; processes 34; processing 26; sorting 21, 33
Almost Famous 137
Amazon 61, 73
Amazon Prime 243
Amazonia 53
analytics 32, 255; ecosystem 33; platforms 35; services 29
Anchorman 135, 137
Anchorman 2 137
Android 24
anime 66
annihilation of space by time 67, 84, 235
anonymity 53, 230n1
ANT 189n1
anticapitalist: critique 121; performance 129
antivirus software 163
Antwone Fisher 137

app: economy 9, 24, 34; ecosystem 34
Apple 35n1, 61, 73
Apple Watch 14, 245–247
Arab Spring 49, 215, 223
Ararat 220–223, 226
Arendt, Hanna 218
Arvika, Sweden 13, 197–198, 200–207, 209, 211
assemblages: body-technology 155; cultural-material 80; energy/object 82; socio-technical 87; technological 50
asylum seekers 217–218, 221, 224–229, 230n1
ATM 55
audience: research 65; studies 63–64
augmented reality 3; applications 31; game 7
Australia 185
automated: processing 32; systems 88
automation 73, 241
avant-garde 253

Badolato, Italy 13, 216, 219–228, 230n1
Baja Norte Studios 138
Bakewell, UK 236
Baltimore, USA 70
Bangalore, India 4
Banjo 21, 25–28, 32–35
Bauman, Zygmunt 116
BBC 240
bear411.com 154
Belgium 223
Berlin, Germany 12, 183
Beverly Boulevard 141
big data 5, 11, 54, 97, 256
biopolitics 88, 160
Birmingham, UK 235
Black Rock Desert 70

Bifrost, Louis 236
border control 216, 227
Borneo 88
Boston Marathon bombings 27
Boys in Company C, The 137
branding 61, 70
Bremen, Germany 187
Breton, André 250
Brightkite 25
Brighton, UK 154
Brisbane, Australia 104–105
British Guiana 88
Burning Man festival 70
Button 34
Buxton, UK 236

cable television 133, 146
Caesars Palace 132
Calabria 216, 220–221
California 62, 136, 147
Canada 147, 185
Canary Islands 215
capital: accumulation of 71, 197; cultural 195, 197, 202–204, 206, 208; network 13, 85, 88–90, 195–199, 202–211; social 54, 196–200, 204, 209, 211
capitalism: fast 84, 241–242, 245, 247; global 234; industrial 244; turbo 241
capitalist: economies 241; modernity 84; order 241; production 241
Caribbean 81
cassette players 190n5
CBS 135–136
CCTV 80, 98
cell: phones 30, 41, 45, 49, 53–54, 84, 86, 90, 115; towers 30, 32, 80, 87
cellular: mobile 24; phones 177
Central Station 126
Ceuta, Spain 215
Champs Elysées 237
check-in 7, 25, 28, 31
Chipotle 36n1
CIR (Italian Refugee Council) 222, 224–225
Cisco 99, 104–105, 110n2
citizen: engagement 97, 104; participation 97; smart 97, 100, 105, 109
city: cinematic 135, 138; cosmopolitan 199; future 11–12, 250; media 4; smart 11, 97–110; the right to the 116, 123; urban 11

CityNext Partners 101, 103, 109, 110n5
climate: change 88, 100; justice 91
CMC (Computer Mediated Communication) 154–155, 239
code/space 9, 31, 87
Cologne, Germany 226
commercialization 6
commodification 110n3
commodity fetishism 247
communication: devices 53, 85, 197, 257; geography 2, 14, 23; industries 196; networks 82, 88–90, 180, 195; satellites 45; services 154; systems 82–83; technologies 52, 54, 67, 166, 152, 177, 245–247, 251
communicational turn in geography 2, 23, 252
communicative: culture 158, 183; exchange 14, 251, 254
Communist Party 221
computational systems 73, 251
computer games 45, 109
computer science 15, 31, 257
connected presence 177, 189
content analysis 46, 252
convergence 3, 8, 22, 27, 30, 33–34, 52; media 61; translocal 73
cookies 9, 50
Copenhagen, Denmark 153–155, 167
Coronado 144
Cortana 34
cosmopolitan: hospitality 13; rights 218; studies 174
cosmopolitanism 218–219, 229
counter-hegemonic: cultures 12, 167; structures 156
counter-urbanization 201, 211
creative: class 196, 199; industries 61, 68, 199; sector 199–200
credit card 49, 53, 55
cross-platform: data sharing 33; partnerships 29, 34
Crowley, Dennis 25
cultural: changes 234; community 195, 204–205, 210; ecosystem 198, 210–211; environments 195; industries 63; intermediaries 73; life 66, 198, 205, 255; politics 206, 236; practices 22, 34, 81, 125, 219, 249; processes 63, 83; production 61, 63, 68, 72; products 134; resources 208; scene 197, 205–206;

Index 269

studies 15, 23, 62–65, 68, 254, 257; theory 46, 179
cyberspace 253

D-Day 239
Dagens industri 224
DARPA (Defense Advanced Research Projects Agency) 45
data: analytics 103, 104, 109; biometric 88; capture 32; centres 84; classification 254; collection 5, 255; extraction 21; feeds 98; flows 41, 88, 102–105, 110n3; matching 27; mining 27, 31; shadows 54, 56, 87; streams 33, 103, 108; transmission 45, 102; visualization 5, 108
data-driven platform 21, 30, 33
datafication 32
De Laurentiis Company 147
Del Coronado Hotel 135
Deleuze, Gilles 129
Denmark 159
Derrida, Jacques 9, 258
deterritorialization 118
deurbanization 89
development: digital 3; economic 70, 134–135; technological 8, 21, 23, 35, 86, 238; urban 134
diaspora studies 174
digital: colonization 8; divide 6; economy 256; era 9, 258; networks 22, 30, 32, 254–255; platforms 251, 258; records 49; signals 5, 42, 45; traces 53
digital media 31, 45, 49, 155, 158, 178, 184, 251, 254–255; industries 70; platforms 249, 256; systems 2; technologies 152, 251
digitalization 1, 3, 52, 55, 217
digitization 1, 8
dividual 9, 48–50, 52–56
Dodgeball 25
domestication theory 155–156
domination 7, 49, 236
dot com bubble 243
drones 14, 83, 243
Dublin Treaty 227
Dunes 132
dystopias 230

echo chambers 50
Edison, Thomas 65
Egypt 223

El Rancho Vegas Resort 132
electronic interface 186
emancipation 6, 235–236
embodied: practices 71, 174; presence 4
Emerson, Ralph Waldo 236
empowerment 2, 6, 11
encoding/decoding 64
energy: culture 82–83; flows 87; systems 83
English Channel 236
environmental: justice 91; protests 236; sustainability 97
EQUITY 240
Ericsson 1–3
Ethiopia 225
Euro 2016 41
European borders 13, 188, 216, 226; politics 14, 226–227
European refugee crisis 13, 215–216, 226, 228–229
European Typology on Homelessness and Housing Exclusion (ETHOS) 190n14
European Union 215
Evernote 29
exclusion: digital 187; social 184–185, 187
experiential bubbles 42
exploitation 2, 6–7, 49, 242, 247
extractive industries 87

face to face 159, 177, 196, 257–258
Facebook 7, 25–27, 33, 49, 61–62, 73, 98–99, 185, 203, 225–226, 239, 256
facial recognition 62
feminist theory 46
field spaces: computational 73; industrial 75; social 10, 64, 72, 74; technical 10, 64, 73–75
fields: artistic 13, 198; cultural 198, 206–207, 211; journalistic 71; media production 72–73; social 13, 187, 197
film industries 11, 136, 139, 141
film production: industry 133–134, 139; markets 134, 139
filmmaking 69, 133–134, 143, 148
filter bubbles 9, 49–51, 54–55
Finland 227
firewalls 47
Flamingo 132
flâneur 121

Flickr 29
Florida 140, 145
Ford 236
Fordism 139
Fortress Europe 215
Four Square Productions 139
Foursquare 21, 25–26, 28–29, 31–35, 35n1
France 41, 176, 179
Frontex 216
FutureLife 100–101, 105–107, 109
Futurist Manifesto 236

Gas Lamp Quarter 144
gay culture 157, 158, 163
Gazzetta del Sud 221
gender equality 91
gendered stereotypes 11, 108
geo-ecology 10, 79–80, 81, 87
geo-politics 10, 79, 81, 85
geo-positioning 2, 7
geo-tagging 3, 7, 24
geodata 26, 29–31, 33, 35
GeoEye 90
geographical: imagination 13, 215–217, 228; order 54–55; organization 23
geolocation 9, 21, 23, 26, 30, 34
Geomedia Studies 92n1
geomedia: studies 1–5, 8, 10, 12, 14–15, 43, 46, 62, 79–80, 91, 173, 211, 234, 250, 257–258; technology 4
geomediatization 6–8, 12, 197; perspective 156; processes 8; research 153; studies 152, 167
geomediatized worlds 13
geosocial: boundaries 197–198; positioning 5
geoweb 24
Germany 41, 188, 216, 220, 223–224
GIS 134
Glancee 25–26
Global North 6, 13, 54
Global South 6, 13, 54
global village 14, 259n2
globalization 6, 14, 65, 84, 217, 224, 234, 241, 248, 250; capitalist 245; studies 234
Gomer Pyle 137
Google 23–26, 31, 49, 61, 73, 239, 256
Google Earth 23
Google Maps 23–24, 175

Gowalla 25
GPS (Global Positioning System) 7, 29, 32, 52, 175; data 255; devices 32, 52
graffiti: culture 114, 117, 119, 124–125; writer 115, 120, 125, 128
Greece 215, 226
Green Dot 25
Grindr 154, 158, *164*
Groupon 25
Growlr 154
Guattari, Felix 9, 129
Gulf War 105

habitus 10, 64, 67–72, 74, 211, 257
hacking 91
Haiti 89–91
Hamburg, Germany 110n5
Hannover, Germany 190n16
Harry-O 135, 137, 144
Hawaii 140
HDmessaging 25
hegemony 7, 155, 157; urban 116, 129
Heidegger, Martin 9, 56n1, 67, 252
Hershey, Barbara 135
Highlight 25–26
Hilton 149n2
HIV/AIDS 167n2
Hollywood 69, 132–133, 136, 147–148
home-entertainment 257
homelessness 173, 184–189, 190n12
Honnold, Douglas 132
hook-up apps 153–154, 157–159, 163, 165–166
How It Works: Internet of Things 104
How It Works: Smarter Cities 104
Hull, Thomas E. 132
humanitarianism 228
humour 11, 71, 242
Hurricane Matthew 89
Husserl, Edmund 56n1
hybrid: ecologies 4; performances 52, 56
hybridity 49

IBM 1–3, 98–101, 103–104, 106–109, 110n2, 110n6
Iceland 9, 41–42
ICQ 154
ICTs (Information and Communications Technologies) 152, 186

identity: collective 56n2; modular 9, 47, 49; modularized 48; personal 41, 48–49, 51, 226; self 51; social 157
IFTTT 34
Il Volo 224
immediacy 14, 235, 242–247, 257–258
immobilities 88–89, 174, 179, 183, 188
Indianapolis, USA 236
individualization 6
industrialization 82
inequalities 88, 174
inflight magazines 5
information: environments 49–50, 255; technologies 85–86, 254; transfer 45, 104
Information Highway, The 1
informational: augmentation 87; systems 80
infrastructures: communication 6, 30, 46, 82–83; computer 3; digital 97, 200; energy 84; media 79, 81, 89–91, 253, 255; network 24, 254; networked 10, 79, 251; physical 80; satellite 5; sensor 32; sociotechnical 88
infrastructuring 10, 80, 83, 91
Ingesund, Sweden 201
Instagram 28, 41, 45, 119
Intel 99–100, 103, 105, 107–108, 110n1, 110n2, 256
interior design 73
International Theater and Stage Employees 141
Internet: access 186, 188, 199, 220; café 186; industry 5; protocol 24; services 187
Internet of Things 24, 100, 103, 106–107
interoperability 33–34
Interreg/EU 212n1
intimacy 153, 156, 160, 167, 178
invisible sorting 88
IoT Made Simple 103
iPad 154, 161
iPhone 24–25, 30, 34, 35n1, 246
IT-hjaelpen 155
Italy 215, 216, 220–226

Japan 179
Jiepang 25

Jordan 215
journalistic culture 69

Kabyle 68–69
Kauhava, Finland 219, 227–229, 230n1
Kearney Mesa neighbourhood 138–139, 146
Keating Building 135, *136*
Key Performance Indicator 98
kinetic elites 82, 88, 90
Konsthantverk 201
KUSI 139
Kyrkerud Folk High School 204

LA *see* Los Angeles
La Cienega Boulevard 141
La Jolla 144, *145*
Lake District 242
Lampedusa, Italy 215, 219, 225–226
Las Vegas, USA 27, 132–133
Last Frontier 132
Lautréamount, Comte de 249–250
Layar 31
Le Corbusier 237–238
Le Courrier 222
Le Figaro 236
Lebanon 215
Lei Cidade Limpa 122
Lemasters, Kim 136
Lesbos Island, Greece 215, 226, 230n2
Libya 223
Limbo 25
linguistic theory 64
liquid modernity 84
Lisbon Biennale 181–182
Living City 100
local: communities 155, 196, 198, 201, 204–207, 210, 227; culture 207, 230; politics 12, 199, 225; press 204–205, 221–222
locality 69, 176, 222
localized: conditions 69; practices 13; situations 62
location: awareness 3, 14, 22, 30, 32, 254; data 28, 102; information 29, 34; marketplace 29
location-based: applications 25; dating 4; mobile social networking (LMSN) 24–26, 28, 31, 33, 35; services (LBS) 2, 9, 21, 25–26, 29–30, 33, 35, 255; technologies 3

locational: data 53–54, 87; information 49, 134
locationally aware: devices 53; technologies 54, 56
logistics: hubs 83; industries 24; networks 84; studies 10, 80, 85, 91
London, UK 122, 235, 242
Long Beach, USA 135
Loopt 25
Los Angeles, USA 133–135, 138–142, 145–147
Louisiana 147
loyalty cards 246
Lucky 146

M-A-D 182
MacBook 82
machine: age 237; learning 24
Macklemore 249–250
Mannello, Gerardo 220–223, 225, 227, 230n1
mapping 1, 23, 46, 188; applications 24; capabilities 24; technologies 9, 23
Marinetti, Filippo Tommasso 236–238
marketization 121
Marriott 149n2
Marx, Karl 65, 84, 247
material: commodities 61; cultures 82; geographies 10, 63, 84; relations 5; textures 70, 74
material turn in media studies 79, 91
materialist approaches 10, 80–81, 91
McCurdy, Kathy 134
McDowell, Roddy 135
McLuhan, Marshall 14, 252–257, 259n2
mechanical: modernity 235; speed 235–236
Med TV 223
media (concepts): affordances 80; archaeologies 80, 85, 91; audiences 64; changes 2, 7; competences 153, 157–159, 162–163; consumption 65; cultures 61, 239–240; dependence 211; devices 2, 6, 22, 30, 254; diet 177; effects 64; environments 9, 61, 152, 225, 255; events 35, 259n3; forms 10, 62, 65–67, 73, 75, 238; geographies 3, 86, 249; industry 10, 12, 63, 68, 70; landscape 7, 14–15; life 2, 31; literacy 158, 198, 203; platforms 34, 249, 251–252, 254–256; power 62, 66; practices 10, 12, 62–64, 73–74, 91; production 9–11, 61–64, 66–75, 257; repertoire 159; representations 5; skills 195, 210; spatialities 63; systems 2, 79, 234–235, 238; technologies 3–5, 7–9, 86, 152, 155, 185, 210–211, 218, 225, 229, 235, 237–239, 242, 247
media (types): biased 253; broadcast 55, 257; domestic 190n5; electronic 3, 244; connected 1–2, 6–7; connective 73; deinstitutionalized 63; fake 9; fast 14, 234, 238–243, 246–248; geo-social 4; global 79, 216–217, 234–235; hyperlocal 68; local 205, 216; locative 3–4, 21, 23–24, 30, 176, 249, 255; mainstream 228; mass 99; mobile 2, 6, 21, 30–31, 87, 155, 173, 175–178, 181; modern 238; networked 33, 185; new 1, 3, 7, 14, 85, 239, 252; old 3, 14, 239; personalized 175; portable 176; print 228; spatial 3, 5; spatialized 4; transportable 253; virtual 85; see also digital media; social media
media-centrism 63–64, 234
mediapolis 218–219
mediated: communication 5, 52, 211; connectivity 198, 211; encounters 219; experience 31, 44, 51; localities 3–4, 249; practices 257; presence 257; representations 4; societies 62; work 244
mediation 4, 49, 54, 61, 82–83, 85, 88, 211, 257–258
mediatization 4, 6–7, 13, 49, 54, 153, 155–156, 167, 187, 198–199, 203, 210–211, 257–258; of culture 152; of society 152, 176
mediatized: experience 241; geographies 85; home 12, 153, 155, 157, 159–160, 162, 166–167; processes 81; society 160; worlds 6, 91
Medion 162
Mediterranean Sea 13, 180, 216, 219–220, 222, 225, 230n2
medium specificity 61, 63
Melilla, Spain 215
men seeking men (MSM) 167n2
men seeking women (MSW) 167n2

Menlo Park, California 62
Metropoli 228
metropolis 132
Mexico 137
MGM 132
Mickey Mouse 246
Microsoft 34, 99, 101, 103, 108–109, 110n2, 110n5
Middle East 226
Milan, Italy 225
military: logic 83; power 85, 91; research 83; strategy 83, 85; supremacy 82
Mission Hills 144
mobile: applications 24, 31; communication 87, 174, 176, 257; connectivity 2; devices 7, 24, 29, 32, 190n9, 255; games 4, 31; Internet 9, 24, 31; life 54, 85, 183, 198, 206, 211; maps 218; medialities 85–86; money 90; networks 1, 24, 31; payment 246; phones 30, 173, 175–178, 181, 186, 220, 225, 239; place 129; practices 31; public 9, 52–56; sensors 32; technologies 30, 45, 176–177; telephony 79, 87; television 31; world 13
Mobile Media & Communication 175
mobilism 12, 173, 178–185, 187–189, 190n9
mobilities (concepts): (in)justice 90; capabilities 87; justice 81, 86–87; paradigm 174, 178, 189n1; regimes 84, 87, 89–90; research 79–80, 85, 87, 91, 175, 177; studies 176, 250; systems 80, 88–90
mobilities (types): augmented 47, 52–53; communicative 174, 183; connected 90; critical 10, 80, 91, 178–179; differential 174; elite 211; geomediated 83; global 88–89; guided 52, 55; homeless 188; informational 83–84; local 89; marginal 179, 183; mediated 10, 52, 80, 86; new 70, 80, 86–87, 173, 195; physical 83–84, 183; social 174, 183–184, 188–189; spatial 174; transnational 90; uneven 81–82, 86–87
mobilities turn in social sciences 12–13, 173, 183, 195
modularization 48, 55

monetization 21, 26, 33
Mongolia 81
Montgomery Field 139, 146
Montgomery Wards 146
motility 34, 85, 88, 174, 176, 179, 188, 189n1, 195
Motograph News Bulletin 239
movements: anarchist 226; anti-immigrant 226; gay liberation 159; indigenous rights 91; political 182
Mr. Wrong 141
Multi-Image 139
Music Innovation Network Inner Scandinavia 212n1
MV 228

Nabors, Jim *137*
Napolitano, Giorgio 222
Nationwide 64
Nazism 67
neoliberalism 121, 156, 160–161
networked individualism 177, 189, 203
Neues Deutschland 222
Nevada 70, 132
New Media & Society 33
New Mexico 140
New Orleans, USA 70
New Year's Eve 226
New York, USA 28, 70, 105, *106*, 116, 124, 134, 136, 139, 147
New York Times 239
Newroz 221
NHS England 108
Nigeria 81
Ninomiya, Sontoku (Kinjiro) 181
Nobel Peace Prize 224, 230n2
nomadic: logic 117, 124; practices 119
nomadology 115, 117, 121
non-media-centrism 178–179
Normandy 239
North America 132–134, 139, 141, 146–147, 252; *see also* U.S.
North Carolina 140, 147
Northern Rhodesia 88
Norway 126
Nostra Mare 216

O'Toole, Peter 135
Ocean Beach 144
Olympics 98

online: adverts 240; banking 155, 159, 161; community 166; habits 49–50; news 49
ontological security 155, 160, 185
Orlando, USA 146
Oslo, Norway 200

Palestine 88
Paris 136, 226, 237–238
Parretta, Nicola 224–225
passports 55, 88
Path 29
Pathé Newsreel 236
pattern recognition 32, 254, 256
Patton, Damien 27
pay phones 220
Penrith, UK 242–243
personal data 50, 53
Peura, Ilkka 227
phenomenology 46, 56n1, 236
phonograph 65, 237
PIN codes 239
Pinpoint 29
Pinterest 26, 29, 34
PKK 220
placelessness 67–68
political: action 89, 125; choices 126; events 126; life 198, 217; practices 234; resistance 49; struggles 89, 129; subjectivity 14, 228
political economy 62, 64, 68, 234
politics: aesthetic 116–117, 128; of hospitality 215–219, 222–230
popular press 221
population management 88
Portland, USA 70
Portlandia 70
post truth 248
postcolonial theory 46
power: asymmetries 9, 61; dimensions 11; dynamics 13; geometries 1, 8, 87, 203, 224; relations 11, 83, 88, 199, 229; structures 2, 7, 11, 195; symmetries 154
PowerPoint 109
practice theory 63–64, 67
practice turn in media studies 63, 67
precarity 61, 167
predictive analysis 27
privacy 34–35, 43, 53–54, 104, 154–155, 158, 160, 185
Pro Badolato 221–222

production: companies 133–134, 146–148, 149n1; industry 144, 147; practices 61, 64, 66–68, 74, 148; processes 144, 241; studies 63, 65
public: advertising 122; anonymity 53; places 4; policy 15, 257; safety 80, 100

quality television 68
queers 156

Rackstad colony 201
radar 25, 119
radio 82, 87, 190n5, 238, 255, 259n3
Railway Mania 243
Rancho Santa Fe 144
Randall, Tony 135
reality television 257
recommendation systems 256
Red Cross 227
Rede Lecture 256
refugee politics 219, 222, 227
Refugees Hospitality Club 226
Refugees Welcome 226
regulatory regimes 35, 89
remediation 4–5, 73,
remote control 85
resource extraction 81, 86–87
RFID (Radio Frequency Identification) 24, 53
Riace, Italy 225
Rio de Janeiro, Brazil 98
rural: areas 199; life 236, 242
Rural Networking/Networking the Rural 212n1
Ruskin, John 236

San Diego Film Commission 134–135, 140–141, 146, 148n1
San Diego Police Department 143
San Diego, USA 11–12, 132–146, 148
San Francisco, USA 62, 136
San Jose, USA 105, 110n5
Sant' Anna, Italy 225
São Paulo, Brazil 122
satellite: communication 82, 85; guidance systems 83; low earth-orbiting 79, 90; transmission 84; uplink 45
Scavenger Hunt 135
Schengen Agreement 215, 227
science and technology studies 83, 189n1
Screen Actor's Guild 141

Scruff 154
Sea World 135
Sea-Badolato, Italy 220
Sears 146
Second World War 13, 215
securitization 88
security: apparatus 88; state 86
selfie 9, 109
sensing devices 32
sensor technologies 24
sensory: experiences 120–121; fragmentation 44
sex culture 166, 167n2
Siegel, Bugsy 132
Siemens 99–101, 103, 105–106, 108, 110n2
Silicon Valley 70
Silk Stalkings 138, 144
Simmel, Georg 189n1
Simon and Simon 135–137
Simon, Paul 119, 126
Siri 246
Situationists International 121
Skype 154
smart: appliances 255; cards 53; solutions 100–101, 108; technology 100, 104
Smart Data 103
Smart Solutions for Smart Cities 108
smart city 97–99, 104, 106–109; governance 104; government 104; technology 98, 110n2; systems 256
Smarter Cities 100–101, 103
smartphones 2, 7, 9, 24–25, 49, 53, 97, 101, 121, 154–155, 162, *163*, 186, 255; applications 21, 97; services 21, 25; users 24, 152
smiley 158
Snapchat 29
Snow, C.P 256
social: action 69; actors 196; agents 197; change 6, 183, 188–189, 230; collectivities 41; connections 27, 45, 205; data 28; exclusion 184–185, 187; inequality 173; justice 91, 217; life 4, 6–7, 12, 198, 207, 217, 252, 256; location 25; norms 66, 178; order 116, 238, 243; platforms 6; practices 88, 132, 143, 255, 257; privilege 195; processes 13, 52, 177, 217, 229; regime 8; rules 66, 74; search 25; simultaneity 22, 33, 255–257; status 174, 196; structures 66, 206, 217, 229
social media 4, 22, 28–29, 31–33, 35n1, 42, 54–55, 99, 203, 218, 226, 228–229, 244; accounts 28, 187; analysis 27; applications 33–34; data 27–28, 31; firms 26, 33; platforms 27, 34; posts 27; profiles 99; systems 256; users 31, 152
social network 24, 27–28, 45, 49–50, 195; applications 25; research 189n1; sites 185; ties 186; topologies 46
social networking 28, 45, 54; services 66; technology 186
Social Semiotics 63
societies of control 48, 61
sociological imagination 217
Soderbergh, Steven 137
Södermalm 116
SoftBank 27
software: applications 73; corporations 99; sorting 85; studies 85
Some Like It Hot 135
Sonar 25–26
spaces: calculative 54; cinematic 143–144; communicative 115; digital 73; domestic 101, 108–109; filmic 132; geographical 51, 72; geosocial 211; home 12, 153, 155–160, 162, 166–167; imagined 8; infrastructural 79–80, 86, 90; infrastructure 79, 81, 83–86, 88, 90–91; lived 8; material 8, 45, 72, 144; mediated 254; networked 73; nomadic 118; online 165; physical 28, 67, 253; planetary 8; platform 73; private 54; public 6, 31, 35, 53–54, 101, 116, 121–122, 124, 126, 128, 252; regional 30; smooth 117–118, 126; social 13, 22, 31, 69, 71, 197; state 124; striated 117–118, 125–126, 129; symbolic 72; technical 43, 72; temporal 72; translocal 30; urban 4, 11, 30–32, 45, 53, 102, 110n3, 114–115, 117–118, 123–124, 129, 254; virtual 41, 46; visual 117
space/place 4, 8, 12, 15, 43, 120
space/time 4, 43, 249, 251, 257–258
Spain 108

spatial: appropriation 126; differentiation 88; forms 217; interventions 115; models 54; organization 43, 53, 104–105, 107; performances 52; politics 116–117, 128; practices 49; questions 79; relations 81
spatial turn in media studies 2, 22, 252
spatialization 3, 85, 89
spectroscope 236
Stardust 132
stigmatization 188
Stockholm, Sweden 115–116, 123, 127, 200, 208
street art 116, 120–121, 129n1
Stunt Man, The 135
Stu Segall Productions 133, 138–140, 144, 146–148
Stureplan 126
subalterns 89–90
subject/object 1, 9, 67, 72
Suomi24 228
surveillance 7, 54, 83, 88, 104, 187, 216, 227; algorithmic 56; CCTV 80; digital 55; mass 255–256; panoptic 98; social 54
surveillant practices 47, 54
Sutton, Frank 137
Swarm 28
Sweden 126, 196, 198, 200–201, 204, 209
Swedish Arts Council 209
Swedish Research Council Formas 212n1
Switzerland 220–221
symbolic: ideal 125; power 5, 203; value 125
Syria 215, 226

tabloids 228
tax: incentives 140, 147–148; policies 134; subsidies 133
Teamsters 141
technical: agency 72; capacities 239; ecologies 74; logic 22, 33; object 258; platforms 10, 62
technological: advances 247; changes 3, 21, 49; determinism 253; modernity 237; regime 2, 4, 6; transitions 83
technoscape 87
telecommunications 1, 24, 27, 82

telegraph 82, 237–238, 255
telemediation 234–235, 239
telephony 255
television: audience 64; industries 62; movies 133–134, 138, 140, 142; productions 61, 133–135, 138, 142, 146–147; series 66, 70, 135, 138, 140, 142, 146; shows 5, 133–135, 137–138, 140, 142, 144, 146–147, 149n1; station 45, 133, 139; studios 146
temporality 14, 86, 249, 255, 257
terms of service 34
territorialization 126
Thales 99–102, 109, 110n2
Tijuana, Mexico 138
time/space 234, 245
Times Square 124, 239–240
Top Gun 135, 137
topological theory 46
tourism 2, 5, 81, 85, 87
Traffic 137
transdisciplinarity 91
transnational: communication 174; corporations 147–148; geographies 86, 89; networks 225; places 217–218
transnationalism 87, 174, 225
Treme 70
Trump hotels 36n1
Tunisia 223
Turkey 215, 220
Turn 29
Twitter 25, 27–28, 33, 98–99, 239, 248

U.S. Department of Defense 45
U.S. presidential election 36n1, 49
U.S. 45, 50, 68, 70, 133–135, 137–138, 147–148
Uber 26, 29
ubiquity 3, 22, 30–31, 69, 255–256
UEFA 9
UK 97, 185
UNESCO 224
uneven: access 6, 85, 87; geographies 90; materialities 81, 87; topologies 10, 80, 86, 89–90
United for Intercultural Action 215
United States *see* U.S.
United States vs Paramount Pictures, Inc., The (1948) 133
unmanned aerial vehicles 83

urban: aesthetic 121, 129; condition 21, 31; culture 196, 242; discourse 116; dwellers 126–127; environment 32, 100, 126, 199; experience 22, 32, 121–122; fetish 110n3; growth 100, 103, 108; landscape 116; life 4, 114, 127–128; places 51; practices 4; policy 97; problems 103; scene 99
l'Urbanisme 237
urbanism 80–81, 254; antimilitary 89; mediated 249; smart 97, 103
urbanization 79, 81
user agreements 50
utopias 70, 109, 230

Vancouver, Canada 134, 140, 144, 147
Värmland 205
Velux Foundations 167
venue recommendations 28
video: cameras 45, 53; feeds 45; games 45, 73
Vienna, Austria 186
Vinci 99–100, 104, 110n2
virtual: gadgets 7; places 41, 44; resources 196; travel 174; world 45
virtuality 44
visual: advertising 51; expression 117, 121, 125, 127; representations 10; traditions 109
visualization 5, 83, 99, 107, 109
Vkontakte 28

Wal-Mart 146
Wales 44
war machine 117–118, 123, 129
Wayne, John 133
web 2.0 256
Wegener, Alfred 180–181
Weibo 28
Wenders, Wim 224
Western Video 139
What Does the Internet of Things Mean? 107
Whrrl 25
Wi-Fi 24, 30, 32, 82, 99
Widmer, Ryan 134
Wilmington, North Carolina 147
Wilson, Pete 135
Wire, The 70
Wired 34, 254
wireless: connection 32, 102; devices 32; Internet 24; networks 32
Withnail and I 242
World Bank 6
World Habitat 224
World Wide Web 1

X-rays 88

YouTube 99, 109, 110n2

Zambia 81
zombification of society 127